Land in African Agrarian Systems

Land in African Agrarian Systems

Edited by

Thomas J. Bassett and Donald E. Crummey

THE UNIVERSITY OF WISCONSIN PRESS

The University of Wisconsin Press
114 North Murray Street
Madison, Wisconsin 53715

3 Henrietta Street
London WC2E 8LU, England

5 4 3 2 1

Printed in the United States of America

Library of Congress Cataloging-in-Publication Data
Land in African agrarian systems / edited by Thomas J. Bassett
  and Donald E. Crummey.
    430 pp.   cm.
    Includes bibliographical references and index.
    ISBN 0-299-13610-8   ISBN 0-299-13614-0
    1. Land reform—Africa—Congresses.   2. Farm tenancy—Africa—
Congresses.   3. Agricultural productivity—Africa—Congresses.
    I. Bassett, Thomas J.   II. Crummey, Donald.
    HD 1333.A35L36   1993
    333.3′16—dc20   92-27696

Contents

Part 3. Radical Agrarian Reform and Agricultural Performance

Figures and Tables

Figures

Tables

Acknowledgments

The papers collected in this volume were first presented at the University of Illinois, Urbana-Champaign, during the Center for African Studies 1988 spring symposium on land in African agrarian systems. We would like to thank the following individuals and institutions for their part in making this symposium so successful. At the University of Illinois, International Programs and Studies provided generous financial support. External funding was also critical for the participation of scholars from Africa, Europe, and North America. We are grateful to the U.S. Department of Education, Title VI program, for their continued support, to the Social Science Research Council for a research planning activities grant, and to the Wenner-Gren Foundation for Anthropological Research for an international travel support grant.

The staff of the Center for African Studies excelled in the planning and coordination of the three-day meeting. Sue Swisher played the key role in managing the event from beginning to end and more. She was also responsible for printing out an early version of the manuscript, which entailed reformatting and making compatible a number of unfriendly computer files. Gladys Robinson and Cleota Cord assisted at all stages in an amazingly calm manner. We also owe our thanks to the members of the symposium organizing committee, Professors Eyamba Bokamba, Mallafé Dramé, William Martin, and Charles Stewart, and to our students, Shumet Sishagne, Maarten de Witte, and Daniel Ayana. Thanks are also extended to Jane Domier of the University of Illinois Cartographic Laboratory who produced many of the maps that appear in this book.

Professor Sara Berry of Johns Hopkins University gave the keynote address for the meetings. Although she may not be aware of it, Professor Berry also played an inspirational role since her writings on the subject of land access and control in rural Africa were the basis of many of the organizing themes of the symposium.

Finally, we are grateful to Barbara Hanrahan, Senior Editor of the University of Wisconsin Press, who has kept our spirits up during the sometimes discouraging delays in the publication process. It has been a pleasure to work with her.

Contributors

Thomas J. Bassett, Department of Geography, University of Illinois, Urbana–Champaign

Peter C. Bloch, Land Tenure Center, University of Wisconsin–Madison

Merle L. Bowen, Department of Political Science, University of Illinois, Urbana–Champaign

John W. Bruce, Land Tenure Center, University of Wisconsin–Madison

Donald E. Crummey, Center for African Studies and Department of History, University of Illinois, Urbana–Champaign

Steven W. Lawry, Land Tenure Center, University of Wisconsin–Madison

Fiona Mackenzie, Department of Geography, Carleton University

H. W. O. Okoth-Ogendo, Population Studies and Research Institute, University of Nairobi

Dessalegn Rahmato, Institute of Development Research, Addis Ababa University

Terence Ranger, St. Antony's College, Oxford University

Michael Roth, Land Tenure Center, University of Wisconsin–Madison

Mahir Şaul, Department of Anthropology, University of Illinois, Urbana–Champaign

Michael J. Watts, Department of Geography, University of California, Berkeley

Richard P. Werbner, Department of Social Anthropology, University of Manchester

Land in African Agrarian Systems

Thomas J. Bassett

Introduction: The Land Question and Agricultural Transformation in Sub-Saharan Africa

New types of crops and new methods of agriculture are transforming the systems of tenure; land is being commercialized; the basis
of holding land is changing from one of community and custom
to one of individualism and contract; wealthy native capitalists
are appearing; agricultural debt is already in full swing, and
many peasants are becoming labourers on lands which were once
their own.

—C. K. Meek, 1946

Together with *histoire des femmes* land disputes are the main
issue dealt with by the tribunals.

—A. Köbben, 1963

Introduction

Until recently, there has been little discussion in the African agrarian
crisis literature on the issues of access to, control over, and, to a lesser
extent, management of rural land.[1] The relative neglect of this subject is
the result of the predominance of two related approaches to the relationship between land tenure systems and agricultural productivity in sub-
Saharan Africa. The first is the common view that in comparison to
population-land densities in Asia and Latin America, sub-Saharan Africa is a relatively land abundant region. Labor shortages are generally
perceived to be a more critical constraint to expanding agricultural output than land availability. The second approach similarly minimizes the
role tenure systems play as a constraint on increasing agricultural productivity by arguing that "customary" or indigenous systems have generally
accommodated the needs of peasant farmers seeking access to land.[2]

Some recent studies on landholding patterns in Africa challenge these
common views. Cohen argues that population densities are much higher
than the frequently cited 10 to 30 persons per square kilometer when
nonarable land is excluded from the equation. The fact that rural population growth rates have been higher than the expansion in area under
cultivation suggests that pressures are greater than generally thought,

3

especially on the best lands.[3] Kenneth Swindell and A.T.B. Mamman's research on land expropriation and accumulation in the Sokoto region of northern Nigeria suggests that landlessness is a growing problem in the peripheries and hinterlands of urban areas.[4] The notion that indigenous tenure systems are sufficiently flexible to accommodate changes in production is the subject of considerable debate to which I will return below. Suffice it to say here that a large number of recent case studies indicate that in some parts of Africa, access to land is becoming difficult for some groups, especially women, pastoralists, and poor households.[5] A common theme of these studies is that African tenure systems are becoming more and more exclusive as the rights to land are (re-)defined more narrowly in the context of new political, social, and economic conditions. In short, Africa is no longer perceived to be an exception to the trends in land concentration and scarcity typical of other Third World regions.

Colonial administrators, African elites, and foreign aid donors have historically viewed indigenous landholding systems as obstacles to increasing agricultural output.[6] These groups have argued that only private, freehold arrangements will provide the investment security necessary to make African agriculture more efficient and productive. Indeed, the World Bank is currently funding a new series of land titling and cadastral projects in sub-Saharan Africa on the assumption that title will confer the necessary security to stimulate agricultural investments and thus increase productivity.[7] The impetus for organizing the conference on land in African agrarian systems was to examine critically such assumptions, especially in light of much recent scholarly research showing that the relationship between security and productivity is complicated by social and political processes that appear to have a greater impact on investments than formal tenure considerations.[8]

The question of whether or not there is a relationship between the current agrarian crisis and access to and control of rural land has been raised but not thoroughly explored.[9] Given the World Bank's renewed interest in tenure issues in its sectoral work and structural adjustment programs, there is a need to transcend its technocratic and theological approaches that posit a direct link between freehold tenure and productivity.[10] The central argument of this volume is that such calls for sweeping tenure changes are misconceived. The notion that tenure reform is the panacea to Africa's agrarian ills is an old idea that ignores critical social dynamics that strongly influence how productive resources are acquired, utilized, contested, and immobilized. Indeed, a major contribution of this volume is the conceptualization of land tenure as a political process. This is most evident in the case studies that document a variety of conflicts over land rights as a result of government legislation and changing economic and political circumstances. The contributions help to illuminate the extent to which the politics of land access and control present problems to individuals and groups seeking to expand agricultural output.

The case studies are pitched at different scales of analysis. Some focus primarily at the level of the household and community, while others are situated at the national level, as in the discussions on the politics of land reform. Most of the papers seek to integrate these various levels to show how land access, control, and management strategies are embedded in social, political, and economic structures that vary and change over time. Any analysis of the links between landholding patterns and agricultural output must therefore consider tenure systems as "embedded systems."[11] The thrust of this collection is that we need to examine the nature of these embedded systems to understand the dynamics of agricultural change in Africa today.

Historical Antecedents

Notwithstanding the remarks of C. K. Meek, it is difficult to generalize about the impetus for and direction of change in landholding patterns. The tendency of colonial apologists to project their own (European) models and concepts of land tenure onto African societies has hindered our understanding of development and change in this area. As noted in the following pages, ethnocentric and ideological biases and their attendant political agendas distort much of the literature. Rather than try to determine the major sources of change in tenure regimes, I attempt here a periodization of official efforts to transform indigenous "communal" tenure systems along individual, private lines as a means of expanding agricultural production.[12] I am interested in identifying periods of interest in this type of tenure reform for two reasons. First, such an approach will help to place this book in a larger historical framework. For example, many contemporary pronouncements on the advantages of individualized holdings are echoed in the official colonial record. An examination of this literature enables one to detect the extent of continuity and change in land tenure policies in sub-Saharan Africa. The second objective is theoretical. How can one explain past and present interest in this subject? How have indigenous tenure systems been portrayed over time? What has motivated officials to promote individualized holdings?[13] The following periodization of reform initiatives shows the emergence of an evolutionary model of tenure change and agricultural development that continues to dominate the approaches of contemporary reformers. This model suggests that freehold tenure offers the most propitious conditions for agricultural investments and heightened productivity. It is based on the assumption that land registration brings the necessary security for producers to obtain credit and to manage their resources more efficiently. Such reforms have been proposed most often during crisis periods when the state has sought to stabilize economic and political conditions by nurturing a mass of producers whose stake in the land would help to buttress both the rural economy and the weakened state.

The first period (late nineteenth century to 1930) is marked by little interest on the part of colonial authorities in transforming African "communal" tenure systems into individual holdings.[14] In fact, this period is dominated by official efforts to preserve what were perceived to be customary rights to land for purposes of political stability.[15] Consonant with the policy of indirect rule, the state sought to maintain the political authority of chiefs and other elites whose status was partly based on their power to allocate use rights to land in "their territory."[16] The fact that the state often concocted this land-controlling power indicates that colonial authorities played an important role in the creation of African customary tenure.[17]

As Elizabeth Colson argues, the development of customary land laws during the colonial period was the outcome of Europeans projecting their notions of tenure as proprietary ownership onto African societies. If no individual owner of land could be identified, then ownership was attributed to the political unit residing in the area, whether or not the leaders of these polities actually held such notions or exercised such authority. Colson cogently argues that

the official search for the owners of all land encouraged the confusion of sovereignty with proprietary ownership and the creation of systems of communal tenure which came into being with precisely defined rules. These rules now inhibited the development of individual rights in waste land because it was deemed that such rights encroached upon the ancient right of some community, lineage, or "tribal" polity. The newly created system was described as resting on tradition and presumably derived its legitimacy from immemorial custom. The degree to which it was a reflection of the contemporary situation and the joint creation of colonial officials and African leaders, more especially of those holding political office, was unlikely to be recognized.[18]

In the tropical forest zone of West Africa where African commercial agriculture was rapidly expanding, new rights to land were claimed and disputed.[19] Many disputes were resolved in "customary courts" over which colonial officials had ultimate jurisdiction. It was in such arenas that European biases and stereotypes of African custom became encoded in new definitions of indigenous tenure systems. One is struck by the narrowness and rigidity of these interpretations in contrast to the apparent openness and flexibility of precolonial patterns of land use, access, and control.[20] Terence Ranger's contribution (chap. 13) provides an excellent illustration of how this process unfolded in Southern Rhodesia (Zimbabwe).

Despite the tremendous diversity of policies among (and within) the colonies, common in both French and British colonies was the monopolization of rights to alienate land by the state. The creation of Crown lands in the British colonies and state ownership of "vacant lands" in the French territories sought to promote political stability and to provide European settlers and companies with sufficient land for their enterprises. As Lord Hailey notes, a major objective of land policies in this first period was to promote colon agricultural development.[21] Immigrant farmers and later industrialists were seen as the main source of the revenues needed to sustain the colonial administrations. African agriculture played different roles from one colonial economy to another. In West Africa, the state promoted peasant commodity production, while in the eastern and southern regions, Africans were generally forced to become migrant laborers on white settler enterprises. As H. W. O. Okoth-Ogendo remarks in his contribution (chap. 9), controlling land was central to the "efficient exploitation" of the colonies in the latter area. Indeed, one objective of the Native Reserves was to generate a steady flow of cheap labor to settler farms and mines.[22] They also served as shock absorbers in that nonproductive members of the community were cared for by residents of the reserves and not by the colonial state.[23] In some areas, settlers even sought to usurp the privileges of African elites by claiming the right to labor tribute, as in the *thangata* system in Nyasaland (Malawi).[24]

The common prohibition on freehold tenure in the reserves was typically rationalized on the paternalistic and racist grounds that Africans were incapable of looking out for their own best interests. The state would serve as the Africans' "protector" to make sure they did not sell off the little that they possessed. Although some officials were sincere in their interest to shield indigenous peoples from the settler onslaught, the ideology of the protector myth is transparent. Its practical implications for the maintenance of colonial rule are equally clear. An exclusive right to alienate reserve land enabled the state to initiate resettlement schemes and soil conservation works as well as to expropriate land for settlers for future agricultural and industrial development.

In summary, despite the official interest in preserving "native law and custom," the interpretation of customary tenure was quite narrow, influenced as it was by European notions of proprietary ownership. Far from preserving customary land laws, the search for individual landowners, the redrawing of community boundaries, and the flood of land laws at the turn of the century created new rights and conditions of access that became the subject of considerable dispute.[25] Ironically, this search for tradition and the European interpretation of customary tenure created the conditions for promoting individualized holdings during the next period.

During the second period (1930–1960), a series of economic and political crises (the Great Depression, World War II, resistance, and decolonization) forced colonial officials to take a closer look at African land use patterns and tenure systems. In repeated efforts to stabilize their regimes during these crises, officials encouraged the expansion and intensification of African agriculture. Despite local differences, a common model of agrarian change in which agricultural progress is measured by the gradual dissolution of "communal tenure" into individual rights in land guided these reformist policies.[26] In the view of colonial officials, like Governor Reste of Côte d'Ivoire, individualization of production was a natural process in which he equated changing social relations of production with "moral emancipation."

It is obvious that we have a great interest in favoring the moral but especially the economic emancipation of the individual so that he [*sic*] will take a liking for his work and become more conscious of his personal interests. . . . We have a great interest in favoring the constitution of an *indigenous peasantry* of small and middle landowners. This is the goal that we must assign ourselves.[27]

When writing in 1932, Reste's main interest was to create incentives for individual producers to increase their output. In the five-year period 1928 to 1932, custom receipts—the primary indicator of the colony's prosperity—had dropped by three-fifths. The governor's solution was to encourage more goods for export. In his view, paying individual producers instead of chiefs was an important step toward intensifying production. He envisioned the emergence of a peasantry, not unlike the French one, that had a stake in the land and thus an incentive to produce.

It was widely believed by colonial administrators and agricultural service personnel that a major obstacle to realizing production goals was the varied system of customary tenure that they continued to have a hand in creating. Although recognized by many administrators to have social and political advantages, customary tenure was increasingly viewed as an impediment to agricultural growth.[28] The primary complaint was that "traditional tenure" did not provide adequate security to producers willing to invest in production. That too many people could claim rights to the same parcel of land discouraged land improvements. A second concern was the difficulty in obtaining credit since land could not be mortgaged. According to critics of communal tenure systems, the commercialization of land rights would solve most, if not all, of these production problems.[29]

In eastern and southern Africa, these criticisms were more attenuated. Although some considered individual holdings to be the ideal form of tenure, political reasons discouraged colonial officials from granting freehold status. Some administrators opposed freehold because it would mean the loss of the right to expropriate lands and the ability to regulate agricultural practices in the reserves.[30] Freehold was available to Africans only in the "Native Purchase Areas" of Northern Rhodesia and Kenya and in the Land Settlement Scheme of Swaziland. Elsewhere, they held land as tenants of the state, as in Southern Rhodesia under the Native Land Husbandry Act, or under customary tenure in resettlement areas, as in Tanganyika (Tanzania).[31]

Colonial authorities were particularly reluctant to grant freehold status to Africans in eastern and southern Africa on the grounds that if their agricultural practices went unchecked, they would destroy the land. As early as the 1920s, district officers and agricultural department personnel cited soil erosion in the reserves as a major problem. Typically, officials blamed African farmers and pastoralists for mismanaging the land in the most pejorative terms.[32] The causes most frequently cited to explain the problem were overstocking, agricultural techniques, the fragmentation of landholdings, and high population growth rates. By the 1940s, soil conservation programs were in full swing throughout the region. In South Africa, "betterment and rehabilitation schemes" involved resettlement and restrictions on livestock raising and shifting cultivation. In Tanganyika, "plow rules" and forced conservation works were financed by a special tax levied on maize producers.[33]

The official reaction to soil erosion and the subsequent conservation policies followed the classic blaming-the-victim approach.[34] The fact that a minority of colonial settlers occupied the most fertile land and that the majority of Africans were forced to work marginal soils did not enter the analysis. The land-extensive nature of African agricultural systems in the context of increasing population growth and relative land scarcity resulted, not surprisingly, in overcrowded conditions.[35] Policies such as the prohibition of livestock raising in certain areas, group resettlement, and compulsory conservation work were strongly resented by rural producers. The highly coercive nature of these policies and the fact that European settlers were their major beneficiaries made soil conservation a major political issue.[36] By the 1950s, African resentment and resistance expressed itself in the abandonment of new settlement areas in Nyasaland and the destruction of contour ridges and terraces in Sukumaland, Tanganyika.[37]

As Okoth-Ogendo underlines in his contribution, colonial soil conservation policies were "diversionary" in that they failed to address the pressures compelling peasants to mismanage natural resources. He argues that they protected the interests of the settler elite to the detriment of the African masses. When one considers how land use regulations served to control people, the ideological content of these policies also appears to be important. Meek's comments lucidly reveal how conservation ideology legitimated continued state control over the reserve lands.

The wide demand for freehold may be regarded as part of the general development of economic individualism. . . . Yet the indiscriminate grant of freehold title may have the most disastrous effects on the welfare of any territory, since it may effectively tie the hands of governments in all schemes of agricultural advance. Ignorant peasants armed with freehold rights may soon destroy the country's capital. An effective system of State ownership, on the other hand, assures to the community the maintenance of the fertility of the soil, as well as such incremental value as may arise, not from the efforts of the occupiers [*sic*], but from the development of the country as a whole.[38]

Such views reflect the efforts of colonial apologists to legitimate the colonial status quo. They also lend support to David Anderson and Richard Grove's point that "the exclusion or the social control of people has been the pragmatic guiding principle if not the original motivation of these (conservation) policies."[39]

The Master Farmer Schemes of Rhodesia and Nyasaland in the 1950s indicate that the colonial position on the relative merits of freehold tenure was ambivalent. While Meek's statements highlight the conservative settler view toward individual tenure, more liberal positions were held by officials seeking to nurture a class of prosperous African farmers during the period of decolonization. The Master Framer Schemes were built on the idea that individualized holdings combined with conservation training would result in greater agricultural output and higher standards of living. Freehold tenure was viewed as providing the security necessary to stimulate increased investment in the land.[40]

In summary, this second period shows evidence of a major policy shift from supporting customary tenure arrangements for largely political reasons during the first period to a growing commitment to individualized holdings for mainly economic reasons. Although this new position was not consistent, especially on the issue of conservation, a change in thinking about the relative strengths of individual versus communal holdings was particularly evident in discussions on expanding African agricultural output. Officials perceived the apparent movement toward individualization of land rights in commercial cropping areas as an evolutionary trend. It was a unilinear transition consisting of a gradual shift from customary to individual rights in land. Moreover, this transition could be encouraged by introducing land laws to promote individualization and expanded production. On the eve of independence, this evolutionary model of agrarian change had become a major policy option for African leaders in their quest for economic development.

The third period of interest in transforming African customary tenure systems into freehold arrangements begins in the early 1980s after a hiatus of nearly twenty years. Yet the 1960s and 1970s were by no means a quiet period. They may rightfully be labeled the land reform decades, a period in which dozens of independent African governments enacted new land legislation. These initiatives reflected considerable continuity with the past in three respects. First, as a number of case studies in this volume note, many postcolonial governments simply retained or revised colonial land laws. Second, ideologues everywhere continued to perceive indigenous tenure systems as hindering the formation of agrarian structures that were both highly productive and congruent with doctrinal principles. To capitalist-oriented regimes, the now-familiar litany of criticisms ranging from farmer insecurity to environmental degradation were basic assumptions behind land laws promoting freehold tenure. To socialist-inclined governments, indigenous tenure systems were condemned not only as inefficient but also as conducive to capitalist class formation if allowed to evolve on their own. Third, the new land laws reflected what Okoth-Ogendo refers to as the "broad-spectrum approach" of land reform. Policymakers during these two decades held the common assumption that a wide range of agrarian ills could be treated with the land reform pill. The curative powers of such prescriptions were, and continue to be, based on the problematic view that land reform is in itself sufficient to transform production structures. This theme is more closely examined by Okoth-Ogendo, Dessalegn Rahmato, Merle Bowen, and Ranger in Part III, on radical agrarian reform.

The timing of this renewed interest in African land tenure in the 1980s agrees with the thesis that attention to the subject is linked to official efforts to resolve economic and specifically agricultural problems. Although the data are highly contentious, agricultural production appears to have stagnated in the 1960s and 1970s in sub-Saharan Africa.[41] None other than the president of the World Bank, Robert McNamara, admitted in his famous Nairobi speech in September 1973 that two decades of development assistance had not measurably changed the lot of the rural poor in the Third World. In fact, their conditions had deteriorated in many areas, notably, in Africa where famine peaked in 1973 in the Sahelian region. The greater emphasis given to rural development during the McNamara years (1968–1981) involved few serious attempts at land reform.[42] Between 1975 and 1981, just 7 percent of the World Bank's agricultural and rural development projects contained landholding and titling components, most of which took place in Latin American countries. Since 1982, the World Bank and other lending agencies have dramatically increased funding to land-related projects in all regions.[43] The greater attention to land tenure systems in this third period must be viewed in the context of the crisis in African agriculture. The outpouring of analytical and prescriptive literature on food and rural development has brought the role of land tenure systems to the forefront of African studies. If recent reviews of the literature are suggestive, there is much continuity in the themes, issues, and approaches between the second and third periods.[44]

An important book bridging the two periods is *African Agrarian Systems,* edited by Daniel Biebuyck. Its main contribution lies in detailed studies of indigenous tenure systems—a topic that was relatively neglected by Meek and Hailey in their surveys of colonial land policies. In contrast to the stereotyping of custom common in these books,[45] the Biebuyck volume emphasizes local variability and the influence of both endogenous and exogenous factors in the making of different systems. Many of the contributors, especially Paul Bohannan and Polly Hill, offer trenchant critiques of the assumptions of the tenure evolution model and call for less ethnocentric concepts and approaches.[46] Bohannan stresses the social nature of land access and control, a recurring theme in recent studies. He urges scholars and administrators alike to view land tenure systems not only in terms of relations between people and land (the "man-thing unit") but also among people (the "man-man unit").[47]

Despite its greater sensitivity to local variability in indigenous tenure systems, the Biebuyck volume echoes Meek's and Hailey's emphasis on the relative strengths of "individual" versus "communal" systems in improving agricultural output. Audrey Richards's and Charles White's contributions, for example, examine the individualization of landholdings in Buganda and Northern Rhodesia.[48] White's study, in particular, reflects the influence of modernization theory in its depiction of freehold tenures as "modern" and communal systems as exhibiting "certain undeveloped features." He argues that continuous cultivation, cash cropping (especially of perennial crops), and population pressure are the three most important factors accounting for "individualized rights"—that is, a land market. Shifting cultivation is considered to be a backward agricultural system since it inhibits the "the full emergence of land rights of individuals."[49] White even ventures into applied anthropology when he hypothesizes that freehold tenure is likeliest to emerge among patrilineal and virilocal societies and least likely to emerge among matrilineal and uxuorilocal groups. In short, the evolutionary model of agrarian change is well represented in Biebuyck, albeit cloaked in the terminology of the anthropology of modernization.

The land tenure studies of the 1980s continue to give considerable attention to the transition between communal and individual tenure regimes and to linkages between land degradation and landholdings. New research directions focus on inter- and intrahousehold struggles over land with emphasis on gender inequalities in landholdings and land concentration by indigenous elites.

Discussions on the transition between indigenous and freehold tenure appear in the literature in two variants. The first encompasses a number of analyses focusing on the apparent shift toward greater individualization of rights in land where land pressure results in relative scarcity. A variety of forces are cited, often in a checklist fashion, to explain this process. Both John Cohen and Robert Hecht follow Biebuyck's general argument, in which population pressure and expanding agricultural commercialization lead to greater individualization of land rights.[50] However, they present more sophisticated arguments. Hecht shows that individualization is not merely a response to changing demographic and economic conditions but also reflects the historically shifting strategies of landowners to strengthen their political and economic position in the community. Cohen similarly urges caution in citing such factors as explanatory variables. He notes that "the causes of population increases rather than the increases themselves may be more important in understanding the nature of land-tenure changes."[51] Despite these caveats and insights, the arguments remain unilinear and constructed on ideal conceptual types of corporate and individual tenures.

The second variant of the transition debate focuses on the relative efficiency of individual versus communal tenure systems in increasing agricultural output. This largely technocratic position is taken by the French geographer, Pierre Gourou, who contends that private, individual tenure arrangements will lead to greater security, efficiency, and productivity in Africa.

Communal tenure protects the individual from indigence. But it is an obstacle to technical progress. If the agricultural future of tropical Africa is intensification, then it can hardly be conceived of occurring outside of private property. How can a farmer invest labor and capital into his field if he is not the owner? Improvements, fertilizers, terracing, drainage, irrigation, all this cannot be realized outside of private and hereditary property.[52]

In its study on the African economic crisis, the World Bank similarly argues that private property is a key incentive for farmers to invest in land improvements. It invokes the evolutionary model of tenure change and agricultural growth to make its case for redefining land rights and funding land registration projects in sub-Saharan Africa: "Since countries (and regions) are at *different stages of this transition,* Africa has diverse and changing land rights. Agricultural modernization combined with population pressure will make land titling necessary."[53]

The critics of this neomodernization model argue that the data are too weak to support such claims.[54] Angelique Haugerud shows that among the Embu of Kenya, land titling has not led to significant investments in agriculture. Although credit is available to titleholders, funds are most often channeled into off-farm investments such as charcoal production, children's education, and land speculation.[55] Further evidence from Ghana and Rwanda indicates that land titling has little effect on productivity.[56] Raymond Noronha argues that neither communal nor individual systems have a direct bearing on agricultural output but that more important variables appear to be security of possession, access to other productive resources (labor, credit, inputs) and institutional rents (subsidies and extension services), and managerial capability.[57] John Bruce's contribution in this volume (chap. 1) evaluates the merits of the opposing views in this debate.

Notwithstanding these findings, it is still widely believed that individual ownership is one key to solving much of Africa's economic and environmental problems; in the meantime, the transition toward it produces much uncertainty, which further exacerbates the situation. This view is well expressed by Paul Harrison in *The Greening of Africa:*

Most of Africa is in the transition phase between communal and individual ownership. It is a no-man's land in which farmers have permanent rights over an area, without legal title to it. Their tenure is uncertain. They cannot offer their holding as collateral for loans, because it is not fully theirs to forfeit if they default. They cannot be sure they will still be farming the same areas in ten or twenty years' time, and so they are more reluctant to invest in permanent improvements to the land, from tree planting to soil conservation works.[58]

The links between land degradation and landholding patterns have received considerable attention since the 1977 U.N. conference on desertification in Africa. Desertification, like coup d'états and famines, has become emblematic of Africa in the distorted news coverage of the continent. Popular writers like Lloyd Timberlake and Paul Harrison devote chapters to "the desertification problem" in their recent books in which they link land degradation to insecurity of tenure.[59] With one important difference, Timberlake presents what Piers Blaikie labels the "classic or colonial approach to erosion and conservation" with his emphasis on environmental factors (soils and climate), mismanagement of the environment, overpopulation, and market integration.[60] In the colonial view, the insufficient development of cash cropping impeded soil conservation. Only when farmers produced for the market would they adopt such "modern" agricultural techniques as soil conservation.[61] Timberlake departs from the classic approach by suggesting that market involvement may accelerate environmental degradation when deteriorating terms of trade push peasants to intensify production on marginal soils. However, he is vague on the nature of this involvement and leaves one with little understanding about the possible links between environmental mismanagement, population growth, and market involvement.[62]

Communal tenure systems continue to be cited as a structural feature of environmental degradation in Africa. In an overview of the anti-pastoralist literature, Michael Horowitz and Peter Little note that their long-standing condemnation by colonialists for destroying the environment is reiterated today in the discourse on common property resources, which blames herders for abusing the privilege of grazing their (private) animals on (communal) ranges by overstocking. The resulting "tragedy of the commons" becomes manifest in land degradation.[63] An often-proposed solution is the privatization of the commons.[64]

Lionel Cliffe notes a similar recourse to the same paradigm in the "conservationist orthodoxy" of Zimbabwe. The degradation of grazing lands there is in part explained by the open access to rangelands by residents of the so-called communal areas. Zimbabwean bureaucrats perceive this free access to pasture and water as a structural problem inhibiting "improved land use."[65] Ranger's discussion (chap. 13) illuminates the opposing sides and issues in this debate.

As many critics have pointed out, the tragedy of the common perspective is flawed by its assumptions about "unregulated" access to productive resources and the corollary that "improved" land use practices will result from privatization.[66] There is much historical evidence showing that pastoralists have regulated access to rangelands, as in the case of the interior delta of the Niger during the early nineteenth century.[67] Horowitz and Little rightly challenge the view that pastoralists are inherently self-seeking individuals with no responsibilities and obligations in the communities to which they belong.

Almost all of the anthropological literature on pastoralism points to restrictions on both access and use of "communal" ranges, and widespread claims on the use and disposition of "private" livestock. In other words, pastoralists, no less than anyone else, live in communities, and these communities have moral bases which do not allow for unchecked personal aggrandizement at the expense of one's fellows.[68]

The second assumption, that privatization will ensure sound land use management, has also been effectively refuted by many authorities. Bruce notes in this volume (chap. 1) that the American Dust Bowl is a prime example of where this logic breaks down. Other observers have pointed to evidence of land degradation in areas of Botswana, Lesotho, and Kenya where privatization of rangelands has occurred.[69] Pauline Peters proposes a more appropriate analytic framework when she argues for viewing commons systems as embedded systems characterized by "multiple or overlapping rights" and by a "combination of individual and group claims."[70] Land rights are rooted not only in changing economic and political structures but also in the interpretation and transformation of meanings associated with access to common property resources. As Peters argues, "Competition among rights and claims takes place through competition in meanings. These are assigned, accepted, and imposed: whose right, which meaning, whose definition are critical questions in deciphering changes in land rights.[71] Michael Watts's paper (chap. 6) shows how such questions are central to understanding the politics of access to and management of irrigated rice land in The Gambia.

A third group of studies that emerged in the 1980s examines the nature and implications of contemporary access and control patterns on land concentration, socioeconomic differentiation, and gender relations of production. The results of this predominantly village-level fieldwork challenge many of the simplistic assumptions underlying the evolutionary model of tenure change and agricultural development. They also raise new questions about the relationship between landholding patterns and agrarian change which are pushing the tenure debate out of its evolutionary cul-de-sac.

Sara Berry's work on the privatization and concentration of productive resources in West Africa emphasizes the centrality of social identity and political power in obtaining and defending rights in rural land. She challenges the notion of progressive individualization assumed in the tenure stage model by showing how multiple claims to the same parcel of land result in incomplete privatization of rights in the highly commercialized tree-cropping zones of West Africa.[72] She notes how labor mobilization strategies and inheritance rules frequently lead to situations where there are "overlapping and open-ended rights" in tree-crop farms. This indeterminancy of ownership often leads to land disputes that are commonly resolved in favor of individuals who wield the greatest political power. Since status is a fundamental basis of political power in Africa, rival claimants in land disputes frequently invest considerable sums to enhance their social position (e.g., finance lavish weddings, obtain locally prestigious titles), to the apparent detriment of agricultural investments.[73] Berry's point is that rights in land are "embedded in multistranded social relationships" that are open to redefinition under changing political, social, and economic circumstances. Land use and rural investment patterns can, in part, be viewed as the result of individual and group strategies to obtain and secure rights to land in these changing contexts.

Jean Davison similarly accentuates the social and political dimensions of landholding rights in Africa in her theoretical discussion on gender relations of production.[74] Specifically, Davison notes that women's access to land is today widely determined by their relationship to men, especially as wives. In the past, this access was not as severely circumscribed since women frequently inherited rights in land from kin. Davison argues that the development of commodity relations during the colonial period led to a restructuring of gender relations in which men benefited from European notions of property in assuming control over cash crop production and primary rights in land. As a result, women are increasingly dependent on their husbands and kin to obtain what are usually secondary rights in land. Even these rights are now being eroded, as many of the case studies in Davison's collection illustrate.[75]

The emphasis given by Berry and Davison to the centrality of power relations in the acquisition of land rights and in the process of social differentiation in West Africa is amplified by other Africanist scholars. For example, Miriam Goheen points to the emergence of new elites in northwestern Cameroon who are able to accumulate land because of their knowledge of national laws and their ability to gain influential positions in local institutions.[76] These "modern big men" profit from the ambiguous coexistence of national and local tenure regimes that, in Paul Harrison's view, only leads to insecurity and land degradation. Further evidence from Kenya and Niger suggests, to the contrary, that relatively wealthy households view uncertain tenure as an opportunity to expand their holdings.[77] These rural elites have their counterparts in urban areas where civil servants, government officials, and merchants acquire rural land through their knowledge, resources, and contacts in government bureaucracies. Allan Hoben accentuates the degree to which the process of rural land concentration by urban elites in Somalia depends on their political influence as opposed to their farm managerial capabilities.[78]

Access to registered land, particularly large tracts of new land believed to have development potential, depends on claimants' ability to mobilize a broad range of political and economic resources, rather than on their ability to generate and reinvest profits from agriculture in additional land. In this sense, land accumulation is thus primarily a political rather than an economic process. The successful individual or agency is one that has contacts in the bureaucracy, knowledge of how to "work the system," clan and personal ties with high government officials, access to government credit and equipment, or is able to obtain support from foreign aid agencies.[79]

The accent of these recent studies on the social and political dimensions of land access and control suggests some important relationships between the nature of landholdings and agricultural performance in contemporary Africa. Berry's work takes us the farthest in this direction in her discussion of the implications of overlapping rights in land and incomplete privatization for agricultural investments. However, these recent collections only indirectly address the relationship between the land question and agricultural performance. Their main contribution lies in the detailed examinations of land access and control in terms of gender inequality and concentration. The Davison and Richard Downs and Stephen Reyna volumes have advanced the discussion on indigenous tenure systems by focusing on important inter- and intrahousehold dynamics relating to resource control and use. This work is the first to take a broad look at the links between land tenure regimes and agricultural performance since the Biebuyck volume published nearly thirty years ago.

Flexibility and Conflict in Indigenous Tenure Systems

One of the basic assumptions held by the tenure evolution theorists is that the progressive commercialization of agriculture inexorably leads to the individualization of rights in land.[80] Cohen questions this view on the grounds that field research shows peasants enjoying considerable individual freedom under corporate tenure systems. He wonders if the supposed shift toward individualization is really not a shift after all but merely a discovery by researchers of "underlying reality."[81]

Bruce's contribution (chap. 1) challenges the major assumptions of indigenous tenure critics with the reality of peasant farmers' rights in land. He systematically analyzes such concerns of reformers as the adequacy of indigenous tenure systems for investment security, efficient resource allocation, obtaining credit, and land transfers. Bruce acknowledges the importance of these concerns but concludes that in only a few cases do they pose serious problems to African farmers today. He offers practical suggestions in the form of a series of questions that force one to consider nonreform approaches to apparent tenure constraints.

One of the criticisms of indigenous tenure systems discussed by Bruce holds that the absence of land markets impedes agricultural development. At issue is the ability of "outsiders" seeking to expand their agricultural operations to gain access to land held under customary tenure. Steven Lawry (chap. 2) and Mahir Şaul (chap. 3) illustrate, to the contrary, that land transfers are commonplace between indigenous landholders and outsiders in rural Lesotho and Burkina Faso. Their case studies highlight the flexibility of indigenous tenure systems by showing how land borrowing and leasing arrangements accommodate the needs of landless and commercial farmers in areas with different population densities. Lawry demonstrates how sharecropping and leasing provide ample security to farmers in densely populated areas of Lesotho. Şaul turns the neoclassical concern with security on its head by arguing that a major reason why transfers take place in Burkina Faso is because the *lender* feels secure that his permanent rights in the land are recognized. The flexibility of the system breaks down only when the lender feels insecure about regaining control over borrowed land.[82] Şaul also challenges the evolutionary model of progressive individualization by noting how the expansion of commodity production has strengthened lineage control over land in Bare. Both illuminate some of the interests and circumstances behind the persistence of customary tenure despite the attempts of government planners and international aid donors to transform these systems.

Conflicts over land use and control in pastoral development is the central theme of chapters 4 and 5. Richard Werbner examines the strategies of elites in Botswana to acquire land for commercial agriculture and livestock raising. What has been condemned by many observers as one of Africa's great enclosure movements is shown by Werbner to be a more complicated and less deterministic process. His attention to power struggles over land access and control among "competitive and disunited elites" reveals a situation of incomplete privatization of land. Borehole owners and those possessing ranch leases continue to practice extensive, open-range livestock raising for political and economic reasons. In fact, it appears that herd mobility across the unenclosed range is greater today than in the past. Yet, these new claims to land conflict with the rights of others like the hunting-gathering San and Barolong agropastoralists whose common land has been eaten up by powerful landholders.

Werbner shows how elites have historically secured land through their political influence and by strengthening their "organic links" with rural areas through such strategies as retribalization and neopatrimonialism. It is only within such cultural, political, and historical-geographic contexts, he argues, that one can understand the forms and outcomes of land conflicts in contemporary Botswana.

My own contribution (chap. 5) examines the origins and failure of a Fulani sedentarization scheme in northern Côte d'Ivoire. The case study shows that the interactive effects of land conflicts between different groups at three overlapping levels (local, regional, and national) undermine both the expansion of Fulani livestock production and the intensification of agricultural systems in the savanna region. The scheme's failure is attributed to the inadequacy of technocratic approaches to solving interlocking political, economic, and human ecological problems.

In summary, the circulation of land via borrowing, inheritance, leasing, and pledging is a key characteristic of flexible indigenous tenure systems. Land was even alienable during the precolonial period, a type of transfer that should not be seen exclusively as an outgrowth of capitalist land markets.[83] The issue of secure rights in land under indigenous control cannot be answered outside of those social systems in which rights are assumed, negotiated, and lost. As Okoth-Ogendo argues, the content and longevity of these rights range along a continuum from "the most temporary and functionally specific allocation of power . . . [to] the full complement of power in respect to some or all functions."[84] The degree of security or individual control can swing back and forth along this continuum of rights, depending on the extent of one's ability to engage in the process of tenure building. By tenure building, Okoth-Ogendo means "the expansion and continuous vindication of particular allocations of power in specific production contexts."[85] In this sense, the process of acquiring and defending rights in land is inherently a political process based on power relations among members of the social group. That is, membership in the social group is, by itself, not a sufficient condition for gaining and maintaining access to land. A person's status (age, gender, ethnic group, elite group affiliations) can and often does determine his or her capacity to engage in tenure building. It is within this realm of inter- and intrahousehold politics that we turn in the next section of this book to examine the implications of changing conditions of production for the struggle over rights in land.

Access to Land and Agrarian Politics

Watts (chap. 6) opens the black box of intrahousehold production relations by focusing on conflicts over access to irrigated rice land in The

Gambia. The catalyst for these conflicts is the intensification of labor associated with the double-cropping of rice. By classifying newly formed rice plots as "household" fields in which all household members must work, Mandinka men attempt to monopolize control over land and crop rights. Mandinka women, however, are shown losing their individual swamp rice fields as their land is incorporated into the irrigated perimeters and reclassified as household fields. Many women have resisted this renaming of fields by withdrawing their labor power and contesting their de facto dispossession through appeals to project personnel and the courts. The complicity of project management in the "interpretive struggles" over land, labor, and crop rights is related to its overriding concern with meeting productivity goals. Watts shows that property rights are defined by social relationships that are represented in cultural forms such as language, gender roles, and labor arrangements. Thus, struggles over land and labor will often take the form of interpretive struggles over meaning in which "the power to name" can be a highly political issue.

In a different context, Fiona Mackenzie (chap. 7) addresses similar issues. Her focus is on how Kikuyu men seek to control land claimed by women by manipulating the tradition of *mbari*, the basic kinship and territorial unit of the past. They do this by invoking customary inheritance rules ostensibly to maintain the mbari territorial integrity. However, Mackenzie shows that the accumulation of land by individuals since the 1930s has considerably weakened this institution. The recourse to mbari authority represents, she argues, a re-creation of custom to mask ongoing processes of socioeconomic differentiation. Like Mandinka women in The Gambia, Kikuyu women are contesting these claims in the courts and are manipulating their own tradition of taking a "female husband" to preserve some of their rights in land.

Like Watts, Peter Bloch (chap. 8) also looks at changing patterns of land access and control in the context of an irrigated rice project, this time among the Soninké in the Bakel area of the Senegal River valley. His study focuses on the distributional effects of the new land use and tenure arrangements on casted people, former slaves, and women in the area. The results indicate that former nobles are seeking to exclude both women and other subordinate groups from acquiring improved land. The dispossessed have responded to these pressures by establishing their own perimeters in a few areas. But the most significant trend appears to be the strengthening of Soninké elite control over land and labor as "former" nobles acquire land in which their "former" dependents work. In sum, despite the purported egalitarian orientation of the irrigation scheme, the landholding elite is currently using new mechanisms of land control to perpetuate their social, political, and economic dominance.

In summary, the papers in Part II highlight the relationship between power relations and rights in land and how these relationships vary and change under different historical situations. Struggles over productive resources have historically taken place between the rich and powerful and the underclasses. The nature and outcome of these struggles are linked to changes in the conditions of production and the ability of individuals and groups to take advantage of new opportunities to improve their social and economic position within the community and household. In the context of these changing conditions, in which the meaning and substance of power relations are frequently contested, the outcome of these struggles is not predetermined by wealth and class.[86] Despite the efforts of men and nobles to reassert their hegemonic control over agricultural resources, women and other subordinate groups are meeting these challenges with some success. The ability of women and former slaves and serfs to open their own irrigated perimeters in the Bakel area of Senegal is illustrative of how the underclasses can alter previously entrenched relationships.

Radical Agrarian Reform and Agricultural Performance

A distinction is often made between agrarian reform and land reform. Land reform generally refers to a reorganization of tenure arrangements and landholdings that often assumes two basic forms: the breakup of large holdings and their redistribution and the consolidation of fragmented holdings into a single field. Agrarian reform often combines some type of land reform with specific interventions designed to promote rural development such as the expansion of extension services, agricultural credit, and improved infrastructure to rural producers.[87] The papers in Part III examine the attempts of colonial and postcolonial governments in eastern and southern Africa to implement agrarian reform programs to increase agricultural output. The case studies concentrate on states that have pursued socialist paths in which the development of collective agriculture (producer co-ops, state farms) has been a central feature of reform policies. Most of the authors concur on the dismal results of agrarian reform in these countries in raising agricultural productivity. The authors analyze the nature of this unimpressive performance and explain why radical agrarian reform has not been the panacea for the production problems plaguing African rural economies.

Okoth-Ogendo (chap. 9) contributes a historical overview of tenure reform policies in eastern and southern Africa. He identifies many continuities in the diagnoses of and prescriptions for various agrarian crises over the past hundred years. Repeated attempts at reform have failed, he argues, because of the view that tenure reform would, by itself, have a "broad-spectrum effect" that would cure the various ills afflicting rural society. Okoth-Ogendo views such prescriptions as illusory because they invariably blame the victim for his or her situation. Because they fail to identify correctly the production and marketing problems facing peasants, he views such approaches as diversionary.

Dessalegn Rahmato (chap. 10) evaluates the impact of the radical Ethiopian land reform decree of 1975 on the agricultural performance of different farm enterprises. He presents evidence showing that "private" peasant production outperformed state farms and cooperatives despite the massive channeling of resources to the collective sector. The overall decline in per capita agricultural output in Ethiopia is attributed to the "double subordination" of the peasantry. Peasants were subordinate, on the one hand, to the state by policies biased toward socialist forms of production and, on the other, to urban populations that were the main beneficiaries of fixed grain prices. Dessalegn acknowledges some of the positive social features of the land reform but is sharply critical of the Ethiopian government's doctrinal views of socialist agriculture. Important agrarian policy changes have recently been implemented in the rural areas. The new thinking is now in favor of peasant endeavor, reversing the earlier emphasis on collectivization. The structure of smallholder agriculture and most of the constraints inhibiting peasant production still remain, but the collective ("socialist") sector has now lost its significance. Dessalegn's contribution is important as a document in the history of agrarian contradictions in Ethiopia and should serve as a useful source to students concerned with Afro-Marxist agrarian history.

As in Ethiopia, land rights were concentrated in the Somalian state following its 1975 land reform. As Michael Roth remarks in chapter 11, the official rationalization for nationalizing land has been to encourage the "modernization" of agriculture and to guide agrarian change in an equitable and economically efficient direction. This process in Somalia entails the elimination of indigenous tenure systems that are perceived to be inefficient, environmentally destructive, and conducive to agrarian capitalist processes such as land speculation and concentration. Roth's study presents the results of a Land Tenure Center study examining the process of land registration and security of tenure in the lower Shebelle River valley. The most important trends he discusses are heightened peasant insecurity due to conflicts between customary and national land systems, rural land speculation by urban elites, and a reduced flexibility of indigenous tenure systems with little progress made toward equity and productivity. Taken together, Roth and Dessalegn show how the *étatist* nature of agrarian reform in the Horn of Africa fostered increasingly rigid land allocation and management practices. It is this rigidity, in contrast to the flexible use of resources under indigenous tenure systems, that partly accounts for the highly inefficient farming systems characteristic of the region in the 1980s.

The final two contributions focus on the processes of agrarian reform in southern Africa. Merle Bowen's study (chap. 12) of Mozambique's recent policy shift from a collective agricultural strategy to one oriented toward private and peasant farming in many ways complements Dessalegn's work on Ethiopia's reform experience. Like Ethiopia, Mozambique initially followed the orthodox socialist path of collective agriculture with a heavy emphasis on state farms. The same problems of poor performance, despite massive capital investments in this sector, have prompted officials of the ruling Frelimo party to seek alternative solutions to increasing agricultural output. Bowen locates the policy shift to a "private" farming strategy within the very difficult circumstances of Mozambique's decolonization process, internal and external aggression, the financial incapacity of the state to sustain the collective sector, and the pressures of foreign aid donors who are only willing to fund private initiatives. She notes that agricultural output has substantially increased in areas where the state has redistributed state farmland to peasants and smallholders. The flexible approach of Mozambican officials toward sharecropping and wage labor markets contrasts with the more rigid position of the Ethiopian government. Indeed, Mozambique appears to be succeeding in creating an "agricultural pluralism" that Dessalegn proposes for Ethiopia. Bowen wonders, however, if the processes of socioeconomic differentiation presently occurring in her study area will ultimately compromise the goals of equity for the sake of productivity.

The contribution by Terence Ranger (chap. 13) on agrarian reform in the so-called communal areas of Zimbabwe is a fitting closure to this collection. It brings us full circle on the debate over the potential of communal tenure systems for promoting agricultural growth. He begins by showing how the notion of communal tenure as it is currently conceptualized was not at all typical of the precolonial period. It emerged as a colonial construct during the 1920s and is shown by Ranger to be continually re-created by agrarian reform programs emphasizing egalitarian landholdings. He views current initiatives to reshape land tenure systems in the Communal Areas as an ironic continuity for a purportedly revolutionary government. He probes into the class nature of the communal area debate and notes that well-established commercial farmers have succeeded in shifting the discussion from land redistribution and resettlement for land hungry peasants to land tenure reform within the Communal Areas. Like Cliffe,[88] Ranger stresses the importance of community democratic control in any restructuring of the existing "flexible communal tenure" system. He concludes by viewing the absence of tenure reform legislation in Zimbabwe since independence as an encouraging sign that the debate about the land question and agricultural performance may be moving in potentially innovative directions. The case of Zimbabwe is illustrative of other countries where future agrarian reform legislation will reflect the outcome of struggles between contending groups such as large-scale commercial farmers and peasants who seek to gain access to and defend their control over productive resources. The papers in this collection suggest that whatever the outcome of these struggles, they will have important implications for agricultural performance in sub-Saharan Africa.

To reiterate the central argument of this book, tenure reform is not a cure-all for improving African agricultural performance. This is not to say that tenure constraints do not exist. As Bruce persuasively argues, there may be a need to modify certain features of indigenous systems when these changes are justified. But rather than attempting to replace these systems with European models, tenure reform strategies should build on the strengths of indigenous systems. Moreover, what appears to be a tenure constraint might in fact be a non-tenure-related problem requiring a nontenure solution. Too often, sweeping changes are proposed from both the left and right wings of the political-economic spectrum without any serious enquiry into the nature of the production problem. Instead, this book calls for pragmatism and a respect for the flexibility of indigenous tenure systems. At the same time, this is not a populist appeal that ignores the complicated issues of state intervention, socioeconomic differentiation, and the social relations of production.[89] The attention given here to social and political processes behind the struggles over productive resources seeks to situate the land question beyond the particularistic features of local tenure systems. This book examines the complicated relationships between these changing systems and agricultural development from a multidisciplinary perspective. Its major objective is to advance the debate over the land question and agricultural performance in Africa. In the process, it also seeks to temper the powerful forces bent on reforming tenure systems in the direction of privatization on the grounds that this is one key to increasing productivity and getting Africa out of its crisis. The case studies collected here argue that these doctrinal responses are inappropriate and are to be resisted.

Notes

For comments on an earlier draft of this introduction, I want to thank Sara Berry, Donald Crummey, Mahir Şaul, and Michael Watts.

1 By agrarian crisis, I am referring to the decline in per capita agricultural production since the 1960s. For two influential analyses of this crisis, see World Bank, *Accelerated Development in Sub-Saharan Africa: An Agenda for Action* (Washington, D.C., 1981), and S. Berry, "The Food Crisis and Agrarian Change in Africa." *African Studies Review* 27, 2 (1984): 59–112.

2 See C. Eicher and D. Baker, *Research on Agricultural Development in Sub-Saharan Africa: A Critical Survey* (East Lansing, 1982): 98; D. Grigg, *The World Food Problem: 1950–1980* (Oxford, 1985): 171.

3 It is estimated for the entire continent that 60 to 70 percent of the land is not suitable for either livestock or crop production due to deserts, mountains, rainfall, poor soils, and disease. See J. Cohen, "Land Tenure and Rural Development in Africa," in R. Bates and M. Lofchie (eds.), *Agricultural Development in Africa* (New York, 1980): 357–358.

4 Swindell, K., and A. T. B. Mamman, "Land Expropriation and Accumulation in the Sokoto Periphery, Northwest Nigeria, 1976–86," *Africa* 60, 2 (1990): 173–187.

5 J. Davison (ed.), *Agriculture, Women and Land: The African Experience* (Boulder 1988); and R. Downs and S. Reyna (eds.), *Land and Society in Contemporary Africa* (Hanover, N.H., 1988).

6 J. Bruce, *Land Tenure Issues in Project Design and Strategies for Agricultural Development in Sub-Saharan Africa,* Land Tenure Center Paper 128 (Madison, 1986); Cohen, "Land," 349–389; Lord Hailey, *An African Survey* (London, 1957): 685–815; and R. Noronha, *A Review of the Literature on Land Tenure Systems in Sub-Saharan Africa.* World Bank, Research Unit, Agricultural Development Department (Washington, D.C., 1985).

7 F. Falloux, "Land Management, Titling and Tenancy," in T. Davis and I. Schirmer (eds.), *Sustainability Issues in Agricultural Development* (Washington, D.C., 1987): 190–208.

8 For an excellent overview of recent social scientific approaches to African tenure systems, see the special issue of *Africa* 59, 1 (1989), "Access, Control and Use of Resources in African Agriculture."

9 For the most insightful inquiries addressing this question see Sara Berry, "Concentration without Privatization? Some Consequences of Changing Patterns of Rural Land Control in Africa," in Downs and Reyna (eds.), *Land,* 53–75, and S. Berry, "Property Rights and Rural Resource Management: The Case of Tree Crops in West Africa," *Cahiers d'ORSTOM Sciences Humains* 24, 1 (1988): 3–16; and H. W. O. Okoth-Ogendo, "The Perils of Land Tenure Reform: The Case of Kenya," in J. Arntzen, L. Ngcongco, and S. Turner (eds.), *Land Policy and Agriculture in Eastern and Southern Africa* (Tokyo, 1986). A network of francophone Africanists is examining the impact of the state and capital on landholding systems in rural and urban areas of sub-Saharan Africa. See E. Le Bris, E. Le Roy, and F. Leimforfer (eds.), *Enjeux fonciers en Afrique noire* (Paris, 1983); B. Crousse, E. LeBris, and E. Le Roy, *Espaces disputés en Afrique noire* (Paris, 1986); and R. Verdier and A. Rochegude, *Systèmes fonciers à la ville et au village* (Paris, 1986). Also, see the special issues of *African Perspectives* 1 (1979) and *Politique*

Africaine 21 (1986) which contain articles on the politics of land reform and agrarian change in sub-Saharan Africa.

10 World Bank, *Sub-Saharan Africa: From Crisis to Sustainable Growth* (Washington, D.C., 1989): 90, 100–104.

11 See P. Peters, "Embedded Systems and Rooted Models," in B. McKay and J. Acheson (eds.), *The Question of the Commons: The Culture and Ecology of Communal Resources* (Tucson, 1987): 171–194.

12 The focus in this historical section on transitions to individualized holdings versus collective forms typical of socialist states such as Ethiopia is based on the fact that most African states have pursued the capitalist road and that the current direction of reform in some socialist states such as Mozambique is toward individual holdings.

13 In posing these questions, I have been influenced by the work of Chauveau et al. on the emergence and depiction of African land tenure systems in the administrative and scientific literature. See J.-P. Chauveau, J.-P. Dozon, E. Le Bris, E. Le Roy, G. Salem, and F. G. Snyder, "Rapport introductif au journés d'études," in Le Bris et al., *Enjeux*, 17–43.

14 The focus here on the official and scholarly literature is linked to my interest in the evolution of land tenure policies and the gap between development theory and reality. The official literature is fundamental to this policy overview, while the scholarly literature illuminates the social and political origins and practical consequences of these policies. The late-nineteenth-century starting date for the first period is due to the fact that most of sub-Saharan Africa was partitioned into European colonies at this time.

15 Even in French West Africa where "direct rule" was the official method of administration, the French government recognized the land rights of indigenous peoples. However, its claim to be the owner of "vacant lands" introduced much ambiguity to this official position. See Hailey, *African*, 743–749.

16 C. K. Meek, *Land Law and Custom in the Colonies* (London, 1946): 10, 22.

17 For examples of the colonial state granting chiefs the right to control land, see Hailey, *African*, 709, 731, 792. For a discussion of the transformation of earth priests into "land lords," see E. Colson, "The Impact of the Colonial Period on the Definition of Land Rights," in V. Turner (ed.), *Colonialism in Africa 1870–1960*, vol. 3, *Profiles of Change: African Society and Colonial Rule* (Cambridge, 1971): 193–215. On the construction of communal tenure by colonial authorities, see A. Cheater, "The Ideology of 'Communal' Land Tenure in Zimbabwe: Mythogenesis Enacted," *Africa* 60, 2 (1990): 188–206. For a more general discussion, see E. Hobswan and T. Ranger (eds.), *The Invention of Tradition* (Cambridge, 1983).

18 Colson, "The Impact," 197.

19 See P. Hill, "Three types of Southern Ghanian Cocoa Farmer," in D. Biebuyck (ed.), *African Agrarian Systems* (Oxford, 1963): 203–223; and A. Köbben, "Land as an Object of Gain in a Non-Literate Society: Land-Tenure among the Bété and Dida (Ivory Coast, West Africa)," in Biebuyck, *African Agrarian Systems*, 245–264.

20 Many observers have commented on the adaptiveness and dynamism of

African tenure systems. See, for example, Colson, "The Impact," 196–197; Hill, "Three Types," 215; Meek, *Land,* 25–26, and Bruce, chap. 1, this volume.

21 To give credit where it is due, Lucy Mair wrote the chapter, "The Land" (chap. 11) in Hailey's *African Survey.* For a discussion on the origins and writing of this monumental work, see J. W. Cell, "Lord Hailey and the Making of the African Survey," *African Affairs* 88, 355 (1989): 481–505; and E. B. Worthington, "Lord Hailey on the African Survey: Some Comments," *African Affairs* 89, 357 (1990): 579–583.

22 A. J. Christopher, *Colonial Africa* (London, 1984): 58–60.

23 Hailey, *African,* 760.

24 Ibid., 711. For a detailed discussion of *thangata,* see L. White, *Magomero* (Cambridge 1987): 99–120.

25 I am grateful to Sara Berry for this observation; personal communication, September 7, 1989.

26 See Hailey, *African,* 802–803; and M. Chanock, "A Peculiar Sharpness: An Essay on Property in the History of Customary Law in Colonial Africa," *Journal of African History* 32, 1 (1991): 65–88.

27 Archives Nationales de la République de Côte d'Ivoire, 5792, Côte d'Ivoire, Rapport politique annuel, 1932. Emphasis in original.

28 See Meek, *Land,* 24–29; Hailey, *African,* 802–809.

29 See Hailey, *African,* 803.

30 Meek, *Land,* 14–15.

31 Hailey, *African,* 803–804.

32 See W. Beinart, "Soil Erosion, Conservationism and Ideas about Development: A Southern African Exploration, 1900–1960," *Journal of Southern African Studies* 11, 1 (1984): 52–83; M. Drinkwater, "Technical Development and Peasant Impoverishment: Land Use Policy in Zimbabwe's Midland Province," *Journal of Southern African Studies* 15, 2 (1989): 287–305; K. Showers, "Soil Erosion in the Kingdom of Lesotho: Origins and Colonial Response, 1830–1950s," *Journal of Southern African Studies* 15, 2 (1989): 263–286; M. Stocking, "Soil Conservation Policy in Colonial Africa," *Agricultural History* 59, 2 (1985): 148–161.

33 Hailey, *African,* 765–766; Beinhart, "Soil Erosion," 69–83; Stocking, "Soil Conservation Policy," 153–156.

34 See P. Blaikie, *The Political Economy of Soil Erosion* (London, 1985): 53–60.

35 According to Noronha, the population of Zimbabwe increased sixfold from an estimated 490,000 to 3.1 million over the period 1901–1962. Kenya's population doubled over the same period, rising from 4 million to 8.4 million. Noronha, *Review,* 84.

36 Blaikie, *Political Economy,* 59; Stocking, "Soil Conservation Policy," 155–160; D. Anderson and R. Grove (eds.), *Conservation in Africa: People, Policies and Practice* (Cambridge, 1987): 5–6.

37 Stocking, "Soil Conservation Policy," 158.

38 Meek, *Land,* 6.

39 Anderson and Grove, *Conservation*, 8.

40 Beinhart, "Soil Erosion," 79.

41 The data are taken from the World Bank, *Accelerated*, 3; the quality of these data is discussed by Berry, "Food Crisis."

42 Falloux, "Land Management," 190–208; R. Ayers, *Banking on the Poor: The World Bank and World Poverty* (Cambridge, 1983): 104–105.

43 Falloux, "Land Management," 193–196. For a useful discussion of the literature on African land tenure systems, see Noronha, *Review.*

44 See Noronha, *Review,* Cohen, "Land," and J. Bruce, *Land Tenure;* World Bank, *Sub-Saharan.*

45 To be fair, both Hailey and Meek admit the appalling ignorance of indigenous tenure systems by colonial officials and call for further study of this topic. Meek, in particular, recognizes that these systems are flexible and have adjusted to changing conditions. Meek, *Land*, 23.

46 P. Bohannan, " 'Land,' 'Tenure' and Land-Tenure," in Biebuyck, *African Agrarian Systems* 101–115; P. Hill, "Three types of Ghanian Cocoa Farmer," in Biebuyck, *African Agrarian Systems,* 203–223.

47 Bohannan, " 'Land,' " 101–103.

48 A. Richards, "Some Effects of the Introduction of Individual Freehold into Buganda," in Biebuyck, *African Agrarian Systems,* 267–280; C. White, "Factors Determining the Content of African Land Tenure Systems in Northern Rhodesia," in Biebuyck, *African Agrarian Systems,* 364–373.

49 White, "Factors," 370.

50 R. Hecht, "Immigration, Land Transfer and Tenure Change in Divo, Ivory Coast, 1940–1980," *Africa* 55, 3 (1985): 319–336; Cohen, "Land Tenure," in Biebuyck, *African Agrarian Systems,* 59–60.

51 Cohen, "Land Tenure," 358–359.

52 P. Gourou, *L'Afrique Tropicale: Nain ou géant agricole?* (Paris, 1991): 156.

53 World Bank, *Sub-Saharan,* 104; my emphasis.

54 For a useful critique, see D. Atwood, "Land Registration in Africa: The Impact on Agricultural Production," *World Development* 18, 5 (1990): 659–671.

55 A. Haugerud, "Land Tenure and Agrarian Change in Kenya," *Africa* 59, 1 (1989): 62–90.

56 S. Migot-Adholla, P. Hazell, B. Blarel, and F. Place, "Indigenous Land Rights Systems in Sub-Saharan Africa: A Constraint on Productivity?" *The World Bank Economic Review* 5, 1 (1991): 155–175.

57 Noronha, *Review,* 199–200.

58 P. Harrison, *The Greening of Africa: Breaking through in the Battle for Land and Food,* (New York, 1987): 59.

59 Ibid., 313–314, 328–329; L. Timberlake, *Africa in Crisis: The Causes, the Cures of Environmental Bankruptcy* (London, 1985): 73.

60 Blaikie, *Political Economy,* 53–60.

61 Beinhart notes that agricultural officials viewed the commercialization of livestock as a way of breaking down the so-called cattle complex, which they

blamed for the erosion of rangelands. However, he also notes that conservation officers in Nyasaland cautioned against the expansion of certain cash crops in areas where land was already under intensive use since their cultivation threatened to erode the land. See Beinhart, "Soil Erosion," 73–75.

62 Watts and Blaikie and Brookfield attempt to forge such linkages in their pioneering work in political ecology. See M. Watts, "Drought, Environment and Food Security: Some Reflections on Peasants, Pastoralists and Commoditization in Dryland W. Africa," in M. Glantz (ed.), *Drought and Hunger in Africa: Denying Famine a Future* (Cambridge, 1987): 171–211; P. Blaikie and H. Brookfield (eds.), *Land Degradation and Society* (London, 1987).

63 M. Horowitz and P. Little, "African Pastoralism and Poverty: Some Implications for Drought and Famine," in M. Glantz, *Drought and Hunger,* 59–82. The tragedy of the commons model is found in G. Hardin, "The Tragedy of the Commons," *Science* 162 (1968): 1243–1248.

64 Blaikie and Brookfield, *Land Degradation,* 189.

65 L. Cliffe, "The Conservation Issue in Zimbabwe," *Review of African Political Economy* 42 (1988): 48–58.

66 A pertinent review is Peters, "Embedded Systems."

67 J. Gallais, "Essai sur la situation actuelle des relations entre pasteurs et paysans dans le Sahel ouest-african," in École Pratiques des Hautes Études, *Études de géographie tropicale offerts à Pierre Gourou* (Paris, 1972): 301–313. Also, see J. Gritzner, *The West African Sahel: Human Agency and Environmental Change* (Chicago, 1989): 74, 108.

68 Horowitz and Little, "African Pastoralism," 67.

69 P. Molutsi, "The State, Environment and Peasant Consciousness in Botswana," *Review of African Political Economy* 42 (1988): 40–47; Horowitz and Little, "African Pastoralism"; P. Little, "Absentee Herdowners and Part-Time Pastoralists: The Political Economy of Resource Use in Northern Kenya," *Human Ecology* 13, 2 (1984): 131–51.

70 Peters, "Embedded Systems," 181.

71 Ibid., 192.

72 S. Berry, "Property Rights."

73 S. Berry, "Concentration."

74 J. Davison, "Land and Women's Agricultural Production: The Context," in Davison, *Agriculture, Women, and Land,* 1–32.

75 See, especially, the chapters by Carney and Bernal documenting the processes through which women lost their rights in land in the context of irrigated agricultural development projects. J. Carney, "Struggles over Land and Crops in an Irrigated Rice Scheme: The Gambia," Davison, *Agriculture, Women, and Land,* 59–78; V. Bernal, "Losing Ground—Women and Agriculture on Sudan's Irrigated Schemes: Lessons from a Blue Nile Village," Davison, *Agriculture, Women, and Land,* 131–156.

76 M. Goheen, "Land Accumulation and Local Control: The Manipulation of Symbols and Power in Nso, Cameroon," in Downs and Reyna, *Land,* 280–308.

77 P. Shipton, "The Kenyan Land Tenure Reform: Misunderstandings in the Public Creation of Private Property," in Downs and Reyna, *Land*, 91–135; C. Raynaut, "Aspects of the Problem of Land Concentration in Niger," in Downs and Reyna, *Land*, 221–242.

78 A. Hoben, "The Political Economy of Land Tenure in Somalia," in Downs and Reyna, *Land*, 192–220.

79 Ibid., 216.

80 V. Uchendu, "The Impact of Changing Agricultural Technology on African Land Tenure," *Journal of Developing Areas* 4 (July 1970): 477–486.

81 Cohen, "Land Tenure," 356.

82 I make a similar point in my chapter about the reluctance of Senufo landholders to lend land to Fulani herders because government-subsidized pastoral infrastructure is viewed as long-term improvements that make it difficult to reclaim land at a later date.

83 Evidence of precolonial land sales can be found for Ghana, Kenya, and Sudan in Hill, "Three Types"; A. Fleuret, "Some Consequences of Tenure and Agrarian Reform in Taita, Kenya," in Downs and Reyna, *Land*, 136–158; and R. O'Fahey, *Land in Dar Fur: Charters and Reliable Documents from the Dar Fur Sultanate* (Cambridge, 1983).

84 H. W. O. Okoth-Ogendo, "Some Issues of Theory in the Study of Tenure Relations in African Agriculture," *Africa* 59, 1 (1989): 6–17.

85 Ibid.

86 I am grateful to Sara Berry for raising this issue, although the analysis is my own.

87 J. P. Dickenson, et al., *A Geography of the Third World* (New York, 1983): 121–126.

88 L. Cliffe, "Zimbabwe's Agricultural 'Success' and Food Security in Southern Africa," *Review of African Political Economy* 43 (1988): 4–25.

89 For an insightful critique of populist approaches to African land use, see M. Watts, " 'Good try, Mr. Paul': Populism and the Politics of African Land Use," *African Studies Review* 26, 2 (1983): 73–83.

PART 1

FLEXIBILITY AND CONFLICT IN INDIGENOUS LANDHOLDING SYSTEMS

1 *John W. Bruce*

Do Indigenous Tenure Systems Constrain Agricultural Development?

O 13 Q 15
Q 24

Africa

Most African farmers cultivate their holdings under indigenous tenure systems. These systems are frequently referred to as "customary" or "traditional," a misleading practice because they change and evolve quite rapidly; often an important customary rule turns out to be only a generation old.

The crisis in food production in Africa has directed new attention toward the question of whether indigenous land tenure arrangements constrain farmer innovation and investment. Some studies answer this question in formal, almost ideological terms: indigenous systems can only obstruct development, framed as they were to meet the needs of subsistence economies. Stereotypes of indigenous tenure systems that often bear little resemblance to reality are judged "imperfect" by comparison with idealized Western property institutions that are conducive to efficiency in market economies. These analyses often assume, incorrectly, that African tenure systems are "communal," participating in many of the characteristics of a commons, including group production. In fact, once shifting cultivation gives way to settled agriculture, a family usually farms a landholding to which it has had exclusive rights of cultivation for generations.

This debate is not academic. Tenure reform is a part of the agenda of those seeking both capitalist and socialist transformations of African society. Advocates at both ends of the ideological spectrum tend to frame their critiques of indigenous tenure systems in terms of divergence from their preferred models. Reformers in the capitalist mode seek tenure individualization and full private ownership of land (through elimination of community or kin group land management), while socialist reformers seek state ownership and control over allocation of land and, in their more thoroughgoing reforms, collective production in communal villages or on state farms. Within all these scenarios, national bureaucratic and economic elites and their local counterparts seek to obtain control of land and the power such control confers, sometimes in cooperation and sometimes in competition. Often a reform is less important for its explicit objectives than for the openings that the confusion accompanying a poorly implemented reform provides for land grabbing. In such a context, critiques of indigenous tenure systems must be evaluated critically.

Where certain tenure features create costs in terms of efficiency, it must be understood that these features are not isolated, inconvenient facts but important cogs in a socioeconomic system that continues to perform important functions for farmers. Indigenous tenure systems place great emphasis on risk management, a concern that receives far too little attention in current economic analysis of land tenure in Africa. The system may be subsistence oriented, but if subsistence means food security under a sustainable pattern of production, then it is still a very relevant objective in much of Africa. At the same time, many African farmers face the possibility of intensified production under greater investments of labor and capital and a potentially more profitable but certainly more risk-prone reorientation toward markets beyond the village. African farmers often stand with one foot in subsistence and one in the market. At this moment in their history, the farmers' well-being and productivity (indeed, their survival) can be adversely affected by focusing too exclusively on either. Moreover, considerable tenure evolution has already taken place under the impact of market forces and other influences during the colonial and postcolonial periods, often in the direction of greater individual control of the holding and alienability.[1]

Here I review the concerns about indigenous tenure systems and seek to identify more specifically and narrowly the situations in which these concerns may in fact be justified. My focus is largely limited to farmland, primarily issues of agricultural productivity, but I do not mean to suggest that other considerations such as equity and the social insurance value of access to land are not very important. Where there does seem reason for concern about tenure impacts on productivity, I note countervailing benefits that the farmer may derive from existing arrangements. Tenure arrangements do not have problems and benefits in the abstract but only in terms of specific strategies, and this discussion assumes an agricultural development strategy that relies on farmers utilizing family landhold-ings, over which they have more or less exclusive rights of cultivation, to innovate and invest to increase production for consumption and the market. Toward the end, a series of questions are set out, the answers to which help test whether major tenure reform is called for in a particular case. Finally, the need for such a relatively careful and instrumental approach to tenure reform is explained in terms of the African experi-ence with major tenure reforms in the past two decades and the evolving policy debate.

Land Use and Conservation

Shifting cultivation has often been denigrated and, with it, the land tenure systems that accommodate it. But it is a natural and efficient response to an abundance of land, the fact that prolonged cultivation exhausts soil, and the absence of an agricultural technology that can counteract that exhaustion. Until such technology is available and afford-able, shifting cultivation and tenure systems consistent with it are appro-priate.[2] They do not, however, involve "commons" situations. They usually involve some social control over new land clearing, and they allow different degrees of continuing household control over bush fal-low, which often involves some less intensive use of it.

Serious problems arise when, in the absence of an appropriate technol-ogy, population densities can no longer accommodate shifting cultiva-tion. In some parts of Africa, natural growth over the last fifty years has created serious pressure on the land resource. Cultivation stabilizes, going over to a rotation system with declining fallow periods, and farm-ers may have difficulty maintaining fertility. When land degradation occurs, it is sometimes characterized as the inevitable outcome of a tenure system that gives farmers no long-term interest in the land and thus encourages them to exhaust rather than conserve it. In economic terms, the cultivator is said to lack incentives carefully to husband the holding; he does not have property rights that internalize the costs and benefits of conserving or failing to conserve the land.[3] It is not clear that this is in fact the case. When the necessity has arisen, most indigenous tenure systems have readily recognized long-term exclusive rights in land for farmers or households. The process of evolution in this direc-tion is well documented.[4]

No matter how responsive the tenure system may be to new needs, population pressure may simply outdistance available technologies for maintenance of fertility. Tenure change cannot create more land. It should not be blamed as an expression of "culture," when the critical need is for new, appropriate technologies that allow a productive and sustainable agriculture. In this respect agroforestry seems to offer the best hope for many African farmers today. Integration of trees into farmers' cropping patterns (for instance, through alley cropping) offers a new source of cash income, green manure for sustainability and fodder for livestock. Research must focus on the specific relationship between land tenure and the adoption of such technologies.[5]

The establishment of a stabilized and productive agriculture will need new tenure rules, which enhance the farmers' rights in the land, to both facilitate and reinforce it. Enhanced individual tenure offers the freedom of action and economic incentive to conserve resources. However, it is important to realize that such change does not offer a panacea for destructive land use. Where technology cannot maintain fertility under the use required for subsistence, individual tenure will accomplish little. Farmers will need to maximize short-term production to survive, despite long-term costs. If the freedom conferred by ownership is coupled with ignorance of proper land use practices and ecological stress, it provides only the opportunity to degrade the resource. Witness the American Dust Bowl experience of the 1930s.

Security of Tenure and Investment in the Holding

A farmer will be disinclined to make long-term investments in his holding unless he is secure in his expectation of reaping the benefits. Insecurity of tenure in African systems is usually attributed to rights having short duration and terminating automatically on cessation of cultivation and to farmers being subject to ouster by chiefs or other community land administrators.

Security of tenure is a very real need, and its importance should not be underestimated. In agriculture, capital formation is an accretionary process. It takes place over a long period of time through incremental investments in the holding of labor, cash surplus, and credit in clearing, leveling, destumping, terracing, drainage, ditching, farm road building, well digging, irrigation works, tree planting, and fencing, as well as in the construction of farm buildings. The land tenure system should speed the formation of capital by creating incentives for investment as opposed to consumption. Security of tenure does this because the farmer can afford to balance a higher rate of return over time from a slow maturing investment in the farm against possibly lower-yielding but quick-turnover investments and to balance appreciation in value of his capital assets against immediate income.

This represents sound and durable reasoning in a market economy with broad farmer autonomy over land use and management decisions. These conditions are not always present in Africa but seem to exist or to be emerging to an extent that justifies cautious use of this model. However, investment is usually only possible where real incomes are rising. Otherwise, farmers will tend to favor consumption and short-term pay-offs, and labor will seek opportunities outside agriculture. There will be situations in which few such alternatives are open to African farmers, but again this is less and less the case as time passes.[6]

Do indigenous systems offer the security of tenure necessary for farmers to invest? Shifting cultivation has been said to provide only "farm tenure," not "land tenure."[7] If under such systems a farmer loses his rights when he moves on to farm other land, he has had as much security as he needed or wanted. Under settled agriculture, most indigenous tenure systems appear to have evolved to provide adequate security, at least in the context of subsistence use of relatively plentiful land.[8] But what happens as population pressure increases? In some societies, chiefs or elders take from existing holdings to provide for new households. This reflects a steadfastness in the widespread principle that any member of the group has a right to land. In other societies, land distribution comes to be governed exclusively by inheritance (and transactions, if these are allowed). It is not readily apparent why reallocations take place in some societies and not others. Often no "official" action is necessary for it to occur. A new household head wanting land will go to relatives with large holdings, and they will give it to him out of a sense of family obligation. The impact on investment is potentially negative but may not materialize where local rules require that an unimproved part of the holding be reallocated.[9]

Can one rely on traditional rules and institutions to provide security as commercial agriculture develops and particular pieces of land come to have different values as a result of investment, or will investment actually attract claims? Emergent commercial farmers often express insecurity in conversation. Under most indigenous systems, a farmer can have as much land as he or she can use, so long as it is available. But jealousies and conflicts may soon develop. If permanent improvements have been made in the holding, others may raise long-dormant claims to it. The emergent farmer may be seen as too wealthy, as a new focus of power and influence in competition with traditional leaders. He may be badgered to use his tractor to plow the chief's or community land. If he refuses when such requests become too burdensome, he may be criticized for a lack of respect, a failure of community spirit. Jealousy can give rise to accusations of witchcraft, which can result in banishment. This is a greater danger if the farmer is not originally from the landowning group and is viewed as cultivating by its permission.[10]

The causes of insecurity of tenure are diverse, and many have little to do with the *rules* of indigenous systems. It may arise from abuse of power by traditional land administrators in hierarchical systems, or from their ineffectiveness in enforcing rules in political or economic circumstances which have undermined their authority. Competition between ethnic groups, land grabbing by new elites, and such arbitrary government action as taking without compensation or granting concessions inconsistent with existing rights are emerging sources of insecurity of tenure that may prove in the long run more serious than deficiencies in the substantive rules of indigenous systems.

Since there is no absolute security, but only degrees of it, how insecure must tenure be before it constitutes a serious problem? The answer is not obvious and probably not generalizable. On the one hand, insecurity is an objective fact, a probability of disturbance that can be determined by research. On the other hand, it is a state of mind, and it is the *sense* of insecurity that affects investment decisions.[11]

Exclusivity of Tenure and Farm Management

In many discussions of security of tenure, one finds a secondary theme, lamenting the African farmer's lack of full freedom to make management decisions concerning his or her farm. Some ways in which indigenous tenure systems so limit farmers are common enough to deserve mention. First, community-sanctioned land use practice may require the participation of all landholders. An example is the turning of the community's livestock onto the fields after harvest to graze crop residues. Because a farmer's livestock is free to range with all the others, it may be considered unfair for him to intensify use of his land in a manner that requires exclusion from such grazing.[12] Similar arrangements for serial use of land are sometimes made by communities of cultivators with groups of pastoralists, or between groups of pastoralists. These relationships may be peaceful and symbiotic but tend to be fraught with tension and conflict in periods of change. In the Sahel, for example, such arrangements have come under pressure as land use intensifies and new accommodations must be sought between ethnic groups.[13]

Planting trees or fencing land may be seen as an attempt by the landholder to arrogate to himself rights inconsistent with those of the community. Planting trees might tie down the use of the land for longer than is appropriate, and fencing might exclude his neighbors' right of commons outside the cropping season. The community may thus seek to prohibit these activities and in this way constrain innovation. The extent to which they do so is a matter for investigation in a particular case, especially because it appears that the durability of such restrictions in the face of real incentives may not be very great.[14]

Efficiency in Resource Allocation

Critics often fault indigenous tenure systems for their reluctance to recognize sales. They claim that they impose unacceptable "transaction costs," that is, risks of loss of the purchased land because of uncertainty as to whether the sale will receive legal recognition. They argue that the distribution of land arrived at through allocations by indigenous land administrators, by inheritance, or by some combination of these is inefficient. They suggest that land would be more productively distributed (i.e., in more efficient factor combinations) if it were a marketable commodity. They assume that the market would transfer it to those with the capital and skills to utilize it most effectively. This "market" they conceive as large, relatively impersonal, and permitting permanent rather than temporary transfers of rights. Critics also suggest that investment in land is discouraged, in relation to other potential investments, if it cannot be converted to liquid assets by sale of the land.[15]

The matter is more complicated than might at first appear. First, it needs to be emphasized that land under indigenous tenure, while often not "marketable" in the sense described above, is usually not frozen in idle hands. Under shifting cultivation, abandoned land can usually be reallocated. Even in situations of settled cultivation, nonuse can sometimes result in loss of a holding, though in practice, family or friends will usually farm the land if the "owner" cannot. Where there are temporary imbalances in factors, such as a household short of labor because of illness or labor migration, there are usually indigenous arrangements to redress the balance. Land can be "loaned" to another farmer, and sharecropping and other forms of compensation for land use are not unusual. These are in fact land markets.[16] Transfers of a temporary nature pose little difficulty to indigenous tenure systems, some of which have free markets in such land rights, with minimal transaction costs. Do we readily assume that permanent alienability is a necessary component of "ownership"?[17] There is, in fact, considerable discussion in theoretical circles in agricultural economics as to whether arrangements such as sharecropping are, as was once imagined, inherently inefficient.[18]

When land assumes value by virtue of productive improvements on it or has value conferred on it by investment or by location near markets and service centers, indigenous law comes gradually to recognize sales of land. At first, sales may be disguised, for instance, as unredeemed possessory mortgages. Later, sales may be sanctioned only among members of the group, then to outsiders with approval of the group or its head, still later without such consent. Sales may initially be subject to a right of preemption by family members or to a right of repurchase by the seller.[19]

Second, all markets are imperfect, and new land markets in Africa are more imperfect than most. We tend to assume that capital and entrepreneurship go together and that if management skills and agricultural acumen do not, they will be hired. In Africa, these assumptions do not always hold true. Most people with capital to invest fall into one of two groups. There is a trade-oriented mercantile class, often of foreign extraction. Sometimes, as noncitizens, its members cannot legally own land. More important, they may not want to own land and are not often interested in agriculture. They do very well out of a rapid turnover of inventories and often prefer to keep their investments relatively liquid, partly out of a sense of insecurity. There are others whose wealth comes from education and consequent employment in government or the modern private sector. These have privileged access to credit, insider knowledge of opportunities, and the ability to use networks of colleagues to move quickly through bureaucratic mazes that daunt others. However, these are commonly men and women who have turned their backs on the land and have little serious interest in farming. Moreover, they usually have access to investment opportunities that offer rates of return superior to farming. If they do purchase land, it is often for speculative or prestige purposes. Their holdings tend to be poorly managed and less productive than smaller farms around them. There are, of course, exceptions, and there would presumably be more if agriculture were more profitable.

Third and finally, liquidity of assets is and will in all likelihood continue for some time to be a matter of limited interest to most African farmers, who lack opportunities to invest outside agriculture. The argument is more relevant as regards investment in agriculture of private capital originating outside the agricultural sector.

These considerations indicate that the benefits of freer marketability of land may in the short and intermediate run be less impressive than is sometimes suggested. It is important that the tenure system provide sufficient land to farmers attempting to move from subsistence to commercial production. A market of some sort will be important in meeting this need, though some indigenous systems do get land to the best farmers and the best farmers to available land.[20]

Will full alienability lead to an increasing concentration of land in the hands of a few people, depriving others of even a subsistence opportunity? There are few land markets in Africa functioning on a scale that generates data helpful in answering this question. Historically, major land concentrations have originated in state action rather than in market forces. In the Kenyan case, perhaps the single vital national land market in sub-Saharan Africa, the trend has been for the market to break up the large estates in former white settler areas through a process of subdivision and sale, thereby probably producing more equitable distribution. However, in the former customary tenure areas, sales appear to facilitate both some land concentration and landlessness.[21]

However, landlessness is not associated only with tenure systems that allow alienation of land. Other systems under heavy population pressure can de facto throw off significant numbers of landless, notwithstanding theoretical rights to the contrary.[22] In many African countries, the state has nationalized all land to prevent growing land concentration, but it is not at all clear that direct state control over land allocation is the solution. Allocation of rights to land by the state invites corrupt practices. It remains to be seen whether in Africa the greater potential for skewed distribution and landlessness lies with the market or in the manipulation of state control over access to land by political elites.[23]

The issue is of utmost seriousness under either system. Tenure change in Africa must avoid the intractable and politically explosive maldistribution of resources that has plagued Latin America and parts of Asia. In addition, recent analysis has emphasized the advantages for agricultural development of unimodal patterns of small holdings. Economies of scale no longer provide a credible argument for skewed distribution patterns.[24] The suggestion that increasing landlessness and a related population flow out of a developing agriculture are "normal" misses the point: there is already a massive exodus from the rural sector taking place in Africa, and it has nothing to do with increased efficiency. It has rather to do with stagnation, the deterioration of even subsistence opportunities, educational systems that denigrate work in agriculture, and real or imagined superior opportunities in towns.[25]

Land-Secured Credit

Discussions of the adequacy of customary land tenure frequently raise the issue of pledging or mortgaging of land as security for a loan. Sales and loans against the value of improvements on land, such as houses or tree crops, are quite acceptable to most indigenous tenure systems and antedate transactions in land itself. Traditional land security arrangements tend to place the land in the hands of the creditor until repayment of the loan and so are not well suited to finance agricultural investment.[26]

Crops provide adequate security for most credit needs of traditional farmers but not for the needs of emergent or commercial farmers for substantial loans for major improvements in their holdings. Where the need for property-secured credit arises, it is important to understand the relationship between this "security in land" for credit and "security of tenure." A banker will not loan to a farmer who does not have a secure expectation of continuing in possession to reap the returns on his investments. However, this security of tenure is only one of the necessary conditions for land to be used as security for a loan. As banks do not wish to become farmers, the land must also be readily transferable to someone who does want to use it, for a price that will satisfy the debt. This requires not only ready transferability and mortgageability of land at law but also the existence of a market and the reliable, effective demand on which it is based. Legislative reforms to permit mortgaging far in advance of the development of the demand side of the land market will have little effect.

There is a further reason why mortgageability may have less impact than expected. Tenure is hardly the only reason commercial banks hesitate to lend to small and emergent farmers. The farmer must be "creditworthy." To determine this, banks ask: Does the borrower have an account with the bank and a good savings record? Does he have a record of repaying previous loans? Does he have some income from a source less variable than farming, for instance, a monthly remittance from a son with a good job in the city? Banks prefer lending against a liable income stream to lending against an asset for which the market is uncertain. Beyond this, commercial banks look for larger opportunities than those the small farmer can provide, opportunities in which administrative costs are low in proportion to the size of the loan and in which the capital lent can be recovered far more quickly than from a farm.[27]

Mortgageability may be a valid long-term objective, but caution is indicated. Unscrupulous or irresponsible lenders can use mortgages to deprive commercially naive smallholders of their land. And tenure change to create mortgageability will not have the positive effects anticipated unless the other conditions that will enable farmers to take advantage of it are satisfied. These include the existence of a rural land market; willing lenders on terms farmers find attractive; the support services that can help ensure success in agricultural innovation; a political situation that permits foreclosure if necessary; and prices for produce which permit recovery of costs of an investment. In the absence of these opportunities, money borrowed against agricultural land will be diverted from investment in agriculture toward other opportunities, such as urban real estate and building projects.[28]

Fragmentation and Subdivision of Holdings

Inheritance rules are an important element in an indigenous tenure system. Critics sometimes blame them for extensive subdivision and fragmentation of holdings, which may prevent adoption of certain new technologies. The terms "subdivision" and "fragmentation" are often used loosely. Here "subdivision" describes the process by which a single parcel of land is progressively subdivided, sometimes into awkwardly small pieces. Excessive subdivision is the result of too many farmers trying to eke out a living on too little land. By contrast, fragmentation describes the situation in which a farmer's holding consists of several noncontiguous parcels. The economic objection to it is clear. If the number of fragments in a holding is large and distances between them great, it can impose serious inefficiencies on the farmer in the use of labor and such scarce resources as plow oxen.[29]

Inheritance generates subdivision by giving several descendants of the deceased shares in his land. This is a concomitant of very broad access to land. Where there are few opportunities outside agriculture, it is hardly surprising that rules of inheritance support this, and changing the law to restrict the number of heirs without creating new opportunities will in all probability have little impact. There is evidence, however, that once inheritance rules reach the point of creating holdings too small even for subsistence, they are bent to reduce the rate of subdivision. After a certain point, increased pressure on the land resource produces not further subdivision but undivided ownership in common by a number of co-heirs, only a few of whom are cultivating the holding—a situation that has its own problems. The real problem is population pressure on a limited resource, not rules, and land tenure reform alone is not a very effective tool in this context. It cannot create more land.

Fragmentation may originate directly in inheritance, where each heir receives a part of each parcel in a parental holding. It can also be caused less directly, if subdivision has progressed until parcels are so small that a holding must include several parcels to be viable. But there are other, more positive reasons for fragmentation, such as access to different soils or, in mountainous areas, even different ecological niches. It is often a critical part of farmers' risk management strategies, intentional and purposeful. Its benefits may significantly outweigh any inefficiencies in resource use associated with it. In Kenya, following individualization and consolidation of landholdings in the 1970s, farmers in at least one area engaged in land exchanges to reconstitute a pattern of fragmentation that had a risk-spreading function.[30]

Where it serves no such useful purpose, what is a "serious" degree of fragmentation? It depends on a number of factors, in particular, the distance between parcels and the residence. Concern should increase if labor is in short supply or a scarce and costly capital item, such as plow oxen or tractors, is used inefficiently as a result. Finally, a given degree of fragmentation affects households differently. Labor-poor households with limited access to draft animals will be affected more adversely than better endowed ones.[31]

If fragmentation is a serious problem, and there *are* some cases in Africa, then the solution may lie in some combination of land consolidation, inheritance reform, more effective land markets, labor-absorbing intensification of production, and, most important in the long run, the creation of new opportunities outside agriculture.

The Tenure Needs of Women Farmers

So many of Africa's farmers are women that any evaluation of indigenous tenure systems must ask how well their needs are met. The literature on women as farmers which has grown so remarkably over the past decade has now begun to spin off a literature concerning women farmers and the terms of their access to land. There are now a number of excellent case studies and some serious comparative essays as well as some path-breaking attempts to relate tenure rules and the impact of new technologies, such as agroforestry, on women.[32]

The burden of the case against indigenous tenure systems, and it is accurate enough, is that the vast majority of African tenure systems give women access to land not in their own right but as their husbands' wives or, in the case of divorce and widowhood, as daughters or sisters of males within their own families. While they may have a right to land from their husbands or other male relatives, they have no right to a particular piece of land and may be shifted from field to field. This position is not much different in matrilineal societies; inheritance rights may pass in the female line, but they usually pass to males, who control land just as they do in patrilineal situations.

A woman farmer often has fields of her own, over which she and not the male head of household make the key management decisions. Where women make these management decisions, of what relevance is the head of household's security of tenure? Does it matter when the woman is making the management decisions but has little or no security of tenure? We now have a few case studies with good descriptions of these situations, though I know of only one serious (but inconclusive) attempt to measure the impact on investment and production of differences in tenure security among field managers within the household.[33] There would presumably be a considerable dilution of any causal connection between the security of tenure the household enjoys and investment in the holding.

It is equally clear, however, that women do not always fare well under tenure reform. Individualization reforms best fuel ownership of household land in the head of the household, who is usually a man. He thereby acquires a right to sell the land, defeating the rights of his wife and children to shares of the land under customary rules. This has been a major problem in Kenya and has only been partly mitigated by land control boards that review proposed sales of land in terms of their economic and social consequences.[34] Individualizing reforms have their positive side as well; they allow women to, for the first time, purchase land and hold it in their own right. Most women, of course, lack the resources to do so. This is a long-run advantage, and so far we lack the data to indicate the extent to which women are becoming landowners.

Specific change in tenure rules may be possible within the general framework of local custom. Options that deserve consideration are inheritance reform, a community property regime for marriage, and credit programs to facilitate land purchases by women. It should be recognized, however, that to alter the rules of the lineage system is in many African societies to undermine the basic principles of social organization and cohesion. Nor will women farmers profit from becoming individual owners if agricultural extension services and access to credit and other facilities is denied to them.

Person/Land Ratios, Population Mobility, and Citizenship

Indigenous tenure systems are generally based in kinship and ethnicity. Some critiques of them suggest that this prevents movement of people from areas experiencing heavy population pressure to areas with low person/land ratios. Victor Uchendu argues for the breaking down of tenure barriers to interrural migration, arguing that "if interests in land are restricted between agricultural areas, it will be difficult to deal with the problems of 'uneven' development which might threaten national unity."[35]

Individuals and families have in the past crossed ethnic boundaries regularly in search of land, in at least some parts of Africa. Their need for land has often been matched by the receiving group's need for new members, and they have been absorbed into landowning groups through marriage or under legal fictions. In West Africa, "stranger farmers"—or in The Gambia, "strange farmers"—have played a major role in agricultural innovation.[36] Where pressure has become intense, "strangers" not yet fully absorbed into the landowning group have been expelled. Such movement is likely to be increasingly constrained in the future, which may retard technology transfer from advanced to more backward agricultural areas.[37]

How serious is this problem of relative person/land ratios, in terms of broad demographic patterns? It is probably not very serious. Areas of relative land plenty will be fully utilized in a generation, even failing immigration. Often the absorptive potential of such areas is overestimated. There are good reasons for their sparse population, not readily apparent to planners. This may be presumed to be the case when an area, in close proximity to crowded areas, remains thinly populated. Shifting large numbers of people is very costly, and existing differences in regional distributions are of an order that will be evened out by population growth and movement into urban areas and toward other opportunities in the space of a generation. Attempts at major movements of people usually only delay hard choices in coming to grips with the problems they face where they are.

Finally, the issue of access to land held by one ethnic group by citizens belonging to another has major political implications. There are countries in Africa where politics are dominated by one or two ethnic groups, and this power may be used to expand access to land. In such circumstances, attempts to achieve demographic balance may implement group expansion and economic hegemony.

Evaluating Tenure Constraints: Some Key Inquiries

Though sometimes exaggerated, each of these concerns about indigenous tenure systems has a kernel of substance. Each will be justified in some cases, though sometimes only a few. These concerns deserve to be taken seriously but should be examined rigorously by those planning development strategies. The series of inquiries that follow can assist in sizing up a suspected tenure constraint and its implications.

First, a dated description of a rule should not serve as the basis for a hypothesized constraint. "Common knowledge" about the tenure system needs to be reexamined carefully. Provisionally, consider anything over ten years old as dated. Custom can change rapidly, and field research must confirm the relevant norms.

Then, instead of simply asking if there is a constraint, ask, "*Who* is constrained?" Is it all farmers, or only certain groups of them (e.g., tree growers, lowland farmers, women farmers, "emergent" farmers)? The seriousness of the constraint and the appropriateness of strategies for dealing with it will depend on the answer to this question.

Is this tenure problem a bottleneck, the binding constraint whose elimination will lead to a change in behavior? Or are there other constraints that are more immediate, stronger, and less maleable, so that tenure change alone will have little impact? If so, then its costs can only be justified as part of a larger package of initiatives that addresses the other constraints as well, or the other constraints may need to be tackled first.

What purpose or purposes are served by the feature of the tenure system that is in question? If in one context it is a constraint, is it enabling in other ways? Does it constitute an important component in risk-avoidance strategies? What are the trade-offs involved in a tenure change to remove the constraint?

How static is the constraint? Is it unlikely to resolve itself in an evolutionary manner in the reasonable future, or is there change already under way in customary rules and practices which may obviate the need for government-initiated reform and suggest a less intrusive, more facilitating approach to tenure change?

Is there a nontenurial solution to the problem? What is referred to as a constraint is often a mismatch between a tenure characteristic and a project or policy initiative. The gears belong to different machines and do not mesh. In such a situation, it is sometimes possible (and far simpler) to develop strategies that accommodate the tenure system, redefining the initiative to achieve the same objective in a somewhat different manner.

Finally, in formulating reform responses to a tenure constraint, we tend to draw too exclusively on models derived from comparative experience. We need to ask whether there are models of tenure or normative change generally in this customary legal system which suggest reform strategies. Are there opportunities posed by the structure of the system and its institutions, of which policymakers could take advantage in planning tenure change?

These questions must be part of a process of applied research that goes beyond simply identifying constraints and allowing donors and national policymakers to make the leap of faith to a reform model consistent with their ideology. Tenure reform on those lines is a costly affair, whether one seeks to move toward registered individual titles or communal villages. Answering the questions set out above should help decide whether such radical tenure reform is needed. It will not entirely dispose of the question because tenure is not only a matter of agricultural production but of the distribution of an agrarian society's most valuable resource. The ongoing policy debate will assume new forms, but underlying it will be a continuing competition for land.

In the Longer Term: Emerging Models of Tenure Reform

I have so far examined tenure change in a very instrumental manner, largely in terms of its impact on agricultural production and resource use. Tenure systems are part of larger political and economic systems, and tenure reform decisions are never dictated just by the facts of the case and development theory. Politics often plays a large and legitimate role, with politicians using tenure reform to build constituencies, to undermine opponents, and to realize their vision of a good society. As different interests compete for land and control over use of land, that competition will find expression both in demands for radical tenure reforms and in debates over the much more modest changes toward which a careful consideration of the issues set out here might lead.

The emphasis, I suspect, will be on the latter level, with more comprehensive reform falling out of favor. Given the current disenchantment with the state farm and communal village models of socialist agriculture in the Soviet Union and Eastern Europe, and the grim experience with these models in Africa,[38] it seems likely that policy discussion in socialist as well as free market circles will focus on the tenure options for an agrarian structure similar to that assumed here: one that consists of a large number of private producers of varying size and complexity but of which the vast majority are compound, household, or individual production units. In the socialist debates over reform, attention is likely to center on tenure systems based on leasehold from the state, at least for most farmland. Such state leasehold is another form of individualization of tenure, and where leaseholds are long enough, they potentially offer many of the same advantages as individual ownership. The experience with this system has, however, been seriously marred by abuse of the state's powers of land allocation to allow bureaucratic and other elites to grab land.[39]

This does not mean that the policy arena now belongs to proponents of systematic individualization of tenure in full private ownership. Indeed, recent research tends to call into question the viability and cost-effectiveness of comprehensive tenure reform generally. The preliminary results of a four-county study of tenure reforms conducted by the Land Tenure Center, University of Wisconsin, suggest that farmer demand for individual title comes less from a desire to change agricultural practices and increase production than from their sense that a title conferred by the state may be the best way to defend against reallocations of land by the state and its local representatives, whom they see as the major threat to their security of tenure. Where such titles have been provided, they appear to have little impact on production, except for larger holders who have other assets and advantages that in conjunction with title increase their access to credit and other investment opportunities. A growth in transactions in land, which is usually associated with individualization of tenure, was found to be developing across tenure categories with less correspondence to formal tenure types than might have been expected. The tentative policy implications of the study point away from comprehensive tenure reform as a not very effective or cost-efficient tool in most cases and toward the exploration of community-based solutions to tenure insecurity and a "state-facilitated" evolution of indigenous land tenure systems.[40]

How do these new reform approaches relate to the growing competition for land? It has been suggested earlier that reforms most often do not resolve these competitions but just redesign the playing fields on which they are carried out. The reorientation of efforts at reform toward community-based and implemented solutions should allow us to do a better job of evaluating assertions by the competitors about indigenous land tenure systems. It would allow questions to be posed more specifically about the impact of particular aspects of a particular tenure system in particular circumstances, along the lines suggested here. This will help bring to an end an era of reform policies based on overgeneralization about complex systems and ambitious reforms that fail to achieve their stated objectives but succeed in creating normative confusion, which the powerful take advantage of to appropriate land.

Notes

1 Economics has found it difficult to do justice to transitions between economic regimes, as do other disciplines. For a sense of different approaches, see P. M. Raup, "The Contribution of Land Reforms to Agricultural Development: An Analytical Framework," *Economic Development and Cultural Change* 12 (1963): 1–21; K. H. Parsons, "The Place of Agrarian Reform in Rural Development Policies," in *Studies on Agrarian Reform and Rural Poverty,* ed. M. R. El Ghonemy et al., FAO Economic and Social Development Series no. 27 (Rome, 1984): 19–41; and Y. Hayami and V. W. Ruttan, *Agricultural Development: An International Perspective* (Baltimore, 1985).

2 The rehabilitation of shifting cultivation has its roots in E. Boserup, *The Conditions of Agricultural Growth: The Economics of Agrarian Change under Population Pressure* (Chicago, 1965). For a more recent consideration, see J. Hunter and G. K. Ntiri, "Speculations on the Future of Shifting Agriculture in Africa," *Journal of Developing Areas* 12 (1978): 183–208.

3 D. E. Ault and G. L. Rutman, "The Development of Individual Rights to
   Property in Tribal Africa," *Journal of Law and Economics* 22 (1979): 163–182.
4 Classic studies include S. Berry, *Cocoa, Custom and Socio-Economic Change
   in Rural Western Nigeria* (Oxford, 1975): 90–125; R. A. Manners, ed., *Process
   and Pattern in Culture* (Chicago, 1974): 266–280; P. Mayer and I. Mayer,
   "Land Law in the Making," in *African Law: Adaptation and Development,* ed.
   H. and I. Kuper (Los Angeles, 1965): 51–78; C. Tardits, "Développement du
   Régime d'Appropriation Privée des Terres de la Palmeraic du Sud Dahomey,"
   in *African Agrarian Systems,* ed. D. Biebuyck (London, 1963): 297–313;
   C. M. McDowell, "The Breakdown of Traditional Land Tenure in Northern
   Nigeria," in *African Agrarian Systems,* 266–278; R. Feldman, "Custom and
   Capitalism: Changes in the Basis of Land Tenure in Ismani, Tanzania," *Journal of Development Studies* 10 (1974): 305. An important attempt to generalize
   about this process is V. Uchendu, "The Impact of Changing Agricultural
   Technology on African Land Tenure," *Journal of Developing Areas* 4 (1970):
   477–486.
5 The Land Tenure Center, University of Wisconsin–Madison, has for the past
   five years been engaged with the International Council for Research in
   Agroforestry (ICRAF) in exploring tenure issues in the adoption of agroforestry. See L. Fortmann and J. Riddell, *Trees and Tenure: An Annotated
   Bibliography for Agroforesters and Others* (Madison: Land Tenure Center
   and International Council for Research in Agroforestry, 1985); J. B. Raintree, ed., *Land, Trees and Tenure: Proceedings of an International Workshop
   on Tenure Issues in Agroforestry* (Madison: Land Tenure Center and International Council for Research in Agroforestry, 1987); and L. Fortmann and J.
   W. Bruce, eds., *Whose Trees? Proprietary Dimensions of Forestry* (Boulder,
   1988). The Land Tenure Center and the International Livestock Center for
   Africa have recently launched a two-year comparative program of research
   on land and tree tenure and alley-cropping in tropical West Africa, with
   studies now under way in Nigeria, Togo, and Cameroon.
6 Raup, "Contribution"; the point about rising real income is made on p. 11.
7 The term "farm tenure" was not meant pejoratively by its originator, Paul
   Bohannan. See his " 'Land,' 'Tenure,' and Land-Tenure," in *African Agrarian Systems,* 101–115.
8 The early 1970s saw a reevaluation of received wisdom on indigenous tenure
   systems for the colonial period. See T. Verhelst, "Customary Land Tenure as
   a Constraint on Agricultural Development: A Re-Evaluation," *Cultures et
   Développement* 2 (1969–70): 627–656; I. Gershenberg, "Land Tenure as a
   Constraint to Rural Development: A Re-Evaluation," *East African Journal
   of Rural Development* 4 (1971): 51–62; R. Barrows, "Individualized Land
   Tenure and African Agriculture: Alternatives for Policy," LTC Paper no. 85
   (Land Tenure Center, University of Wisconsin–Madison, 1973); and R. Bar-
   rows, "African Land Reform Policies: The Case of Sierra Leone," *Land
   Economics* 50 (1974): 402–410.
9 This was the case with reallocations of *chiguraf-gwoses* land in Tigray, Ethio-

pia, in the early 1970s. J. W. Bruce, "Land Reform Planning and Indigenous Tenures: A Case Study of the Tenure Chiguraf-Gwoses in Tigray, Ethiopia," SJD diss. (Law), University of Wisconsin–Madison, 1976, 255. There is a dearth of information on the point in other tenure systems.

10 A good description of this set of circumstances is provided in A. J. B. Hughes, *Land Tenure, Land Rights and Land Communities on Swazi Nation Land in Swaziland* (Durban, 1972): 148–149. In Zambia's Southern District, increasing population pressures on land have led to eviction of some migrants imperfectly absorbed into the tenure system. J. W. Bruce and P. P. Dorner, *Agricultural Land Tenure in Zambia: Perspectives, Problems and Opportunities*, LTC Research Paper no. 76 (Land Tenure Center, University of Wisconsin–Madison, 1982): 32.

11 Suggested measures of security might be length of residence in the settlement, incidence of evictions, incidence of land disputes, or security perceptions. See World Bank, "Land Title Security and Farm Productivity: A Case Study in Thailand" (Washington, D.C., 1983): 12.

12 See, e.g., Hughes, *Land Tenure*, 225–226; D. R. Phororo, *Land Tenure in Lesotho, Soil Use and Conservation, Water Use and Irrigation* (Maseru, 1979): 14–20; and H. M. Nour el Zubeir, *Fur Customary Land Law in Southern Darfur*, Customary Law Monograph no. 4 (Khartoum, 1979): 75–82.

13 A number of such situations are examined in J. C. Riddell, *Land Tenure Issues in West African Livestock and Range Development Projects*, LTC Research Paper no. 77 (Land Tenure Center, University of Wisconsin–Madison, 1982). See also T. Bassett, "Land Use Conflicts in Pastoral Development in Northern Côte d'Ivoire," chap. 5, this volume.

14 For a review of the literature on tree and tenure interactions, see J. W. Bruce and R. Noronha, "Land Tenure Issues in the Forestry and Agroforestry Project Contexts," in *Land, Trees and Tenure: Proceedings of an International Workshop on Tenure Issues in Agroforestry*, ed. John B. Raintree (Madison: Land Tenure Center and International Council for Research in Agroforestry, 1987): 121–160. For a collection of readings on these issues, see Fortmann and Bruce, *Whose Trees?* Such prohibitions on tree planting or fencing may not be very durable. Where use is recognized as conferring tenure, it appears that once prohibitions on tree planting begin to weaken, tree planting becomes an attractive way to establish tenure of long duration. In research by the Land Tenure Center in Swaziland in 1986–87, not yet published, prohibitions on fencing of holdings were found to have collapsed in the last two decades.

15 See Omotunde E. G. Johnson, "Economic Analysis, the Legal Framework and Land Tenure Systems," *Journal of Law and Economics* 15 (1972): 259–276; and Ault and Rutman, "Individual Rights," 174.

16 J. M. Cohen, "Land Tenure and Rural Development in Africa," in *Agricultural Development in Africa*, ed. R. F. Bates and M. F. Lofchie (New York, 1980): 349–400.

17 See D. King, *Land Reform and Participation of the Rural Poor in the Develop-*

ment Process of Africa, LTC Paper no. 101 (Land Tenure Center, University of Wisconsin–Madison, 1974).

18 The debate has been generated by S. N. S. Cheung, "Private Property Rights and Sharecropping," *Journal of Political Economy* 76 (1968): 1107–1122.

19 For discussions of transactions in customary tenure systems, see S. Famoriyo, "Land Transactions and Agricultural Development in Nigeria," *East African Journal of Rural Development* 7 (1974): 177; and Cohen, "Tenure and Development," 349–400. For mortgaging of improvements on land where land itself cannot be mortgaged, see R. O. Adegboye, "Procuring Loans through Pledging of Cocoa Trees," LTC Reprint no. 94 (Land Tenure Center, University of Wisconsin–Madison, 1969).

20 A. Hoben, "Social Anthropology and Development Planning—A Case Study in Ethiopian Land Reform Policy," *Journal of Modern African Studies* 10 (1972): 561–583.

21 H. W. O. Okoth-Ogendo, "African Land Tenure Reform," in *Agricultural Development in Kenya: An Economic Assessment,* ed. J. Hayer, J. K. Maitha, and W. M. Senga (Oxford, 1976): 179. For a thoroughgoing examination of the functioning of factor markets in Kenya, see P. Collier, "Malfunctioning of African Rural Factor Markets: Theory and a Kenyan Example," *Oxford Bulletin of Economics and Statistics* 45 (1983): 141–172. See also F. Mackenzie, " 'A Piece of Land Never Shrinks': Reconceptualizing Land Tenure in a Smallholding District, Kenya," chap. 7, this volume.

22 Lesotho, which has not had a significant rural tenure reform, exhibits a high population density on a mountainous land base and major labor migration to South Africa. Under the indigenous tenure system, landlessness, defined as that proportion of households without land, had risen to 25.4 percent by 1986, up from 20.7 percent in 1980. J. Bruce, "Reflections on Agricultural Land Tenure Issues Raised in the Quthing Workshop," in *Government of Lesotho, Ministry of Interior, Proceedings of the Land Act Review Seminar, 27–30 January 1981* (Maseru, 1987): 7.

23 From a long-term historical perspective, state action would seem to have produced most major concentrations, often, though not invariably, as the result of conquest and division of the spoils. See E. H. Tuma, *Twenty-Six Centuries of Agrarian Reform, A Comparative Analysis* (Berkeley and Los Angeles, 1965): 168–179.

24 Evidence on the relative efficiency of different sizes of farms in Africa comes from Kenya and Sierra Leone. It is presented in J. Levi and M. Havinden, *Economics of African Agriculture* (Harlow, Essex, 1982): 80. The evidence from Kenya is from settlement schemes, and that from Sierra Leone concerns shifting cultivation. If it comes from specialized circumstances, it is supported by considerable evidence from other continents. See A. R. Berry and W. F. Cline, *Agrarian Structure and Productivity in Developing Countries* (Baltimore, 1979); and B. F. Johnston and P. Kilby, *Agriculture and Structural Transformation: Economic Strategies in Late-Developing Countries* (New York, 1975).

25 See J. R. Harris and M. P. Todaro, "Migration, Unemployment and Development: A Two-Sector Analysis," *American Economic Review* 60 (1970): 126–142.

26 This is most common in countries of Africa in which Islamic legal influence is strong. The possessory mortgage does not pay "interest" as such and so has usually been considered more consistent with Islamic law's prohibition of any interest as usury. The possessory mortgage also occurs in non-Islamic contexts and in circumstances as diverse as Botswana and highland Ethiopia. In neither case does it appear to be a recent innovation. See I. Schapera, *Native Land Tenure in the Bechuanaland Protectorate* (Lovedale, South Africa, 1943): 140. In highland Ethiopia, a possessory mortgage that is never repaid is sometimes the mechanism used to accomplish a surreptitious sale (Bruce, "Land Reform Planning," 233–235).

27 For a discussion of putting the cart before the horse (i.e., legal mortgageability before a land market) in the village housing context, see J. W. Bruce, *Observations on Land Tenure and Housing Development in the Major Villages of Botswana,* LTC Research Paper no. 75 (Land Tenure Center, University of Wisconsin–Madison, 1981).

28 Okoth-Ogendo, "African Land," 139; and H. W. O. Okoth-Ogendo, "The Perils of Land Tenure Reform: The Case of Kenya," in *Land Policy and Agriculture in Eastern and Southern Africa,* ed. J. Arntzen, L. Ngcongco, and S. Turner (Tokyo, United Nations University, 1986).

29 On the economic impacts of fragmentation, see O. E. G. Johnson, "A Note on the Economics of Fragmentation," *Nigerian Journal of Economic and Social Studies* 12 (1970): 115–184; M. U. Igbozurike, "Fragmentation in Tropical Agriculture: An Overrated Phenomenon," *Professional Geographer* 22 (1970): 321–325; and E. H. Jacoby and C. F. Jacoby, *The Essential Revolution: Man and Land* (New York: Knopf, 1971): 264–274.

30 See A. Haugerud, "The Consequences of Land Tenure Reform among Smallholders in the Kenya Highlands," *Rural Africana* 15/16 (1983): 25–53. A balanced review of fragmentation is provided by R. King and S. Burton, "Land Fragmentation: Notes on a Fundamental Rural Spatial Problem," *Progress in Human Geography* 6 (1982): 475–495.

31 D. F. Bauer, "For Want of an Ox . . . : Land, Capital and Social Stratification in Tigre," in *Proceedings of the First United States Conference on Ethiopian Studies, 1975,* ed. Harold Marcus (East Lansing, 1975): 235–247.

32 The best source to date is J. Davison (ed.), *Agriculture, Women, and Land: The African Experience* (Boulder, 1988). See, in particular, the concluding chapter by J. Knowles and K. Cloud, "Where Can We Go From Here? Recommendations for Action," 250–264. On agroforestry technologies and women, see L. Fortmann and D. Rocheleau, "Women and Agroforestry: From Myths and Three Case Studies," *Unasylva* 36 (1984): 145–169; and J. W. Bruce and L. Fortmann, *Agroforestry: Tenure and Incentives,* LTC Paper no. 135 (Land Tenure Center, University of Wisconsin–Madison, July 1989).

33 One of the more careful descriptions comes from Swaziland: A. Black-

Michaud and F. Simelane, "Small Farms in the Central RDA, Case Studies of Twelve Small Farms on Swazi Nation Land in the Central Rural Development Area of the Middle Veld in Swaziland," Malkerns Research Studies no. 1 (Malkerns, Swaziland, January 1982). The attempt to measure the impact of security of tenure differentials among household members on investment was made by E. H. Golan, "Land Tenure Reform in Senegal: An Economic Study from the Peanut Basin," LTC Research Paper no. 101 (Land Tenure Center, University of Wisconsin–Madison, January 1990). While the differences in security of tenure were demonstrated, the lack of any new investments in a depressed agricultural sector prevented impacts from being measured.

34 A. O. Pala, "The Joluo Equation: Land Reform = Lower Status for Women," *Ceres* (May–June 1980): 37–42; and S. F. R. Coldham, "The Effect of Registration of Title Upon Customary Land Rights in Kenya," *Journal of African Law* 22 (1978): 91–111.

35 V. C. Uchendu, "The Conflict between National Land Policies and Local Sovereignty over Land in Tropical Africa," Seminar on Problems of Land Tenure in African Development, Leiden, Netherlands, December 13–17, 1971 (Leiden: Afrika-Studiecentrum, 1971).

36 See, e.g., K. Swindell, *The Strange Farmers of the Gambia* (Norwich, 1981).

37 This was happening in 1981 in densely populated areas of Zambia's Southern District. See n. 10, above. It has also been reported in Ghana. See J. C. Riddell, "Dynamics of Land Tenure and Agrarian Systems in Africa: A Synthesis of Findings," discussion draft (Rome, 1984): 26–29.

38 On Ethiopia, see J. M. Cohen, "Agrarian Reform in Ethiopia: The Situation of the Eve of the Revolution's 10th Anniversary," HIID Development Discussion Paper no. 164 (Cambridge, 1984); on Tanzania, see J. W. Harbeson, "Tanzanian Socialism in Transition: Agricultural Crisis and Policy Reform," UFSI Reports no. 30 (Hanover, N.H., 1983), and Z. S. Gondwe, "Agricultural Policy in Tanzania at the Crossroads," *Land Use Policy* 3, 1 (January 1986): 31–36; and on Mozambique, J. W. Bruce, "Land Tenure Policy and State Farm Divestiture in Mozambique" (Land Tenure Center, University of Wisconsin–Madison, 1990).

39 See the discussion in J. W. Bruce, "The Variety of Reform: A Review of Recent Experience with Land Reform and the Reform of Land Tenure, with Particular Reference to the African Experience," Paper prepared for the Conference on Human Rights in a Post-Apartheid South African Constitution, Columbia University, New York, N.Y., September 25–28, 1989, 8–11.

40 J. W. Bruce, ed., "Security of Tenure in Africa: Preliminary Findings of a Program of Comparative Research and Their Policy and Programmatic Implications," Proceedings of a Workshop for the Agency for International Development, April 19–20, 1990, Washington, D.C. (Land Tenure Center, University of Wisconsin–Madison, June 1990).

2 *Steven W. Lawry*

Transactions in Cropland Held Under Customary Tenure in Lesotho

$\overline{O}$ 13

Q 15

Lesotho

Introduction

An important subject for tenure research and policy in many parts of Africa is the strategies used to secure land by people unable to attain sufficient or suitable amounts through traditional mechanisms. This issue emerges especially in areas of shortage, where rural families possessing traditional rights find there is no longer any land to be allocated and where entrepreneurial farmers, often outsiders, would like to take advantage of new commercial opportunities by purchasing suitable agricultural land but run up against customary prohibitions to sales.

Landlessness and commercialization generate social and political pressures that can lead to fundamental changes in tenure systems. De facto selling land to strangers or buying and selling among villagers may become accepted practice, receiving ultimate sanction in land reform. Alternatively, basic change may be forestalled. Other mechanisms may evolve partially to accommodate the new demands placed on the system. Moreover, many rural people may resist fundamental change, even when supported by law, because they perceive the customary system to assign and protect land rights in ways preferable to those implied by reforms, particularly ones that encourage land markets.

This chapter explores these issues in the context of a case study of

Lesotho. Despite high levels of landlessness and pressures for reform from donor agencies and commercial farmers, the country's political leadership has adroitly protected the integrity of the customary land tenure system. This is largely because of continuing support at both the elite and the popular level. This support, however, is not necessarily based on the perception that the system still succeeds in allowing most Basotho households to earn adequate, independent livelihoods. For, generally speaking, the productivity of agriculture has declined steadily since the 1960s, and the small average size of holdings coupled with badly depleted soils give yields totally inadequate even for subsistence, let alone the generation of cash income.

For most landed households, the principal source of income is remittances from men working in the South African mines. But long-term opportunities there and in urban centers in Lesotho are sufficiently insecure as to disincline rural Basotho to cut their ties to the land. Moreover, apartheid and immigration controls prohibit workers from bringing their families to live with them in South Africa. Direct investment in agriculture remains low, but people retain their customary interests in land, expecting that it will provide an important source of income in an uncertain future. An informant to the research reported here describes this situation well:

The tendency is for people here to cling to the land. They are not ready to forfeit it altogether. It is a sort of security. People mostly rely on working in the mines [in South Africa], and one starts thinking about the time he will be coming home and having nothing to live on. He will just get a few bags of grain [from his land] but it's much better than getting nothing. [There are] no pensions, nothing. That is the problem.

Under these circumstances, agricultural land is both underutilized and in short supply in relation to demand. About two-thirds of Lesotho is mountainous, and only 13 percent of its area is arable. About 85 percent of the 1.4 million population of Basotho is rural, residing mostly in the so-called lowland zone in the west of the country, bordering on the Orange Free State. According to the 1986 census, 71,000 rural households, or 25.5 percent of the total population, are landless. This is a marked increase since 1970, when 27,000 households, then representing 12.7 percent of the total population, were without land.[1] Many of these are younger and not necessarily destitute. The able-bodied men who head these households frequently secure jobs in the mines and accumulate pieces of land, often through inheritance, as their households grow. But data presented below suggests that increasing numbers of landless are middle-aged, returned mine workers.

Popular commitment to the customary tenure system has affected the evolution of policy and how landless people and commercial farmers deal with shortages. This chapter describes how policymakers, despite pressure from donors and elsewhere to sanction sales through land reform, have ensured the preeminence of customary rules. It then describes informal and formal "borrowing" mechanisms—including sharecropping and leasing—that have given landless and commercial farmers access to agricultural land in ways that do not threaten the basic tenets of the system yet fall short of sales. The terms and conditions of these arrangements vary depending on the special requirements of the borrower. Commercial farmers require more formal, longer-term agreements than subsistence producers.

The 1979 Land Act

Moshoeshoe I (r.c. 1830–1870), the founder of the Basotho nation and its first paramount chief, formalized Lesotho's customary tenure system. He established the principle that all land belonged to the nation, to be held in trust by the paramount chief (today the king). He delegated land allocation rights to a hierarchy of area and village chiefs. The system operated to assure Basotho access to land for subsistence purposes and stressed an overall theme of welfare.[2] In 1903, the Laws of Lerotholi, named after the then paramount chief, codified its basic tenets. These laws provided that land could not be allocated to non-Basotho and proscribed sales of any kind.[3] The Basotholand Council periodically revised the laws to take account of changing requirements and to incorporate rulings made by higher traditional courts.

In the 1950s and 1960s, certain provisions of the laws that applied to agricultural land were the target of criticism by (usually) expatriate scholars and analysts. For instance, section 7(2) provided that chiefs could revoke rights in "excess of subsistence requirements" and allocate the land to families in need. Critics interpreted this provision as a restriction on the adoption of commercial practices. Landholders, they felt, would not produce crops in excess of their subsistence needs out of fear of having the land taken away. Actual experience did not support this interpretation. Since the turn of the century, many farmers have produced wheat and other crops for cash and have not lost their land as a result, and it is likely that framers of the Laws of Lerotholi had a more generous definition of "subsistence" than that assumed in the economic development lexicon.

Section 7(3) provided that rights to land not properly cultivated for a period of two years could be revoked and allocated to another. Critics argued that this provision led many landholders, especially those reliant on remittance income, to farm in a desultory fashion to ensure they kept their land. This criticism took on added currency in the mid-1970s, when mine wages increased by 500 percent over a period of thirty months. According to Jerry Eckert,

The result was a sharp decline in planted area, a tendency to slight proper husbandry practices on remaining land, and a general stagnation in the agricultural sector. Coinciding with the mine wage increase, planted acreage dropped 38 percent to the lowest levels ever recorded. The situation as seen by the farmers surfaced in the 1978 National Farmer's Conference in terms of a widespread perception that agricultural resources were being very poorly used or wasted. This was coupled by strong demands from [commercial] farmer representatives for corrective action.[4]

Critics also attacked the customary provision that on the death of a holder, the land would revert to the chief for reallocation on the basis of need. In practice, land passed to the widow and on her death was divided among surviving sons. Practice almost never contradicted this de facto inheritance process, and precedent-settling court cases recognized the land rights of widows. However, there was concern that disputes between a chief and a villager arising in nonland matters could be played out over land rights, and this was seen as contributing to farmer uncertainty over his or her long-term rights. Uncertainty, it was alleged, discouraged investment in soil conservation measures, in soil fertility, and in other land improvements that had a long-term payoff.

In sum, the tenure system was criticized for two failings. First, farmers' uncertainty about their long-term tenure rights discouraged investment in land. Second, progressive farmers willing and able to employ land and other factors at higher levels of productivity than subsistence were unable to secure land because of the general prohibition against sales.

Agencies such as the World Bank and U.S. Agency for International Development (USAID) generally accepted these criticisms, and the press reported in the late 1970s that donors were demanding reforms as a precondition for further development assistance. Basotho leadership, however, was reluctant to accede to a thoroughgoing reform for several reasons. First, it felt that the customary system had been badly misinterpreted. Customary tenure did not restrain adoption of commercial agriculture. Poor performance was more properly attributable to other, mainly economic factors, such as low product prices, competition from South Africa, and high opportunity costs of labor. Second, though rare cases of abuse by chiefs could be cited, in practice, land rights were secure. Third, allocation of land was one of the last vestiges of power retained by the chiefs. Land titling to increase security would heighten civil authority in relation to the chiefs, and the latter would resist. Sanctioning of markets would deal chiefs completely out of any meaningful role in land matters. While government was clearly ambivalent in its attitude toward the chieftainship, it was not looking for a fight over rights to allocate land.

The government's eventual answer was the Land Act of 1979. This piece of legislation was carefully calculated to account for some of the more obvious criticisms of the customary system while preserving its basic tenets, particularly the right of all Basotho to free allocations of agricultural land in their village of residence. The main provisions of the Land Act are:

(1) Land remains the property of the nation and is held in trust by the king.

(2) The entitlement of all adult married males to a "customary" allocation of land for residential and agricultural purposes. (This tenure is for all intents and purposes the same as provided by the Laws of Lerotholi. Customary allocations are certified on a Form C, copies of which are held by the village chief and the landholder, and are commonly referred to as "Form C allocations.")

(3) The recognition of inheritance rights and the establishment of procedures for them. (Surviving widows and then the oldest adult son inherit.)

(4) The strengthening of individual rights against chiefs who are prohibited from revoking or subdividing land for reallocation.

(5) The creation of a new agricultural leasehold tenure. (The law gives customary holders the option of converting their allocations to a lease-right, which they can mortgage and even sell, subject to approval by the minister of interior.)

(6) The creation of land committees empowered to allocate land and chaired by chiefs.

In sum, there are three distinguishing features of the Land Act as it applies to agricultural land. First, it encoded in law features of customary practice that authorities had not always applied consistently. This addressed the major criticism that uncertainty about inheritance and capricious actions by chiefs created insecurity in the minds of landholders.

Second, the act created a new tenure in the form of agricultural leases. Persons with a customary Form C allocation could convert their holding to a lease-right. The holding would be surveyed and registered with the commissioner of land. Subject to the approval of the minister of interior, the holder could mortgage the lease or sell it. This provision appears to meet demands for a more fungible land title. But on closer examination, its usefulness disappears. Conversion to a lease required the initiative of the landholder. Critics saw the problem as the inability of entrepreneurial farmers to secure good land. To purchase rights under the Land Act, the entrepreneur would first have to convince the current landholder to convert his Form C right to a leasehold. For the land transaction to occur, he would next have to secure the approval of the minister of interior, who had very limited administrative capacity. By enveloping the transfer process in multilayered administration, the Land Act contributed very little to the increased marketability of land. The law did not ease the basic supply problem of entrepreneurs.

Third, the Land Act diluted the allocation rights of village chiefs. However, the government did not press the adoption of the land committee model in rural areas and was ambivalent in defining the real nature of the relationship between it and the chiefs, most of whom chose to see the committee as strictly advisory.

Transactions in Cropland Held Under Customary Tenure

On January 20, 1986, a military coup overthrew the government of Leabua Jonathan, in power continuously since independence from Great Britain in 1966. The new military leadership accorded heightened status to the king, Moshoeshoe II, whom Jonathan had limited to a nonpolitical role. The king and the chieftainship never supported the Land Act, principally because of its provisions that committees allocate land. Many in the civil service, normally supportive of limits on chiefly authority, were unhappy about the sometimes corrupt application of the act in urban areas. Nor had the act been fully implemented in rural areas through failure to promulgate many of the necessary regulations to bring it into force. The change of government provided a propitious climate for a critical review of the Land Act, and the high-level Land Policy Review Commission was established for that purpose.

In 1984, the Land Tenure Center (LTC) had been involved in a workshop in Lesotho which considered the application of the act in rural areas. In January 1987, two staff members of the LTC returned to Lesotho for a second workshop that inaugurated the commission's program of work. Transactions of cropland were a principal concern of the commission. Certain transactions, especially sharecropping, were commonplace. But anecdotal evidence suggested that customary holders of cropland were renting and leasing it under fairly formal contract arrangements. Hitherto, this was almost unheard of, though it was not inconsistent with tenure rules prohibiting sale of land rights. But there were also some reports of such sales. Commissioners wanted to know whether greater mobility of land and greater access by commercial farmers were developing in ways that were consistent with customary tenure but that were also less expensive to administer than the Land Act. A staff person from the LTC was asked briefly to study current transactions under customary tenure, with two issues in mind: (1) sharecropping, its prevalence, the terms and conditions of its contracts, and the demographic and farming characteristics of parties engaged in it; (2) new renting, leasing, and sales arrangements, their terms and conditions, the characteristics of the parties to them, and the mechanisms used to secure them.

Limited time and resources dictated a rapid assessment. The study relied heavily on interviews with such knowledgeable informants as leading farmers and government officials. We interviewed nineteen village chiefs, forty sharecroppers in two farming areas in lowland Lesotho (thirty who shared land out, ten who shared land in), and several commercial farmers who were renting and leasing land near Maseru.

Sharecropping

Sharecropping arrangements have been a common feature of agriculture in Lesotho for many decades. A. F. Robertson[5] has estimated that in any given year they involve about one-third of holdings. The Lesotho arrangement is quite distinct from the conventional model, in which a large landholder enters into farming-by-shares contracts with landless and generally asset-poor tenants. In Lesotho, the landholding party typically lacks necessary assets other than land while the party sharing-in would often already have land plus other assets such as draft power and cash in excess of his own requirements. Classically, sharecropping allowed landholders who lacked draft oxen to get their land cultivated. Patrick Duncan describes the typical arrangement, also known as half-share plowing or *lihalefote,* in Sesotho.

This is a contract between land-occupiers who have no cattle and owners of ploughing oxen. The contract may take any form, although the usual agreement is as follows: occupier to provide the land, plougher to provide the oxen; each to share the purchase of seed in equal shares; each to share equally the expenses of bird-scaring, hoeing, and reaping; and, each to get half the crop.[6]

The survey collected data on sharecropping arrangements with respect to (1) the characteristics of households entering into them, including the age and sex of their heads, ownership of land, cash income, labor supply, and ownership of farming assets in addition to land; and (2) their terms and conditions, particularly how both input and labor contributions and the harvest are divided. We collected information from village chiefs on their perceptions of trends in sharecropping as a farming arrangement and on the kinds of dispute it generated.

The Characteristics of Sharecroppers

Age and sex of the household head and cash income. Households contributing land to share arrangements tended to be headed by older women. Nineteen of thirty heads, or 63 percent, were women. The average age of all heads sharing out was 63 years. In contrast, all of the households sharing land in were headed by men, with an average age of 50. Seven of the ten men had formerly worked in the mines in South Africa. Average cash income of those sharing out was Maluti (M) 292 per annum, as compared with M766 for those sharing land in. Low levels of cash income of those sharing land out suggests that lack of cash to hire oxen or tractors may be a major constraint on their ability to farm independently. With one exception, male heads of household sharing land out were resident and not absent for wage work, suggesting once again poor access to cash income, an important factor enabling participation in agriculture in Lesotho.

Labor availability. Households sharing land out had less resident adult labor available than households sharing land in. Households sharing out reported an average of 2.76 persons above 14 years of age resident during the growing season, as compared to 3.7 adults resident in households of those sharing land in. Thus, households sharing land in had about 30 percent more labor power, roughly defined, theoretically available to work in agriculture.

Landownership. Of those sharing land out, 40 percent owned one field, 43.3 percent owned two fields, 13.3 percent owned three fields, and 3.4 percent owned four fields. In contrast, only two of the ten households sharing land in owned any cropland, and each owned one field only. Sample size is much too small to draw general conclusions, but if this relationship were to be borne out by a larger sample, it would support the view that those sharing in are more land poor than in past times.

Terms and Conditions of Sharecropping Agreements
Division of traction contribution. The conventional terms of sharecropping matched landholders without oxen with owners of oxen, to plow, plant, and cultivate the landholder's land on a half-share basis. We asked sharecroppers to identify which party was responsible for providing traction for these operations. Their responses are presented in table 2.1.

An interesting feature of the data is that plowing relied on tractors with greater frequency than oxen. Nearly 60 percent of the cases involved hired tractors for plowing. Only four of the ten respondents sharing land in owned oxen. Two of these owned only two oxen, while the remaining two owned four. In seven cases (about 17%), the landholder provided the traction to plow fields, suggesting the party sharing in was responsible for providing some other essential input, perhaps labor, seed, or fertilizer. A minimum of four oxen is considered necessary to plow. While plowing frequently used tractors, planting used oxen to provide traction, though in several cases seed was broadcast planted. Oxen weeded just over half of the fields. A third of the time the landholder provided for oxen-cultivated fields.

Division of labor contributions. The conventional sharecropping model provided that the parties to the agreement equally divided the labor. Data in table 2.2 suggest that, with the exception of plowing and planting where the provider manages the traction, this remains the case.

Division of equipment and input contributions. Table 2.3 presents responses to questions on the division of equipment and input contributions to sharecropping agreements.

As would be expected, those sharing land in, who are normally responsible for traction, also provide plows and planters. There appears to be no obvious convention governing which party provides seed, with actual

Table 2.1. Sharecropping party providing traction for plowing, planting, and cultivating (n = 40)

	Plowing[a]		Planting[b]	Cultivating[c]
	oxen	tractor	(oxen only)	(oxen only)
Share land out	3.0	4.0	7.0	8.0
Share land in	16.0	22.0	18.0	7.0
Provided jointly	1.0	26.0	4.0	8.0
Average no. oxen used	4.4	—	2.9	2.0

[a]In 5 cases, both oxen and tractors were used.
[b]Seed was broadcast planted in 11 cases.
[c]In 17 cases, oxen were not used to cultivate.

Table 2.2. Labor contributions to major tasks by sharecropping parties

	Plowing	Planting	Cultivating	Harvesting
Labor provided by:				
Share out only	6	8	6	1
Share in only	15	15	6	1
Jointly provided	19	17	28	38

Table 2.3. Division of input and equipment contributions

	Plow[a]	Planter	Seed	Fertilizer	Pesticides
Input provided by:					
Share out only	3	6	15	3	1
Share in only	16	16	14	10	11
Jointly provided	—	3	11	8	6
Input not used	—	15	—	19	22

[a]Oxen plows only.

practice dividing more or less evenly among the three possible alternatives. Those who share land out rarely provide fertilizer or pesticides on their own, underscoring the extent to which sharecropping landholders tend to be short on cash to purchase farming inputs of any kind. In about half of all cases, neither party provided fertilizer or pesticides.

Division of the crop. All but two sharecroppers said their agreements provided that the two parties equally divide the crop. Equal labor contribution was the most common justification for equal division of the harvest, and no attempt was made to provide for the relative value of other inputs. In the two cases where the crop was not divided equally, it was split 60/40 in favor of the parties sharing land in because they had provided a disproportionate share of labor. About one-quarter of respondents said that disputes over the division of the harvest in relation to labor contribution had led to discontinuance of sharecropping agreements in the past.

Trends in Sharecropping
Eleven of nineteen chiefs believed that sharecropping was becoming more frequent in their areas. Six thought it was declining, but three of them attributed this to the presence in their villages of a government project to subsidize the costs of tractor hire. Three thought rates of sharecropping were unchanged over the recent past. The chiefs of Moletsane ha Makaba in densely settled Berea District and Makhosi in Mohale's Hoek District estimated that one-half of farmers in their vil-

lages sharecropped. The chief of Majaeng village in Berea District put the figure for his area at 40 percent.

Reasons given by chiefs for the increase in sharecropping included less land for allocation to newly established households; more widows and female-headed households with too little cash to farm on their own; declining livestock ownership and fewer available oxen for plowing; increasing farming costs; and population growth generally.

About two-thirds of sharecroppers believed that sharecropping was becoming more frequent in their villages. About one-half of this group cited lack of sufficient cash to engage in independent farming as the principal reason people enter into share agreements. Other causes mentioned included landlessness and declining ownership of oxen.

Sharecropping in Lesotho appears on the way to becoming a commonplace farming strategy and is the result of shortages both of land and of farming assets such as draft power, labor, and cash. In fact, census and survey data suggest that only a small percentage of households have sufficient land and inputs to farm independently. According to the 1986 census, only 41.2 percent of them in lowland Lesotho own both land and livestock. Since possession of only one sheep or goat would allow for inclusion in this category, households owning sufficient oxen to plow would be considerably fewer.[7] An analysis by Mavuso Tshabalala and David Holland[8] of ownership of assets among households in three farming system research sites in the lowlands found that 37.5 percent of all fields were managed by households owning one ox or less and two or fewer farming implements. Defining sufficient farming assets conservatively as two fields, two oxen, and three farming implements, they further found that only 6.1 percent of households managing just 11.6 percent of all fields were in a position to farm independently.

The same study discovered that a group of households with at least two fields but one ox or less and fewer than two implements held 65.7 percent of all land shared out and 61.3 percent of all fallow land. Women headed 55 percent of households within this group, while males headed 80 percent of households in the group owning the full complement of farming assets. Tshabalala and Holland are of the view that the poor match between the ownership of land and other farming assets implies severe limits for the potential for technologically-led increases in agricultural production in Lesotho.

In a social formation where the [resource] rich control most of the land a large production increase can be expected from a biologically oriented agricultural technology improvement program. In a social formation like Lesotho, however, the production response will be small because the likely adopters control only a small proportion of the land.[9]

New Forms of Land Transaction: Renting,
Leasing, and Sales of Customary Land Rights

In the general absence of a market in cropland, entrepreneurial farmers must turn to mechanisms other than purchase to secure land. A few have tried to follow the procedure for transfer of lease rights as set out in the Land Act of 1979. They found it heavy going. Prospective sellers were intimidated by the procedure for converting their customary right to a leasehold. Prospective buyers found the process expensive and time-consuming, with no guarantee that they would ultimately succeed in their goal. Sharecropping is equally unsatisfactory because it is a joint farming operation generally associated with subsistence field crops. Commercial farmers are looking for greater control over operations and profits than this model affords. It is within institutional constraints such as these that entrepreneurs demonstrate their resourcefulness in creating new forms of land transaction consistent with customary rules. We will see that some of their arrangements even go beyond the bounds of acceptability and raise problems for the customary system which policy must address in one way or another.

Members of the Land Policy Review Commission were inclined to see in renting and leasing evidence that the customary system was in fact adaptive to current requirements, specifically to the need to employ more land at higher levels of productivity. But they were also concerned that unregulated sales would lead to greater landlessness and that if sales were in fact taking place, they should take steps to control them. They asked me to learn what I could about the terms and conditions of these new types of transaction, to get a sense of their prevalence, and to help assess the implications of the findings for land policy.

It was clear from the outset that these transactions were not only new but as yet fairly uncommon. The commercial farming sector in Lesotho is still relatively small. Large-scale sampling of commercial farmers was not appropriate or even possible. Rather, I used a case study approach in which I sought out and interviewed representative commercial farmers working under nontraditional arrangements. Three case studies generally representative of the new kinds of transaction emerging are selected for presentation here.

Case Study 1: Farmer A
Farmer A is a former civil servant. He was one of the first commercial farmers to experiment with renting and leasing agreements unconventional to Lesotho, and his experience illustrates a process of trial and error. Farmer A has used three types of agreements.

1. Annual leasing agreements. Here the farmer pays rent to the land-holder. The agreement is for one season only and may or may not be extended. Rent is usually paid in grain or in-kind farming services, not in cash. When he first started, Farmer A would guarantee payment in grain equal to the average annual production achieved when the landholders farmed on their own. This soon led to problems. The farmer cited an agreement in which the holder agreed to rent in return for seven bags of maize a year, his previous annual average production. Farmer A grossed 35 bags the first year and 75 bags the second year, after which the holder wanted his land back! The ensuing dispute was resolved by an agreement allowing Farmer A to farm a third year with no further renewal. Such experiences have soured Farmer A on annual agreements, and he now views long-term leases as clearly preferable where he is contemplating large investments in improving soil fertility.

2. Written lease agreements for multiple years. Multiple-year leases ensure Farmer A that he will accrue the returns from such investments as enhancing soil fertility. The lease is written in clear, nonlegalistic Sesotho. The village chief witnesses it, and both parties to the agreement as well as the chief keep copies. Terms vary. Length is from three to five years. Depending usually on the preference of the landholder, full rent may be paid out in advance or on a year-to-year basis. In-kind payments prevail over cash.

3. Sharecropping. Farmer A also enters into modified sharecropping agreements. Unlike the traditional ones, Farmer A provides all inputs including labor. The crop is divided equally after deduction is made for costs.

Of the three types of arrangement described above, Farmer A clearly prefers the multiple-year written lease. This allows a longer-term planning and investment horizon. Farmer A least prefers sharecropping, wherein landholders still assume certain rights over the timing of operations, especially harvesting. Moreover, disputes often arise over the division of the crop. He ranks the annual renting arrangement somewhere between long-term leasing and sharecropping, despite its year-to-year uncertainties. Farmer A believes that landholders' preferences are in reverse order of his own.

Case Study 2: Farmer B
Farmer B is a well-known entrepreneur with diversified interests in farming, vegetable marketing, and retail sales. He concentrates his farming activities around his own village, which is about 25 kilometers outside of the capital, Maseru. He is extraordinarily enterprising and has gained access to extensive areas of cropland using long-term leases. He

has separate arrangements with about one hundred holders, encompassing about 500 acres of land. Farmer B uses a pro forma typed and duplicated agreement, which describes terms in detail. Copies are held by the landholder and Farmer B, who employs a clerk full-time to maintain these and other farming records. The village chief witnesses all agreements.

The majority of the agreements are for five years. They use a variety of terms, usually depending on the particular circumstances and wishes of the holder. Rental is most often paid in kind. Some typical forms include (a) payment of school fees from Form A through matriculation for one of the holder's school age children; (b) provision of funeral services; (c) provision of plowing and other farming inputs for part of a holding in exchange for the right to farm the remainder; (d) sharecropping, where one-third of the harvest is deducted to cover costs and the remaining two-thirds is divided equally between the two parties; (e) construction of housing for the holder; (f) cash. Farmer B has also entered into a few lifetime agreements, usually with widows who are without family and lack the minimal resources for farming. He provides all basic subsistence requirements, including food and clothing, in return for which the holder designates him as heir to the holding.

Farmer B uses lease land mainly for field crops such as maize and sorghum. He also owns a small irrigated holding where he produces cash crops like cabbage, carrots, potatoes, beet root, and lettuce. He markets all the vegetables through his wholesale outlet in Maseru. He has expanded his irrigated perimeter by bringing in neighbors' land under five-year lease agreements. Farmer B is reluctant to farm land outside of his village area for fear of increased supervisory costs and losses due to crop damage and theft.

Case Study 3: Farmer C
Farmer C wanted to go into dairy production near Maseru but had no customary rights to land in the area. Dairying involves high levels of fixed infrastructure investment, and he felt that a long-term lease agreement would not provide him with sufficient security of tenure. He thus purchased customary land rights from an existing holder by using a procedure, described below, that is still uncommon. It is also illegal, but it may suggest future trends.

Euphemistically speaking, sales involve a "reallocation" of land rights one person to another. In Farmer C's case, a mutually agreed price was negotiated. Farmer C and the holder then approached the village chief and advised him that they had agreed that the customary rights should be transferred to Farmer C. A new Form C was issued to Farmer C.

Views of Commercial Farmers Toward the
Customary Land Tenure System

Obviously, the entrepreneurs interviewed in the course of the research are not typical of the Lesotho farmer who is oriented to subsistence and highly reliant on off-farm sources of income. Although the commercial farmers felt that ad hoc renting and leasing had provided some access to land, they see the absence of sanctioned land markets and the difficulties associated with reallocation as major obstacles to the development of commercial agriculture in Lesotho.

They interpret government's reluctance thoroughly to reform the system to permit land sales as indicating a lack of commitment to meaningful agricultural development, which should be led by people like themselves and not by subsistence farmers whom they perceive to be underutilizing and abusing land. In the view of one entrepreneur, only 10 percent of people holding land "farm it effectively or productively." Many farmers offered examples of how they increased yields dramatically over levels achieved by the landholders.

One of them characterized the growing group of commercial farmers as "pioneers" driven by the "spirit of self-sufficiency." He asked, "If they are self-sufficient across the border [in South Africa], why can't we do it here?" All of them argued that commercial cultivation of land would realize higher levels of social welfare when measured in terms of increased agricultural production, employment, and income. One farmer argued that "equity should not be expressed in terms of landownership but in terms of the benefits of new jobs accruing to those who don't own [any] land." At the same time, commercial farmers recognize the social security role of the customary tenure system and, as a result, expect that far-reaching reforms in support of land markets would meet stiff political resistance. They used an idiom of social obligation when describing their relationships with landholders. One aspirant, who had not yet secured land, proposes to offer widows "some kind of pension" to be paid monthly in return for use of their land.

Interestingly, all entrepreneurs felt that a Form C allocation provided them with sufficient security to farm commercially. None of them perceived a customary allocation as inadequate or a disincentive to investment. Despite the potential advantages of mortgageability, they viewed the procedures for securing a lease under the Land Act as too expensive and time-consuming to justify conversion of a customary title.

Commercial farmers were of the view that rentals can be handled apart from the Land Act. There is a clear trend toward written agreements, but there was a general perception that the language used in any documents emanating from the Land Act would intimidate small farmers. Witnessing of clearly written agreements by village chiefs appears to provide sufficient assurance to both parties. In most cases, the five-year terms that were becoming standard for leases appear optimal to both parties and especially to the landholders, many of whom feel that a longer-term commitment would seriously compromise the options of absent family members to return to farming from mining or other jobs.

Conclusions: Lesotho's Land Policy Dilemma

Although agriculture as a source of income has declined in importance where the head or other adult household members are working off-farm and sending home remittances, land continues to have value as a form of capital that can be used to produce even a modest crop. But more important, many families expect agriculture to increase in importance after the head returns from the mines or other remittances come to an end. The economic system within which most Basotho operate does not provide long-term assurance of access to nonfarm employment, of pensions on retirement, or other forms of economic security that might incline holders to surrender their land to others who would be able to farm it more productively. Widows especially, who have lost the income earning capacities of their husbands and who may or may not be able to rely on their sons or daughters for support, see land as the only productive asset over which they retain control. Lacking other farming assets such as traction, implements, labor, and cash, they will often use land as their contribution to sharecropping arrangements.

In broad economic terms, land in Lesotho is seen less as a source of primary subsistence than as a source of supplementary income, one of last resort for households that cannot secure more conventional types of income outside of agriculture. Against this background, an emerging group of commercial farmers who can farm at higher levels of productivity had difficulties securing land. In part, this is because formal markets for land do not exist. The 1979 Land Act provides that lease rights to agricultural land can be bought and sold, subject in each instance to approval by the Ministry of Interior. But regulations for doing so have not been promulgated, and many commercial farmers see the process of converting a customary allocation allocation to a lease as too costly and onerous.

A more significant constraint is the continuing importance of land as a source of security to current holders in a generally insecure economic environment. In a fair reflection of popular opinion, the final report of the Land Policy Review Commission explicitly advised against relaxing the procedures by which land rights could be bought and sold. The commission made much of the spontaneous emergence of renting and leasing as evidence that the customary system was sufficiently responsive to current needs. It advised government to encourage holders not farming their land to seek out rental partners.[10] It is doubtful that policy will go much beyond exhortation. Policies for increasing the costs of holding idle land, such as land tax, would be widely resisted for the same reasons that basic reform to the customary system is opposed. The right to free land is a central feature of the long-term income and economic security strategies of households. The fact that land is in increasingly short supply serves only to galvanize support for the basic tenets of the system, at least among those who have land and who stand to inherit it. Lesotho's political leadership is attuned to the broad public support for customary principles of access and is not likely to endorse any reforms that seriously compromise them.

The interests of those in favor of the status quo as opposed to those who support increased marketability are fairly easy to discern. The balance of power currently favors the former. As it gains strength, the nascent commercial farming sector may exert increasing pressure for reform, particularly for the kind that eases marketability. The growing class of landless returning mine workers probably will not press in this direction. Only a small percentage will see commercial farming as a viable strategy, and in the main it will pursue nonfarm income strategies.

An economic analysis that evaluates the customary land tenure system strictly for its impact on agricultural production may conclude that it contributes to an inefficient allocation of resources. But, as we know, such systems do not function solely to serve this end. They also establish certain principles or rules governing how opportunities to participate in agriculture are distributed. Customary land rights are an important element in Basotho household income strategies, which presume heavy reliance on nonfarm sources but which also rely on agriculture to help keep food costs down and on land as a relatively secure economic asset in a generally uncertain environment. Despite an economy that strengthens popular commitment to basic traditional tenets, the system is accommodating new forms of contractual arrangement better suited to commercial farmers.

In considering the long-term shape of tenure change, factors very much beyond direct control will be of great importance. There is no escaping the fact that Lesotho's economy is almost wholly integrated with South Africa's. It will remain so after apartheid goes. Its neighbor's industrial economy will continue to be a magnet for rural Basotho. If a post-apartheid South Africa were more sympathetically to accommodate Lesotho's long-term economic and social interests, and there is good reason to think it would, we might see many Basotho permanently leaving the land, giving scope to fairly far-reaching changes in the customary system. These changes could extend to legally sanctioned "re-allocation" of customary rights, with village decision bodies reviewing applications for land transfers to nonvillagers. Given the flexibility that custom and village institutions have shown in accommodating share-cropping and renting and leasing, it is likely that the best models for managing such transactions will emerge out of the very complex workings of an evolving "customary" land tenure system.

Notes

1 Lesotho, Bureau of Statistics, "1986 Population Census, Preliminary Results", mimeo. (Maseru, 1987).
2 J. Eckert, "Lesotho's Land Tenure: An Analysis and Annotated Bibliography" (Maseru: Lesotho Agricultural Sector Analysis Project and Colorado State University, 1980).
3 P. Duncan, *Sotho Laws and Customs* (Cape Town, 1960).
4 Eckert, "Lesotho's Land Tenure," 3.
5 A. F. Robertson, *The Dynamics of Productive Relationships: African Share Contracts in Comparative Perspective* (Cambridge, 1987).
6 Duncan, *Sotho Laws,* 94.
7 Bureau of Statistics, "1986 Population Census."
8 M. Tshabalala and D. Holland, "Recommendation Domains: Some Considerations for the Design of On-Farm Research and Extension in Lesotho" (Maseru: Research Division, Ministry of Agriculture).
9 Ibid., 24.
10 Government of Lesotho, "Report of the Land Policy Review Commission" (Maseru, October 1987): xi.

3 *Mahir Şaul*

Land Custom in Bare: Agnatic Corporation and Rural Capitalism in Western Burkina

Introduction

Our understanding of traditional order in Africa has undergone considerable change in recent decades. What observers previously described as a remnant of an early stage they now see as a response to conditions of colonial existence and incorporation into the world economy. We look beyond tradition, to the interests on which it rests or the compromises of conflicting claims that it represents.[1] We are sensitive to the discourses that shape these interests and also give expression to them. This new attitude provides inspiration for a fresh look at such old problems as the one that guides this discussion: the relationship between African land-holding practices and the development of both production for the market and incipient differentiation. If traditions are also responses to recent or current developments, we need to be cautious about overly dramatizing the potential incongruity between inherited structures and present practices. We need to be alert to how accommodation and conflict may be located in the synchronic plane of today's interpersonal and intergroup relations, rather than something that occurs between integrated systems pertaining to different historic times. We should also restrain our temptation to see custom as something quickly receding into irrelevancy or as veiling and distorting modern reality.

Among the southern Bobo communities of Burkina Faso, relations involving the use of land did not crystallize into their present form until several decades after the establishment of colonial administration. For example, there is evidence of a struggle over the norms regulating access to land between agnatic and uterine descent groups.[2] Nevertheless, by the time of independence in 1960, when development efforts started to take place and current economic patterns of commodity production and consumerism became overwhelming, the local normative bases of agrarian structure had stabilized. At the center of this structure was the unchallenged supremacy over land of patrilineal groups with rights that had both economic and ritual content.

This stabilization coincided with important changes in the relationship of the community to the wider market, and it is these links, rather than the gradual process of sharpening the institutional bases of land control, that concern us here. Administrative intervention in the form of law enforcement did not directly strengthen agnatic claims. Colonial policies in the French West African savanna encouraged "individualization" and privatization as abstract goals but were half-hearted and contradictory in practice. The provisions for the acquisition of title to land by *immatriculation* according to French law, as well as the softer *constatation des droits fonciers des indigènes,* which left the land subject to native law, remained largely inapplicable and without effect. Whatever changes occurred resulted from political forces within the communities themselves, influenced by the outside world to the extent that it shaped the visions and interests of the actors in the local scene. The most important of these influences were the possibilities of personal monetary income through wage employment, which forced recruitment to public works and to the army impressed on villagers, or income from the sale of produce, stimulated again by grain requisitions.

Marx noted that production for the market has a more or less dissolving influence on the producing organization. More recently, Claude Meillassoux has sketched how the process might occur in West Africa.[3] In his study of changing property relations in Senegal, Francis Snyder notes that the extent and direction of dissolution depends on the character of the old mode of production.[4] Martin Chanock adds that an additional factor is the availability of a new legal discourse and institutions to redefine social relationships.[5] We could further add that these catalyzing rhetorical resources need not be borrowed from the encroaching social order; they can be drawn from the heterogeneous notional repertoire of the community itself. Being indigenous makes them no less new. This is the case with the agnatic corporation of the Bobo, which despite its formal rigidity proved highly flexible in the face of an incipient rural capitalism.

Reflecting the climate of opinion that ruled in the colonial period, Hailey avers that African landholding practices will transmute into commercialized land rights when subsistence gives way to the cultivation of marketable crops.[6] This belief rests on the idea that there is a direct link between the form of resource control and production techniques. For example, according to this logic, group ownership is the result of shifting cultivation practices which involved the combined labor of a number of individuals. This view reveals a curious inability to consider something that was well documented by that time, that in many African communities land control units and units of production are not identical. Commonly, land rights are invested in large corporate kinship groups, whereas farming is undertaken by smaller social units, which in the course of production rely on networks of collaboration that may crosscut the land corporations. Today we do not necessarily read this lack of isomorphism as evidence of a recent (and inevitable) developmental trajectory. The vision that stresses the narrow correspondence of customary normative practices to production techniques misses their political and legal content.

The links between agnatic landholding norms and market-oriented rural production in Bobo country are many-faceted and contradictory. Nevertheless, they explain the remarkable consensus that exists on the validity of these norms, underlying the well-observed tenacity in matters of land tenure which defies expectations of evolutionary change. The relationship hinges largely on one vital point that I feel the current literature does not make sufficiently clear. The control of land by descent groups does not imply that the only way a person can acquire farming rights is as a member of such a group. The linchpin of the links between group control of land and private production for the market is that temporary access to land by nonmembers of the agnatic corporation *is* possible, as long as the permanent rights of the descent unit are securely recognized. Modern conditions have stimulated a more precise definition of the nature of rights and of boundaries. Under these circumstances, at the heart of the malleability of land custom lies the question of "security," but under an unexpected guise, meaning almost the opposite of what this term usually implies. The support for customary land tenure in Bobo country, as well as its adaptability to enlarged production, is related to the free lending of field sites. When administrative intervention or legal ambiguity makes it risky to grant temporary rights, those who hold permanent rights restrict access to land by nonmembers, production units cannot adjust their capacity, and land may lie idle while

potential farmers feel a scarcity of farm sites. Information obtained in
Bobo country clearly illustrates both of these situations. Landholding
practices may appear to encourage or hinder agrarian capitalism, depending on circumstances or what one chooses to stress.

In turn, the availability of freely borrowable land has two polar consequences. First, it allows widespread access to farming. Whatever disparity
one finds in the size of farms, it arises largely from causes other than
claims to land by virtue of agnatic membership. Easy access to farmland
limits the number of those who depend on wage earnings because they are
unable to establish their own farm. It is often repeated that the chronic
shortage of labor in Africa, even in well-populated areas, is really a
"problem" of few constraints on the availability of land. However, one
should understand availability not only in its ecological meaning but also
in its jural/legal meaning. As a consequence, the supply of outside labor is
effectively limited to age grades and other work groups offering their
services by the day, poor foreigners who make long-term service contracts
in multiplex relations with their employer, and old women who find themselves incapable of engaging in autonomous production.

Yet, second, the availability of land also makes it easier for prosperous farmers to enlarge their scale of production, thereby creating a
conflicting demand for outside labor. This pressure shifts to dependent
members of production units, to work groups of young people, and to
women who offer their services by the day. In turn, this creates difficulties for heads of production groups in the control of the labor power
within their unit. The increasing vitality of work groups is one mechanism through which some successful farmers can enlarge their production scale beyond what would be possible with only the labor of their
own dependents. The modest advances of small-scale commodity production in the village depends on the redefinition of community organizations for labor mobilization. None of this is new, but it is worthwhile to
stress that landholding practices strongly condition the whole complex.

The following discussion has two components. I begin with a detailed
description of the institutions regulating access to land and their relation
to farm practices in the Bobo village of Bare. This description follows
the mode of presentation villagers adopt in their daily discourse. In the
second part, I present a complementary analysis of the results of a
survey conducted on a sample in this village.[7]

Landholding and Agriculture in Bare

In the village of Bare, agnatic groups, or sets of agnatic groups, hold
rights to land. The villagers express the relationship of the group to the

land by using a possessive construction with the plural of the term *laga* 'soil, land': *Bɔ kɔ-ta lagare?* 'Whose lands are these?' The answer is always the name of a person, the head of the agnatic group, its most senior member in terms of age grade, who manages the patrimony. This expression contrasts with: *Bɔ kɔ-ta lo?* 'Whose field is this?' The answer to this question would be the name of the farmer, man or woman, who cultivates the area without necessarily possessing permanent rights acquired through agnatic membership.

The relation of an agnatic group to its land is not only economic but also ritualistic. It is in fact the ritual links that provide the justifications, sanctions, and clearest expressions of what we would recognize as the economic facet. The whole territory is divided into named tracts. Not only these large tracts but also smaller areas, such as seasonal ponds on the course of seasonal rivers, spots that support uncommon vegetation such as a high concentration of trees of a certain species, or unusual topographic features or microenvironments, have their own name. A very vast territory, including the farms as well as uncultivated bush, is thus humanized almost with the precision of our urban street maps. Most of these names refer to a shrine (*feeno*) that "governs" the area or the particular resource in question. The control of particular groups over these resources is justified by their complex historical relationship to these shrines. Oral traditions make occasional reference to the transfer of a shrine and the associated resource from one group to another but never in the form of a purchase or explicit economic exchange.[8]

To the named tracts or resources are associated interdictions and ritual prescriptions of various kinds. Some of these regulate the economic use of the resource in question and privileges the group that appropriated it. For example, the land has to be rendered fertile by specific ceremonies that its members must undertake, or its natural abundance can be enjoyed only by members of this group or by others with their permission and ritual intercession. In other cases, the economic content of ritual prescriptions is less evident. To certain spots, for example, are attached interdiction to play some musical instruments, or to cross them in masquerades, while other spots, of course, are the places where such masquerades must originate. Some places are sanctuaries on which violent pursuit or armed confrontation is forbidden on pain of severe spiritual sanctions. Certain animal species cannot be killed on certain tracts. The group that controls the shrine is considered responsible for making these ritual prescriptions available to those who exploit its resources and also claims for itself the right to vouchsafe for them.

When a farmer wants to open a new farm on a tract of land, the head of the agnatic group in whose custody it is has to give him permission, make the ritual killing over the *Sɔgɔ* shrine, and give him the stuff (a small bundle of branches of the *tɔnkalɔ* plant, *Gardenia ternifolia*) with which the farmer establishes a personal Sɔgɔ shrine in his farm, usually under a shea butter tree.

The specific roles in the performance of these rituals over the vegetation shrines can be delegated to people of other descent groups, even in perpetuity. Neither this, however, nor the filling of this role by a particular lineage mate gives this person or his descendants privileged access to a particular section of the tract.

This is also true for the use of land for farming purposes. Today individuals cannot claim specific portions of a tract because they or their immediate kin established a farm on it. All of these resources are managed as *indivisible* corporate goods. The land of the corporation remains undivided even when agnatic sets undergo fission. I encountered two contrasting examples of this in Bare. In the first case, that of Yaworo-wenema, an agnatic segment seems to have split from the larger descent unit under unfriendly terms. It remained in the same village but took its shrine of twins and placed it in another temple house (*kɔnsa*). By doing this, they lost their rights to the lineage land, even though all parties still recognize the agnatic tie. In the second case, a man moved to the other ward of the village where he established a new *kɔn,* or house, in association with members of another patrilineage. He did not, however, sever his ritual ties with the rest of his agnatic group. This split occurred three generations above the current senior one. Today his descendants still live in the ward to which he moved and, when it comes to administrative and political matters, are members of the kɔn that he established, whereas the rest of the agnatic group lives in the original ward and is organized as a separate kɔn. However, in terms of landownership, the agnates of both segments constitute one single corporation. The most senior member, who can be from either of the two branches, oversees the patrimony.[9]

Like most Bobo villages, Bare includes several agnatic as well as uterine sets. Some of these have very old roots in the region and are considered hosts, while others have traditions of having arrived more recently and are considered foreigners. The "old" lineages trace their origins to no longer existing smaller settlements in the vicinity. They are the founders of Bare, which as a center must date at least to the early nineteenth century, and base their land claims on the notion that their ancestors initiated the shrines and cultivated the territory of these earlier settlements. In contrast, many of the descent units with traditions of having arrived later do not possess permanent land rights around the village.

One result of this pattern is that a small number of lineage elders in fact control all the village farming land.[10] One recent instance made clear this concentrated structure. In the 1960s, a multilateral international development project associated with the Matourkou extension training school tried to convince Bare villagers to change to a system of permanent cultivation with household-owned farms. They failed on both accounts, but initially they even had difficulty in getting the elders to allocate farm plots to the young heads who were willing to try the new production techniques. In the long course of negotiations, the project staff were confronted by a small number of lineage heads acting in strong solidarity. Many people whom this structure excluded from the control of land were not opposed to it but rather supported it. This was just as true of members of "foreign" lineages, who had to borrow farm sites, as it was of the junior members of landowning groups. Otherwise the Matourkou experiment might have led to different developments. Not only the residents of the village but also outsiders accept without challenge the normative order justifying ancestral claims to land. I will return below to the relationship between farming scale differentiation in the village and the different ways of acquiring farming rights. Here, I would like to elaborate briefly on outside farmers.

The interest in farmland is very keen in Burkina Faso. The village of Bare is under pressure, not only from people who return to it after a period of residence elsewhere but also from unrelated outsiders who are seeking farm tracts. This territory is particularly attractive because of its proximity to a large city and a highway. Among those who seek sites in the vicinity are, first, people who hail from the village but have spent most of their lives away, in school or in city employment. Many retired civil servants or soldiers come back either to settle permanently or they live in Bobo-Dioulasso and maintain a farm in the village. Usually they find an appropriate site without too much difficulty, on land either of their own lineage or borrowed from another group. Then there are other civil servants or merchants who were born not in the village but in the area and request land to maintain farms in Bare or its vicinity. They usually approach the elders using as intermediaries the villagers with whom they had developed friendship in the city or during their years of army service.

The third group is made up of farmers from other regions who come as migrant settlers. The most numerous of them are Mosi from the central plateau. The elders who control the land tracts are most alarmed about this type of outsider. They fear a flood of them and have responded with a concerted effort to deny them rights to settle and farm. They have succeeded in setting a formal prohibition in the village against accepting migrant settlers. The Mosi influx, which is stimulated by the possibility of attractive returns to commercial farm production, is of course itself a function of the flexibility inherent in customary practices concerning land everywhere in the country. These people are not destitute immigrants in search of land to eke out survival, as sometimes assumed, but resourceful and motivated farmers looking for better conditions to increase their output.[11] Nevertheless, the collective action of the landowning lineages of Bare has effectively blocked further settlement on their territory, as a result of which the villagers enjoy an abundance of land despite surrounding pressure.

Because the village has a strong corporate character in other respects, residents sometimes speak as if it also had its own territory. This is not accurate, however, because there is no public domain belonging to the village community in its entirety. In economic and ritual matters, the relevant attribution of a tract or resource is always to a specific agnatic set. For example, the villagers explain that Bare enjoys vast lands while the neighboring village to the north, Tondogoso, possesses very exiguous tracts with a humorous story according to which Tondogoso got first choice to set its boundaries. Its people threw a rock and claimed all the land up to where it fell, which was not very far. When their turn came, the people of Bare set fire to the dry grass and claimed all the bush up to the point where the fire stopped, which was the very limit of Tondogoso in the north and vast areas in all other directions. They tell this trickster tale for fun and not as an etiological narrative supporting claims. In fact, the claims of some descent sets in Bare extend very far from the village, to Semehon in the east, Sare in the south, and Kopena in the west, places sometimes more than 20 kilometers distant. All these claims are related to former habitation in these areas, whereas in the immediate surroundings of the village there is land controlled by nonvillagers, such as the people of Piere. Even though there is no village land as such, this humorous story does make metaphoric reference to the notion that permanent farming rights are rooted in clearing the virgin bush with the help of fire and asserts the foolishness of stone throwing instead of using time-tested farming techniques.[12]

When villagers or outsiders borrow land from the members of a lineage that claims permanent rights, this relationship is expressed by the term *mɛ* 'ask for': *Ma dɔ laga mɛ* 'I went and asked for land'. When a young male dependent or a woman is looking for a little land, usually less than 0.1 hectare to open a personal garden of earth peas or peanuts, the request can be made to the farmer who most recently cultivated there or who has fields in the vicinity. But when the head of a production group (or, rarely, a woman who has an important autonomous farming activity) contemplates opening a major cereal farm he (or she) has to ask permission from the head of the lineage that possesses permanent land rights; no other member of the group has the authority to grant it. Before opening the farm, the borrower brings a specified number of chickens, usually two or three, for a ritual that is performed by the head of the granting lineage or a sacrificer appointed by him, and he also gives the borrower the stuff for the Sɔgɔ shrine on the farm. Thereafter, the borrower brings yearly harvest gifts to the elder who holds the office. The amount of these is not negotiated, but there are conventional expectations such as a 20-liter measure of grain (about 17 kg) in years of good harvest.

Members of the lineages in the village who do not have permanent land rights freely resort to this method of obtaining land loans for cultivation. So, too, do many farmers whose lineages do claim permanent rights. The reason is convenience of the site, or because they are attracted to a particularly suitable tract. Current cultivation practices and the distribution of land rights over the village space lead many villagers to borrow a site rather than to farm vacant land that belongs to their group.

When a farmer receives temporary farming rights, the loaned area is not circumscribed with precise boundaries. Normal cultivation practice in the village is such that a field is expanded over the years. After the initial clearing, in each farming season the farmer enlarges his fields by adding some adjacent area and plants the new portion with sesame or earth peas to cover the ground and condition the soil. In subsequent years, he clears the area of wild vegetation more thoroughly and plants cereals. The land remains under mixed cereal-cowpea cultivation for three or four consecutive seasons if no manure or fertilizer is used. Finally, the land is planted with fonio (*Digitaria exilis,* Stapf.) for one more season and, after that, abandoned to rest. As the farmer enlarges the field with recently cleared areas, he abandons the older parts that have completed the rotation cycle. Thus boundaries of the cultivated area, and of the sections devoted to specific crops within it, shift from one season to the next.

These shifts occur in a specified direction and result, over a number of years, in the movement of the farm along a linear track. The farmer considers that he has a zone of expansion in front of him and leaves behind a stretch of abandoned fields that separate him from the point where he started. When a farmer is granted permission to farm, the understanding is that he will follow this course of expansion. Therefore, temporary cultivation rights are granted not for a specific site but for a larger tract of land that the farmer and his production group will exploit for a number of years until they reach its natural boundaries.

These large tracts are defined with reference to topography. Current practice always start a farm at the lowest point of the sequence, by the side of an area that becomes inundated in the rainy season. In the following years, the farm gradually moves toward the ridge, where the soils are lighter. Even if the slope is barely perceptible, this practice has advantages in weed control. Because the wash from the upper reaches of the tract deposits wild seeds, farmers prefer to leave the weed- and parasite-infested abandoned portions of their fields down in the direction of the torrent flow. Farmers also like to cultivate in company of each other for reasons of security, to reduce damage by animals and birds, and also for social reasons such as labor exchange or to undertake common ceremonies to bush shrines. A farmer who is left alone in a tract will often abandon his farm there even if he still has room for expansion.

This means that often the small valleys along the temporary water courses are farmed by a few men expanding their fields over the years in roughly parallel tracks in a movement from the bottom of the valley toward the watershed. The texture and quality of the soil changes over the years as the farm shifts, and farmers have to take this into consideration in their cropping decisions. Sometimes neighboring farm owners compete over the area of expansion. Because the speed of expansion, as well as the size of the farm in any year, depends on the arduous task of initial clearing, which is often undertaken by work parties, those who can mobilize a larger amount of labor can move ahead by clearing areas that block or channel the movement of their neighbors. They can thus push them into a less desirable surface or reserve for themselves larger contiguous areas for expansion in future years. Even though villagers pointed this out to me, I never heard of conflicts or bitterness for such a reason. All seems to be done with decency and good humor.

These tracts are very large. The axis of the movement of a farm can be 10 kilometers long. It is not uncommon for a farmer to spend twenty or twenty-five years in one such tract, to continue to farm up to his mature years in the same location where his father started a farm, or to spend most of his productive life in only one such zone. For example, Do, a farmer who was part of the sample, started a farm in a tract in 1963, and in 1983, when I interviewed him, his farm was near the end of it. Before him his father had farmed in the same place and abandoned it in the early 1940s. Thus, Do returned to this location twenty years after his father left it, and it took him another twenty years to go through the tract. The spot where his farm was in 1983, therefore, had laid fallow for about forty years. Another farmer, Namanyi, kept a notebook recording the places he farmed. In 1942, he and his father had started to farm in a tract that they abandoned in 1966, completing thus the long cycle in twenty-four years. After that, he went to a smaller tract in the Sare zone to the south of the village territory where he farmed for another eleven years. In 1978, he returned to the first tract. At the starting point, the ground had laid fallow for thirty-six years. But since Namanyi can shift his farm either faster or slower than his father did, for the rest of the tract the length of the fallow period will depend on the speed of his advance. Both Do and Namanyi have their fields on land they claim by agnatic membership.[13]

The large tracts that circumscribe the long farm cycle are not always controlled by a single agnatic corporation. Two or more descent groups may divide them. The dividing line can also be such that as the head of a production group shifts his farm along the topo-sequence, he can cross from the territory of one lineage to that of another. Some people may start farming on their lineage land but several years later, as they enlarge their field, may have to move into that of some other group. Others start on borrowed land but cross the territory of different lending groups as they shift their fields.

The borrowing of farmland gives flexibility to farming units as they try to respond to the changing productive potential in different points of their developmental cycle. The loan relationship does not establish, in itself, political clientship or subservience between the parties. The ethos is fiercely against inequalities that do not follow from the status distinctions of age, gender, and ritual office in appropriate contexts.

For the borrowing of land to be viable, the lending group must feel secure that its permanent rights will not be lost. When this is challenged, the system no longer functions smoothly. When it comes to individual farm operators, security of land tenure seems rarely to influence their decisions, and they undertake similar types of production whether on lineage or borrowed land. Actually, I will provide evidence that in Bare, "modern" and intensive agriculture is undertaken more frequently on borrowed field sites. Insecurity is a perceived problem not so much for the borrower with regard to the management of the farm but for those who claim permanent ancestral rights with regard to their political context. In matters of tenure land-controlling lineages fear interference by the administration inspired sometimes by the political clout of an outsider or of an organization. Those who lend farm sites usually will not allow their tenants to plant permanent crops such as fruit trees, because they are afraid that these could be used to press claims of personal ownership. Nevertheless, some tree planting on borrowed land does take place with the agreement of both parties. For example, the settled Fulani of the village have the largest mango plantations, all on borrowed land since they do not possess any permanent rights to the soil.

As long as the borrower is a member of the village, or a person who is part of the same social and ritual universe, a possessing lineage feels safe in granting temporary cultivation rights. For example, land is frequently loaned to people from neighboring villages such as Pala and from around Bobo-Dioulasso with whom the old lineages of Bare recognize cultural affinities. This is the case with many of the urbanites, such as retired soldiers or traders, who come from Bobo-Dioulasso. People cannot advance counter land claims qua individuals, and an outsider who is not a member of a landholding lineage in the village is not likely to develop a case. But the elder of the lending lineage is careful to maintain the symbols that are reminders of the grantor and grantee relationship, even in loan agreements with local people. The animals brought by the grantee for the ritual of the initial clearing certainly express this relationship. The yearly postharvest gifts play a similar role. The substance of the gift itself is of secondary importance as long as the borrower makes clear his status with regard to the land.

Otherwise, the head of the lending lineage has powerful sanctions that he can apply. For example, in 1983, the head of a land-rich lineage in Bare asked one of the villagers, who was farming on land borrowed from him, to bring a chicken to be killed in a special ritual. This was occasioned by his supposition that the farmer had unknowingly killed a little reptile, *kuzu,* one of the two forbidden species of the tract. The farmer denied that this happened and refused. The elder declared that he could not tolerate somebody "spoiling his bush" and asked the farmer to stop cultivating. The latter went to farm elsewhere. Events such as this may be a way for elders of land-granting lineages to test the limits of their economic leverage, but the concern to assert periodically the temporary nature of the grant is also very real.

The evidence for the effectiveness of the jural complex established around access to the land is that land conflicts are virtually nonexistent within the village itself. The position of borrowers is such that their access to land and their security in it usually lies in recognizing the claims of the granting lineage rather than in contestation. The situation, however, is different when it comes to settlers from different regions, because with them potential problems cannot be contained within the village polity.

Like elsewhere in western Burkina, most settlers are Mosi, but there are now also some farmers from neighboring Bobo communities. The

Mosi have a pattern of colonizing. They come first as individuals who make a friendly request for land. These settlers then act as hosts to large numbers of relatives and village mates who become their dependents or obtain further farmland. Finally, when their number has increased considerably, they take over politically, often imposing their own institutions, including a village chiefdom. Once such a stage is reached, it becomes very difficult for the lineages that originally granted farming and settlement rights to revoke them. The villagers of Bare are quick to point out the village of Soumousso, which is some fifteen miles to the south, as an example of this pattern. It used to be a sparsely populated Tiefo village, but today, after two decades of immigration, it is indistinguishable from a crowded Mosi town. The settlers are now encroaching on the territory of Bare from the south. This led to two litigations, one involving a Tiefo lineage that lives close to Bare.

In the late 1970s, the head of a lineage in the small satellite settlement of Piere, which is of Tiefo and not Bobo ethnic origin, went against the agreement and loaned some land interspersed between tracts Bare lineages controlled to some northern migrants. This led to a long and bitter litigation between the lineage head and some Bare elders who claimed the land for their own lineage. When the influence of the district office in Bobo-Dioulasso was added to the feeling widespread in the village that this was legitimately land belonging to the people of Piere, the conflict resolved in favor of the Tiefo elder and the migrants.

In 1987, there was another more serious conflict, indirectly related to the earlier one, between a group of Mosi squatters and the villagers. In this case, the situation was more complicated because as part of his attack on the traditional "feudal" system, the revolutionary president of the time, Captain Thomas Sankara, also took a position against lineage control of the land. Ordinance no. 50 of August 4, 1984, abolished customary rights to rural land and declared that it will be allocated by the elected village committees (CDRs). In the following year, the president himself and other high officials made repeated announcements that land belongs to everyone. The Mosi squatters seem to have been encouraged by all that talk, and with the help of a few settled Fulani families who have integrated into Bobo life by living in the village for several generations, they co-opted one village farmer and occupied some farmland, thus creating great commotion in the village. As the conflict developed, the squatters tried to elicit the support of district officials, whereas the great majority of the villagers and the village sons and daughters in employment in the city allied themselves strongly with the landowning descent groups and their elders. This litigation provides fascinating material for understanding local level politics and the limits of administrative interference in the face of strong community positions. In the end, the villagers were able to evict the squatters and impose severe sanctions on their allies within the village. The incidence also marked the return of the Tiefo segment in Piere into full solidarity with Bare lineage heads. The story needs to be told in detail elsewhere. The point in summarizing it here is to show that such conflicts are closely tied to the larger national context established by the administration and that they are not internal to the jural order to which the adult men of the village universally subscribe.

Among the Bobo, land conflicts, like all other contestations, are first discussed by the heads of the "house" and descent groups of the parties. If this discussion does not resolve the problem, it comes to the head of the ward, the custodian of the Kiri shrine and administrative chief. Late in the colonial era, after the hold of the canton system weakened, the administration also recognized an official village chief who is from the ward of Konwuna, and theoretically the holder of this office would be the next authority to whom the problem would be referred. However, up until the time of the fieldwork, village chiefs did not have much authority, and the village always had to make decisions by consensus in public gatherings, even though there may also be a less visible informal structure whereby a group of influential villagers wield power behind a front of elders with age seniority who hold ritual offices. An unsatisfied party, however, has the option to go to the district office in Bobo-Dioulasso. It is only at this point that serious accommodation with the administration becomes obligatory. Even though the Burkina administration has not developed a clear and unambiguous policy concerning agricultural land even after the 1984 ordinance and the Sankara episode, it tends to favor settlers, especially when they are also locally politically powerful and furthermore appear to be highly productive and innovative farmers. It is this tendency that leads the lineages that claim permanent rights on the basis of their agnatic identity to be very cautious with foreign immigrants colonizing the place in large numbers.

This caution reduces the flexibility that local practice is capable of producing. But for the villagers of Bare, it secures their vast patrimony against encroachment under the pressure of immigration and the expansion of a grain market. So far they have succeeded in keeping the village territory largely free of outsiders. This, in turn, allows a fallow period long enough to fully regenerate the natural productivity of the soil. According to field histories obtained in the village, tracts opened up in 1982 (n = 31) had an average preceding rest period of at least forty-three years (actually longer, because in some cases people did not know when the tract was last cultivated, usually because it had been a very long time ago; these cases have been dropped for the computation). Similarly, for tracts that were reported to have been opened in 1975 (n = 16), the average rest period had been about forty years.[14]

We can, then, look at the way local landholding practices in Bare have allowed a response to economic changes within the village itself, leaving aside for the rest of this discussion the effect of migration on national scale and the effect of part-time or retired farmers who come from the cities, a topic with which I have dealt elsewhere.[15] The data that will be analyzed here were obtained in a survey conducted on a sample that included fifty-one production units.[16] I particularly want to ask whether or not there is evidence that differences in landholding status by virtue of membership in agnatic corporations have a significant effect on the scale of production. This is part of a larger issue, the relationship between incipient capitalism and customary landholding in Bobo county. The purpose is to document the consequences, in the face of changing production circumstances, of the mechanisms for access to farmland that I have described above.

Differentiation and Local Landholding Practices

To frame the discussion, I will briefly summarize farming scale differentiation among the production units included in the sample. For all fifty-one of them, production units have an average of 9.6 members and farm slightly more than 6 hectares. But this average can be misleading, because there is large diversity in terms of farm sizes among households. Twenty of the fifty-one units farm much larger areas than the rest.[17] These units also have more people in them, but their farm area per worker is 59 percent larger and their farm area per consumer 72 percent larger than in the remaining households. Of these aggregated areas, such dependent members of the households as wives and adult sons control a small proportion. If we disregard the autonomous production of dependent members, the difference in cultivated area between the two groups increases because in the large units the heads also control a greater proportion of the household aggregated farm area. The farms they personally manage have an area 68 percent larger per worker and 83 percent larger per consumer compared to the area managed by heads of other units. Many of the large farm operators also have larger non-farm incomes. These differences cannot be explained by age, the development cycle of the household, or other factors internal to the social organization of the community. The polarization is moderate but undoubtedly related to the existence of a market for grain and to differential participation in a capitalist economy.[18] How does this differentiation relate to the institutions regulating the control of land?

The importance of land borrowing not only in the organization of farming in general but also in facilitating scale differentiation is borne out very clearly in the data at hand. Overall, the fifty-one production units borrowed 53 percent of the area they farmed. However, large production units rely on borrowed land more heavily. The area they borrowed amounts to 60 percent of their total farm, whereas for small units, it is only 52 percent. Actually, the twenty large farms in the sample borrow 1.6 times more land than the remaining thirty-one households. Nevertheless, on the aggregate, these farmers also cultivate more of their own lineage-owned land, because they have larger fields.[19]

Neither of these two subgroups is homogeneous, because both contain some farmers who rely almost exclusively either on lineage-claimed land or on temporary use grants. But in 1983–84, there were many more large operators who depended heavily on borrowed land than there were small ones. Only five of the large farms (25%) had no portion on borrowed land, while this was true for eleven of the small farm units (35%). More than half of the large farms were established almost completely on borrowed tracts, and another 10 percent had at least one main cereal field on such land. Fewer small farm units depended on borrowing to that extent (table 3.1).

While most of this land is borrowed from lineages of Bare and a small portion from the Tiefo lineage in neighboring Piere, only 2 percent of the aggregated area for the sample is granted by matrilateral relatives. In other respects, matrilineages play an important role in these communities. They are corporations holding joint movable wealth and cult elements. They still play a role in the inheritance of personal property. And they are also the units within which women are bestowed in marriage.[20] That matrilineal links are not frequently mobilized for access to farmland arises from an ambiguity in the very matrilineal/patrilineal contrast. Today this issue seems to have been settled by entirely excluding matrilineages from land issues.

Table 3.1. Dependence on borrowed land (in percent)

	No borrowing	Up to 10% borrowed	10–50% borrowed	50–90% borrowed	More than 90% borrowed
Large farm units (n = 20)	25	10	0	10	55
Small farm units (n = 31)	35	10	12	3	39

To understand the various modalities of free access, it is necessary to elaborate on the details of the relationship between different agnatic groups and the land within the community. The core patrilineal units in Bare are generally defined by reference to a family shrine called Wuro-Meleke. These are agnatic categories in a very strict sense which have a collective name derived from a cult place (*warɔ*) and which possess a set of personal forenames and prohibitions related to this cult. They can split into segments, but the segmentary structure is not elaborate. The agnatic segments, in turn, can associate themselves with other unrelated agnatic segments and thus establish larger groupings. These associations are formed with varying degrees of moral and political strength.[21]

At the strongest level, the grouping of the segments is explained by reference to a pact between the respective ancestors who in early times acted toward each other as host and guest. Even though the boundaries of the constituent Wuro-Meleke segments remain intact, because agnatic identity cannot be changed and is transmitted to the next generation by way of unambiguous ritual practices and symbols, within such groupings constituent segments can share offices and for practical purposes pool their land resources. Thus, subsidiary lineages participate in the exercise of land rights by virtue of their association with an authoctonous agnate group that provides the basis for them. The members of such groupings fear severe retribution from the ancestors for stating in public that specific tracts belong to one or the other of the constituent Wuro-Meleke units. Members of constituent agnatic segments may be instructed in private about such matters, and this knowledge is to some extent shared in the village. Yet in such cases, it would be wrong to talk about borrowing, because every man within the larger grouping considers himself a member of the land corporation by right. The oldest man in the grouping manages the whole patrimony even if he belongs to a subsidiary lineage, even though important decisions are always taken by a council of elders including necessarily the elders of the agnatic unit to which land is specifically attached.

At a looser level, agnatic segments or the larger groupings formed by their association may be united with each other, creating an administrative unit called *kɔnkɔn*. Members of a kɔnkɔn have a joint temple house where they keep cult objects, and constitute the primary set of agricultural cooperation because farm production groups within it harvest the major crops jointly and organize work parties. There is no pooling of land resources or sharing of offices within the kɔnkɔn, but members can borrow land from each other. Bare has some kɔnkɔn composed of agnatic groups that are complementary in that one of them controls large tracts of land while the other does not. Members of the group who have no land rights borrow the lands of those who do. Therefore, the kɔnkɔn serves as a frame for exchanging group loyalty for privileged access to land.

One example of this is the kɔnkɔn of SuroNyena which includes two major agnatic segments. One of them is the Yaworowenema, mentioned earlier because they lost their rights in the agnatic patrimony to their clan brothers. The second segment is the Monowenema, mentioned earlier in the same context. They share their patrimony with the agnatic relatives organized as a separate kɔnkɔn. In SuroNyena, there are also farmers who belong to descent groups other than these two. Some of them derive from landowning lineages in the village, and some do not. Nevertheless, most of them farm borrowed land. Kɔnkɔn members who belong to Yaworowenema in particular mostly farm land held by the Monowenema. The Yaworowenema members of the kɔnkɔn do not borrow from their agnatic relatives in the village who control vast lands in highly productive areas. Again, this is so because those who claim permanent rights try to avoid situations that could provide grounds for future contestations. The result is that people more commonly borrow land from those who are not patrilineally related than from relatives.[22]

The processes described are not unique to the SuroNyena, but this kɔnkɔn has a particular relevance to the present discussion because it happens to include a disproportionately large number of the prosperous and highly productive "modern" farmers of the village, even though most of its household heads do not have rights in farmland. This kɔnkɔn provides leaders who link the village with the national extension service. For example, the highly influential president of the Village Group and most members of its executive committee belong to it. Most of them farm on borrowed land, and some of them are among the large farm operators in my sample.

The large farm units also have a greater tendency to lengthen the number of years of uninterrupted cultivation before abandoning a site to fallow. Newly introduced technology has created opportunities for lengthening the use of farm sites. The Bobo also have an old tradition, to which they attach great moral value, of intensifying farming through greater expenditure of labor per unit area by more thorough weeding, rigorous mounding and ridging, and so on. Even though, like many other groups in Burkina Faso, the southern Bobo seem to have extensified their land use in the colonial period, people can return to such demanding intensive techniques if they see an advantage.[23]

At present, one of the advantages of extending the uninterrupted use of fields results from the introduction of plows about twenty years ago. Four or five years of cultivation largely frees the soil of stumps and roots and allows it to be plowed with less effort. Yearly plowing lengthens the useful life of an old field. In the case of cotton, farmers even consider an older field preferable. They always plant a cotton parcel (from 0.5 to 2 ha) on an older portion of the farm that has been carefully plowed. If a farmer does not own draft animals or a plow, he will rent the equipment just for this purpose while using older techniques for the major part of his farm that is under cereals. Those who plant cotton reuse the parcel in subsequent years for growing cereals to take advantage of the subsidiary effect of fertilizers. Thus, a parcel on which cotton has been one of the rotated crops can have an uninterrupted use of eight or nine seasons, almost twice as long as usual. Commercial cultivation of cotton, however, is not the most important factor in the length of field use, because around Bare it is only a subsidiary crop, and the area allocated to it is relatively small even among the commercially oriented operators. There are a number of additional factors that jointly make longer use possible.

One of them is the recent growth in the number of herded cattle in the village and its environs. This increase is related to a complex set of interrelated phenomena in social structure, economic climate, and perhaps veterinary care. With the exception of draft animals, cattle in Bobo country are herded by Fulani caretakers. In the postharvest season, large farm operators often have herders pen their animals on their fields in exchange for the fodder that residues of the harvest constitute. This improves the texture as well as the nutrient level of the soil. Some successful farmers have pointed out that with a combination of measures such as plowing, use of fertilizer, penning cattle, and different crop rotations, one could reduce the necessity of investing the large amounts of labor necessary for clearing new fields. By shifting fields less frequently, farmers not only save the effort of clearing new areas but also of building new farm residences, a considerable additional drain on labor, for, unlike some other Voltaic populations, the Bobo are not satisfied with makeshift shelters on farms but construct relatively involved multiroom structures where all household members spend the largest part of the growing season.[24]

Finally, development projects of the last twenty-five years have continuously publicized the virtues of permanent cultivation. For example, the Matourkou project attempted to establish farms along European lines. These efforts were undertaken without a good understanding of local farming systems, involved misjudgments of an economic nature, and were overly optimistic about the capital and logistic support that was necessary to achieve a major leap in small-scale farming. The Matourkou experiment failed in its primary objectives, but certain isolated elements of such development packages have proved to have a more lasting influence. Draft labor is one of them. It is also possible that the project message about the role of systematic crop rotation and the use of chemical fertilizers in extending field life has had an impact, not in its originally formulated form, which, besides being dubious on technical grounds, also ran up against the barrier of the customary landholding institutions, but in a modified form adapted to local conditions.

In addition to a longer number of years of uninterrupted use, among large farm operators one also finds shorter fallow periods. A shorter fallow period does not necessarily cause lower yields, as it is sometimes assumed. In fact, it has been claimed that depending on the type of soil, a relatively short fallow period can lead to a larger output.[25] Large farm operators take advantage of these economic opportunities. The tracts opened to cultivation in 1982 by the small farm units in the sample had an average prior rest period of 43 years (n = 23), while the comparable figure for tracts opened by large farm units is 24 years (n = 9; see n. 4). The evidence for fields said to have been opened in other years confirms this conclusion. For example, fields opened by small farm units in 1975 had an average prior rest period of about 40 years (n = 5), while those of large farm units had a period of only 18 years (n = 11).

There is evidence, then, that the most intensive use of the soil achieved by increasing the ratio of cropping to fallow years—either by longer uninterrupted use, or shorter rest periods, or the combination of both—is associated with large farm production units. What is not very clear and needs further study is whether this development can solely be accounted for by the technical advantages described so far or whether it is also due in part to the difficulty of finding sites appropriate to larger-scale agriculture.

An alternative way of analyzing the importance of borrowing in the organization of farm life arises from the recoverable history of currently used fields. The survey included questions to identify the user of the farm site prior to the last rest period for each field included in the sample. This information allows us to study the land transactions over two consecutive use periods. For about 10 percent of the total measured area, it was not possible to recover the identity of the previous user, and these were usually sites that had remained unused for very long periods of time. Of the rest, only 38 percent had been used by members of the agnatic corporation claiming permanent rights both in the previous cultivation cycle and at present, while 52 percent had been lent out at least in one of the two cycles (table 3.2).

Table 3.2 indicates that agnatic members tend to reserve some tracts for their own exclusive use [a], while lending out others in successive production cycles [d and e]. It is possible that tracts included in [a] have a higher natural fertility or have been reserved for longer periods to

Table 3.2. Borrowing of land in the last two farming cycles

a.	Farmed by members of the agnatic corporation both in Cycles I and II	125.25 ha (38%)
b.	Farmed by members of the agnatic corporation in Cycle I, loaned out in Cycle II	42.25 ha (13%)
c.	Loaned out in Cycle I, farmed by members of the agnatic corporation in Cycle II	14.76 ha (4%)
d.	Loaned out in both cycles and to people of one single receiving lineage	16.32 ha (5%)
e.	Loaned out in both cycles but to people of different lineages	99.85 ha (30%)
f.	Previous user unknown	32.88 ha (10%)

restore them more fully for use by members. However, a relatively large portion of the area (17%, [b] + [c]) has been farmed by both agnatic members and outsiders in the last two cycles. But even in this case, the area used by agnatic members in the first cycle and loaned out in the second is much larger than the area where the reverse happened. That is, the group holding permanent rights is likelier to loan out a tract that one of its members had previously used than to return to a field that it had loaned out in the preceding cycle. All of this can be taken as an indication that there are some advantages to having first choice to location as a member of landholding lineage.

These advantages are modest, however. Some permanent rights holders do return to fields that were previously loaned out.[26] Many people who presently farm on borrowed fields belong to agnatic groups that have rights to some other territory. Only a few agnatic corporations enjoy a vast and highly productive land patrimony, but these do not have a proportionately larger number of "large farm" production groups. There is no evidence that in Bare the differences in the amount and quality of the land controlled by virtue of membership in agnatic corporations have been translated into the production scale of farming units.

The low value of [d] compared to [e] is related to the unwillingness to let any ambiguity emerge as to the holder of permanent rights on a tract of land. While grantors repeatedly loaned out some tracts in successive cycles, they preferred not to let them be associated with the same borrowing agnatic group, revealing again the concern to avoid future challenges to their own claims.

Conclusion

What emerges from this discussion is that competition brought about by commodity production and the pressures of immigration do not necessarily lead away from older corporation-based types of land control, in the direction of private tenure. On the contrary, in Bare, they set off an interest in a less ambiguous definition of lineage-based norms of access to land and in the strengthening of corporate control. The recent African development literature exhibits some confusion concerning the development of land rights because of the use of vague terms like "individualization." Some researchers have confused the breaking up of farm management units (from large ones including several adult brothers to more restricted ones that belong to conjugal sets) with the altogether different matter of acquisition of land use rights.[27] In some other cases, analysts have mistakenly perceived "individualization" of land tenure because their observations differed from what their hypothetical models of the traditional led them to expect. If individualization means the tendency for the size of corporate groups asserting permanent rights to farm land to become smaller by undergoing fission, it is clear that this is not happening in Bare. The village is not atypical for Burkina Faso in this respect.

An equally important conclusion is that administrative practices influence developments concerning access to land even when the government does not interfere in its allocation by such drastic measures as expropriation, alienation, registration, or forced enclosure. Because litigations are ultimately resolved in the district office, even in the absence of universally enforced legal codes, the attitudes of administrators, local political balances, and the ethos of development all influence villagers' decisions. The factors that land-granting lineages of Bare take into consideration when they screen the requests for the loan of field site show this very clearly.

Finally, perhaps the most important issue emerging from this discussion is the existence of strong links between customary landholding practices and commodity production in agriculture. A growing number of researchers are now questioning the colonial dogma that formal private tenure is necessary for and necessarily results in greater agricultural output.[28] We need to assert even more forcefully that nonprivate land control not only allows growing commodity production thanks to the flexibility of use made possible by mechanisms such as loan agreements but may also facilitate it by reducing capital requirements for commercial farming. Whether the current situation is seen as one of rural development in an ameliorative perspective, or in a more critical vein as greater integration into the market and the capitalist world economy, a finer-grained and more socially informed analysis will show that it has a close relationship to the maintenance of "informal" means of access to land. Actually, for a clearer view we need to distance ourselves from the current preoccupation with the agrarian crisis and redirect our attention to the reasons for the endurance of custom in different parts of the continent. To avoid falling back on treating African rural populations as cultural dopes instantiating structural inertia, we need to consider the interests and conditions that lead to the persistence of given patterns of land control, sometimes in the face of government- and project-induced plans for transformation. The practices described for Bare can operate only in a context of widespread support for and commitment to customary norms on the part of very different sectors of the rural population. In Burkina Faso, even where the number of cases of land litigation has increased, one finds a remarkable consensus on the normative order justifying land claims. What we find is a discourse and practice of ancestors and tradition that, at the same time as it allows the reproduction of a subsistence contingent, also supports patterns of differentiation and commands the allegiance of newly emerging strata to the moral order encoded in it.

Notes

1 S. F. Moore, "Explaining the Present: Theoretical Dilemmas in Processual Ethnography," *American Ethnologist* 14 (1987): 727–736.
2 B. Cire-Ba, "Les Bobo, la famille, les coutumes," *Education Africaine: Bulletin de l'Enseignement de l'Afrique Occidentale Française* 42ᵉ année, 23 (1954): 61–75. I have discussed some aspects of the social organization of southern Bobo communities in "The Bobo 'House' and the Uses of Categories of Descent," *Africa* 61 (1991): 71–97, and in "Corporate Authority, Exchange, and Opposition in Bobo Marriages," *American Ethnologist* XVI (1989). See also G. LeMoal, *Les Bobo: Nature et fonction des masques* (Paris, 1980).
3 C. Meillassoux, Introduction to *The Development of Indigenous Trade and Markets in West Africa* (Oxford, 1971): 19–20.
4 F. Snyder, *Capitalism and Legal Change* (London, 1981).
5 M. Chanock, "A Peculiar Sharpness: An Essay on Property in the History of Customary Law in Colonial Africa," *Journal of African History* 32, 1 (1991): 65–88.
6 L. Hailey, *An African Survey,* rev. 1956 (London, 1957): 803.
7 I have conducted research in Bobo country since 1983 with grants from the National Science Foundation (BNS 83-05394 and BNS 88-15676), the Wenner-Gren Foundation, and the University of Illinois Research Board. In 1983–84 in addition to participant observation, I conducted a formal survey with the help of three enumerators on a sample of 51 production units in the village of Bare, a large village that had a resident population of about 1,900 people during fieldwork. It is situated about 30 kilometers southeast of Bobo-Dioulasso, on the highway to Diebougou.

8 Even though land is now always associated with agnatic groups, some other
   natural resources may be controlled by uterine groups. For example, the
   Telena ponds where the villagers organize joint fishing expeditions in the dry
   season, and the shrine that governs it, are the property of a matriclan.
   Matriclans also claim other cults, some of great public relevance, and have a
   special relationship to the *do* cult. For further details, see M. Şaul "The
   Bobo 'House.' "

9 I give more details on these cases below.

10 Nevertheless, the political relationship between lineages within the village is
   fairly democratic. Decisions within the village are made in assemblies in
   which most of the men participate but only elders of kɔn groups or their
   representatives speak. The village has a corporate existence in its collective
   shrines and in the decisions made by such assemblies, and the collectivity can
   impose constraints and sanctions on its constituent units and members.

11 See M. Şaul, "Money and Land Tenure as Factors in Farm Size Differentiation," in R. E. Downs and S. P. Reyna (eds.), *Land and Society in Contemporary Africa* (Hanover, N.H., 1988): 405–450.

12 The oral repertoire of one of the authoctonous groups in Bare includes
   another tradition of a more historical nature on the migration of the original
   population of Tondogoso. They maintain that the first settlers of Tondogoso
   were their "foreigners" who were placed by a large pond to enforce the
   fishing rights of their hosts. Later, having committed an infraction, they were
   chased away and had to seek refuge in the present location of their village,
   which is a small mound within a basin inundated during part of the year. I do
   not know what the people of Tondogoso think about these stories.

13 In fact, the relationship of agnatic groups to each other and to land is more
   complicated than the outline provided so far. I will give some further details
   below. Namanyi belongs in reality to a subsidiary lineage that is part of a land
   corporation by virtue of its association with another lineage.

14 The figure for the average years of rest is calculated by weighing the reported
   number of years during which the tract has remained uncultivated prior to
   the most recent initial clearing by the area of the field in 1983 or 1984, when
   the information was collected [$(y*a)/a$, where y = years of rest prior to
   cultivation and a = area of the field in question during the survey]. This
   abstract figure is useful in that it summarizes information for all the measured area more accurately than does a simple mean of the reported number
   of fallow years without consideration of the area in question.

15 Şaul, "Money and Land Tenure."

16 The 51 production units in the sample represented roughly a quarter of the
   village population. They were drawn randomly from two strata established
   on the basis of farming scale according to the opinions of the members of the
   Village Group (a precooperative voluntary organization provoked by the
   rural development agency). After the fields of the people in the sample were
   measured, the production units were reclustered into two subsamples according to the area cultivated by the head of the production group. It is these

subsamples, labeled large farm units and small farm units, that I am contrasting in this chapter.

17 The large farm units include those where the head of the household farms an area of more than 6 hectares.

18 Şaul, "Money and Land Tenure."

19 The total farmed area was 180.7 hectares for large farm units and 151.2 hectares for small farm units. I included in the sample a somewhat higher number of large production units compared to the village universe to arrive at comparable subsamples.

20 See Şaul, "Corporate Authority."

21 See M. Şaul, "The Bobo 'House.' "

22 A corollary observation is that in parts of Burkina where land conflicts have become more common, the parties in litigation are usually patrilineal relatives. J.-L. Boutillier, "Les structures agraires en Haute Volta," *Études Voltaïques*, mémoires, 5 (Ouagadougou, 1964): 61.

23 That increasing the scale of production in the colonial period went hand in hand with the adoption of more extensive production techniques has been described for the Mosi by G. Ancey, "Recensement et description des principaux systèmes ruraux saheliens," *Cahiers ORSTOM*, sér. sci. hum. 14, 1 (1977).

24 With all this it is not easy to say that large farm operators invariably obtain better yields. It is even more difficult to decide whether they obtain better returns to labor and especially to capital. What is certain is that they produce larger quantities, and they achieve this by cultivating much larger areas and using greater inputs of labor and capital. Yields are very much influenced by the thoroughness of weeding and timely planting (related to labor inputs) and by the use of fertilizers. Plowing can save weeding labor but may cause a delay in planting. The practice of sowing in lines can also save weeding labor by allowing the substitution of draft power but again causes a delay in the beginning. The quantitative comparison of all this with the time saved over a number of years on long-term investments by extending the use of the same soil is empirically very complicated and cannot be undertaken with data presently at hand. For an account of farm practices in Bare and differences in this respect among farmers, see M. Şaul, "Farm Production in Bare, Burkina Faso: The Technical and Cultural Framework of Diversity," in G. Dupré (ed.), *Savoirs paysans et développement* (Paris, 1991): 301–329.

25 S. Jean, *Les jachères en Afrique tropicale: Interprétation technique et foncière* (Paris, 1975): 34.

26 There is a remote possibility that extraneous concerns may have affected farmers' answers and lowered [c]. Since villagers could have taken the survey as an infringement on their internal organization, members of lineages claiming permanent rights to the fields they cultivate may have hesitated to recognize that a nonmember had previously used the site.

27 An example is S. Sanou, *Land Tenure in the Agricultural Sector of Hounde, Burkina Faso* (Ph.D. diss., Michigan State University, 1986).

28 See, for example, J. W. Bruce, *Land Tenure Issues in Project Design and Strategies for Agricultural Development in Sub-Saharan Africa* (Madison, 1985). In the case of Kenya, which has had one of the most ambitious privatization programs in Africa, Haugerud concludes that changes in land tenure rules "are unlikely to have substantial or predictable effects on agriculture." See A. Haugerud, "Land Tenure and Agrarian Change in Kenya," *Africa* 59 (1988): 84.

4 *Richard P. Werbner*

From Heartland to Hinterland: Elites and the Geopolitics of Land in Botswana

Introduction

By accumulating land on a vast and unprecedented scale, competing elites in a new nation-state put received definitions of hierarchy and inequality at risk. Even if disunited and competing, the elites are locked together in testing—and thus in rejecting or renewing—their underlying premises and perceptions of value. The dynamics of the resistance they confront depend on, among other things, long-established cultural oppositions. The expansion of elite landholding is a cultural phenomenon, tied, as such strategic interaction regularly is, to economic, technological, and political change. Hence to study the geopolitics of elites in Botswana as a new nation-state is to uncover the cultural reconstruction of a renewed nexus between power, privilege, and wealth, the nexus that is patrimonialism or, rather, neopatrimonialism. More generally, it is to examine the remaking of certain basic relationships between state and civil society.

In Botswana, elite competition over land takes place in old polities given a new guise, tribes turned districts or subdistricts. "Tribe" and "tribesman" are not merely colonial conceptualizations or the bywords of bygone times. They have a renewed currency in Botswana, backed by the authority of the country's constitution and transacted in the everyday realities of citizenship. The state is a polity of renascent polities. The extent to which such polities develop locally specific relations between center and periphery, between heartland and hinterland, and between various sociogeographic zones is an important problem. How and in which respects do they become distinctive arenas of neopatrimonialism? This problem is all the more important where, as in much of Botswana, the dominant elites base themselves at great centers, their home villages, and yet pursue expansion by commanding major resources in remote hinterlands. Botswana is exceptional among African countries in that its governing elites, both nationally and in most districts, are dominantly cattle keepers, tied to commercial production for the beef market.[1] This political and economic bias owes much to the colonial policy that favored and subsidized pastoralism at the expense of agriculture in most of the country.

The extent of landholding by elites in Botswana has increased on a vast scale during the past few decades. The surge of expansion has had its greatest force in once inaccessible pastures in tribal or communal areas. There, in the past, cattle could not graze, due to a lack of surface water, for all or most of the year. The drilling of deep wells or boreholes has overcome that limitation. As private property, the boreholes are strategic points for control of the surrounding land. Some of them, being publicly financed, were originally property of the colonial state, but many of them—indeed, all since Independence—have been paid for privately. They have enabled their owners to maintain cattle posts from which they can command as much as ten square miles or more. In such areas, certain fields have been extended hundreds of acres for commercial agriculture, which is mechanized, with tractors, and sometimes heavily capitalized also. In addition, a small minority among the elites have very rapidly become ranch owners on freehold land or leaseholders on tribal or state land, some having more than one ranch of twenty-five square miles or more. The colonial state did not allow tribesmen, with the apparent exception of the chief, to own freehold land. Huge farms and ranches were a settler monopoly.

The immense increase in elite landholding, which began toward the end of the colonial period, has been accelerated, with some fits and starts, even in the face of severe drought and inflation, during the economic booms since independence. Productivity, reckoned in gross and aggregate terms, has risen sharply, one measure being the tripling of the national herd from about one million to more than three million head of cattle in the decade following independence.[2] An obvious factor in this expansion has been the introduction of new technology: the widespread adoption of the tractor and the borehole, coupled with favorable credit from the national government, agricultural subsidies, and a massive growth in the government's investment in the development of livestock and beef production, in turn, a response to a highly profitable, buoyant market.[3]

All of this seems to imply radical social dislocation. "By the early 1970's the situation in the rural areas was nearly chaotic," Jack Parson writes, "yielding the possibility of long-term damage to the environment and apparently providing absolute limits to the further development of capitalist cattle production."[4] It has also been described apocalyptically as an "enclosure movement," "an ecological disaster," "dispossession," "polarization," "intensified class conflict," "exploitation," and so forth. But is this really so? Perhaps. But there are less obvious political and social continuities from the colonial state and, indeed, the precolonial polities also. And, oddly enough, the dire tidings and apocalyptic visions echo fears following the introduction of the plow and the subsequent scarcities in the colonial period.[5]

Looming large in all this expansion is the legacy of the low-cost, minimalist state of the colonial period. By a minimalist state, I mean here a state that has a radically limited capacity to intervene or regulate, given its rudimentary organization, its small, fairly constant staff, its considerable reliance on agencies not of its own invention and other than those of an autonomous bureaucracy. Its legacy is disjointed. Not only does that manifest itself differently at different levels of the state but it is highly localized and very specific in the various parts of the country. It is also a legacy that catches people in old dilemmas and continuing struggles for power, all the more forcefully when an avowed aim is an attack on the colonial legacy in the name of reform or development.[6]

The labels have changed. "Native Land" is now "communal"; the "Reserve" or the "tribe," a "district" or "subdistrict"; "European Areas" of farms, "freehold"; "Crown Lands," "state lands." But they are not always consistent; some of the discards keep slipping back into use. Even more, many of the old underlying presuppositions and ideological oppositions prevail, though significantly modified by new ones, or by a recombination. Thus, ideological contrasts between the individualistic or private and the collective or "communistic," long current among local, modernizing elites as well as missionaries and officials in the colonial state, are being re-created in a recent division of tribal land into the communal and the commercial.[7]

Retribalization and the Organic Link of Elites

The hope that the end of the Protectorate would prove the end of the tribe has turned out to be false. Given the force of the colonial legacy, the shift from the low-cost, minimalist state has reinvigorated the tribe and tribesmanship. This has not been entirely the unintended consequence of unplanned action: the opposite is closer to the truth. It stems largely from conscious and highly successful efforts by members of the educated salariat, including the rich and the "super-scale" rich, who have gone to great lengths to extend the organic link between themselves and the countryside.

Within the countryside, many of the elite have been based in great centers, once chiefly capitals and now the main towns of districts. But until recently, the salariat largely lacked other urban origins or permanent homes in centers other than those identified with particular tribes, their cultures, their rural social organization. The colonial period introduced no major new urban centers, only small towns along the line of rail. The country had no capital of its own prior to Independence. It was administered from Mafeking, over the border of South Africa. In Robert Redfield and Milton Singer's terms, the longest established tribal and district centers were more orthogenetic than heterogenetic. They carried forward a common cultural matrix with the hinterland instead of creating new or alien cultural modes with authority beyond or in radical conflict with those in the hinterland.[8] Nor is it clear how heterogenetic the small railway towns are. We have been grossly neglectful in not studying them, and research is urgently needed on their actual relation with the countryside.[9] Allowing for that, the initial point I want to make, for most of the salariat, is this: their home, in the most compelling sense of the word, is still in the countryside. Heterogenetic towns are, at most, homes away from home.

An ever-increasing stream of investments has mediated this organic link between the salariat and the countryside—investments in cattle, in boreholes, in retail stores, in the education of close relatives, and most recently, under freehold or leasehold, in the land itself. The salariat are a new type of labor migrant; but, like so many of the past, they continue to send home remittances. The change is in scale, toward greater capital investment. It is now long enough since Independence for the first generation of the postcolonial elites to have gone through a major part of their life cycle. In accord with aging, some of them have let their organic link bring them even closer home, just as retiring labor migrants have done in the past.

A number of the first generation, having reached their peak in government service, as principals, permanent secretaries, ministers, became, in turn, local directors of major multinational companies or managers and owners of other private enterprises. Gradually, they have come to spend more and more time managing their cattle, land, and other rural investments. Prominent in the more home oriented first generation are former long-term residents of the capital who seemed in the first postcolonial decade to be settled in the town, at least for some purposes. Now they have virtually retired to the countryside, where they tend to pursue interests more tied to the district and its environs. Nevertheless, they do so not merely with the benefit of their past privileged perspective on development planning in the state but also with the benefit of a great flow of information, rumor, and pragmatic wisdom from their sustained contacts with their successors and other elites in the capital.

The largely expatriate development planners, according to their different factions within the government, are no longer the only ones calculating the odds for development priorities and agendas, if ever they were. They now must cope with the higher political learning of the elites of a tribal district, some of them formerly and others still well placed in the central government. Such elites now use inside information and effective political leverage to plan and pursue preemptive counterinitiatives within their tribal home district.[10]

As citizens, people belong to the state as a whole. It is national policy, often reiterated, to eliminate tribal barriers to landholding. Under the Tribal Land Act of 1968, land boards succeeded the chiefs or tribal authorities, during 1970, in the administration of tribal land.[11] The act, which is not merely tribal in name, preserves tribal land for "the benefit and advantage of the tribesmen," subject to the overriding power of the president. That power enables exemptions to be made through a minister. In practice, each district or subdistrict as a tribe restricts its grants of land and sites for deeply drilled wells or boreholes to its own people. The requirement is acceptance as a tribesman by the Tribal Authority, the grounds being birth or domicile. Without such tribesmanship, a person cannot actually get a grant from the land board. Some tribes, such as the Kgatla, virtually lack the virgin tracts needed for a ranch under the Tribal Grazing Land Policy. A member of such a tribe who seeks the leasehold for a ranch from another tribe does so in vain, although in the past some wealthy Batlokwa and Barolong did get boreholes on Bangwaketse land.[12]

The attachment to tribe and the home district or subdistrict extends further for its competing elites who buy commercial ranches on freehold land or take up long-term leases in state land. They do so almost invariably in areas surrounding or adjacent to their home district. Each such area is usually dominated by members of one or at most two tribes, so that even on nontribal land, landholding is not by citizenship irrespective of tribe. There is thus a process of retribalization that goes beyond the assertions of ethnic difference so familiar in the literature on ethnicity.[13]

Tribe and District

Some details of tribe and district are necessary to clarify the importance of retribalization for strategic interaction over land. There have been political demands to split up a tribe, the publicly stated grounds being that it is "too large and diverse to be a single district for democratic participation and administrative efficiency."[14] But effective resistance has prevented the postcolonial state from cutting the powerfully renascent tribe down to size. At the other extreme, even change toward tribal federation has sustained and not subverted retribalization.

There are two illuminating cases of the amalgamation of colonially recognized tribes into a single district. In one case, a couple of the smallest, Batlokwa and Balete, have been federated to form a wider district, the South-East. Neither tribe is large or powerful enough to dominate the other. Although one is somewhat closer to the national capital, and thus has the more valuable residential land, neither has pasture or arable land prized by the other. Both are highly congested. Each has its own land board; and each retains considerable autonomy or semiautonomy.

In the second case, the Southern District of the Bangwaketse and Barolong, most of the district, including the great village capital, belongs to one of the country's most powerful tribes, Bangwaketse. Some of its members are now at the forefront of the expansion into ranching and, to a much lesser extent, commercial agriculture. The rest of the district, known as the Barolong Farms, is now relatively short of pasture, but it contains the country's biggest area of elite expansion into commercialized agriculture on the largest scale.[15] The Barolong Farms belong to a tribe, Barolong, which gained its own official autonomy with a resident chief shortly after Independence. Before that, it was a hinterland of a tribe with a great capital village on the other side of the South African border, and it still lacks a major village as a center of its own.

In this second case, the imbalance between the two tribes is much greater; the commercially valuable land of certain elites is at risk; and the potential consequences of reduced autonomy, or of one tribe encroaching on the other, are strongly resisted by those who consider they have much to lose. Political arguments about the relative autonomy and interests of the parts of the district are often put in terms of tribe. This case will reappear in a discussion of relations between heartland and hinterland.

Here I must stress a simple point. Its rich and politically powerful members have reinvigorated the tribe in the guise of the district or subdistrict as an entity with its own public resources and territory and

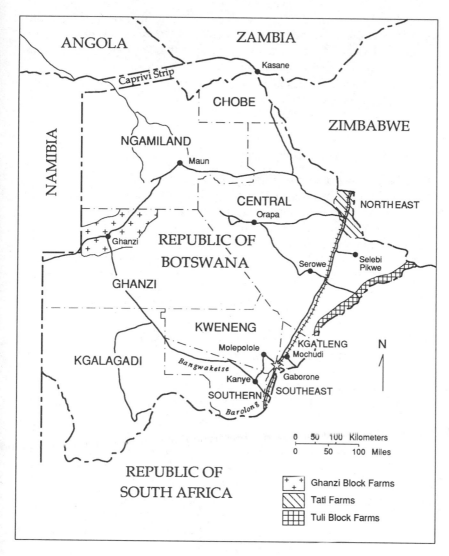

Figure 4.1. Map of Botswana

beyond that its own sphere of interests, to be defended against the perceived threat of encroachment from outsiders, particularly members of other tribes.

The question of who controls the land, how and for what purposes, has become more salient, increasingly more so. Uncertainty of control has arisen from, and in turn become an important factor in, a spiral of contradictory processes, often involving incompatible uses of land and sometimes the conflicting interests of hunter-gatherers and ranchers, or commercial farmers with tractors and other villagers with plows. Predatory expansion by some elites has met counterexpansion by others. Once again, as Hitchcock[16] points out, we need to appreciate that unofficial initiatives have confronted and, particularly in the case of the Tribal Grazing Land Policy, subverted official counterinitiatives.

The Galactic Polity and Patrimonialism

Much of our own understanding of the strategic interaction over land depends on how we conceptualize the polity within which people defend or expand their interests, accumulate land and wealth, seek power, and act strategically. We must be careful lest the labels we use falsely imply a radical shift in values or in the felt qualities of life. We need to keep in mind how the later polity is the old in a new guise, that we are studying transformation and not revolution in our approach to the strategic interaction over land in districts or subdistricts as tribes. For that reason, I find it useful to borrow an image Tambiah uses for expansion and counterexpansion, for centripetal and centrifugal tendencies, in Southeast Asian kingdoms. It is an image of "the galactic polity."[17]

From one aspect, the galactic polity is a recurring design of central places in a hierarchy, each modeled on the capital. In the case of Tswana tribes, the capital as traditional model has the chief at the center and at increasing distance, his relatives and commoners, with serfs somewhat beyond the pale. The hierarchy of central places is downward from the chief's capital, from the greatest center with tens of thousands of villagers and with the greatest differentiation between them, including the greatest concentration of the rich, the politically powerful, and the people of the highest rank. Below that are villages that are big and politically important and that now may be subdistrict capitals but have a maximum of roughly ten thousand people, usually forming, in the main, a satellite community of ethnically cognate immigrants. At the bottom of the central place hierarchy, the villages are small and relatively unimportant, with at most hundreds of residents. The small village is often ethnically distinct, its people regarded as inferiors by people of big villages.[18] In many cases, the villagers are immigrants, former hunter-gatherers or herdsmen, former serfs, and servants of the chief or men of rank.[19]

Overlapping in the outermost areas are also hunter-gatherers or agropastoralists who live in dispersed settlements of homesteads or hamlets. Such people, lacking nucleated villages, are somewhat outside the hierarchy, yet within its sphere of influence or actually under the command of its rulers.[20]

A scheme for the representation of center-oriented or concentric space recurs. Among Tswana, it extends each village outward from its nucleus. At least, this is how it has been traditionally conceptualized, if not always operationalized. The nucleus is a center of administration, politics, ritual, consumption, and redistribution. It extended to its surrounding areas of production, where, according to the centrist plan, the innermost arable areas are separated from the outermost areas of pasture and hunting. The center around the chief and his close relatives is the locus of greatest value and greatest power. It was a place from which serfs, in the precolonial and even colonial periods, were excluded, except as immediate servants. Their place was in the hinterland at the frontiers. As a traditional design, this concentric scheme represents political inequality and social distance by spatial distance.[21]

From another perspective, the galactic polity is a competitive arena of a patrimonialism predicated on the premise of a nexus, transmittable from one generation to the next, between political status or political power, rank or recognized prominence, wealth, and privileged access to land. Pauline Peters points to "the reciprocally reinforcing effects between political and economic power: political authority and influence ensured access to valued resources and the material advantages derived from the latter facilitated a continuing hold on political status and privilege."[22]

The relation between the privilege and responsibility of a patrimony, between its exploitation and its guardianship, is a political and economic question, to be answered anew in each generation.[23] Depending on the answer, quite different patterns of social mobility emerge. In turn, instability in center-periphery relations is a function of social mobility along with patrimonialism. A correlate of this is that social and spatial mobility intimately intertwine.

In the past, the chief could attempt to regulate competition and centralize the arena more strongly by creating patrimonies for chief's men out of his own patrimony of the chiefdom as a whole. He had the power to appoint overseers of pasture and of arable land. With their appointments to political status came patrimonies that they could pass on to their successors and that gave them privileged access to land and thus, depending on manpower, to wealth. The overseer was not a trustee in the Western sense of someone holding a trust on behalf of others, to the exclusion of his own personal and proprietary interest. I must stress his privileged interest, lest the importance of patrimonial strategies be obscured.

The danger to successive rulers was that the staff of overseers could become entrenched in their own right. In that case, they could represent a force counter to the ruler's own interests. This danger is as endemic in the galactic polity of the present as it was in the past. Against the danger, the chief could hold the appointees and, even more important, their successors in a direct debt relationship by giving them his own cattle on agistment.

The postcolonial state has yet to subvert the galactic polity by a total end to patrimonialism. If anything, the subversion may be said to run in the opposite direction. Admittedly, the postcolonial state has taken the power of patrimonial appointment out of the chief's hands. But so far, it has endorsed the legitimacy of the existing chief's men as overseers of arable land.[24]

The chief's men now represent persons around whom opposition may rally against the land board as the chief's successor under the Tribal Land Act of 1968. It is a fresh development in the continuing opposition between the entrenched staff of a ruler and his successor. The further stage is that prior ruler and successor actually share power and authority, given the chief's membership in the land board and the chief's continued jurisdiction in court cases over land. After the Tribal Land Act of 1968, the ruling party's 1969 election manifesto proclaimed that it had "no intention of excluding traditional authority." The manifesto denounced "the arbitrary decisions of the Chiefs" (a code phrase for strategic action against the interests of a new elite?) as a reason for making them members of the land board along with elected representatives of the tribe.[25] In the face of a general mistrust of the district land boards,[26] the chief's men assert their own autonomy, subject to pressures from elders and other influential people who advise them on the basis of local knowledge. In certain areas where the chief's men hold virtually unused tracts of a square mile or more, the land board cannot directly redistribute land because it has no reserves under its immediate control. The board makes its grants subject to a letter of authorization from the local overseer or headman. If anything, this endorsement by the postcolonial state along with the freedom from the chief's official control has strengthened the privilege in holding land as a patrimony. I must stress that this is the case, so far. But there is also a countertendency, an opposition to banking of land by the privileged overseers for future use while validating rank in the present.[27]

It appears in many areas that land is already thought to be scarce, or the threat of a coming shortage is felt to be immediate. According to Ørnulf Gulbrandsen, some people consider that "an artificial shortage of land" is being created. Writing of Bangwaketse in the context of a wider report on southern Botswana as a whole, Gulbrandsen observed, "There are, of course, a number of commercially oriented, politically articulate people who have no immediate access to a large, traditional holding, and who are therefore highly critical of the prevailing lack of check upon the tribal overseer."[28] However, some smallholders tie their high regard for overseers to the very fact that they are bankers, holding back a reserve for the future; that they are not expanding their actual use of land and thus represent no present threat to the smallholders.[29] The invidious comparison is to the commercial operators who "eat up the land."

Gulbrandsen himself was concerned about the dangers of an over-centralized regulatory agency. More bureaucratic decision making at the district headquarters was, he feared, unlikely to improve the administration of land under increasingly crowded conditions. Land registers would be more a problem than an answer.[30] Instead, as the anthropologist advising the Land Access Reference Group of the Ministry of Local Government and Lands, Gulbrandsen recommended that in each small, highly localized farming community, "there should be elected an arable lands advisory committee into which the lands overseer is co-opted as an ex-officio member."[31] This recommendation carries forward the attack on chiefly patrimonialism to the local level of the chief's men, as do some of his others on the enforcement of a Tribal Land Act rule canceling grants of land unused for more than five years. Although the central government has accepted these recommendations, it is too early to say what their local impact will be. The implementation will probably be met by preemptive counterinitiatives because elite and powerful members of certain land boards have themselves got substantial patrimonies in land, "large, traditional holdings," that are largely unused.

Without predicting far into the future, this much can be said: patrimonialism, an underlying premise of the galactic polity of the past, is alive and well in the present; it is still a powerful factor in the most recent strategic interaction over land.[32]

Expansion and Geopolitics

In addition to its central place hierarchy, concentric design, and competitive patrimonialism, it is characteristic of each galactic polity that is a constellation manifestly unlike any other, and yet, according to a simple logic of expansion in geopolitics, all are variations on the history of a theme. The theme is one of transition toward defined boundaries, fixity of a once impermanent capital, and elimination of any surrounding "no-man's land" (in reality, often the land of hunter-gatherers).[33]

As Isaac Schapera reports,

The territories of the various tribes [before the Protectorate] were not clearly defined, and disputes about water and grazing rights were frequent along the borders where their cattleposts overlapped, In addition, portions of the territory occupied by one tribe were sometimes claimed by another. Even after the proclamation of the Protectorate [in 1885], the Administration on several occasions found itself obliged to intervene in territorial disputes that threatened to result in war. . . . But the establishment of the Protectorate imposed a check upon further territorial expansion, and boundaries were gradually defined that had to be accepted.[34]

Expansion from the southeast to the north and the west was predatory in the nineteenth century. Great villages spread outward and, with smaller satellites at their frontiers, encroached on bands or less centralized polities without hierarchies of nucleated villages. Advantage in gaining territory was to the most centralized.[35]

I find it useful to represent the logic of expansion, and thus its variations, externally in terms of the closure of frontiers and internally in terms of the relation between heartland and hinterland. First, externally, a galactic polity emerges as a specific constellation according to its relative freedom from being surrounded by other such polities.

The smallest tribes, Balete and Batlokwa, exemplify polities with the least such freedom, with extreme congestion, marked homogeneity, a simple central place hierarchy and administrative structure, and a severe limitation on the production of wealth from cattle and cereal crops. Currently, they are also distinguished by a high level of investment in people, as reflected in the generally high level of education and, of course, employment at the nearby national capital. Together they form the South-East District.

At the other extreme is the greatest of tribes, Bangwato, now the Central District, which has largely open frontiers.[36] It has the least congested areas, the greatest ethnic and economic differentiation, the greatest elaboration of the central place hierarchy and administrative subdivisions, and the least limitation on both cattle and cereal production. It is mostly free of any other galactic polity around it, although it meets several for relatively short stretches. Around it, instead, are bands of acephalous hunter-gatherers (Basarwa or San),[37] agropastoralists who are egalitarian villagers, without rank or chiefship or central place hierarchies (Kgalagadi),[38] and others who live in dispersed hamlets and homesteads under petty chieftains (primarily Kalanga) and now have their own tribal district (the North-East).[39] It also incorporates peoples originally belonging to these categories. The current openness of its frontiers is represented by most of its surrounding land belonging to the state, unlimited by the control of another state-recognized tribe.

This openness represents a strategic advantage given the postcolonial policy of converting state land increasingly into tribal land. The Central District as tribe, along with the other big cattle-holding districts, North-West and Southern, continues to benefit most from such "tribalizing" of land.[40] Further potential for expansion is tied to the past geopolitics of the galactic polity. In the postcolonial state, it is the largest tribes and the ones with the greatest openness of frontier that gain the most in increased access to surrounding pasture.

The more total the closure of its frontiers by the frontiers of others, the more the galactic polity is smaller, more congested, more homogeneous, more rudimentary in administration, and more limited economically in terms of agropastoral production; and also, in the precolonial period at least, the more its autonomy was threatened by a neighbour. At the other extreme, the converse also holds. The formation of each galactic polity is within a chain that, in extending to its outermost limits, encompasses politically less centralized outsiders, incorporates them, or, even beyond its frontiers, impels them to convert toward greater centralization and nucleation.[41] In turn, with such galactic encompassment and influence beyond the frontiers come reactions; there is resistance by the outsiders in collaboration with certain insiders, and there are countertendencies toward decentralization.

Much also depends on the internal relation between heartland and hinterland. Around the capital is the heartland, the great village with its neighbors, where the population becomes densest, congestion is recognized first, and the pressure for arable land first threatens to eat away the reserve for pasture. Beyond that lies the hinterland, which has the main potential for expansion. It may be a more or less extended series of hinterlands according to the relative conversion into heartland.

If the conversion is complete, as in the smallest tribes, the hinterland is consumed. It all becomes heartland, without extensive or adequate pasture for large herds, and virtually all the landholdings are small. But the value of the land, the assessment of shortage, and the responses to that are all closely tied to the changing nature of the center at the top of the hierarchy. For the southern tribes without a hinterland, the center is now the national capital, the country's first city. In effect, the great villages now form a periurban or suburban area around the city. Hence urban employment has inflated the demand for the value of residential plots and housing; it also means that the quite small plots typical here are viable because they are merely the source of a supplement to cereals bought from earnings.[42]

The small plots are usually plowed by tractor for a fee by the very few commercial farmers and not by the urban employed owners themselves.

The concentration of the mechanized means of production in the hands
of the few does not result in the dispossession of the many. There is a
valuable increase in the food supply for the city, given that otherwise
staples are rarely grown in its gardens or fields. In the heartland without
the hinterland, the main tendency is toward a decrease in the scale of
landholding; expansion is restricted; and the accumulation of land in the
hands of an elite is not tolerated. It simply does not occur.[43]

Where the conversion is least, as in the largest tribes, the hinterlands
become the major zones for the increasing accumulation of land by
elites. Expansion is based in the big villages, but it largely takes place in
their hinterlands, and it is usually initiated from the heartlands outward.
Generally, both the social and the central place hierarchy develop and
become elaborated with predatory expansion from the center outward,
with encroachment on areas outside the big villages themselves. In turn,
competition within the big village drives expansion beyond it, although
the rich, the politically powerful, and the privileged are not exclusively
concentrated at the center. Even the more decentralized hinterlands
may have their own elites. But if the prizes they win in the hinterlands
are major landholdings, they always win in competition with elites encroaching from the big villages of the heartlands.

This predatory expansion has developed along with a change in the
importance of internal boundaries.[44] The introduction of boreholes facilitated movement across what had formerly been separate grazing areas.
It also undermined the capacity of overseers to control grazing within
smaller areas around pans or surface water. Partly in response to this,
and at the time of considerable public investment in boreholes toward
the end of the colonial period, the Protectorate administration introduced at certain tribal capitals small committees sometimes known as
Committees for the Conservation of Natural Resources.[45] In its concern
with the allocation of land and water supplies, it was a forerunner of the
land board. Power and influence became even more centralized, instead
of dispersed among overseers with much more localized interests and
responsibilities. Politically influential elites, based at the capital or elsewhere in the heartland, strengthened their grasp on the hinterland.

In general, the recent tendencies are clear. Once a hinterland appreci-
ates in value for the elites, because its pastures are no longer beyond
reach or because of a leap forward in mechanized and commercialized
agriculture, its former automony comes under attack. Elites from big
villages use their political influence at the center to command major
prizes for themselves in the hinterlands. There they often seem virtually
to shed their sense of noblesse oblige and to feel even freer to be individualistic, competitive, and exploitative and to maximize their self-

interest than they do at home in their heartland. Usually, they retain a base at the center in a big village and rarely attempt to dominate expansion at the periphery by becoming "immigrants," residing exclusively in a hinterland.

The hinterland is now subjected to increasing pressure toward greater centralization, although resistance may mitigate its effects. Sometimes, the pull of the hinterland is the greater, and elites from the capital and the heartland are co-opted into the defense of the hinterland qua hinterland.[46]

An account of heartland-hinterland relations within an actual district will further our understanding of such strategic interaction over land. I would like to consider the Southern District. Although I do not know it from firsthand observation, there are good reasons for choosing it. It enables us to appreciate certain major landmarks of transformation in the country as a whole. The two tribes, Bangwaketse and Barolong, that form it represent extreme alternatives in their heartland-hinterland relations and are to some extent mutually constitutive within the chain of galactic polities. In addition to this representative importance, it has a substantial literature, rich in acute studies of both the long-term and the very recent strategic interaction over land. For the sake of clarity, I will start by discussing each tribe somewhat separately, beginning with the larger one, Bangwaketse, which has the potential to dominate the district as a whole and in which the pull and influence of the heartland is now the stronger. In addition to the earlier work by Schapera,[47] the important studies on which I rely are primarily by Gulbrandsen.[48]

Zonal Relativity, Expansion
From the Heartland, and State Intervention

Among Bangwaketse, the expansion of elite landholding has shaped, and in turn been shaped by, a hierarchical ordering of conflict from the heartland to the hinterland. I want to stress that it takes us beyond the views familiar in the literature of the central place hierarchy as an order of function or of the gradient in dominance by which political inequality is represented in spacial distance. I argue that the Bangwaketse heartland has grown stronger, at the expense not merely of the hinterland but also of a displacement of conflict, such as over land, outward. Hence within the heartland, people with very different interests, from smallholders to the richest and most powerful elites, have continued to negotiate a modus vivendi, without gross dispossession or marked social dislocation.

The heartland is not conflict-free, of course. On the contrary, I would infer that here, too, there is what, in *Land Reform in the Making,* I called "defensive enclosure":

Barbed wire is fast becoming as familiar as the thornbush. The new permanent fencing, largely financed by government loans, subsidies or outright grants, is at once a symptom and a cause of the re-defining of the relations between men over land. Visible boundaries matter as never before, whether between whole communities or between the lands of individuals. Much of the fencing is defensive enclosure, rather than encroachment on other's land, though it often does become provocative in the eyes of neighbours. . . . Sometimes people who never permanently fenced their fields before do so now to protect what they believe—or insist—would have been already theirs, on the basis of locally acknowledged claims.[49]

However, given the pressures within the heartland, elites have looked beyond it, both for their major expansion into commercial agriculture and for the fresh pastures where they have been recently making vast capital investments in herds and new boreholes. As a consequence, there has come to be a zonal relativity in the certainty or definition of rights and claims, in the nature and intensity of conflict, and in the span of interests represented. Who is involved in the strategic interaction over land, and for what purposes, has come to be relative to location in a series of sociogeographic zones. Each shades off into the other, roughly from northeast to southwest, and each corresponds roughly to a tier in the central place hierarchy (the remote hinterland also has its own middle-sized village as a subdistrict center). The main distinctions are between the heartland, the transitional hinterland, and the remote hinterland. I consider each of these in turn to clarify the importance of zonal relativity.

The heartland largely manages its own affairs in matters of land. Rights and claims are fixed according to local knowledge and local understanding and within, of course, the local power structures. In some of the most congested parts of the heartland, where the people are predominantly subsistence farmers, they continue to lend land,

and a community consensus has developed on the redistribution of unused land. Accordingly, when a young man has identified a piece of land which has not been cultivated for quite some years and whose holder or his descendants are not apt to use it in the foreseeable future, he will make a plea to take it over with a minor compensation for the work put into de-stumping and clearing the land acccording to traditional rates.[50]

In the arable areas of the heartland, the land board's policy has been laissez-faire, with virtually no attention to land use planning. In the pasture areas, especially where the heartland shades off, the land board has made more gestures toward regulation but without effectively blocking rich commercial farmers from converting tracts into vast fields.

The sharper conflicts along with greater uncertainty about rights and claims have emerged in the transitional hinterland. The pressure from commercial farmers based in the capital has set up a chain reaction. The local villagers, many of them with hunter-gatherer or serf origins in small subordinate communities, see themselves threatened by politically dominant outsiders as "land eaters"; "this conflict is locally cast in terms of ethnic and class suppression."[51] In their turn, these villagers have encroached on the pasture of other villages even farther into the hinterland to the south, creating major disputes that have involved the Ministry of Local Government and Lands. Within the villages themselves, there has been an increase in disputes over land, a greater reluctance to lend it, and a greater emphasis on banking it, with an eye to sharecropping arrangements with commercial farmers, some of whom have found these arrangements the only way to expand farther. The idea that land is about to become very scarce is widely shared.

In the remote hinterland, the competition has been the fiercest. The political and economic stakes have also been highest and the uncertainties in rights, in privileges, and in prospects greatest.

On one thing almost everyone agreed, although they came at it from very different perspectives: the prime value of virgin land. The elites prized it for fresh grazing. The land use planners needed it, because they had to lay the ranches down according to a preordained scheme of paddocks, rather than designing them on the spot to accommodate local patterns of tenure and use. I say almost everyone, because it does not include hunter-gatherers and those, in government and outside it, who spoke for their interests. Their prime value was mobility across the territories the hunter-gatherers recognized as their own. However, the prime value of the others prevailed over theirs; and it was their rights and claims that became the most ambiguous or, as Sanford put it, "obscure,"[52] when the attorney general ruled that they were not tribesmen for purposes of the Tribal Land Act and thus could not claim their own territories against allocation for a commercial ranch or cattle post. No ruling in court has clarified the obscurity further.

Within the government, district officials, especially the expatriate field staff of district land use planners (district officer for lands), have been at loggerheads over the remote hinterland with capital bureaucrats, most prominently the office-bound economists of the Ministry of Finance and Development, under the then vice-president (now president and himself from the heartland, with his own expanding interests in the hinterland). The Ministry of Finance economists fought for ranches, for large-scale commercialization as the way forward for the nation, the gross national product, and the balance of payments. The resistance rallied around the Ministry of Local Government and Lands, around its minister (said to be a political rival of the finance minister), and around its expatriate field staff whose opposition arose as much from professional reasons as from reasons of "social justice." They had to do the groundwork for ranches they knew not to be designed or adapted for local conditions.[53]

The land board itself was divided, most obviously along party lines, apparently with the ruling party members in favor of leasehold ranches in the hinterland and the opposition against. A prominent influence was former Chief Bathoen II Gaseitsiwe, a leader of the opposition party. "After several years of seriously attacking what he once denounced as 'robbery of the people's property,' he has been compelled to apply for a ranch to ensure sufficient grazing for his large herd."[54] Laissez-faire was not an option. The national and tribal pressure for at least the appearance of control by an agency at district headquarters was too great. Instead, regulatory planning for the remote hinterland became all-consuming, and the Land Board was left virtually no manpower to do anything else elsewhere.

Given its factional division, the land board tried to eat its cake and have it too. First, it gave in to demands from the rich and politically influential for new borehole sites, despite a central government "freeze" on such allocations. Later, it proceeded as if it still had a "virgin area" and could take a decision based on having made no allocations. "By these allocations, the land board informally acknowledged that in due course these borehole allocations could be turned into commercial ranch leases."[55] "It was not only H. E. the [current] President who was allocated two boreholes here, but a number of other, prominent, influential Bangwaketse."[56] This was a preemptive move. It left virtually no virgin area. While the planners were busy planning, the actual decision was taken out of their hands. Having gained rights to borehole sites, few people wanted to take ranch leases around them. Their preference was for free range areas. The ranch leases would have imposed unwelcome requirements for enclosure of the grazing, investment in expensive fencing, and maintenance of paddocks. The evidence of extensive use gave concerned professionals a welcome reason for revised plans. They decided the barest number of ranches, instead of the intended two hundred, were to be allocated. Finally, when the land board did try to make the allocations, it was evident to all that the whole planning exercise had been a costly fiasco; it had to be largely scrapped.

This account implies conflicting interests among elites themselves, not merely between them and the underprivileged, the weak, or the rest of the tribe. Gulbrandsen rightly highlights this elite disunity, as does John Holm, and I must stress it also,[57] because of the past misrepresentation of "the political unity of the elite."[58] Opposition to the tactics of the wealthy brother of the man who was soon to become head of state, then the minister of finance and the vice-president, expressed this disunity. Despite a land board rule of "one-man-one ranch," the vice-president's brother got more, besides the two he already owned on freehold land. As a sleeping partner, he acquired the extra ones in the names of front men, including the current chief and a servant at his cattle post. For various reasons, the expatriate district officer for lands became suspicious and raised the matter with the land board.

Gulbrandsen reports,

Since the Paramount Chief was also directly involved, the Land Board was very reluctant to follow up this case. This officer, however, unsatisfied with this response brought the case informally to his Ministry (MLGL) and it ultimately reached the Minister of Local Government and Lands. This minister, who, ostensibly, was not entirely enthusiastic about the TGLP [Tribal Grazing Lands Policy], presented the case to H. E. the President, Seretse Khama and a Presidential commission of enquiry was set up. . . . The commission's findings revealed, among other things, the suspected instances of strawmanship. Hence, the question was whether these allocations should be re-drawn. The Attorney General's verdict was that there was no legal basis for cancellation as the allocations were only in disagreement with the Land Board's provisional rules and not in conflict with Botswana's legislation.[59]

The more it became plain how very few ranches actually could be allocated, the more disaffected about ranching and the more divided among themselves the elites became. In addition, almost none of the ranch holders kept to the projected "techno-ecological production regimes." Instead, they virtually converted their lease holdings to cattle posts, by not maintaining the rotation between paddocks or their perimeter fences.[60]

The fenced ranch is the orthogenetic mode, the free-range cattle post the homogenetic mode. The ranch is for the exclusive use, and the cattle post is for negotiable use, more or less exclusive according to the current circumstances of the borehole owner and those attached to him.[61]

In preferring cattle posts over ranches and in converting the latter into the former, elites have been making the mode more appropriate in cultural terms. Thus, they have been harmonizing with their relationships to others less privileged than themselves. In prevailing conditions, they have also been making it a more economically viable and productive mode for absentees, a development very much in the interests of a salariat with organic links to the countryside.[62]

But does it all boil down to greed, the motive for all "land grabs"? We must appreciate the preference for expansion based on cattle posts in terms of interests wider than those narrowly of the elites. Gulbrandsen observes, "Patently, to a considerable degree, the borehole owners have, through their apparently generous supply of water to local people and to less wealthy people from the east, paved the way for far more extensive communal land use (both arable and pastoral) than would otherwise have been possible."[63] In accord with this, I agree with his conclusion "that the tremendous expansion of commercial pastoralism had, in fact, generated conditions which prevented full privatization of vast tracts of the communal grazing land through extensive enclosures."[64] If that is greed, then it is transformed by being embedded in the obligations of ongoing social relationships: the organic ones that elites have with the communities of the countryside.

The Pull of the Hinterland Against the Heartland

To discuss the rest of the district, where commercial and mechanized agriculture has had its most extensive impact, I turn to the once disputed hinterland, now known as the Barolong Farms. I derive my account from studies by Schapera, John Comaroff, Patrick Molutsi, and Gulbrandsen,[65] although our interpretations differ. I divide the account into two periods, each of which began with a translation of political inequality into inequality in the control of land. During both periods, the powerful and the privileged turned large tracts of land that were previously tribal assets into patrimonies, the difference being that in the second period, the hinterland came more into its own. In addition to immigrants from the heartland, some of its long-term residents commanded the major prizes.

Toward the end of the nineteenth century, dominance of this hinterland was uncertain for two reasons. First, two tribes disputed its territory. One, Bangwaketse, came to be wholly in the Bechuanaland Protectorate and the other, Barolong, mainly in South Africa. A colonial decision awarded the territory to the South African tribe that thus had to control its hinterland from across the colonial border. Second, there was the recognized danger from encroachment by white settlers with their special privilege of setting up farms under private ownership, to forestall which, the Barolong chief tried to make such ownership a privilege associated with rank and power within his tribe. In doing this, he had the example of a related tribe in the Orange Free State, which had divided its land into individually owned farms.[66] Some of its privileged landholders eventually used the proceeds from the sale of land for educating a professional elite of lawyers and doctors.[67]

Dividing up the hinterland, the Barolong chief created his own farms, with titles registered under leasehold. In the main, they were rewards for his close relatives and for other favorites with important political status in the heartland. Over time, privileged titleholders from the Barolong heartland appealed to the protectorate to let them pursue fully the Orange Free State example. Their evident aim was to cash in on their land in the hinterland. In the face of opposition from the Protectorate administration, the sale of land was prohibited, as in all the Protectorate's tribal land. Although some titleholders did manage to rent farms to white settlers, most had to allow other tribesmen to use their land for a fixed and low fee, and very few extracted any substantial income in this way. Virtually none came to live on their farms in the hinterland. They delegated immediate control to local overseers or "de facto headmen."

The nature of the holders' title remained somewhat ambiguous, one thing in their view, another in the views of successive chiefs or the Protectorate administration. "The history of the Barolong Farms is the history of an unsatisfactory experiment in 'individual' land tenure," Schapera argued in his role as anthropological advisor to the administration in 1943.[68] In his influential report to the administration, "The System of Land Tenure on the Barolong Farms,"[69] Schapera championed the common people; he took the side of the tribesmen of the hinterland and defended "the interests of the tribe" against those of "landlords" and "private enterprise." Schapera recommended

that the policy of the Administration should be to treat the Barolong Farms like the other recognized tribal areas in the Protectorate and that immediate steps should be taken towards doing away with the two main features in which the Farms differ from those areas—the leasing of land to European farmers and the payment of rent by Native tenants.[70]

Eventually, the chief in South Africa, apparently with some urging from the protectorate administration, declared all rents to be owed to the Tribal Treasury. His political motive was to weaken his opponents in the heartland by capturing their assets in the hinterland. In response, the titleholders increasingly lost interest in their farms; and, according to Comaroff, despite the appointment of a chief's representative over the hinterland, the links between it and the capital "grew increasingly tenuous."[71]

If we ask about the overriding tendency in heartland-hinterland relations throughout most of this period, the answer is this: remoteness counted. For people in the heartland, the pull and influence of capital or the center was greatest, with the pull and influence of the hinterland being minimal; and conversely for the people of the hinterland, it was the hinterland that had the greater pull. However, toward the end of this period, that balance of centripetal and centrifugal forces became ever more precarious, with a tilt toward the hinterland.

From the late 1950's onward, the value of land in the hinterland appreciated astronomically, as elites began to utilize increasingly mechanized forms of commercial agriculture. In part, this was due to a number of so-called exogenous factors, the most important of which were from the state, subsidies and beneficial credit along with improved extension services; and from the proximity to South Africa, profitable labor migration for earning initial capital, cheap seasonal labor by South African immigrants living as landless workers near the railway, better access to the then higher paying South African market through cooperatives in nearby towns, cheaper secondhand tractors and expert maintenance services from the town mechanics, and training in the use of tractors on South African farms.[72] No less important were "endogenous factors," including the more competitive individualism of elites at the hinterland, their settlement in households relatively more autonomous than in the heartland, and the availability of largely denuded tracts best in soils and rainfall for large-scale mechanized agriculture. The interaction between these exogeneous and endogenous factors strengthened the pull of the hinterland.

In response, South African immigrants came from the heartland and became among the most prominent, perhaps even a majority, of the large-scale farmers in the hinterland.[73] The rest were long-standing residents. It is a moot point how far such immigrants actually took the lead in making the leap forward in commercial agriculture. My sources are not conclusive. But it was not a return of the old titleholders or a restoration by a "traditional" aristocracy of its past hold over the Farms. Shortly after Independence, the administrative tie to the South African chief was cut; the Farms became a state-recognized tribe. Comaroff stresses that the majority of the large farmers "have no kinship connections" with the tribal royalty or the 'traditional' authorities across the border."[74]

By the time of independence, a major shift in landholding was already under way, with the large farmers each coming to command land on an unprecedented scale, one thousand acres or more. It remained for them to get this hold ratified and to regularize the position of newcomers to their numbers. The opportunity to do so came with the establishment of land boards in 1970, which in their initial stages were agencies of an ad hoc kind.[75] In general, the early land boards were ambiguously accountable, highly politicized within the local government and well beyond any national close supervision. The members of the Rolong Land Board were dominantly the new Barolong chief and his allies among the commercial farmers. They soon realized that they had a relatively free hand to make large-scale grants of unoccupied land and thus to reward favorites among the rich and politically powerful. The chief may have regarded such rewards as part of his efforts to build up the chiefship and a more centralized chiefdom. Some of the board members themselves benefited greatly from this. Once again, close links to the chief, though this time not necessarily of kinship, counted for access to control over major shares in tribal land.

Having been brought from the South African heartland as the reigning chief's younger brother, the old chief himself refused to leave his great capital, and the new chief was oriented toward the centrist model from the heartland. In the early 1970s, he tried to make the fledgling chiefdom more in the image of its source and planned to concentrate it in five villages under headmen of his own appointment. This policy represented an attack against the established Barolong overseers. Their hand against him was strengthened by the fact that given their recognized political status, they were the authorities around whom popular opposition to the venal land board could and did rally. The chief considered a public good what was popularly considered venal. That was the plan's further undoing. Having come as a poor man, he relied on rewards of land both to make the powerful indebted to him and to extract the "tribute" that he needed to become rich and powerful, to be truly a chief. Eventually he fell out with his own headmen, and in the face of popular resistance, his plan failed. The Farms remained a hinterland without great concentration of settlement, a major capital, or centralized administration.

During the 1970s, when Comaroff carried out his research, polarization seemed to be in progress. Households "caught in the middle, being neither subsistence farmers nor large-scale commercial operators," feared they were being squeezed out.[76] Yet, despite this specter of increasing impoverishment, middle range and small Barolong farmers do not now have less access to land than in the mid-seventies. Or rather, they have not had their land expropriated to any great extent by large farmers.[77] There has been encroachment, but it has largely been on areas once set aside for shared use as pasture.

In this period, elites became immigrants, gave up the heartland, and did not capture the new value at the hinterland the way, in the first period, the rich and powerful did as absentees. I must say more about the reasons for this and its implications for strategic interaction over land. My argument is economic, organizational, and political.

In economic terms, during the first period, it was open to the rich and powerful as titleholders to reap the benefits of their large landholdings at a distance. This needed no investment or careful management to gain some income, albeit small, from fees and rents. Even the larger return from investing in cattle and using the land for cattle posts required only occasional supervision, not constant residence or maintenance of a household year-round to keep track of the investments. Secondly, there is the organization of services, which was primarily in terms of long-term relationships of kinship or status, such as between patron and client, master and serf. This organization was also skewed toward the center, according to the central place hierarchy within which it operated. Complementary to that, the value of the center was politically overriding. It was from the capital that the chief distributed rewards, perhaps cattle even more prominently than land. It was the supreme locus of intrigue and palace politics. It was successfully exerting its sphere of influence against a rival on its tribal frontier. In political terms, therefore, the rich and powerful were strongly pulled toward the center, from which they could not be permanently absent without endangering their tribal standing.

In the second period, these relations were economically, organizationally, and politically reversed. It became exceptional in the Farms to have major investments in cattle as remote assets. Successful management of the land, the labor, and the machines under commercial production virtually required having a permanent household within the hinterland, often one under a wife's daily control. Organizationally, an absentee was also likely to be disadvantaged, given the fact that many services and relationships, including the very important ones with sharecroppers, were on an ad hoc or contractual basis. Sharecroppers often found it in their interest to change or break off the relationship from time to time. One had to be at hand to negotiate the best terms and hold people to them. Politically, the old heartland, if ever a power base for controlling the hinterland, lost its influence. Even in administration, the writ of the old capital ceased to apply when the new state of Botswana, unlike the old colonial Protectorate, could not tolerate tribal rule across its problematic borders with South Africa. Under these conditions, the logic of combining power and wealth, of using one for the sake of securing the other, when applied by elites to the hinterland, drew them away from the heartland into the hinterland.

But what are we to make of the fact that the hinterland remained autonomous qua hinterland? It did not become a centralized heartland or fall unambiguously within the sphere of influence of another heartland. After all, each galactic polity develops within a chain of others; and a hinterland out of the control of one heartland is vulnerable to pressures from another expanding outward.

This has indeed been the case. Contemporary Barolong are fearful of being vulnerable to pressures from the other tribe in the district. They express resentment in terms of a fear of tribal domination.[78] They are quick and effective in resisting measures that they see as attempts to subordinate their tribe within the district. Partly, they resist by raising claims to virtually all the arable land. No superior or unitary land board could redistribute land to outsiders. They are also defensive against the interest of nationally powerful elites from the country's capital. The eyes of such outsiders, too, are on the prize land in the hinterland, which is relatively near the capital.[79] The struggle over relative autonomy and greater or lesser centralization within the district continues even now. And the struggle between the strong polity and the weak, the centralized and the decentralized, is by no means settled. Time will still tell.

Conclusion

We must analyze strategic action over land within the distinctive polity that provides its context. Otherwise, the basic cultural premises on which it is predicated remain obscure; or worse still, rhetoric, which is actually a force in the strategic action, replaces analysis. In Botswana, it is all too easy to condemn the elite expansion around boreholes as nothing more than "a land grab," "a land rush," a state-legitimized stampede by "cattle barons." Expatriates, consultants, and civil servants first passed these Western judgments, for purposes of their own political rhetoric. As Western judgments, they have indeed shaped policy, its public presentation, and in some measure its implementation. But such rhetoric mystifies the very objects of our analysis: the realities of the power struggles among competitive and disunited elites in a state, very much an exception in Africa, not heavily in debt. And, no less, these realities are the cultural and organizational achievements made in the hinterland by elites with an organic link to the countryside.

My discussion confronts the need to locate the strategic action within its distinctive context. My method typifies the polity according to an image that represents the continuities and discontinuities from the precolonial through the colonial to the post colonial states. It is an image deliberately borrowed from South Asian kingdoms to free the analysis of geopolitics from the ethnocentric rhetoric of apocalyptic crisis in Africa: the image of the "galactic polity."[80]

It follows from my argument that heartland-hinterland relations have a long-term momentum of their own in a chain of galactic polities; that zonal relativity structures the nature and intensity of conflict within a galactic polity; and further, that neopatrimonialism, along with its nexus between political and economic power, is, and long will be, a major force in the expansion of elite landholding in Botswana.[81]

Notes

1 Ø. Gulbrandsen, *When Land Becomes Scarce,* Bergen Studies in Social Anthropology, no. 33 (Bergen, 1986); *Privilege and Responsibility* (Bergen, 1987).

2 C. Colclough and S. McCarthy, *The Political Economy of Botswana* (Oxford, 1980): 119.

3 On the beneficial impact of preferential treatment by the European Economic Community, see Colclough and McCarthy, *The Political Economy,* 123; and on the costly hazards for cordoned ranchers, see I. Mazonde, *The Development of Ranching and Economic Enterprise in Eastern Botswana,* (Ph.D. diss., University of Manchester, 1987): 217–225.

4 J. Parson, "Cattle, Class, and the State in Rural Botswana," *Journal of Southern African Studies,* VII (1981): 245.

5 See I. Schapera, *Native Land Tenure in the Bechuanaland Protectorate* (Alice, 1943): 134–138.

6 For an important case in point, see the most recent and comprehensive review of the rise and fall of the Tribal Grazing Land Policy in Gulbrandsen, *When Land;* Gulbrandsen, *Privilege;* Gulbrandsen, "Changing Property Relations: Inequality of Wealth and Land Scarcity in Tswana Society," paper presented to the Workshop on Changing Property Rights and Problems of Pastoral Development, Manchester, 1987; and the earlier critiques in S. Sanford, *Keeping an Eye on the TGLP N.I.R.* (Gaborone, 1980); R. Hitchcock, *Kalahari Cattle Posts* (Gaborone, 1978); R. Hitchcock, "Tradition, Social Justice and Land Reform," in R. Werbner (ed.), *Land Reform in the Making* (London, 1982); U. Almagor, "Pastoral Identity and Reluctance to Change: The Mbanderu of Ngamiland," in Werbner, *Land;* A. Sutherland, "Grass Roots Land Tenure Among Yeyi of North-Western Botswana," in Werbner, *Land;* R. Werbner, "The Quasi-Judicial and the Absurd: Remaking Land Law in North-Eastern Botswana," in Werbner, *Land.*

7 For a major analysis of the intellectual continuities and political meanings involved, see P. Peters, "Cattlemen, Borehole Syndicates and Privatization in the Kgatleng District of Botswana" (Ph.D. diss., Boston University, 1983); P. Peters, "Embedded Systems and Rooted Models: The Grazing Lands of Botswana and the 'Commons' Debate," in B. McCay and J. Acheson, *The Question of the Commons: The Culture and Ecology of Communal Resources* (Tucson, 1987).

8 R. Redfield and M. Singer, "The Cultural Role of Cities," *Economic Devel-*

opment and Cultural Change III (1954): 53–73. See also the discussion in U. Hannerz, *Exploring the City* (New York, 1980): 87–89. On indigenous "urbanization" in "traditional" towns as prior to recent urbanization, see P. Molutsi, "Social Stratification and Inequality in Botswana" (D. Phil. thesis, University of Oxford, 1986): 262ff.; S. Grant, "Resettlement and Large Villages," *Botswana Notes and Records* IV (1972): 267–270.

9 The first major study of the largest of these towns, Francistown, is now being carried out by Dr. Wim van Binsbergen of the Afrika-Studie Centrum, Leiden.

10 The country's first city in the making, the capital Gaborone, is at once an extreme and also exceptional in its development. Luxurious "castles" of the super-rich, built while this paper was in press, have become homes, in new senses. Moreover, real estate for renting and speculative development has become a prime ground for strategic competition by elites.

11 R. Werbner, "Production and Reproduction: The Dynamics of Botswana's North-Eastern Micro-Regions," in R. R. Hitchcock and M. Smith (eds.), *Settlement in Botswana* (Gaborone, 1982); Ø. Gulbrandsen, *Access to Agricultural Land and Communal Land Management in Eastern Botswana* (Madison, 1985).

12 Personal communication, Ornulf Gulbrandsen, Bergen, 1988.

13 For an overview, which came to my attention after this essay was written, see L. Vail (ed.), *The Creation of Tribalism in Southern Africa* (London, 1989).

14 N. Parsons, "Settlement in East-Central Botswana, c. 1800–1920," in Hitchcock and Smith, *Settlement,* 127.

15 J. Comaroff, *The Structure of Agricultural Transformation in Barolong: Towards an Integrated Development Plan* (Good Hope, 1977); "Class and Culture in a Peasant Economy: The Transformation of Land Tenure in Barolong," in Werbner, *Land;* Molutsi, "Social Stratification."

16 Hitchcock, "Tradition."

17 S. Tambiah, *Culture, Thought and Social Action* (Cambridge, 1985): 252–286.

18 See my account of the center-periphery relations of a small village: R. Werbner, "Small Man Politics and the Rule of Law: Center-Periphery Relations in East-Central Botswana," *Journal of African Law* XXI (1977): 24–39.

19 On the elaboration of the central place hierarchy in the primary, secondary, and tertiary centers of the National Settlement Policy of 1980, see Molutsi, "Social Stratification," 17lf.

20 For a discussion of the strategic action over land that outsiders take, see R. Werbner, "Local Adaptation and the Transformation of an Imperial Concession in North-Eastern Botswana," *Africa* XLI (1971): 32–41; "Land, Movement and Status among Kalanga of Botswana," in M. Fortes and S. Patterson (eds.), *Essays in African Social Anthropology* (London, 1975); "Small Man"; "The Quasi-Judicial"; "Production"; idem, *Ritual Passage, Sacred Journey* (Washington, 1989).

21 See Peters, "Cattlemen," 97ff., and "Embedded Systems"; Molutsi, "Stratification," 19–21; Gulbrandsen, *Privilege.*

22 Peters, "Cattlemen," 264.

23 Peters, "Embedded Systems,"and "Struggles over Water, Struggles over Meaning: Cattle, Water and the State in Botswana," *Africa* LIV (1987): 24–59; Gulbrandsen, *Privilege;* Gulbrandsen, "Changing Property Relations."

24 Overseers of pasture had to give up their patrimonies toward the end of the colonial state, a change I say more about later.

25 Q. Masire, *Botswana Democratic Party Election Manifesto* (Gaborone, 1969): 14.

26 Comaroff, *The Structure,* and "Class"; Sutherland, "Grass Roots"; Werbner, "The Quasi-Judicial"; Gulbrandsen, *Access,* 8.

27 For an account of this countertendency toward more immediate beneficial tenure and its regulation by a chief in the colonial period, see Schapera, *Native Land,* 137.

28 Gulbrandsen, *Access,* 9.

29 For this view of overseers or "informal headmem," see Comaroff, "Class," 105.

30 See also, R. Werbner, Introduction, in Werbner, *Land,* x; and on the positive value of registration, Comaroff, *The Structure,* 66.

31 Gulbrandsen, *Access,* 72.

32 This hypothesis has already proved predictive. As this paper goes to press, the struggle over neo-patrimonialism as a national phenomenon has reached a greater height, marked by the resignations of the Vice-President and a senior minister in response to a land scandal.

33 On expansion at the expense of hunter-gatherers, see Hitchcock, "Tradition"; Gulbrandsen, *When Land.*

34 Schapera, *Native Land,* 8–9.

35 A. Sutherland, "Economic Differentiation and Cultural Change among Yeyi in North-West Botswana, (Ph.D. diss., University of Manchester, 1984).

36 For an account of its precolonial and early colonial geopolitics, see Parsons, "Settlement."

37 Hitchcock, *Kalahari.*

38 A. Kuper, *Kalahari Village Politics* (Cambridge, 1970).

39 Werbner, "Local Adaptation"; "Land, Movement"; "Production."

40 Molutsi, "Social Stratification," 162.

41 Werbner, "Small Man," and "The Quasi-Judicial"; N. Mahoney, "Birwa Traders and Neighbours" (Ph.D. diss., University of Manchester, 1977); Sutherland, "Economic Differentiation."

42 Gulbrandsen, *Access,* 57.

43 One important qualification is needed, at least for the city of Gaborone. There is a heightening struggle for elite accumulation of residential and commercial sites; see also footnotes 10 and 32.

44 For those making the commons a series of ranges, see Peters, "Embedded Systems."

45 Peters, "Cattlemen," 270.

46 Werbner, "Small Man."

47 Schapera, *Native Land.*
48 Gulbrandsen, *Access;* Gulbrandsen, *When Land;* Gulbrandsen, *Privilege;* Gulbrandsen, "Changing Property."
49 Werbner, *Land,* x.
50 Gulbrandsen, *Access,* 32.
51 Ibid., 37.
52 Sanford, *Keeping an Eye.*
53 For an insightful account of the internal arguments over the TGLP, see L. Picard, "Bureaucrats, Cattle and Public Policy," *Comparative Political Studies* XIII (1980): 313–356.
54 Gulbrandsen, *When Land,* 139.
55 Ibid., 139.
56 Ibid.
57 J. Holm, "Botswana: A Paternalistic Democracy," in L. Diamond, J. Linz, and S. Lipset (eds.), *Democracy in Developing Countries,* vol. 2, *Africa* (Boulder, 1988).
58 On "this small, rather tightly knit group," see Parson, "Cattle," 90.
59 Gulbrandsen, *When Land,* 131; italics in original.
60 For similar conversions of freehold ranches, see Mazonde, *The Development.*
61 See my discussion of the modes as exclusive and incorporative, Werbner, *Land,* iv–v; and the improved conceptualization of this in Peters, "Cattlemen."
62 On ranching as disadvantageous for absentees, see Mazonde, *The Development.*
63 Gulbrandsen, *When Land,* 133; italics in original.
64 Ibid.
65 I. Schapera, "The System of Land Tenure on the Barolong Farms (Bechuanaland Protectorate)," *Botswana Notes and Records* XV (1983, reprinted from the original report to the Bechuanaland Protectorate Government, 1943): 15–37; Comaroff, *The Structure;* Comaroff, "Class"; Gulbrandsen, *Access;* Gulbrandsen, *When Land;* Molutsi, "Social Stratification."
66 Schapera, "The System," 16.
67 C. Murray, "Land, Power and Class in the Thaba Nchu District, Orange Free State 1884 to 1983," *Review of African Political Economy* xxix (1984): 30–48.
68 Schapera, "The System," 32.
69 Ibid.
70 Ibid., 35.
71 Comaroff, "Class," 92.
72 Comaroff, *The Structure,* 32–33.
73 Personal communication, P. Molutsi, 1987.
74 Comaroff, "Class," 98.
75 Comaroff, *The Structure,* and "Class"; Werbner, "Quasi-Judicial"; Gulbrandsen, *Access.*
76 Comaroff, "Class," 192.
77 Gulbrandsen, *Access,* 47.

78 Comaroff, *The Structure,* 103–4.
79 Ibid., 77.
80 For reviews of the recent literature, see A. Adedeji and T. Shaw (eds.), *Economic Crisis in Africa* (Boulder, 1985); and N. Chazan and T. Shaw (eds.), *Coping with Africa's Food Crisis* (Boulder, 1988).
81 State-backed efforts towards the commodification of land have increased markedly, while this paper has been in press. National legislation, and associated land policies, extended lease holding and the privatization of land in communal areas.

5 Thomas J. Bassett

Land Use Conflicts in Pastoral Development in Northern Côte d'Ivoire

Introduction

A remarkable change in the agricultural geography of West Africa over the past twenty years is the southerly migration of Fulani herds from the Sudano-Sahelian region to the subhumid savannas of Sierra Leone, Côte d'Ivoire, Cameroon, and the Central African Republic.[1] This southerly "migratory drift" of herds and herders represents a new migration pattern for the Fulani.[2] It is a remarkable development because it is occurring well within the tsetse belt—an area avoided by Fulani herders in the past because of the hazards of animal sleeping sickness (trypanosomiasis) transmitted by the tsetse fly. To explain this migration pattern, authorities cite a number of factors such as land use competition between peasants and herders in the Sudano-Sahelian region, land degradation linked to changing social relations of production and demographic pressures both human and animal, protracted drought, and restricted access to formerly open rangelands.[3] Jean Gallais reports that this multiple squeeze on range resources has resulted in both northerly and southerly herd movements.[4]

In the case of Côte d'Ivoire, Fulani herd owners from Burkina Faso and Mali have been attracted to the country by the lure of better pastures, low population densities, proximity to markets, and the veterinary

131

care and subsidies provided by the Ivorian livestock development corporation (SODEPRA).[5] The large average size (145 head) of Fulani herds in Côte d'Ivoire suggests that the southerly migration has been chosen by the wealthiest of herd owners. According to Thierry Quéant and Cécile de Rouville, the largest herd owners were among the first to move out of the Barani and Nouna regions of northwestern Burkina Faso in the 1940s toward southern Mali and Burkina. The first of these herds entered Côte d'Ivoire in the late 1950s in the Tengréla area. Most arrived in the early 1970s in the wake of the Sahelian drought.

The Fulani's contribution to national livestock production has been an unexpected boon to the Ivorian economy. Between 1970 and 1985, the number of Fulani zebu cattle increased at an annual rate of 10 percent, twice the rate of peasant-owned taurin cattle.[6] The Fulani herd accounts for one-third of domestic beef production, which the government would like to see increase. SODEPRA, established in the early 1970s to promote livestock raising in the country, provides extension services and pastoral infrastructure to cattle owners. Two major objectives of SODEPRA's development projects have been to increase local beef production in order to reduce the country's dependence on fluctuating foreign beef supplies and, second, to reduce conflicts between peasants and herders over the issue of crop damage by regulating the movement of Fulani herds at critical periods in the agricultural and pastoral calendars.

The resolution of peasant-herder conflicts is crucial to meeting the beef production goal because the Fulani's access to range resources depends on their maintaining good relations with Senufo landholders. Tensions between the two groups have been explosive, especially in election years when northern politicians promise to banish the Fulani from the country to win popular support. The most recent and serious outbreak of violence occurred in spring 1986 when Senufo peasants killed more than eighty herders throughout the Korhogo region. This civil disorder and the massive emigration of the Fulani toward the Malian and Burkina borderlands forced the Ivorian government to reformulate its livestock development policies. Since the early 1970s, the primary strategy has been to sedentarize Fulani herders through a variety of pastoral development projects. From an initial policy of isolating herds in pastoral preserves to one that sought to integrate Fulani pastoralism with Senufo agriculture through the rotation of manured corrals and cropland, SODEPRA's projects have been characterized by a strongly technocratic orientation. This chapter examines the inadequacy of pursuing technocratic approaches to solving interlocking political, economic, and cultural-ecological problems affecting land use in the context of the Senufo-Fulani Tandem Project, the most recent sedentarization scheme. The case study shows that the interactive effects of land use conflicts at three overlapping levels (local, regional, and national) continue to undermine both the expansion of Fulani livestock production and the intensification of agricultural systems in the savanna region.

After introducing the study area, I provide an overview of the evolution of SODEPRA's Fulani sedentarization schemes that have led up to the Tandem Project. I then look at land access and control patterns among the Senufo of the Korhogo region to provide the sociocultural context for the Tandem Project. In the remaining sections, I focus on the multiple land use conflicts at the regional and national levels which have been integral to this pastoral development debacle.

The Study Area

Fulani pastoralism in Côte d'Ivoire is centered in the north-central savanna region where conditions for raising livestock are most favorable. Herds move frequently within this area in response to the changing quality of range resources (pasture and water), disease hazards, and sociopolitical tensions. This section emphasizes some of the most important human ecological determinants of Fulani pastoralism in the area. The political, cultural, and economic dimensions are taken up later in the discussion of Fulani sedentarization schemes and peasant-herder conflicts.

Rainfall and pasture quality are the most important environmental conditions influencing both the distribution and movement of Fulani herds in northern Côte d'Invoire. The unimodal rainfall regime generally begins in May, peaks in August, and ends in October, with annual averages ranging between 1,100 and 1,400 millimeters. The amount of rainfall and the length of the rainy season determine the savanna types found in the region. Tree and shrub savannas are found in both the Guinea and Sudanian zones, with the major difference being the range of certain species. For example, annual grasses gradually replace perennial grasses in the northerly transition between these two zones. Differential growth cycles result in considerable temporal and spatial variation in the palatability of grasses within each zone. One of the main attractions of *Andropogon guyanus* to Fulani herds is that its nutritive value lasts into the late rainy season when other grasses have lost their palatability. The fact that *Andropogon* is largely found in fallow fields partly explains why Fulani herds are often found near peasant farming areas during the late rainy season when much crop damage occurs.

Another environmental factor that influences the distribution of

Fulani herds is the presence and density of tsetse flies, the most important vector of trypanosomiasis. The two dominant flies in the region
(*Glossina palpalis gambiensis* and *G. tachinoides*) are riverine species
whose numbers fluctuate with the seasons. Fly populations increase during the rainy season and decline during the long, hot, dry season. Their
prime dry season habitats are the riparian woodlands (gallery forests) of
the middle and lower courses of major rivers. During the rainy season,
the flies spread to upper tributaries and move out of the gallery forests
to adjacent woodlands and brush, from where they feed on reptiles and
mammals, including humans.[7] Because of this seasonal expansion of
tsetse flies, Fulani herders move their cattle away from major rivers
during the high rainy season months of July, August, and September to
graze them near agricultural areas where there are fewer fly habitats.
Denis Lagrue notes that herd movements to upland areas in this period
also correspond to herders' attempts to break parasite cycles that pose
serious health problems to herds remaining in lowland areas. In sum, the
concentration and movement of Fulani herds near agricultural zones are
fundamental livestock management strategies aimed at maintaining herd
health in a hazardous environment.[8] It is this seasonal distribution and
mobility of Fulani herds that SODEPRA has sought to regulate through
its various sedentarization projects. A major impetus to control herd
movements has been to reduce the high incidence of crop damage in
Senufo fields caused by Fulani cattle.

The Senufo agricultural system combines bush fallow farming in upland areas with swamp rice cultivation in stream bottoms. Upland fields
are cultivated for 6 to 10 years before a new parcel is cleared. Cotton is
the major cash crop and accounts for 45 percent of the cultivated area.
Other major upland crops are maize, yams, and rain-fed rice. In lowland
areas, swamp rice is the major crop. It is transplanted from nurseries in
July and August and harvested in December. Swamp rice accounts for 10
percent of the total area under cultivation.

Savanna soils are of medium to poor quality and pose severe fertility
and conservation management problems under intensification. Intense
and concentrated rainfall favors the leaching of basic elements (calcium
and magnesium), resulting in soil acidification and weed infestation. Soil
fertility and structure are also adversely affected by the loss of organic
matter stemming from both inadequate restitution of crop residues and
soil erosion.[9] The intensification of agriculture through the use of commercial fertilizers tends to exacerbate these soil management problems
in the absence of corrective amendments such as dolomite and organic
matter.[10] The association of livestock with agriculture offers a potential
remedy for conserving soil structure and fertility under these condi-

tions.[11] SODEPRA's Tandem Project represented a potentially sound environmental management solution to difficult land conservation problems. However, as the case study reveals, a number of social, political, and cultural-ecological obstacles to Fulani sedentarization severely constrained the realization of these technical objectives.

Early Fulani Sedentarization Projects in Côte d'Ivoire

The emergence of the Senufo-Fulani Tandem Project in 1984 as the model of sedentarization came after a decade of unsuccessful attempts to control herd movements in northern Côte d'Ivoire. SODEPRA's first attempt to regulate Fulani livestock raising began in 1976 in the Boundiali region where it established a pastoral preserve of some 180,000 hectares (the Palé Grazing Zone) replete with pastoral infrastructure (dams, improved pasture, dipping tanks), housing, and even mosques. The objectives for creating this grazing zone were both economic and sociopolitical. First, the Ivorian government sought to increase domestic beef production by encouraging the Fulani to settle in the region permanently. By granting herders access to uninhabited and "improved" land as well as to veterinary services and housing, SODEPRA hoped to induce Fulani herd owners to remain in the country. The livestock agency also hoped to reduce tensions between peasants and herders over uncompensated crop damage by geographically separating the two groups in the Boundiali area.[12]

SODEPRA estimated that the Palé could accommodate at least 30,000 head of cattle, but by 1981, there were less than 4,000 head formally registered there.[13] In fact, there were even fewer animals in the preserve because of the Fulani's practice of grazing their herds outside the area. High tsetse fly densities and difficulties in marketing milk were two major reasons that herders preferred to raise their cattle elsewhere. In response to the Fulani's disinterest in the Palé, SODEPRA embarked on a highly technocratic course to eradicate tsetse flies from the area. Between 1978 and 1979, it devoted half a million dollars to an aerial pesticide spraying campaign. The results were negligible, as SODEPRA reported no changes in infestation rates just a year later.[14]

The project was equally unimpressive in reducing peasant-herder conflicts in the Boundiali region. A project evaluation team learned that the herders attracted to the Palé were not from surrounding Boundiali but recent immigrants from Mali and Upper Volta (Burkina Faso).[15] Moreover, the team discovered that many wealthy and politically influential non-Fulani Ivorians were grazing cattle in the preserve. In fact, the project itself was managing the cattle of one absentee herd owner. The scheme set aside more than 25,000 hectares for these "entrepreneurs," some of whom were still in the process of building their herds in 1980.[16]

Unabated crop damage and political campaigns to expel the Fulani heightened tensions between peasants and herders in fall 1980. Numerous camp burnings and a few deaths were reported throughout the north that year.[17] In light of these violent incidents and faced with the prospect of a total desertion of the Palé zone by Fulani herders, SODEPRA was forced to reconsider its approach to sedentarization.

The new approach was the obverse of the pastoral preserve model. Rather than trying to isolate herders from agricultural zones, SODEPRA sought to integrate Fulani livestock raising with local farming systems. This scheme, known as the Agro-Pastoral Units Project, was inspired by the realization that most Fulani herds could be found at the outskirts of agricultural zones where tsetse fly densities were low and economic exchanges more feasible. The emphasis of the new project was again highly technical. It involved the construction of small dams, dipping tanks, and improved pastures as well as the provision of veterinary services (Fig. 5.1). The northern savanna was quickly demarcated into twenty-seven Agro-Pastoral Units. The number of cattle within each unit was to be limited by the area's carrying capacity. SODEPRA believed that it had a better chance of controlling Fulani herd movements in these areas, and thus of reducing crop damage, by regulating the number of animals utilizing its infrastructure. Within each unit, a committee of Fulani herders was supposed to oversee the entry and exit of cattle to maintain pasture quality and control crop damage. It was envisaged that cattle would graze in the improved and fenced-in pastures and take water at the dams during the period from October to December to avoid crop damage. After a 5- to 7-year period, local peasants would farm the heavily manured improved pastures and the Fulani would create another grazing block with SODEPRA's assistance. Funding for the project came from both domestic budget allocations and foreign aid donors (French and German).

The technocratic orientation of the Agro-Pastoral Units strategy soon became apparent as SODEPRA focused on building dams and fencing in pastures. In its annual report, SODEPRA judged its progress by the number of dams built and hectares under improved pasture. It did not report the Fulani's lack of interest in the projects. Herd owners were reluctant to invest their time in maintaining grazing areas for two reasons. First, they were wary of keeping their cattle in one area at a time when declining pasture quality and disease factors compelled frequent herd movements. Second, they realized that their access to and control over improved land was highly insecure. This insecurity had been highlighted in the past when peasants seeking to cultivate the heavily ma-

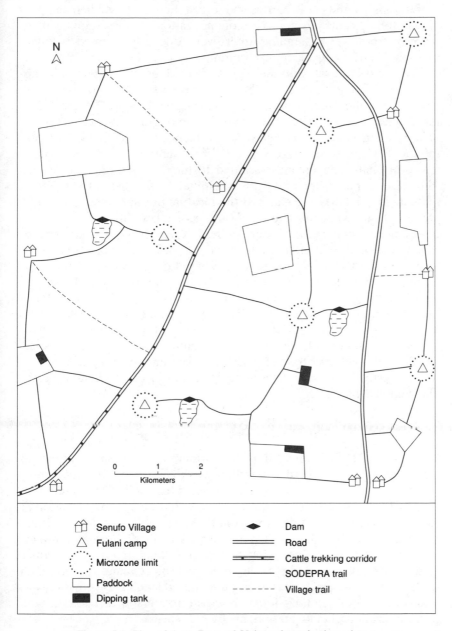

N

🏠 Senufo Village	◆ Dam
△ Fulani camp	═══ Road
⬡ Microzone limit	▬▬▬ Cattle trekking corridor
☐ Paddock	─── SODEPRA trail
■ Dipping tank	- - - Village trail

0   1   2
Kilometers

Figure 5.1. Plan of Agro-Pastoral Units sedentarization scheme

nured soils around cattle corrals had forced them to move their camps.[18] These forced removals and the monopolization of cultivation rights to improved pastures by Senufo farmers were especially resented by Fulani households who engage in mixed farming.[19]

The Agro-Pastoral Units strategy resembled the pastoral preserve approach in that in both cases the technocratic solutions to controlling Fulani herd movements involved a high degree of spatial engineering. Both schemes emphasized the manipulation of grazing space to resolve complex human ecological and social problems. Despite the delimitation of the Palé pastoral preserve and then twenty-seven distinct Agro-Pastoral Units, the Fulani continued to move their herds and camps throughout the north. SODEPRA estimated that half of the Fulani herders in Côte d'Ivoire changed the location of their camps every two years.[20] Underlying the failure of both sedentarization schemes was a poor understanding of the nature of herd movements.[21] The attempts to first isolate and then integrate herders with peasant farming communities, even on technical grounds, were based on poor information. For example, Fulani herd movements in Côte d'Ivoire were typically viewed as resembling herd transhumant patterns common in the Sudano-Sahelian region.[22] The most obvious shortcoming of the technocratic approach was that it ignored the social, political, and economic dimensions of peasant-herder conflicts. The failure to address these issues would continue to frustrate SODEPRA's well-intentioned plans to associate livestock raising and farming in the form of the Senufo-Fulani Tandem Project.

The Senufo-Fulani Tandem Project

In 1984, SODEPRA unveiled its third attempt to sedentarize the Fulani and reduce peasant-herder tensions in the north.[23] Like the Agro-Pastoral Units Project, the Tandem Project promoted the integration of livestock raising and crop production through the systematic rotation of corrals and cropland. It differed from the earlier schemes by specifically addressing the problem of insecure access to land. Formal contracts were drawn up clearly specifying the responsibilities and rights of farmer and pastoralist. For example, the Tandem Project's land rotation plan gave the Fulani equal access to cattle-manured land. This provision was designed to end both their forced removal from manured lands and the monopolization of cultivation rights by peasants.

SODEPRA played an intermediary role in bringing peasants and herders together to engage in the project. It subsidized 90 percent of the costs of the tandem infrastructure by developing 25 hectares of fenced improved pasture, two corrals totaling an additional 25 hectares, and a 12.5 hectare parcel allotted for cropland. SODEPRA hoped that this new spatial arrangement would reduce tensions and facilitate sedentarization in two important respects. First, because cattle would be fenced in at night and have access to improved pasture, the project would theoretically lead to a reduction in crop damage during the early dry season months (a peculiar problem discussed below). Second, planners hoped that their mutually advantageous participation in the scheme would improve Senufo-Fulani relations. SODEPRA launched a pilot project in 1984 to test the feasibility of this scheme as well as to attract further funding from foreign donors. Forty tandems located throughout the region were created by the end of that year (Fig. 5.2).

Cattle-owning candidates wishing to participate in a tandem were supposed to fulfill a number of criteria, namely, they must (1) be "stabilized"; (2) cultivate their old corrals; (3) utilize "off-farm" cattle feeds (e.g., cotton seeds); (4) agree to pay SODEPRA $1,000 over a three-year period for their share of project costs; (5) maintain and use the improved pastures and corrals; (6) agree to allow the participating Senufo farmer to cultivate the manure-rich land of former corrals; and (7) permit the customary landholder to plant trees around the perimeter of each improved block to serve as both a living fence and a symbol of the landowner's control over the land. The last requirement is important, because in Senufoland, private land is rare in rural areas and the establishment of trees signifies a permanent improvement connoting personal control over land. In the end, the ability to pay 10 percent of total project costs was the single most important criterion used for selecting candidates. What type of herder made up the first group of forty to participate in the tandems?

Less than half were Fulani. Fifty-two percent were native (Senufo and Jula) herd owners seeking to benefit from SODEPRA's subsidies. This group was composed of prosperous peasants, civil servants, wealthy businessmen, and politicians, including a minister, a deputy in the National Assembly, and two "canton chiefs'." Their average herd size amounted to 122 head. Fulani participants were among the wealthiest livestock owners in the country, with an average herd size of 302 head, twice the size of the average Fulani herd in Côte d'Ivoire.

There were four types of herd owners among the initial forty. Twenty percent were absentee herders who hired salaried herders and a manager to look after their animals. Thirty-three percent were farmer-herders who owned cattle but were primarily farmers who hired Fulani to guard their herds. With the exception of ox-drawn cultivation, this group did not integrate livestock raising with cultivation. Another 33

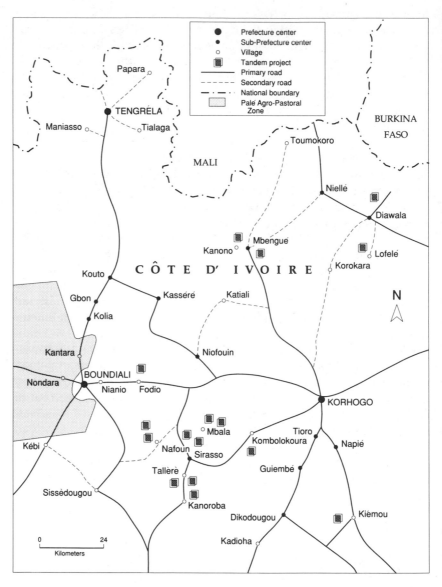

Figure 5.2. Map showing location of Fulani-Senufo Tandem Projects in northern Côte d'Ivoire

percent of the participants were herder-farmers who relied almost exclusively on livestock raising for a living. They frequently cultivated their old corrals with the help of hired labor, but their total area under crops was commonly less than 1 hectare. A fourth type (15%) was composed of agropastoralists who seriously engaged in both farming and livestock raising. The first two types were dominated by native herders, while the latter were largely Fulani.

On the basis of these data alone, it is clear that SODEPRA's tandem project was off to a poor start by the end of 1984. First, the project involved more native cattle owners than Fulani, which contradicted its stated goal of forming Senufo-Fulani partnerships to reduce land use conflicts. Second, SODEPRA appealed to a small and prosperous minority of Fulani herders who were not serious about mixed farming. Yet this was to be the catalyst of greater cooperation between farmers and herders as well as the basis for the intensification of indigenous farming systems. Third, on the basis of their settlement history, there was little evidence that these Fulani were sedentary herders who would utilize the pastoral infrastructure.

Just two years into the tandem program, the results were still not promising. Ninety percent of the Senufo-Fulani tandems broke up in spring 1986 during the Senufo revolt, and no new ones have subsequently been established, although some have been created between native herd owners and local farmers.[24] Why is it that less than half the tandems were between Fulani herders and Senufo peasants? Under what conditions were these tandems formed? Why, despite the potential benefits to both parties, did they fall apart? As the following discussion indicates, land use conflicts at the local, regional, and national levels help to account for this development debacle.

Land Access and Control in Senufoland

Outside of urban areas, individual ownership of land hardly exists in the Korhogo region. The Senufo view land as a collective resource bequeathed from the ancestors and held in trust for future generations. The *tarfolo,* or earth priest, is a religious figure who has customary authority to allocate land rights.[25] With some exceptions, he is the oldest living male member of the village founding matrilineage.[26] Senufo religious thought holds land to be sacred and only to be worked after faithful observation of a number of ritual practices. For example, the tarfolo must perform annual sacrifices to the bush spirits of the area under his control. Certain places where the bush spirits reside are viewed as sacred and cannot be exploited. Also, each place has a specific rest day when no one can work the land without bringing harm to them or their family.

In the past, only the tarfolo could distribute land to those who requested to cultivate it. He typically allotted it to *katiolofolo,* the heads of lineage-based production and consumption units called *katiolo.* The katiolo was the basic social unit during the precolonial and early colonial periods. Its members worked in a collective field (*segbo*) four days out of the Senufo six-day week. The katiolofolo controlled crops and any income originating from segbo production. He also had the right to redistribute land to individual members of the katiolo, most often the heads of lineage segments, who were allowed to cultivate a personal field (*kagon*) one or two days a week. In sum, the sacred value of land and its restricted distribution to lineage heads by the tarfolo represented both ideological and political-economic dimensions of the Senufo organization of production.[27] The creation of new production and exchange relations during the colonial period under a coercive regime of requisitions and the development of commodity relations led to the breakdown of katiolo as the basic unit of production.[28] In its place, smaller social units composed of maternal brothers and their families worked in a collective field three of four days a week and the remaining day(s) in fields belonging to conjugal households. This fragmentation required the further redistribution of land rights from the lineage head to his maternal brothers and married nephews. However, unlike the katiolofolo, the heads of lineage segments were not considered "landholders" in that they did not have the authority to allocate land to others. If the son or nephew of a lineage segment head requested land, it had to be obtained from either the former katiolofolo or the tarfolo. The final authority of the former katiolofolo over these lands was sanctioned by his performing ritual sacrifices to the bush spirits of the areas under his control.

Today, the predominant unit of production is the conjugal family. Most household heads cultivate land that was allotted to their lineage many generations ago. Lineage heads who inherited land from former katiolofolo legitimate their power to control its access by performing the same rituals observed during the precolonial period. They currently allocate land to married male kin on a usufruct basis in the areas under their control. The village tarfolo recognizes the rights of these lineage heads, which results in the fact that there are a dozen Senufo "landholders" in Katiali who claim control in the region. However, when a sample of thirty-eight households was asked who controlled the land they were working, the number of declared holders increased to forty. When asked to explain this proliferation of landholders, the tarfolo of Katiali responded by saying that some people think they control land because it has been in their family for generations, but if they were confronted in a public meeting on the issue of control, they would admit that it "belonged" to someone else. Despite these assertions, it appears that a further fragmentation of village land is occurring coinciding with the continuing individuation of production units at the conjugal household level.

The development of commodity relations through the intensification of cotton cultivation has been the driving force behind these fundamental sociocultural changes.[29] One of the changes most relevant to this study is the increasing monetary value of land that has been improved in the context of the cotton development program. Specifically, the spread of ox-drawn cultivation and the more limited expansion of tractors depend on costly and time-consuming land clearing practices like tree stump removal. The Ivorian cotton company (CIDT)[30] offers, for example, an extraordinary subsidy ($35,000) to tractor owners by clearing thirty hectares of land free of charge in its cotton mechanization program. Even peasants who practice ox-drawn cultivation can benefit from these services by requesting stump removal in fields they cultivate. The economic value of such improvements partly explains the extension in the number of years a field is farmed in the savanna region today.[31]

When strangers arrive in a Senufo area, they are expected to inquire who controls the land they wish to utilize. However, one of the major findings of SODEPRA's land tenure studies was that more than half of the twenty-seven Fulani interviewed in the Dikodougou and Napié regions south of Korhogo did not seek permission to settle. Eleven percent of this group had relatives residing there and did not feel obligated to obtain authorization since it had already been granted to their kin. The largest percentage (44%) claimed to be the guests of the Ivorian government and did not feel compelled to inform village chiefs and earth priests of their presence. The Senufo view this entire group as "squatters" on their land. They feel particularly incensed by the many Fulani who declare they are the guests of the president. The Senufo view these "arrogant" Fulani as "invaders," a hostile view reinforced by the havoc associated with crop damage.[32] Below, I show how land use conflicts at various levels hinder the integration of Fulani livestock raising with Senufo agriculture with unfortunate human and economic consequences.

Local Land Use Conflicts

The right to control and distribute land is currently a contentious issue in Senufoland. SODEPRA discovered during its tenure inquiries for the

Tandem Project that many dormant disputes over rights quickly flared up when questions were asked about the "true landowner of a land parcel under negotiation."[33] As the following examples illustrate, the authority of customary landholders is constantly being challenged at the local level.

In Katiali, I was presented with two accounts of the village founding that conflicted with the most widely accepted oral history. A person who sought to legitimate his family's claim to large tracts of land presented one version. The Jula chief presented another to support his claim that he and other Jula notables control land in the Katiali region. Another Senufo elder asked me to map the boundaries of the area he claimed to control to support his side in a border dispute with another Senufo landholder. Land disputes are especially common between the Senufo and Jula. The tarfolo of Katiali assured me that no Jula could claim to control any land in the region because the Senufo were the first settlers in the area. Yet, a few Jula elders argued that their ancestors had re-quested and received land from Senufo in the past and that they now had the right to redistribute it to others. When presented with these claims, the tarfolo acknowledged that they were special cases but that all other Jula claims were invalid. He was particularly adamant about a Jula herd owner who only a few years ago requested and received land to corral his animals and who was now claiming to "own" the land. The tarfolo said other Senufo elders strongly criticized him for "giving away" this land.

The SODEPRA tandem study provides further examples of tension over land access and control at the local level.[34] In Nondara in Boundiali Subprefecture, the locally elected representative of the country's then single political party[35] gave land use rights to two strangers, a banker and a Fulani herder, when in fact someone else was the customary landholder. The representative received a number of large gifts in ex-change for this favor. When the true landholder learned of these trans-gressions of his authority, he threatened to force the strangers to leave. The dispute was settled only after the strangers formally recognized the true landholder's rights and promised not to claim some day those rights themselves.

In the village of Kombolokoura in Korhogo Subprefecture, a custom-ary landholder became an outcast when he allowed a locally despised Fulani herder to settle on his land over the objections of village elders. Another Senufo who claimed to be a customary landholder in the village of Kanonon in M'Bengué Subprefecture was ridiculed and spat on by elders during village meetings over his granting land use rights to a Fulani herder. SODEPRA realized that this native tandem participant was not a locally recognized landholder and only possessed usufruct rights. The Senufo claimed he inherited the land under question from his *father.* He cited Ivorian inheritance laws that recognize children and the surviving spouse as the legal successors of an estate as the basis of his claim. The elders of Kanonon disagreed with this interpretation and succeeded in convincing SODEPRA that someone else was the legitimate landholder.[36] In two other villages, Kolia and Nondara in Boundiali Subprefecture, local elders recognized as legitimate the patrilineal line of transmission. This acceptance among a customary matrilineal people suggests that land now has a different meaning and is valued less as a collective good to be held in trust for future generations of the matrilineage and more as an object of personal appropriation to be passed onto the members of one's immediate family.

The important point here is that access to and control of land are hotly contested issues among the Senufo. In particular, customary landholders are sensitive to claims made by others. Development projects involving land improvements are especially worrisome, particularly if the beneficiaries interpret these as legitimating their "ownership" of land. SODEPRA's pastoral development projects are perceived as potential threats to the rights of customary landholders precisely because they entail medium- to long-term improvements such as small dams, cattle-dipping tanks, corrals, and pasture. Before granting land use rights to herders enrolled in SODEPRA's tandem program, customary holders insist that the herd owner make a verbal agreement that the land does not belong to him but is simply a loan. When the Senufo refuse to grant rights to Fulani herders, the state intervenes on behalf of the latter, invoking a law dating from the colonial period which grants it the right to dispose of "unused lands."[37] Indeed, the subprefect periodically visits villages when tensions rise to reiterate that only he (the state) has the right to refuse Fulani herders access to land.

Regional Land Use Conflicts   Ivorian livestock Development Corporation

If there is one factor that can account for the failure of Fulani sedentarization in Côte d'Ivoire, it is uncompensated crop damage. A major objective of SODEPRA's schemes has been to reduce tensions between peasants and herders over this issue. However, politicians have exploited it in their electoral campaigns and peasants have used it in the attempt to expel the Fulani from the country. Here I examine crop damage and show why it continues to give rise to explosive land use conflicts at the regional level.

SODEPRA annually collects data on crop damage on the basis of

[handwritten margin note: social divide between elites and non-elites]

formal hearings conducted by a special committee at the subprefecture level. These committees are composed of five persons: the agricultural officer of the subprefecture, a local SODEPRA extension agent, the village secretary of the PDCI, a representative of the local Fulani community, and a guard from the subprefecture. During a formal hearing, committee members converge at the crop damage site in the presence of the herder and field owner to assess the damages. Theoretically, the site is measured and the damages are calculated based on the estimated yield and market value of the damaged crop. The results of this hearing are recorded at the subprefecture, and it is these data that comprise the source of SODEPRA's statistics on crop damage.

The problem with them is twofold. First, probably no more than 10 percent of all crop damage cases are brought before such committees. Second, for those incidents that result in formal hearings, it is unlikely that the true value of the damages is recorded at the subprefecture because of corruption. According to some members of the Niofouin subprefecture committee, both the peasant and herder are informed during the field hearing of the damages to be paid. In fact, neither one is aware of them until the subprefect's administrative assistant tells them individually in his office. He first summons the Fulani herder and informs him of how much he must pay. Then he summons the field owner and gives him a sum that theoretically equals the damages estimated during the hearing and the sum paid by the herd owner. In fact, interviews with herders and peasants involved in two separate crop damage cases revealed a 10 to 20 percent difference between the sum paid by the herder and that received by the field owner.

Rather than rely on underestimated and dubious data, I collected information on crop damage from a sample of thirty-eight households in Katiali over a four-year period: 1980, 1981, 1985, and 1987. A questionnaire was administered to these households on three different occasions (1982, 1986, and 1988). Data were collected on the type of crop damaged, the month and time of day of the incident, the type of animal involved, and compensation. The following statistics represent the average values of this four-year data set.

Two-thirds of the crop damage occurred in cotton (40%) and swamp rice (27%) fields. If one includes damage to sorghum (5%) and millet (6%), then close to 80 percent of the incidents took place in fields where long-cycle crops were planted.[38] Related to this finding is the observation that more than two-thirds of the cases occurred during November and December. As noted elsewhere, there is a strong correspondence between this occurrence of crop damage and Fulani herd movements in the region.[39] Indeed, informants attributed more than 80 percent of the damages to Fulani humped cattle (*Bos indicus*) whose hoofprints and grazing areas are distinct from the smaller, peasant-owned cattle (*Bos taurus*). Finally, more than half of the damage occurred at night, especially during the early dry season months of October, November, and December, which corresponds to the period when Fulani cattle begin to graze over a wider area during the day and into the night.

Crop damage continues to be an explosive issue for four reasons. In close to two-thirds of the reported cases in Katiali, field owners did not receive compensation. In most cases, the peasant did not know who committed the damage; in the others, the herder refused to pay. Just a quarter of the cases involved some compensation. This issue infuriates the victims of crop damage.

Second, local and national politicians in their quest for office have stirred up generalized animosity toward the Fulani. The most violent conflicts in 1981 and 1986 coincided with electoral campaigns in which candidates running for party posts, local mayoral offices, and the National Assembly gained rural votes by supporting the populist movement to ban the Fulani from the country. Candidates toured the north assuring village chiefs that they would expel the Fulani from the country if elected. At the same time, these politicians expressed their loyalty to the state and its venerated leader, Houphouet-Boigny, by declaring their commitment to "peace and dialogue." In sum, what were originally localized tensions between farmers and herders over crop damage became an explosive interethnic conflict in the wake of these electoral campaigns.

Third, differences in economic status between the Fulani and Senufo sharpen the conflict. An average herd size of 145 head represents a substantial amount of wealth from the Senufo's perspective. With the expansion of ox-drawn cultivation in the region over the past fifteen years, peasants appreciate the value of cattle. They correctly judge that crop damage is enrichening the Fulani at their expense.

Fourth, efforts to resettle the Fulani in conflict zones in 1987 and 1988 have been opposed by both communities. During a tour of these zones in April 1987, the minister of animal production unveiled SODEPRA's program for "reinstalling" the Fulani in the north. It involves seven points: (1) the obligatory construction of night corrals; (2) the employment of one herder for every fifty head of cattle; (3) the banning of nocturnal grazing during the agricultural calendar; (4) better training and control of hired herders by cattle owners; (5) better working conditions and pay for salaried herders; (6) prompt payment for any crop damage caused by the Fulani; and (7) greater respect for local customs. Interviews in the Katiali region conducted in summer 1988 suggest that the local Fulani did not take seriously these conditions for returning. For example, there had been no change in salaries offered to hired herders; the ratio of one herder per fifty head of cattle is not practiced; no modern night corrals had been built; and herd owners did not ask permission from landholders to graze their animals in any given area. The only noticeable difference was the greater Fulani willingness to pay for crop damages. In contrast to 1980 and 1981 when just 7 percent of crop damage victims received some compensation, 54 percent managed to obtain some payment in 1987.

National Land Use Conflicts

Earlier, I described the customary system of land control and distribution among the Senufo, stressing its changing nature and particularly the fragmentation of landholding rights coinciding with the development of commodity production. The deepening of capitalist relations continues to erode the "sacred" value land had in the past. The new land use patterns and production relations associated with the intensification of cotton have involved major sociocultural changes, one of which has been the perception of land, especially improved land, as having greater monetary value. I suggested that the persistence of precapitalist land rituals reflects the concerns of contemporary landholders to legitimate their claims. Earth priests and lineage heads continue to express their control over land by claiming that only they have the right to performing rituals to appease the bush spirits residing in a disputed area.

In contrast to these transitional processes of capitalist transformation in the northern savanna, one witnesses more advanced stages in the southern forest region where wage labor and land transactions are commonplace in the export cropping zones. Yet it is widely recognized that despite the frequency of land sales in the south, very little land is legally transferred under formal Ivorian land laws.[40] The major reason cited for this incongruity are the general population's ignorance of these laws and the high costs associated with registering land. However, such factors do not explain why the state does not enforce land. A closer look at the formal tenure system in Côte d'Ivoire and patterns of land concentration will help to explain this clear rejection of land laws and their nonenforcement.

Current law is largely based on two colonial decrees dating from the 1930s, some aspects of which were modified by a 1971 decree. Under these laws, the state is the owner of land that is either "vacant and without an owner or that has not been used for more than ten years."[41] Individuals seeking legal possession of land can obtain it either on a temporary or definitive basis from the state. Temporary concessions such as "occupation permits" and "concessions subject to claims by a third party" are the simplest and least costly legal means of obtaining land for private use. Definitive land rights are obtainable only after survey and registration, a costly and time-consuming process. Just 12 hectares can be registered at any one time. Therefore, an individual seeking to purchase a large area would have to survey and register the tract in 12-hectare parcels.[42]

The high costs involved in registering land and the fact that one can only obtain 12 hectares per title both help to explain the pervasiveness of customary transactions, especially for large holders. It is common knowledge that members of the Ivorian political elite are among the largest holders in the country.[43] In short, the nonenforcement of official land laws stems from the possibilities that politically influential individuals enjoy of accumulating capital in informal land markets.[44] The end result is the coexistence of informal and formal tenure systems, which introduces tremendous uncertainty in anything having to do with transferring land rights to strangers. Disputes are rampant in the forest region where it is often unclear what rights are being transferred when land is sold. Some owners claim that they are only selling cultivation rights and that they still possess the land. Others argue that sales are actually short- to medium-term leases and that the land must be returned after a certain period.[45] Land use conflicts in the savanna region are also related to this ambiguous tenure system. There the state promotes both formal and informal land rights in the Fulani sedentarization program.

In the tandem program, SODERPA approaches customary landholders to obtain their authorization for the construction of pastoral infrastructure for the Fulani. It also recognizes indigenous landholders' rights to "vacant land" by encouraging them to plant trees for the living fence enclosing improved pastures and cropland. However, in contrast to this approach based on cooperation, the subprefect asserts the land rights of the state. On at least three occasions in 1986, the subprefect of Niofouin visited Katiali to inform the population that only he had the right to chase the Fulani from the area. At the same time that these representatives of the state give mixed messages to the Senufo concerning who controls land in the region, their locally elected representatives are chosen partly for their promises to support the Senufo's desire to drive Fulani pastoralists from the north.

Conclusion

The failure of SODEPRA's Senufo-Fulani Tandem Project stems from land use conflicts at three interlocking levels: local, regional, and national. Locally, conflicts appear among the Senufo themselves over who controls land in the changing indigenous tenure system. At the regional level, the essential conflict is between the Senufo and Fulani over land use competition and crop damage. Nationally, a major conflict exists between the Senufo and the state over land access and control issues. These various conflicts adversely affect agricultural performance in Côte d'Ivoire by blocking the expansion of Fulani pastoralism and hindering the development of more intensive agricultural systems based on the integration of livestock raising and crop production.

The instability of Fulani pastoralism in the country has hampered the Ivorian government's goal of increasing domestic beef production. With the exception of veterinary interventions and a few herders participating in pilot livestock development programs, there has been little intensification of pastoralism in the country. The Fulani continue to practice an extensive, semitranshumant form of cattle raising. Their impressive contribution to national beef supplies largely results from more cattle entering the country rather than from improvements in herd productivity.[46] Seasonal variations in pasture quality and the susceptibility of zebu cattle to a host of endemic diseases in the subhumid savanna will continue to force the Fulani to follow their strategy of frequent herd movements within agricultural zones.

Ironically, the integration of livestock raising and farming appears to be a viable solution for the long-term intensification of both Fulani pastoralism and Senufo agriculture. The Fulani's preference to settle close to agricultural zones is evident. The Senufo could also benefit from mixed farming through the improvement and continuous use of agricultural land. Efforts to extend the period of cultivation through the use of commercial fertilizers have failed because of the acidification of soils.[47] The alternative method of rotating cropland with improved pastures on which cattle graze has proven to be a sustainable system of continuous "cultivation," at least in experiment stations.[48] Of course, these ideal conditions are invariably lacking in rural areas. The failure of SODEPRA's Tandem Project indicates that land use conflicts at various levels present major obstacles to improving agricultural systems through the integration of Fulani livestock raising and Senufo agriculture in the Ivorian savanna.

Notes

1 J. Gallais, "Essai sur la situation actuelle des relations entre pasteurs et paysans dans le Sahel ouest-africain," in *Études de Géographie tropicale offeretes à Pierre Gourou* (Paris, 1972); T. Bassett, "Fulani Herd Movements," *Geographical Review* 76, 3 (1986): 233–248; J. Boutrais, "L'expan-

sion des éléveurs peul dans les savanes humides du Cameroun," in M. Adamu and A. H. M. Kirk-Greene (eds.), *Pastoralists of the West African Savanna* (Manchester, International African Seminars, New Series, 2, 1986), 145–60.

2 In his classic study of the Wodaabe Fulani of northern Nigeria, Stenning notes three broad patterns of Fulani herd movements: a west-east "migratory drift" of herders beginning in the eleventh century in Senegal; north-south movements of cattle and herders during transhumance treks between dry and rainy season pastures; and the sudden migratory movement away from conflict areas. The relatively recent southerly migration of Fulani herds to subhumid savanna regions of West Africa represents a fourth pattern of Fulani herd movements. D. Stenning, *Savannah Nomads* (London, 1959).

3 P. Burnham, "Changing Agricultural and Pastoral Ecologies in the West African Savanna Region," in D. Harris (ed.), *Human Ecology in Savanna Environments* (New York, 1980): 147–70; D. Campbell, "Land-Use Competition at the Margins of the Rangelands: An Issue in Development Strategies for Semi-arid Areas," in G. Norcliffe and T. Pinfold (eds.), *Planning African Development* (Boulder, 1981): 39–61; M. Benoit, *Le Chemin des Peul de Boobola* (Paris, 1977). Restricted access to rangelands is related to (1) the expansion of livestock raising among farmers; (2) the year-round cultivation of wetlands important to transhumant livestock raising; and (3) the resurgence in tsetse flies in some areas. C. Frantz, "Contraction and Expansion in Nigerian Bovine Pastoralism," in T. Monod (ed.), *Pastoralism in Tropical Africa* (London, 1975): 338–352; C. Toulmin, "Herders and Farmers or Farmer-Herders and Herder-Farmers?" *Pastoral Network Paper* 15d (1983); Boutrais, "L'expansion."

4 Gallais, "Essai," 309.

5 Société du Développement de la Production Animale.

6 Zebu cattle (*Bos indicus*) refer to the large, humped animals commonly raised by the Fulani in the Sudano-Sahelian region of West Africa. Taurin cattle (*Bos taurus*) are the dwarf, trypanosomiasis-resistant animals raised by different peoples within the more humid savanna and forest regions.

7 D. Lagrue, *La sédentarisation de l'élevage peul dans le nord de la Côte d'Ivoire: Difficultés sociologiques, zootechniques et pathologiques* (Thèse pour le Doctorat Vétérinaire, Ecole National d'Alfort, 1977); D. Cuisance, *Enquête sur les Glossines dans la Zone de la Palé et au Niveau des Postes d'Entrée du Bétail dans le nord de la Côte d'Ivoire* (Maisons-Alfort, 1975); W. Kupper, A. Manno, A. Douati, and S. Koulibali, "Impact des pièges biconiques imprégnés sur les populations de *Glossina palpalis gambiensis* et *Glossina tachnioides,*" *Revue de l'Elevage et Médcine véterinaire des Pays tropicaux* 37 (1984): 176–185.

8 Other important herd management practices designed to control animal diseases include cross-breeding zebu animals with indigenous cattle that have a higher tolerance to local diseases, the use of trypanocides to control animal sleeping sickness, the use of cattle-dipping tanks to kill ticks, and finally, migration to a potentially more salubrious environment.

9 Y. Bigot and J-F. Poulain, "Evolution des sols sous culture pluviale 'encadré' sur défriche recente dans l'extrème nord de la Côte d'Ivoire: Comparison avec l'évolution sous culture traditionnelle" (Côte d'Ivoire, Ministère de la Recherche Scientifique, Institut des Savanes, Départment des Cultures Vivrières, Octobre 1981, mimeo).

10 G. Sement, "Etude des effets secondaires de la fertilisation minérale sur le sol dans des systèmes culturaux à base de coton en Côte d'Ivoire: Première résultats en matière de correction," *Coton et Fibres Tropicales* 35, 2 (1980): 229–248; G. Sement, "La fertilité des systèmes culturaux à base de cotonnier en Côte d'Ivoire," Supplément à *Coton et Fibres Tropicales* (1983), Série Documents, Etudes et Synthèses, no. 4.

11 M. Berger, P. Belem, D. Dakou, and V. Hien, "La maintien de la fertilité des sols dans l'ouest du Burkina Faso et la nécessité de l'association agriculture-élevage," *Coton et Fibres Tropicales* 42, 3 (1987): 201–210.

12 République de la Côte d'Ivoire, Ministère de la Production Animale (MPLA), *Amenagement de la zone pastorale de la Palé: Etude soci-economique de l'impact sur la population sedentaire environnante* (Abidjan, 1975).

13 SODEPRA, *Situation de l'Élevage Peul—1981* (Korhogo, 1982).

14 SODEPRA, *Operation zebu, Rapport annuel 1980* (Korhogo, 1980); Development Alternatives, Inc., *A Mid-Term Evaluation of Two Ivory Coast Livestock Projects* (Washington, D.C., 1980).

15 MPLA, *Amenagement,* 9–23.

16 Development Alternatives, *A Mid-Term Evaluation.*

17 SODEPRA, *Operation zebu,* 16.

18 P. Bernardet, "Dix ans de développement de l'élevage en Côte d'Ivoire. Stratégie et organisation de l'encadrement: Réalisations et échecs," *Cahiers Ivoiriens de la Recherche Economique et Sociale* 1 (1987): 41–56.

19 P. Berarndet, *Association Agriculture-Élevage en Afrique: Les Pauls semi-transhumants de Côte d'Ivoire* (Paris, 1984).

20 SODEPRA, *Situation,* 11.

21 Bassett, "Fulani."

22 M. Barry, "Les Peuls en Côte d'Ivoire," *Cahiers Ivoriens de la Recherche Economique et Sociale* 5 (1978): 75–81.

23 The major sources of information on the Tandem Project derive from the work commissioned by SODEPRA undertaken by the Institute of Tropical Geography of the National University of Ivory Coast. For specific references, see SODEPRA, *Evolution des Rapports entre les Paysans et les Éleveurs-Peul en pays Sénoufo, Rapport de Synthèse I* (Korhogo, 1984); SODEPRA, *Aspects Fonciers et Sociaux des Amenagements Pastoraux, Rapport de Synthèse II* (Korhogo, 1984); SODEPRA, *L'opération tandem Peul-Sénoufo, Dossiers Individuels* (Korhogo, 1984).

24 Interviews with SODEPRA officials, Korhogo, August 13, 1987.

25 S. Coulibaly, *Le Paysan Sénufo* (Abidjan, 1978); Société d'études pour le dévelopment économique et sociale, *Région de Korhogo, Etude de Développement Socio-Economique,* vol. 2, *Rapport Sociologique* (Paris, 1965): 61–72.

26 Some villages in the Korhogo region were founded by Jula migrants who, in the past, devoted most of their time to commerce. There are a number of examples of Jula chiefs giving stranger Senufo farmers total control over land in these villages (see SODEPRA *L'opération*).

27 T. Bassett, "Food, Peasantry and the State in Northern Ivory Coast, 1898–1982" (Ph.D. diss., University of California, Berkeley, 1984): 27–34.

28 T. Bassett, "The Development of Cotton in Northern Ivory Coast, 1910–1965," *Journal of African History* 29 (1988): 267–284.

29 Ibid.

30 Compagnie Ivorien du développement des fibres textiles.

31 In the early 1960s, a field was cultivated for 5 years before being returned to fallow. Today it is not uncommon for fields to be worked 8 to 10 years.

32 S. Coulibaly, *La Difficile mais Nécessaire Integration de l'Élevage Zébu dans le Monde Rural Sénoufo (de la zébuiste)* Université Nationale de Côte d'Ivoire, Institut de Géographie Tropicale, Document Provisoire no. 42 (1980): 12–14.

33 SODEPRA, *Aspects,* 44–46.

34 SODEPRA, *L'opération*.

35 PDCI—Parti Democratique de la Côte d'Ivoire (Democratic Party of the Ivory Coast).

36 Granger notes that the 1964 inheritance law is not widely accepted and that matrilineal principles are still operable in many places. R. Granger, "Étude des Problèmes Foncières dans le Développement de Côte d'Ivoire," mimeo. (n.d.): 9.

37 For an overview of Ivorian land laws, see A. Ley "L'expérience Ivoirienne," in E. Le Bris et. al. (eds.), *Enjeux fonciers en Afrique noire* (Paris, 1983): 135–141.

38 Long-cycle crops are those with a long growing season in comparison to short-cycle crops, which mature sooner. In the Katiali region, cotton is a long-cycle crop because it is planted in June and harvested in November and December. Maize is a typical short-cycle crop that is planted in June and harvested in mid-August.

39 T. Bassett, "The Political Ecology of Peasant-Herder Conflicts in the Northern Ivory Coast." *Annals of the Association of American Geographers* 78, 3 (1988): 453–472.

40 Granger, "Etude,"; C. Blanc, "Le foncier rural en Côte d'Ivoire," mimeo (1981); R. Hecht, "Immigration, Land Transfer, and Tenure Change in Divo, Ivory Coast, 1940–1980," *Africa* 55, 3 (1985): 319–336.

41 Blanc, "Le foncier," 26.

42 Alternatively, one could purchase 12 hectares and lease the remaining area from the state.

43 Blanc, "Le foncier," 41–43.

44 J. Baulin, *La Politique Intérieure d'Houphouet-Boigny* (Paris, 1980): 93–94, 151.

45 Blanc, "Le foncier," 41–44; Ley, "L'expérience," 140.

46 The national herd grew at a rate of 9.5% over the period 1976–1985. More

than half of this increase was due to migration of Fulani cattle to Ivory Coast. The annual growth rate of both taurin and zebu cattle was 4.4% over the same period. FAO, *Livre Blanc de l'Élevage en Côte d'Ivoire, Document Provisoire* (Rome, 1986): 35–36.

47 Sement, "L'étude."
48 Sement, "La fertilité."

PART 2

ACCESS TO LAND
AND AGRARIAN POLITICS

6   *Michael J. Watts*

Idioms of Land and Labor: Producing Politics and Rice in Senegambia

> Society is a battlefield of representation on which the limits
> and coherence of any given set are being fought for and regu-
> larly spoilt. Thus it makes sense to say that representations
> are continually subject to a test of a reality more basic than
> themselves—the test of social practice.
>
> —T. J. Clark

Introduction

One of the curiosities of British colonialism in West Africa is the dramatic volte-face in land and labor policy that occurred at the turn of the
twentieth century. Fred Cooper has described, for example, how the
European debate over slavery pioneered what he calls "a new international discourse" in which free labor provided the universal metric for
imperial conduct in the colonies.[1] Free labor necessitated not simply the
eradication of all forms of servility but the tight control of *land* to ensure
that former slaves sought wage labor, not petty proprietorship. The
imperial emphasis on discipline, order, and free labor was all of a piece
in this regard because free labor ideology might only be realized through
a radical break with local custom, social structure, and culture. It was
none other than the architect of indirect rule, Lord Lugard, who wanted
to convert the Muslim elites of northern Nigeria into late Victorian
agrarian capitalists and the millions of slaves into disciplined wage
workers[2]—the backbone of Chamberlain's colonial estates.

This particular vision was undermined quite dramatically. On the one
hand, former slaves became peasants and former slave owners mercantile capitalists or salaried bureaucrats. And on the other, European
populists and mercantile political interests within the Colonial Office—

157

in part influenced by the ideas of Henry George and backed by certain sectors of British manufacturing capital who preferred to leave production to the natives—successfully negotiated a peasant-based colonial strategy, a smallholder road rooted in local custom and communal tenure.[3] Under the influence of Edward Morel and Josiah Wedgewood, the Land and Native Rights Proclamation of 1910 in northern Nigeria, for example, effectively overturned Lugard's original vision. The unreleased West African Lands Committee report of 1917 recommended concessions and the transition to individual tenure. By the 1920s, then, the European representation of Africa was less of slave-ridden barbarity than harmonious and stable social structures grounded in some sort of organic harmony with the traditional African community.

Like other West African colonies and protectorates, The Gambia experienced a remarkable turnaround in land policy. In 1895, the governor of The Gambia proposed that the state take over all colony land and all unoccupied protectorate land and rent it to Africans or interested European parties. The 1896 and 1897 Public Lands Ordinances brought all land under government control such that all occupants had to obtain a land certificate and pay annual rent. It was hoped that these ordinances would bring to the attention of capitalists the "chances . . . in The Gambia for acquiring landed property and safely investing capital."[4] The prevailing ideology saw West Africans as largely slothful and unindustrious, however, and the difficulty in mobilizing and recruiting wage labor in a largely peasant society fed the notion that the free labor/ capitalist vision could only be sustained by importing a better class of laborer. The acting governor of The Gambia accordingly noted in 1901 that "we will never get the full value out of the land . . . until a people more intelligent, industrious and ambitious is imported such as the India coolie."[5] But the gradual ascendancy of cocoa and cotton interests which required neither concessions nor a mass of wage labor destroyed the case for English land law as a precondition for the growth of export commodity production. Hence by 1912, the governor of The Gambia could say that "there is . . . no doubt in my mind that the tribal system of communal tenure of land is the most suitable for West Africa."[6] The Land Act of 1946, which still provides the legal architecture for contemporary land transactions in The Gambia, states that ultimate rights to land are vested in and administered by the district authorities as representatives of the state and that the occupation and use of land "is governed by customary laws obtaining in the localities."[7] The act does not, of course, specify what the customary laws are.

The slide from freehold to customary tenure was, as Anne Phillips rightly notes, little more than a cloak for inactivity. What was at stake was the fundamental inability of the colonial project to effect its claims:

[Colonial states] could not impose conditions which would create free labor without destroying communal land tenure, and they could not destroy communal land tenure without weakening the chiefs upon whom they relied. . . . The fragility of their control made them dependent on pre-capitalist relations . . . [and] fortunately the reluctance of capital to engage in direct investment and the discovery of alternate peasant production allowed them to retreat with honor.[8]

This was, of course, a Pyrrhic victory because the continuity of something called customary tenure was quite mythical in two senses: there was no continuity, and there was no unified nonindividualized communal control of land. As Karl Marx pointed out, precapitalist property relations contain an enormous variability within the confines of something called communal property. As he put it, "membership of the commune remains the presupposition for the appropriation of land and soil but, as a member of the commune, the individual is a private proprietor. He relates to his private property as land . . . but at the same time as a commune member."[9] This tension explains why the early colonial officers found, but typically dismissed, so much evidence for complex land transactions and individual control of land. The imperial commoditization of many aspects of local economy and society simply furthered, in inordinately complex ways, individual, familial, and community rights of access to land. As Marx suggested, individual rights in African land (which could be quite stable and even bought and sold) are framed in some way by the community and hence are based on social identity. As Sara Berry pointed out, "the definition of property rights hinges on the demarcation of social boundaries."[10] It was precisely these boundaries that were threatened, undermined, and refashioned by the growing commercialization associated with colonial rule, and hence the state's reliance on customary tenure simply obfuscated the complex struggles within African communities over the meaning and contours of these social boundaries. The withdrawal of colonial regulation over land tenure in the name of local custom simply opened up the possibility of multiple, overlapping, and sometimes contradictory sets of rights of access and control over land and as a corollary, struggles over the meanings of those social relations (kin, community, wife, etc.) that regulate access to land.

Manufacturing Dissent Over Land

Returning to The Gambia from home leave in late 1952, the director of the Wallikunda Irrigation Project[11] discovered that a substantial slice of the project rice harvest, some 400 bags of paddy, had mysteriously disappeared during his absence. Petty theft and pilferage by female Mandinka[12] tenants had been commonplace since the scheme was hatched in 1949 by the Colonial Development Corporation (CDC), but the scale of the latest popular appropriation implied, at the very least, collective organization and collusion by local chiefs. Given birth by the postwar West Africa Rice Mission, the Wallikunda enterprise represented a heady vision: to introduce and foster mechanized double cropping of rice through the largely Mandinka middle river districts of The Gambia, a region in which swamp and tidal rice production[13] was of some antiquity. Wallikunda actually linked to adjacent swamps—Jahaly and Pacharr—and in its original blueprint proposed extensive bund and canal construction designed to bring 10,880 acres under irrigation. It proved to be an expensive and embarrassing failure. The CDC alone was implicated to the tune of over US$500,000, and the entire development was plagued by a comical succession of basic design flaws. Massive rice theft following close on the heels of extensive flooding, inadequate surveying and leveling, canal collapse, and rumors of the exploitation of child labor and wild debauchery by the British construction crew quite literally brought the project to its knees. "If these Gothic predations are to continue," observed the exasperated director, referring to the rice theft, "we may as well pack the whole thing up."[14] Indeed they did.

The Gothic predations grew and flourished in the fertile soil of colonial folly and ignorance, notably, in the large-scale appropriation of rice lands by the CDC—initially on a thirty-year lease from the local Native Authority (NA)—which imperial administrators quite wrongly assumed to be "uncultivated." The land seizure initiated a flood of property claims and disputes; indeed, it was the belief of the peasants themselves that they were taking the rice "because the *tubabos* [whites] had taken their land." The collapse of the CDC scheme in 1953 ushered in direct government control and the creation, on a much more modest scale, of the Gambia Rice Farm, which was in essence a state farm with limited water control employing largely female wage labor for most farm operations, particularly rice weeding and harvesting. Local resistance once more proved intractable. Wage workers were almost impossible to recruit and discipline because rice labor bottlenecks conflicted directly with the primary demands made by the work routines of other rain-fed upland crops (groundnut, millet, and sorghum). In addition, the productivity of hired labor was low, and rice pilferage was endemic. In desperation, in 1954 the farm management introduced women sharecroppers onto the farm, many of whom had lost, and were then contesting, their claims on swamplands in the wake of signing of the thirty-year lease. But extensive underreporting and the retention of too much paddy by ornery sharecroppers led to the dissolution of share contracting after only two years. A return to direct cash rental persisted until 1958, by which time the explosion of farm debt, owed by the women tenants to the Department of Agriculture for tractor plowing and other services, marked the final humiliating demise of the Gambia Rice Farm.

These first, and somewhat farcical, efforts to introduce mechanized rice production in the 1950s constituted an important watershed in the changing nature of farm work and peasant land rights in The Gambia. In exploring these complex transformations over the last century, I shall focus on a largely Mandinka region in central Gambia, a traditional swamp rice area whose technical and social relations of production have been radically challenged by the introduction of irrigated double cropping of irrigated rice. The current phase of large-scale, mechanized irrigation, emerging from the ashes of thirty years of land efforts to expand domestic output of rice, contracts household growers as sharecroppers. This represents a form of social integration under state auspices in which households gain access to irrigated plots and critical inputs, while project management taps a "peasant labor market" in the absence of a landless class. Household labor continues to be the dominant social form in which labor power is mobilized but under conditions directly determined and shaped by production management. The project is, as a Gambian administrator informed me, "rather like a factory." Irrigated rice production is labor intensive and hence makes new demands on customary structures of domestic labor recruitment. But new economic practice tests the culturally dominant representations of household work, labor obligations, and property rights, the very stuff of custom and tradition.

In my examination of Mandinka rice growers, I suggest that the battlefield of representations referred to by Tim Clark[15] is a contest over gender roles and the bases of the conjugal contract in which complex configurations of property rights, including land and labor claims, are at stake. This suggestion rests on two critical assumptions. First, property rights must not be seen as narrowly material, for they represent rights with respect to people, including rights over their labor power. Rights over resources such as land or crops are inseparable from, indeed are isomorphic with, rights over people; to alter property rights is, as Robert Bates[16] says, to redefine social relationships. And second, by seeing economic life as a realm of representations, we perceive struggles over land and labor to be simultaneously symbolic contests and struggles over meaning. In the case I examine, such interpretive contests revolve around the intersection of work, specifically, who works where under what conditions, and the conjugal contract. In conditions in which households are contracted as the basic unit of production, the consequences for the labor process (the social organization of work) and property are always domestic in character, reflecting the dominance of kinship and gender in the access to, and control over, resources. Not unexpectedly, production politics[17]—that is, struggles over the labor process—are conducted in the idiom of customary representations of gender, conjugality, and patriarchal control.

While the food crisis in Africa of the last fifteen years has been debated as an epochal moment in the continent's history,[18] The Gambia has been a major importer of staple foodstuffs, primarily rice, for a century and half.[19] The erosion of self-sufficiency in the nineteenth century elicited a series of import-substitution strategies starting in the 1890s, designed to expand domestic rice production. These state interventions embodied three goals: first, to exploit a variety of rice ecologies (from the improvement of indigenous mangrove and swamp systems to large-scale heavily mechanized double cropping under systems of full water control); second, to induce men into production systems that have been, since the middle of the nineteenth century, almost wholly dominated by women; and third, to produce marketable surpluses of rice. On balance, wholesale failure distinguishes the history of rice development in The Gambia. Occasionally, it rises to Chaplinesque fiasco. As I shall show, this checkered past is central to understanding both the social organization of rice production in its most recent and ambitious form and the enduring nature of local struggles over land and labor.

The most recent attempt to expand rice production, the large-scale Jahaly-Pacharr irrigation project, has ironically emerged on the same site as the first, rather theatrical, failure of irrigation thirty years before. I will discuss this latest foray into peasant subordination in The Gambia, specifically, the forms of production politics that emerge in a new, complex, and expensive program to institute double-cropping. The Jahaly-Pacharr scheme is a form of share contracting in which the project management contracts smallholders to produce rice under specified technical and work conditions, providing green revolution inputs for a share of the harvest. The closely supervised production routine has been superimposed on the work rhythms of indigenous upland and lowland farming systems. These routines conflict directly with groundnut, millet, and maize cropping activities. Therefore, in its most immediate impact, the project has amplified labor demands and created dry season farming practices for which there are no established (i.e., customary) rules for mobilizing household labor. The regimented labor regime of the Jahaly-Pacharr project vastly expands intrahousehold labor demands. This amplification has assaulted the customary nexus of crop and property rights and the reciprocal claims on labor, which collectively constitute the social organization of Mandinka domestic production. Therefore, it transforms the domestic arena, and the "multiple-claim property system,"[20] into a terrain of particularly intense struggle. The fulcrum of these struggles is gender, and their focus is the terms and conditions of the conjugal contract, one aspect of which is land entitlement.[21]

I wish to argue that state interventions to improve productivity or to transform the relations of production must, given the prevalence of precapitalist property relations among peasantries, confront what Robert Brenner calls the "internal solidity" on noncapitalist societies.[22] That is to say, economic actors "cannot be assumed to find it in their self-interest to adopt new, more effective techniques . . . or . . . in their self-interest or capacity to make the necessary changes in property relations required to adopt the new techniques."[23] Communities organized themselves in quite specific ways to reproduce stable property relations and to protect the access of some individuals to the means of production. The history of state intervention in rice production in The Gambia is very much the story of the internal solidity of peasant forms of production. In the case of irrigated rice since the 1950s, the state experienced limited success in both controlling peasant labor and challenging deeply sedimented work patterns and property relations. In the same way that Marx and Weber talk of the problem of controlling free labor at the point of production under capitalism,[24] so the similar control of peasant labor has been problematic for a Gambian state intent on increasing food output. The struggle between state and peasantry in this context produced an enhanced work burden for women and intensified efforts by men to subert women's claims on resources, especially over land. However, in the recent past, regimented contractual schemes such as Jahaly-Pacharr have directly challenged local property relations and animated struggles within the household over access to land.[25] These conflicts have largely occurred between genders and specifically between husbands and wives. In other words, a new tightly regimented production routine has failed to create consent but has *manufactured dissent,* conflicts within social relations which threaten not only the performance of the project but the reproduction of customary relations in the sphere of domestic politics.

The discussion consists of three parts. First comes a skeletal history since the 1890s of Gambian policies toward rice import substitution and of the strategies pursued by colonial and postcolonial states to expand rice production within a variety of rice ecologies. The object of this reconstruction is to establish the current class of rice schemes, of which

Jahaly-Pacharr is the archetype, as the product of successive interventions, designed to control and subordinate peasant labor, in which the land-labor nexus has been a theater of conflict and struggle. Second is a description of the contract farming system and of the sorts of domestic conflicts and production politics articulated around labor, land, and crop rights and the conjugal contract. Third and finally, I examine how we can, to employ James Scott's language, see the politics of rice growing as a struggle over custom and usage. However, these struggles are less "a long drawn out campaign . . . based on relationships of force"[26] than they are interpretive struggles over socially dominant representations. I suggest that these representations pertaining to gender, the cultural order of the household, and property rights conflict with the new experiences of material life. As Henrietta Moore points out,[27] such contradictions are rarely contained through coercion but rather through negotiation, what I call *symbolic contests* and *struggles over meaning*. Such negotiation is not a contest between equals because it is framed by the socially dominant representations that attempt to "contain contradictions and conflicts and so to contain the vagaries of lived reality."[28]

Contradictions Between Land and Labor:
Food and Rice Politics, 1830–1980

Has the work force been sufficiently prepared by famine, impoverishment, and proletarianization to constitute a reliable, hardworking, paddy-field peasantry? My assessment is that it has not. Agricultural intensification means getting people to work harder, and that undertaking usually requires coercion.
                    —Keith Hart, *The Political Economy of West African Agriculture*

The African species of rice (*Oryza glaberrima*) is an ancient and culturally elaborated cultigen in The Gambia. Prior to the first European presence, rice was cultivated both as an upland rainfed crop and, more extensively, as wet or paddy rice in both the tidal saline and freshwater swamps (*bafaro*) and in riparian depressions (*bantafaro*). The fifteenth-century Portuguese travelers who waxed lyrical on the flood recession rices cultivated on the tidal flats and in floodplain swamps (*leos*) of the Gambia River were agents of agrarian change in their own right bringing to Senegambia, between the sixteenth and eighteenth century, robust and productive Asian rices (*Oryza sativa*).[29] By the eighteenth and early nineteenth centuries, traveler-explorers like René Caillié, Richard Jobson, and Francis Moore marveled at a flexible and adaptive native technology capable of sophisticated diking, elaborate bunding and flushing, water (and salt) management, transplanting, and, in some locations, even double cropping. By the 1760s, the French were buying large quantities of indigenous paddy at Albreda, and in 1778, the commandant of the province of Senegambia could write that "rice may be produced here as much as in the Provinces of Carolina and Georgia."[30]

As British acquisition of the Gambia River basin inched forward in the first part of the nineteenth century, rice was first given serious consideration as a commodity to diversify a small export base dominated by beeswax, gum, hides, teak, and ivory. Paddy had been exported in 1829 to the West Indies amounting to 5 percent of total export revenues, and rice seed was subsequently distributed in 1834, with much élan, to liberated Africans to encourage "the new branch of trade."[31] Whatever the likelihood of the wholesale conversion of the discontinuous territories along the lower reaches of the Gambia River into a "new Carolina," the explosive birth and subsequent growth of the groundnut industry in any case cut short the nascent rice export trade. Merchant firms from Britain and France such as Foster and Smith and Maurel and Prom actively encouraged groundnut production in the 1830s, notably, in the North Bank districts of Niuni, Baddibu, Niani, and Saloum, and exports began in earnest after 1843. The groundnut boom rested on the use of both servile farm labor by Gambian peasants, especially in the wake of the British control of the river and their dowsing of the French slave trade from Juffure and Albreda, and platoons of seasonal migrants or strange farmers (*samalaalu*) employed under labor share contracts who frequently worked alongside the slaves of their Gambian hosts.[32] Groundnut exports leaped by 400 percent between 1843 and 1857, and, with the exception of an ominous setback in 1857 due to a food shortage that required the import of £6,099 of rice,[33] production and labor migration were both buoyed by intensified mercantile competition and favorable prices up to the crisis of the early 1880s.

The rapid proliferation of commodity production initiated radical transformations within the Gambia River basin prior to the establishment of a colony under British rule. Three broad socioeconomic processes were of direct significance for an understanding of twentieth-century rice politics. First was the demise of the rice export trade after 1843 (fig. 6.1). The allocation of domestic labor to groundnut production and the large-scale employment of strange farmers who as part of the share contract were to be fed (and granted land), in return for their labor power, had the effect of simultaneously expanding food requirements and eroding upland food production of millet and sorghum. Household subsistence needs placed expanded demands on rice, and

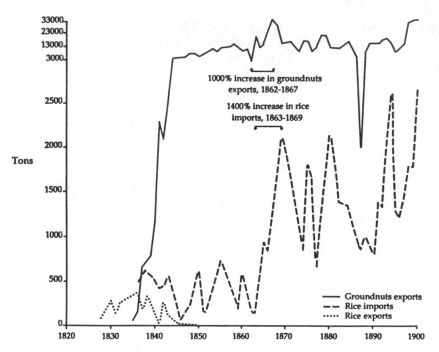

Figure 6.1. Groundnut and rice exports, rice imports for The Gambia, 1827–1900

surpluses for export rapidly disappeared by the 1840s. The 1857 famine threw into dramatic relief the extent to which food production had been undermined. In 1861, Governor D'Arcy noted that peasants from the North Bank, the heart of the fast-growing groundnut industry, were increasingly dependent on food, especially rice, grown in the South Bank districts and from Dyula communities across the border in French territory.[34] But the early growth of regional food specialization could not keep pace with the internal deepening of food demand stimulated by the explosive growth of groundnut production.

Second, around 1860, a rapid transformation occurred in the Mandinka sexual division of labor from task-specific to crop-specific gender roles.[35] In the early nineteenth century, rice formed the basis of an important conjugal fund at marriage and was produced through close cooperation between spouses. Rice production was primariily the domain of women, who appropriated the product individually,[36] but men had the responsibility for certain tasks, most notably, preparing rice land prior to transplanting for which they were reimbursed or reciprocated in some way. However, the monopolization of groundnut production by Mandinka men marked the genesis of a much more singular sexual division of labor by crop. Rice became women's work and, unlike groundnuts, largely noncommoditized. In other words, the growth of groundnut export after 1843 represented a watershed for labor in terms of its domestic division and in its patterns of recruitment and household organization. By 1860, the annual report noted that men were "growing groundnuts and leaving the much heavier work to women" but that twenty years before, in the 1840s, women were "not getting enough to eat and started to cultivate rice on their own account . . . and men encouraged this."[37]

The third process was the rise of the rice import trade in the 1830s and the genesis of a groundnut seed-rice advance system. The burden of strange farmers on household food supply (estimated at 1 ton per season for 11 strange farmers) and the diminished emphasis on upland food crops vastly expanded domestic demand for staples, a hunger satisfied from the early 1840s onward through imported rice.[38] By the late 1860s, rice imports amounted to £10,000, a weighty sum seen by the British administrators as an irritant necessary to maintain the flow of strange farmers in the face of stiff Senegalese competition and to compensate for the quite rapid demise of household self-sufficiency especially on the North Bank and in the upper river districts. The trade was controlled by the French and British merchant houses who distributed rice, through their agents, at their wharfside depots, often on credit.[39] Local nut buyers often deliberately purchased all available groundnuts from peasants so that seed could be fronted for the following season. Cloth, trade goods, and rice were frequently advanced both to "tie" producers for subsequent groundnut sales and as lucrative short-term investments. By 1860, Governor D'Arcy saw these enormous mercantile advances as a "pernicious" system that engendered "lax and immoral views and reck-lessness.[40] Ten years later, Brown and Quinn merchants alone were reputed to have £35,000 in outstanding credit upcountry. Thirty years later, the state found itself heavily involved in seed and rice credit, prompted in the first instance by crop damage. It first advanced seed to peasants in 1894 and regularly after 1896–97 in tandem with a reduction in export tax. The severe drought of 1901 compelled the state to provided 4,000 bags of rice on credit largely because merchant companies terminated their subsistence credit. From 1908 to 1933, the state reluctantly advanced both seed and rice as a matter of policy, in parallel with the huge mercantile system. Public and private sectors constituted a labyrinthine web of debt that subsequently fueled what Governor Arbitrage colorfully referred to as "orgies of speculation."[41]

These three developments suggest that by the turn of the century, the Gambian political economy was structurally unstable. Rice imports had grown dramatically, not least because rice credits were integral to the sustenance of what by 1915 was in excess of 20,000 strange farmers.[42] In 1908, close to 7,000 strange farmers accounted for £2,346 of rice issues; by 1919, the number of strange farmers was 24,000 and absorbed over £38,000 of rice for consumption and seed purposes. The rash claim of Richard MacDonnell, that in spite of overcultivation of groundnuts "there would be no danger of natives suffering . . . from famines,"[43] was shown to be fraudulent by food crises in 1857, 1876, 1894, and 1901 and by the deepening of the "hungry period" in the months prior to the new harvest. Rice importation and subsistence credit was overdetermined despite considerable ambivalence by colonial officers. The government and the companies depended directly on groundnuts for revenues and for the internal demand they generated; but half the harvest was accounted for by strange farmers for whom food was the central axiom of their contracts. The district chiefs and the colonial state also gained from the presence of strange farmers through taxes. In sum, unless food was available to capture migrant labor, and the Gambian climate made local production something of an annual lottery, the colonial house of cards would collapse.

The colonial state facilitated rice imports. But deepening food insecurities and a proliferation of peasant debt[44] necessitated a series of efforts to expand domestic food production. Swamp programs in the 1920s represented the government's first effort at rice import substitution. Developed after World War II along the central Gambian floodplain where rich alluvial soils, tidal flooding, and seasonal freshwater conditions favor high yields, state programs funded mangrove clearance, the construction of causeways and footbridges to improve access to the deep-water swamps, the distribution of improved seeds, and new methods in seedbed preparation. These efforts resulted in a vast expansion of swamp rice production by the mid-1950s when the planted area doubled to 49,000 acres, reducing milled imports by 80 percent to 2,000 tons.[45] This remarkable achievement required the intensification of female labor.

Despite the colonial role in channeling cereal production to the swamps, officials recognized that gender posed the primary obstacle to food self-sufficiency, what Governor Blood referred to in 1943 as "the anthropological problem." The state sought to recuperate losses from diminishing groundnut export values by reducing dependence, and therefore expenditures, on milled imports. The success of the strategy rested on the "extent to which the male population can be persuaded to take an active part in rice cultivation."[46] Persuasion consisted of bringing a group of male farmers to The Gambia from Sierra Leone, where men grew rice, to instruct Mandinka men in swamp rice cultivation techniques, including rudimentary irrigation based on waterwheels and lifts for dry season cultivation and, in the postwar period, targeting for development a lowland rice agroecosystem that had a complementary cropping cycle with groundnuts.[47] But instead of giving a boost to rice cultivation and raising its "status from a women's crop to a family endeavor,"[48] the postwar swamp project failed to transform the gender basis of rice production. In fact, the longer cultivation cycle of the tidal over the rainfed swamp zones and their distance from villages combined to augment the number of months and hours per day women labored in agriculture.[49] In other words, the projects lacked a mechanism to compel men to work in the paddy fields. Men resisted government efforts to intensify their labor by invoking tradition, arguing that rice was "wet work" and a "women's crop," and consequently the burden they were able to shed was shouldered by their wives, mothers, and daughters.

In the wake of these first hesitant efforts to encourage domestic food production, the colonial state further intensified its efforts to expand rice output, but as the experience of the 1920s revealed, a general labor shortage and a marked sexual division of labor by commodity were obstacles to rapid commercialization in this area. As a consequence, throughout the postwar period, the state targeted a variety of rice ecosystems and labor sources to expand production. Beginning in the early 1940s with the saline mangrove systems in the estuarine west and efforts to compel stranger farmers into the swamps, rice strategies evolved toward mechanized small-scale irrigation perimeters in the 1960s in which double cropping of high-yielding varieties rested on the creation of a disciplined male and female paddy field peasantry.

1942–1965, The Mangrove Campaign: Converting Strange Farmers into Rice Growers

The outbreak of war and the disruption of world trade prompted area consideration of the food situation. While as early as 1940 the Department of Agriculture announced self-sufficiency in food as one of its objectives, in 1942 departing Governor Southam could still remark on the gravity of the situation.[50] Two wartime reports by C. J. Rae and Charles Roddan targeting the improvement of existing swamp rice systems were endorsed by Governor Blood, who believed, in the final analysis, that the problem of the crop-specific sexual division of labor was a price question, not a cultural one. Roddan's report was seminal because it elevated the mangrove ecosystem to a privileged position in rice production strategy for a labor-scarce regime.[51] Mangrove rices were higher yielding, while salinity restricted weed growth and hence alleviated the arduous cultivation routines. Roddan estimated that

54,000 acres of tidal swamp were available for development, an endeavor in which the state could provide infrastructural (i.e., causeway)
and seed improvement. In the context of the radical changes heralded by
the Second World War,[52] the mangrove campaign, whose origins lay in
indigenous efforts twenty years earlier, was consistent with many of the
populist sentiments within government. While Roddan's views were far
from uniformly supported, various commissioners argued vociferously
for the neglected upland crops and for the need to "stabilize the strange
farmer." The government did establish a rice research station at Genoi
in 1945 using the CDWA funds to conduct mangrove trials. It also embarked on an ambitious program of mangrove clearance and rice development, doubtless hastened by the widespread local hunger of 1946,[53]
and the frenzied, and fearsome, colonial memoranda of 1947 on the
impending world food crisis resulting from the wartime collapse of Asian
supply areas in particular.[54] Between 1953 and 1960, the government
spent £250,000 on rice projects,[55] and the area devoted to swamp production increased substantially from 23,000 acres in 1946 to 65,000 acres in
1965. While Charles van der Plas believed that the introduction of early
varieties relieved labor bottlenecks between groundnut and rice tasks
with the result that men and strange farmers were entering the rice
system, a view shared by the *seyfolo* (chief) of Dankunku, in fact the
burden of this new production was largely shouldered by women.[56]
Haswell's research shows that in Genieri village, the average tidal
swamp area per female worker increased from 1.0 to 1.19 acres between
1949 and 1962, and the total rice area increased from 168 to 263 acres.[57]
But more women were working longer. The total days per female
worker increased from 90 to 102. And Margaret Haswell's data highlight
dramatically how women were entering rice production at a younger
age. Men were indeed involved in mangrove clearance, but the opening
up of lands became a political issue in two related senses. First, men
were reluctant to have women establish individual claims over the new
rice plots; and second, men and women from founding lineages were
systematically excluded from land access.

In the early 1950s, the mangrove swamps of Eastern Jarra, Niamina
West, Dankunku, and Lower Saloum produced rice surpluses estimated
to be in the order of 4,000 tons. Much of it flooded the Bathurst market,
confronting importers with rigorous domestic competition and reduced
profit margins. In 1954, under pressure from commercial interests, the
state prohibited the export of rice from the protectorate and stopped
completely its flow from the provinces.[58] However, by the mid-1960s,
geography and the limits of labor combined to exhaust the mangrove
strategy. On the one hand, western and lower river districts faced en-

hanced salinity as reduced rainfall forced some of the tidal flats out of cultivation. And, on the other hand, as Rae predicted in 1943, swamp production ran aground on the reefs of labor, which "more than any other factor will be found to dictate future [development]."[59] Efforts to give titles to strange farmers to clear mangrove or to work in rice fields for less tax and less labor obligation all came to nought. Unless men could be "persuaded to take an active interest in rice," and they would not be, the mangrove campaign rested on, and was ultimately limited by, the exploitation of women.[60]

1947–1951, CDC Irrigation: Large-Scale Mechanized Rice Production at Wallikunda

In the context of the 1947 world food shortage and the local scarcity of 1946, two missions, the West African Oilseeds Mission in 1947 and the West Africa Rice Mission in the following year, drew attention to the compelling need to revolutionize production and to introduce mechanized dry season irrigation, that is, double cropping. Against this backdrop, the creation of the CDC in 1947, itself a product of the abandonment of territorial self-sufficiency in the colonies and the need to create nondollar sources of materials supply,[61] must have appeared to Gambian officials as the angel of history in relation to the often-quoted but habitually ignored "irrigation potential" of the Gambia River. The Rice Mission's aims were grandiose, to convert The Gambia into West Africa's "rice bowl,"[62] and despite the grave reservations of Governor Wright pertaining to scale, practicalities, and "political economics,"[63] the British Treasury moved ahead in conjunction with the CDC to develop a large-scale project in The Gambia. In 1949, a CDC team identified the Pacharr-Wallikunda and Kudang swamps in the central, salt-free, region as an ideal site for 23,000 acres of full irrigation development. The Wallikunda pilot site was to be fully mechanized, operated from one primary pump and drained through massive drains and two sluices.

With a capital grant of £300,000 and 10,800 acres of local swamp on a thirty-year lease from indigenous cultivators, work commenced immediately almost as a war operation.[64] The outcome was calamitous. With almost no hydrological and ecological data, no contour survey, and astonishing technical and design flaws, the project ran into immediate labor problems, poor work conditions, and deteriorating relations between the CDC and local villages. In 1951, the Pitt Report reviewed the CDC land appropriation and managed to avoid or misunderstand all of the critical issues and "compensate" farmers indirectly through community infrastructure funded by local NA (i.e., farmer) taxes,[65] ignorant of the fact that the Wallikunda swamplands were themselves already contested among and between villagers. Within one year of the lease signing, the local chiefs (*seyfolu*) and angry peasants were demanding the return of their lands.[66] Imported machinery proved to be expensive and often useless, and costs escalated. By 1951, it was estimated that the scheme would cost an astronomical £780,000. But CDC had already spent £300,000, and floods had devastated the first experimental harvest of 150 acres. In 1952, the assets stood at £349,240, with a cumulative trading loss of £34,914.[67] It was clear by 1952 that CDC required government assistance to advance even in a modest way at Wallikunda, and it smartly entered into a joint partnership called the Gambia Rice Farm to develop mechanized irrigation on a limited scale, about 200 acres according to the Gaitskell Mission. At this point no dry season crop had been obtained or indeed was likely in the foreseeable future; wet season production was a debacle; labor was almost unobtainable; and land conflicts were rife.

1952–1965, the Gambia Rice Farm:
Sharecroppers, Tenants, and Tractors

Between 1952 and 1958, the Gambia Rice Farm scaled down from 4,000 to 200 acres, was established as a joint venture between CDC and the Gambian government, and thereafter converted into the Sapu Rice Research Station. While operating on a less ambitious scale, the Wallikunda project adhered to its original mandate to grow rice under conditions of full water control through contracted wage labor. But farm labor was almost impossible to obtain. There was only one full-time laborer in 1954.[68] The roll call every morning produced little in the way of serious farm labor, and "each year the farm has to be content to wait for women . . . until such time as they are free from work with their own rice crop."[69] In 1954, late rains meant that no labor was available until August, and weed-infested plots produced only one-third of a ton of rice from 30 acres.[70] As a consequence, management followed up a recommendation of the 1952 Gaitskell Report which advised sharecropping to avoid burdening "the system with the cost of daily labor" which "cannot compete against peasant agriculture" (22). Project management could only attract women sharecroppers ("men will have nothing to do with rice growing," remarked the farm manager[71]) who were ornery and recalcitrant. The growers obfuscated crop output, and rice theft by peasants was rampant, because "the tubabos [whites] had taken their land."[72] Rice theft and everyday resistance so jeopardized the project that a formal tenant relationship rapidly superseded sharecropping.

Lands originally leased to CDC were rented to women growers, who were provided with tractor plowing services. In practice, this meant that the rice appropriation by farm management had declined from roughly 1,000 pounds of paddy per acre under sharecropping in 1955, to 400 pounds under tenant arrangements in 1957, and finally to only 160 pounds per acre by 1962.[73]

In any case, the tenancy system proved to be a financial and litigious nightmare. On the one hand, land redistribution was baroque and unfathomable in the context of complex intervillage conflicts over who exactly had "traditional" rights in the swamps prior to the CDC appropriation. By 1964, the situation was "explosive," and in Brikama Ba, "some of the villagers were out with sticks and axes."[74] Faced with real land bitterness, the Ministry of Agriculture and the local government passed the buck back and forth, neither willing or able to resolve land conflicts stemming from, and in part actually predating, the original lease. On the other hand, tenant farmers steadfastly refused to repay government credit. By the mid-1960s, the tractor plowing service was costing £24,000 per year, running at a significant annual loss, and at the mercy of indebted women tenants. More critically, the schemes in MacCarthy Island Division (M.I.D.) simply were not producing commercial surpluses. Rice imports grew rapidly after 1954, exceeding 10,000 tons per annum immediately prior to independence.

1966–1979, Mechanized Irrigation Revisited:
Small-Scale Perimeters and Double-Cropping

Rice import substitution entered a new phase in the 1960s in which the productivity and labor crises were to be resolved through (1) the development of small-scale mechanized production under full water control; and (2), the double cropping of high yielding, green revolution, varieties. Focused on the central and eastern swamp districts in which the river was fresh year-round, the small-scale perimeters of about 10 to 20 hectares in principle returned to the goals of CDC, namely, simultaneously revolutionizing the technical means of production by the deployment of small pumps, rototillers, and threshers and enhancing productivity by extending farm work into the slack dry season to capture male labor. The major difference now was that peasants controlled their own labor process and maintained direct use rights on newly leveled land that they helped to clear. Between 1966 and 1979, some 2,900 hectares of land were leveled and reclaimed for irrigation and some 311 irrigation associations or perimeters established, under three different auspices: the Taiwanese Agricultural Mission from 1966 to 1974; the World Bank from

1973 to 1976; and the People's Republic of China Mission from 1975 to 1979.[75] The organization of both missions and perimeters was heterogeneous but in general rested on the provision of water, fertilizer, pumps and fuel, seed, and rototiller services on credit, at heavily subsidized rates, estimated in 1981 to be between 60 and 80 percent for pumping and power tilling, to be repaid at harvest.

The history of these projects is too complex to be recounted here, but in summary, they failed to meet performance expectations. Cropping intensities were low,[76] productivities fluctuated wildly, and wet season yields were significantly lower than dry season (table 6.1). And while men were indeed induced into rice production, a new temporal division of labor emerged. Men worked in the paddies in the dry season but diverted their labor to the upland groundnut fields in the rains, while women predominated in new wet season rice fields they no longer controlled. By the late 1970s, large numbers of perimeters were effectively abandoned, and the growth of unpaid debt, most of which was systematically written off by the state, was astonishing (table 6.2). Sales of surplus rice to the Marketing Board were insignificant. The state proved incapable of ensuring the technical means to ensure double cropping, which led to constant fuel, spare parts, and credit crises,[77] and unable to regulate either the peasant labor process or surplus extraction. Rice producers successfully resisted being captured by the state. But insofar as the irrigation schemes generally failed to resolve their food deficits, peasants were captured by the market. The government instituted hard-line credit restrictions leading to the abandonment of more perimeters,[78] and the attendant struggles between state and rice producer were paralleled at the point of production by struggles between men and women over land and labor. As swamps were cleared for irrigation, women lost access to their customary rice lands, and the newly developed perimeters became new forms of property: male through rights of disposition,[79] and *de facto* freehold as flourishing rental and share cropping arrangements emerged.

Overall, this survey of rice production in The Gambia yields two important morals. The first is that the state completely failed to capture the rice surpluses of peasant producers and to control and discipline the labor of rice-growing households. This is reflected not only in the failure to radically expand production in the postwar period but also in the explicit resistance and orneriness of the peasants. Men were rarely seen in the paddy fields; women tenants regularly subverted state claims; and the mechanized schemes that began in the 1960s were distinguished not simply by low cropping intensities but also by the massive growth of debt that growers steadfastly refused to repay. This successive failure of rice

Table 6.1. Cropping intensity and rice purchases: Gambian irrigated perimeters, 1974–1984

Year	Area (ha) cultivated (wet)	% of total[a] reclaimed	Area (ha) cultivated (dry)	% of total reclaimed	Cropping intensity[b]	Total production (tons)	GPMB purchases[c] (tons)	% of total irrigated rice production
1974(W)/1975(D)	52.4	4	468.0	39	.43	2429.8	736	33.3
1975–76	46.8	4	848.79	71	.75	4332.29	543	12.5
1976–77	446.38	22	624.59	31	.53	4657.69	718	15.4
1977–78	62.45	3	706.4	35	.39	3124.44	1946	62.5
1978–79	70.64	3	730.8	37	.40	4111.95	2511	61.3
1979–80	73.08	3	1833.11	74	.77	9327.83	4314	46.2
1980–81	964.08	39	1875.67	76	1.15	15576.88	7854	50.5
1981–82	353.93	14	1010.83	41	.55	6755.67	4969	74.0
1982–83	54.28	2	810.04	33	.35	3511.42	n.d.	n.d.
1983–84	83.18	3	1021.48	41	.44	4500.00 (est.)	n.d.	n.d.

Source: Department of Agriculture, Banjul; University of Michigan, Gambia River Basin Studies, 1985, p. 173.
[a]The total development/reclaimed area was roughly 1,200 ha until 1976, 2,000 in 1976–1979, and 2,450 ha in 1980–1984.
[b]Full, i.e., double-cropping of the entire reclaimed area would yield a cropping intensity of 2.00.
[c]Official rice sales to the Gambia Produce Marketing Board.

175

Table 6.2. Farmer debt: ADP project, 1973–1976

		Statement of Loans Summary[a]			
Year	Production of paddy (tons)	Total due	Total repaid	Balance	% repaid
1973	n.d.	7,497.10	5,000.74	2,495.36	66.7
1974	582	60,011.88	19,766.85	40,245.03	32.9
1975	2,978	128,014.27	38,414.12	84,359.83	30.5
1976	3,678	165,077.03	0	0	0
Total	7,238	358,600.28	63,182.71	127,100.22	32.6

Source: Agriculture Development Program (ADP), Project Completion Report, IBRD/IDA, Banjul, May 1977.
[a]All figures in dalasis.

schemes to regulate the household labor process provides the broad canvas on which the Jahaly-Pacharr project, a centralized and regimented production system in which peasants are captured under contract, must be situated.

The second moral, less evident to functionaries, is the intensification of conflicts between family members over access to and control over domestic resources, specifically, swampland. Mandinka households held land under two broad forms: collective (*maruo*) fields on which family members are expected to work to provide domestic subsistence, the disposition of which the male head controls; and individual fields (*kamanyango*) that the head grants to family members for their own use and disposition. In other words, family members receive property and crop rights over a portion of the household patrimony in return for claims on their labor power. Mandinka women cultivate rice on both the individual and collective fields, but their usufructuary rights to *kamanyango* property are a central element of the conjugal contract. Colonial rice projects deepened latent tensions over swampland and more generally over the conjugal contract. Women, who provided the vast majority of labor in the colonial schemes, viewed new rice lands as a means to augment their *kamanyango* holdings, since swamp clearance traditionally confers ownership. Men resisted these claims not simply because expanded domestic rice production could reduce their obligations to purchase food but also because individual rights by women permitted their wives to sever a part of their labor from household control. In sum, individuation of rice lands threatened the patriarchal property-labor system. Men responded by claiming all new lands, reclaimed swamp or irrigated perimeters, as collective, subject to their control and disposition, and providing grounds for claims on domestic labor.

These intrahousehold conflicts became particularly vivid in the pump irrigation schemes, since double cropping introduced labor demands for which there were no customary arrangements. Men gained control of the irrigated plots through clearance and designated these holdings as collective, thereby drawing on female labor obligations. Women fulfilled their new *maruo* obligations during the dry season but withdrew to their own individual swamp fields during the wet season, resisting the efforts of their husbands to draw on their labor for two successive cropping seasons. Women contested claims over the definition of collective property and tenaciously clung to their *kamanyango* rights as a means to preserve their own autonomy.

Contracting Peasants and Producing Conflicts[80]

The Jahaly-Pacharr project, located in central Gambia near Sapu, 280 kilometers east of the nation's capital (see fig. 8.1), began operations in 1984, emerging from the ashes of the land-labor struggles and the poor performance of the earlier small-scale perimeters.[81] As dependence on imported rice continues to grow, the state has pioneered a new strategy based on the social integration of peasant households through contract production designed to secure double cropping and full repayment of production credit, the two Achilles' heels of the earlier schemes. The emergence of Jahaly-Pacharr as a new form of social integration of peasant production must be situated not only in relation to the uncaptured smallholders of the earlier irrigation efforts but also on the larger canvas of the internationalization of fordist production and "more mobile and flexible capitalist [and state] organization of production."[82] The insertion of agriculture into a new international division of labor is captured in the transition from peasant production socially integrated through the market to predominantly microeconomic and extramarket systems of control. Direct producers can, in other words, be integrated "personally" into agroindustrial or corporate entities—private or state—via contracts and institutional relations of vertical coordination between growers and capital.[83] Jahaly-Pacharr contracts peasants to grow double-cropped rice under conditions rigorously specified and regulated by the project management. The allocation of land rights was centralized through a thirty-year state appropriation and the use rights subsequently redistributed to growers in the form of long-term tenancies. This corporatist form integrates direct producers through sharecropping arrangements specified by project management who gains access to a peasant "labor market" in the absence of a landless class.[84] The contract contains different levels of direct control of the labor process; prices, delivery times, irrigation practices, and labor allocation and technology may all be determined by management.[85] But there are also hidden forms of control and subordination as sharecropping households are in effect self-policed—household members are less likely to shirk than wage laborers since they share in profits—and have the Chaynoavian capacity to work harder and longer, frequently with the assistance of child labor, to cheapen unit costs of production.

Completed in late 1987, the project involves over 2,000 rural households from seventy villages and relies on leasing out land, which gives it eviction as a strategy for subordination. Project officials set the rhythm for productive activities by establishing the calendar for cropping, weeding, transplanting, and harvesting as well as by specifying the application dates and types of seed varieties, fertilizers, and pesticides. The project's extension agents, who provide technical assistance, inform small holders of these decisions. Government's cooperatives market the project's paddy. The Jahaly-Pacharr project was predicated on the availability and intensification of family labor, but from its inception, the project anticipated that female labor would be critical to meeting its production targets:

Women are better than men as far as transplanting is concerned and they are also better than men as far as working in the water . . . so quite frankly we expect a lot of labour from women, more so than from men.[86]

In responding to a growing international sensitivity to the adverse consequences of development interventions for women, in particular, to the failure of previous Gambian irrigation schemes to reach women, the donors viewed Jahaly-Pacharr as an opportunity to promote equity objectives. Funders intended not only to integrate women into the project but also to make female growers its primary beneficiaries by awarding them access to irrigated plots. In practice, however, the project's potential threat to family property control in conjunction with its new production routines conflicted directly with these admirable objectives.

In keeping with the contractual conditions, the retention of plot usufruct on the Jahaly-Pacharr project depends on compliance with cropping schedules, production targets, and loan repayment. The new labor process, which rests on domestic labor but amplifies demands on household supply, has ensured that women skilled in rice growing become critical to fulfilling production targets.[87] Growers are under pressure to conform to a regimented work schedule, in which partial mechanization nonetheless rests on farm operations that are arduous and demanding. The labor intensity is reflected in the fact that under fully water-controlled conditions, rice production requires 60 percent more labor per unit of land then in traditional swamp production, even allowing for the deployment of machine plowing.[88] Since the onset of the project, men's wet season work has actually decreased, reflecting a shift in their labor time from upland crops to rice; conversely, women's total agricultural work has increased. Women's experience of mechanized rice production implies radically new claims on their bodies. Its enormously demanding work routines produce a commodity that they see as "women's sweat."

Project implementation has, nevertheless, placed Mandinka women in a particularly vulnerable position that transcends onerous work demands. The absorption of preexisting individual and household fields into the project restricted the ability of Mandinka women—the only ethnic group in The Gambia in which women have no individual crop rights on the uplands—to activate their crop rights, which now rest on access to the project's plots. Unless their extant property rights were protected, Mandinka women possessed no alternative cash-cropping plots in the project area and hence no protection from household claims over their labor. Women fully understood the erosion of a fundamental social right, namely, that a household member is compensated with an individual field in exchange for the labor they provide on household fields. The project's first land distribution revealed the centrality of property control in activating claims to female labor. Donors had specified, in fact, that the original female rice tillers were to receive title to the irrigated plots. This proved difficult to achieved since less than one-third of the plots were registered as women's property. As in previous rice schemes, men opposed women's ownership on the grounds that divorce would alienate land from household control. The project's failure to adhere to its primary objective prompted the major donor, the International Fund for Agricultural Development (IFAD), to intervene. In early 1984, a mission sent to The Gambia succeeded in reregistering the project's plots in women's names, and IFAD accordingly received widespread praise. But its emphasis on land registration obfuscated the real changes that had occurred in household property control.[89]

IFAD's reregistration was a "success" because male heads of household had already achieved *de facto* control. The project management concurred with male heads of household that the household, not the individual woman, should be granted final control over the fully irrigated plots. Officials invoked "tradition" for designating the developed area as household land, but their overriding concern was with productivity. Because the production routine requires the intensification of family labor, government officials were unwilling to champion principles that might reduce its availability. As a labor category, *maruo* alone provided the institutional base for claims within the household. The project mamagement allowed men to declare the plots *maruo,* with the result that "women not only end up growing the crops with technologies that result in lower net returns to their labor time but also exhibit lower average labor productivity."[90]

The importance of naming and classification in establishing control over both land and female labor soon became evident, as the work of Judith Carney has shown.[91] During the first cropping season, all the pumped plots were considered *maruo.* Women provided most of the labor, but household heads refused the customary *kamanyango* crop rights. By the second rainy season cropping period, when it became clear that women were not going to receive rights on the pumped plots, they began to press for official designation of the project's tidal and rain-fed areas as their individual fields.[92] Despite the earlier avowal of women's individual crop rights, management was reluctant to support these claims, nor did IFAD safeguard women's rights. Consequently, women were forced to negotiate for *kamanyango* crop rights through the same land entitlement institutions—the patriarchal village and household social structures—that sought to deny them.

Technological innovation and a restructuring of the labor process funda-mentally affected the micropolitics of the Mandinka household. Male heads manipulated crop and labor rights to expand their hegemony. Con-versely, women faced an attenuation of their customary rights or an actual loss of individual fields and additional labor claims. Von Braun and Webb estimate that the acquisition of an average-size plot of rice land in Jahaly-Pacharr results in an effective 22 percent "tax" on women. In the guise of communal food production, men also appropriated large investable sur-pluses.[93] This recomposition of labor and reclassification of property rights perturbed the architecture of the Mandinka household. In short, many of the new claims, new rights, and new obligations were contested on a variety of material, symbolic, and ideological terrains. Emotion and material interest arose from the same social matrix and, as David Sabean and Hans Medick point out, are deeply embedded in "property relations, working processes and the structure of domination."[94]

Struggles Over Land, Struggles Over Meaning

The issue is rather one of the on-going struggle over meaning. The struggle is formed in the context of the social relations of individuals, groups,

classes and cultures which at the same time are constituted by the struggle. Reciprocity, dependency and resistance . . . are not "structurally given" . . . they come into being only in the struggle for meaning.
—Hans Medick, "Missionaries in a Row Boat"

By the end of the first cropping season, women had received no *kamanyango* rights in the project. Neither had they been remunerated in cash or kind for their labor on the pumped plots. However, the importance of their labor to usufruct retention provided the basis for a struggle to improve women's position within the household. At the onset of the second year, women began to bargain and negotiate for remuneration from their husbands.[95] In doing so, they contested and renegotiated the basis of the conjugal contract, namely, the right of their husbands to control their labor power, thereby challenging patriarchal family relations and culturally dominant representations of gender.

According to Carney, three primary factors have conditioned women's bargaining for remuneration: (1) ethnicity; (2) the economic position of their household; and (3) the terms of conjugal relations. The primary factor was whether or not women retained access to individual fields. Project development did not radically transform the rights of Wolof and Serrahuli women who retained upland groundnut *kamanyango*. Like junior males, they may still withdraw their labor from the household during the rainy season, a consideration that enhanced their bargaining position. As a result, in households with land adequate to generate marketable surpluses, women generally received a share of the plot's paddy as labor remuneration.

The pattern is more complex and contradictory among the Mandinka, most of whose women lost their *kamanyango* fields with project development. The *maruo* designation left them without alternative land, rendering them vulnerable to their husband's efforts to capture their labor for commercial rice production. The struggles that Jahaly-Pacharr precipitated were over the degree to which females would bear the family work burden; that is, the conditions under which work is worth doing. Even though the Mandinka received more land than other ethnic groups, due to their dominance in preproject rice cultivation, the subordinate negotiating position of Mandinka women has constrained their capacity to negotiate compensation for new claims on their labor.

Carney's research near Sapu shows that by the end of the third cropping year, three sorts of resolution had occurred:[96]

1) The provision of labor by women as required on pump-irrigated plots and compensation through the usufruct of tidal-irrigated and rain-fed plots.

2) The provision of labor by women as needed on the pump-irrigated plots, and individual compensation in paddy, receiving a fixed share of the pumped plot's yield in return for their labor.
3) The withdrawal of female labor from the household *maruo*. The household head cannot, or refused to, offer labor remuneration in paddy via access to nonpumped plots.

In the first adaption, the households were usually resource-sufficient, controlling adequate project land for both subsistence and cash needs. Given that nearly seventy villages are involved in the Jahaly-Pacharr project and that tidal land was still being developed in January 1987, it is difficult to estimate the overall percentage of Mandinka households in the first category. In one village intensively surveyed by Carney,[97] which received land in both the pumped and nonpumped areas, women have received *kamanyango* rights to the tidal-irrigated plots. However, four considerations have shaped the impact of these acquisitions. First, one-hectare plots are characteristically not individually cultivated but are shared by several women. Second, in contrast to the pumped plots, the majority of tidal and all the rain-fed areas are cropped for one season only, which limits their income-generating possibilities. Third, these nonirrigated plots tend to be 40 percent less productive than the pump-irrigated areas.[98] Finally, a woman's *kamanyango* crop rights are protected while she remains in the household, but on divorce, she typically does lose control of them. *Kamanyango* usufruct to tidal and rain-fed plots provide Mandinka women with some form of labor compensation, but their labor productivity is 70 percent less than men, and their income-earning potential is accordingly reduced.

The second resolution was associated with households that had ample pump-irrigated land but little tidal or rain-fed land. Through the conjugal contract, women have sometimes successfully negotiated rudimentary sharecropping relations that reward them for their overall productivity. In exchange for their unrestricted labor on the pumped fields, women receive a fixed percentage of its yield. The percentage of households involved in this kind of arrangement in one village intensively surveyed by Carney was about 20 percent. The share women received averaged about 10 percent, with a paddy value that ranged between 150 to 500 dalasis per year (US$20–$70). However, most households fell within the third category, namely, women who were unsuccessful in receiving any form of compensation. In some cases, this was due to the households' land scarcity since 15 percent of the households did not receive project land. Frequently, they shared a plot with other households which was used primarily for subsistence rather than income generation. Material poverty and land shortage constrain women's ability to compensate for their *kamanyango* loss and have compelled them to pursue such other activities as hiring themselves out as wage laborers, cultivating market gardens, and/or engaging in petty trade. The impact of changing intrahousehold resource control on Mandinka women is most clearly visible in the majority of households, which have sufficient land for subsistence and cash needs but which have failed to remunerate women for work on household plots. Women, as a consequence, have withdrawn their labor from the rice fields, a development with far-reaching implications for households and project alike.

First, many households have experienced difficulty adhering to cropping schedules, which has contributed to lower yields. In the project's first year, average dry season pump-irrigated rice yields were 7.5 tons per hectare. In the 1985 and 1986 dry seasons, yields have averaged 5.7 tons. While the decline does not directly jeopardize the Jahaly-Pacharr project, it has reduced anticipated productivities and is the basis for the management's often-repeated remark that the Mandinka are poor and uncommitted growers. Second, female withdrawal has meant an intensification of male labor in rice cultivation.[99] But given the high rate of polygamous marriages in the project area, these men cannot guarantee that household labor covers all on-farm requirements. Hence, there has been a dramatic increase in labor hire by these households, particularly in the rainy season when men also plant groundnuts.[100] Even in the project's first year when women practiced remunerated work, only 25 percent of their village's households completed transplanting without hire labor. By its third year, when the impact of female labor withdrawal was felt, more than half the village's households were also hiring help for harvesting and threshing. For the 1986 cropping year, an average household spent between US$30 and $85 on hired labor, vastly in excess of project expectations. This closely approximates the value of paddy women receive in sharecropping arrangements. Female withdrawal has, in short, systematically undermined the capacity of the household to intensify its labor.

And third, most of the wage laborers in Mandinka villages are females whom the project has, in effect, proletarianized. That is to say, the project has *created a labor market* in which women are central. They now concentrate their economic activity on working for a wage on the project's plots, which in turn has contributed to an erosion of their reciprocal labor networks. Traditionally, village women's age grades (*kafos*) provide large labor groups for rice transplanting and generate income for common purposes such as financial assistance in time of need or for ceremonies. At other times, these reciprocal networks functioned as an auxiliary labor reserve for women who were sick, childbearing, or otherwise unable to go to the fields. The project's impact on the labor process is especially visible in the transformation and individualization of women's *kafos*. For females dispossessed of rice land and currently working for hire on the project's plots, the *kafos* now operate as gang labor or "companies." They provide an organizational framework in which women pool their labor for hire in transplanting, weeding, harvesting, or threshing. In contrast to the preproject period, the group no longer retains the money collected for mutual purposes but divides it up among participatory members as an individual wage. By working collectively, women actually receive a higher wage than they would as single workers. A group of twenty women usually charges 80 dalasis for transplanting one irrigated plot and typically can complete two plots per day. In this fashion, each woman receives 60 percent more than the prevailing daily wage rate.

These transformations of work, property rights, and labor entitlements are evidently material, but they are also simultaneously cultural and symbolic. The new labor process and its production politics can be situated on a larger cultural canvas colored by two dominant themes. The first pertains to the Mandinka notion of *semboo,* or "power/ capacity," the heart of which is labor power. A triad of interlinked core concepts shapes and defines the claims over labor within the domestic sphere: notions of ethical/community standards linked to broader patterns of Islamic ethics (*adoo*); historically sedimented traditions (*tarakuo*); and idiosyncratic customs (*dalikuo*). The concepts are distinguished in terms of the antiquity or heritage of certain cultural practices, by personal preferences, and by the canons of prevailing belief as articulated by elders. As A. F. Robertson observes,[101] these ideological tenets are invoked in the negotiations between hosts and strange farmers to determine the conditions of labor contracts. They are also increasingly visible in the confluence of production politics and conjugal bargaining among Mandinka growers. The second domain draws on an essential duality, the two moral axes of Mandinka domestic life, *badingya* and *fadingya,* which the new labor process has realigned. *Badingya* represents cooperation, obligation, and harmony; and *fadingya* connotes ambition, selfishness, conflict, and at the limit, a domestic or community anomie.[102] The oscillation between these poles naturally carries a strong cultural current but also an interpretive one. Whatever is normal or just, or simply "tradition," is established through discursive practice.

These two broad cultural domains bear on the new work conditions experienced by rice-growing households. The loss of the material basis of women's economic autonomy has produced the threat or actuality of labor withdrawal, a major contravention of *badingya* custom. Husbands and wives bargain over the share of rice women deserve from the irrigated plots, a domain in which there is in fact no customary practice. Domestic conflict can escalate in such circumstances, and divorce is commonly related to labor withdrawal by wives or renegotiations of the conjugal contract. Women take land claims to local courts when intrahousehold conflicts cannot be resolved, and men explicitly use surpluses accumulated from rice production for the acquisition of other wives to resolve the domestic labor crises. Accusations of infidelity have also surrounded the loss of female individual property and income: "There are some married women who take lovers. . . . It's all based on economics," noted a women from Kerewan Samba Sire.

In other words, the Jahaly-Pacharr project has animated this discursive realm and manufactured a sort of symbolic discontent. This is not surprising because every field is the site of a struggle over the definition of legitimate principles of its division. As Pierre Bourdieu remarks,

In the symbolic struggle over the production of common sense, or more precisely, *legitimate naming,* . . . agents engage the symbolic capital they have acquired in previous struggles . . . [that is] all the power they possess over instituted taxonomies.[103]

Local practices are largely instituted through language, but meanings are never fixed, and outside forces can often determine what is to be endowed with meaning. In the context of naming and the power to name, one can appreciate why in Mandinka society the naming of irrigated plots is so charged and so political. While it is within the language of everyday life that meaning is mobilized in the defense of domination, the outcome of struggles such as those initiated within Mandinka farming households is far from overdetermined. Not only may the wage relation have liberating consequences for women but more generally, culture contributes toward the creative, tense, and uncertain social reproduction of diverse kinds of relationships: "cultural reproduction always carries with it the possibility of producing . . . alternative outcomes."[104] The discontent manufactured by the Jahaly-Pacharr project suggests the beginnings of a subtle transgression that threatens the customary discipline of everyday domination. The politicization of women's communal labor groups, the presence of women on land allocation committees, the rumblings of juridical change, female deputations to government ministers, and the like, all suggest that, to use the words of Mariama Koita, a woman rice farmer from Kerewan Samba Sire, "[women] were asleep then. Now we are awake."

Conclusion

The labor demands of irrigated contracting in Jahaly-Pacharr have perturbed the internal structure of Mandinka households, exacerbating the
tensions and contradictions intrinsic to domestic social structure. As
Ellen Wood has suggested in quite different circumstances,[105] the external relations of coercion and discipline are concentrated within the
household and are inseparable from the day-to-day relations of the family. In this sense, the male household or *dabada* head becomes the
"agent of his own exploiter," converting the domestic terrain into an
arena of explicit contestation.[106] However, to fully understand this process requires prying open the black box of the household and examining
the circuits of economic, symbolic, and cultural capital that lie inside.
These internal circuits shape, and are shaped by, the ways in which
capital takes hold of agriculture.[107] As Berry notes in her discussion of
land rights in Africa,

State intervention to redefine conditions of access to land tends to provoke new
struggles over meaning and power which are as likely to inhibit growth . . . as to
release the productive energies of small-scale enterprise, market competition or
capitalist accumulation.[108]

The case of Jahaly-Pacharr reveals that the questions of land rights are
inseparable from a radically new labor process that has given rise to
contradictory, not to say conflictual, developments in the land-property
complex in Mandinka society. Further, it is entirely unclear whether
these contradictions, displacements, and conflicts are compatible with
the agricultural performance and the regimented work routines anticipated by project management.

A particularly compelling aspect of the Jahaly-Pacharr project is that
the external production relation between the household and management is *internalized* as a sharecropping relationship within the household
and specifically within the conjugal contract. The new labor process
imposed from without is, nevertheless, an object of domestic negotiation and bargaining, typically articulated in the idiom of customary
rights and obligations. Efforts to improve land productivity and transform land rights are always mediated by such local cultural idioms. But
as Keith Hart points out, agricultural intensification is about getting
people (women?) to work harder, and that usually requires coercion and
discipline.[109]

Whether one can actually produce a disciplined peasant "labor force"
or a quiescent female contract worker is, however, always an open issue.
The experience of irrigated rice production in The Gambia strongly

suggests that if technical innovation enhances labor productivity and returns to labor in relation to rain-fed crops such as groundnuts, then men will endeavor to take control of irrigated property even if women have prior land entitlements.[110] If successful, these male claims in effect transfer labor from personal, individually "owned" property to domains directly controlled by men in the name of collective goods and domestic security. Men attempted to wrestle control from women by manipulating various rights and obligations rooted in local development agencies. To the extent that women were able to contest male claims over land, their bargaining power was shaped by a variety of factors including women's access to land, the availability of nonhousehold labor and off-farm income, the "traditional" obligations associated with the conjugal relation, and the penalties for noncompliance. All of these negotiations and contestations speak powerfully to the robustness of individual rights in land in Africa and how these rights are themselves rooted in multiple and polyvalent social and cultural relations, which, to return to T. J. Clark, are regularly fought over as they are put to the test of social practice.

Notes

Most of the ideas in this paper have been developed in joint work with Judith Carney, whose field research I cite extensively. Some of the ideas presented here appear in J. Carney and M. Watts, "Manufacturing Dissent," *Africa* 60, 2 (1990): 207–241, and "Disciplining Women?" *Signs* 16, 41 (1991): 651–681.

1 F. Cooper, "From Free Labor to Family Allowances," *American Ethnologist* 16, 4 (1989): 745–765.
2 See M. Watts, *Silent Violence: Food, Famine, and Peasantry in Northern Nigeria* (Berkeley, 1983); L. Lennihan, "Rights in Men and Rights in Land," *Slavery and Abolition* 3 (1982): 111–139.
3 A. Phillips, *The Enigma of Colonialism: British Policy in West Africa* (London, 1989).
4 Public Records Office, London (PRO), CO 87/153, February 8th 1897.
5 Public Records Office, London (PRO), CO 87/164, August 8th 1901.
6 Cited in Phillips, *Enigma*, 72.
7 Cited in J. Dey, "Development Planning in The Gambia," *World Development* 10, 5 (1982): 377–396.
8 Phillips, *Enigma*, 78.
9 K. Marx, *Grundrisse* (London, 1973): 91.
10 S. Berry, "Concentration Without Privatization? Some Consequences of Changing Patterns of Land Control in Africa," in S. P. Reyna and R. E. Downs (eds.), *Land and Society in Contemporary Africa* (Hanover, 1988): 63.

11 Located in MacCarthy Island Division, Wallikunda is some 300 kilometers east of the capital, Banjul, in the middle river region.

12 The Gambia covers 10,000 square kilometers and is nominally part of a confederation with Senegal. Its current population is 695,000 (1983); 40% are Mandinka, the most numerous ethnic group.

13 Swamp rice refers to several traditional, nonintegrated, rice ecologies regulated by daily, monthly, or seasonal tides and by the presence of salinity that may extend at least 160 km upstream during the dry season (i.e., low volume) period.

14 National Archives (NAG), The Gambia, Banjul, File 2/3313, n.d.

15 T. J. Clark, *The Painting of Modern Life* (New York, 1984).

16 R. Bates, "The Agrarian Origins of Mau Mau," *Agricultural History* 61 (1987): 1–28.

17 M. Burawoy, *The Politics of Production* (London, 1985).

18 See, for example, J. S. Whitaker, *How Can Africa Survive?* (New York, 1988); A. Hansen and D. McMillan (eds.), *Food in Sub-Saharan Africa* (Boulder, 1986); P. Lawrence (ed.), *World Recession and the Food Crisis in Africa* (London, 1986).

19 See A. Jeng, "An Economic History of the Gambian Groundnut Industry, 1830–1924: The Evolution of an Export Economy" (Ph.D. diss., University of Birmingham, 1987); H. Barett, *The Marketing of Foodstuffs in The Gambia 1400–1980* (Avebury, 1988).

20 C. Okali, *Cocoa and Kinship in Ghana* (London, 1983).

21 See J. Guyer and P. Peters, "Introduction to Conceptualizing the Household: Issues of Theory and Policy in Africa," *Development and Change* 18, 3 (1987):197–214; see also H. Friedman, "Patriarchy and Property," *Sociologica Ruralis* 26, 2 (1986):186–193. 192ff.; J. Gubrium, "The Family as Project," *The Sociological Review* 36, 2 (1988):273–296.

22 R. Brenner, "Social Basis of Economic Development," in J. Roemer (ed.), *Analytical Marxism* (Cambridge, 1985): 23–53.

23 Ibid., 47.

24 This is the focus of the so-called labor process debate. For a good overview, see S. Wood, "The Deskilling Debate, New Technology and Work Organization," *Acta Sociologia* 30 (1987): 3–24.

25 The research in The Gambia was supported by the Center for Research on Economic Development, University of Michigan, Ann Arbor. A part of the argument developed in the second part of this chapter appears in M. Watts and J. Carney, "Disciplining Women?" I am particularly indebted to Carney's work, cited in the text, which was also conducted under the auspices of the University of Michigan project. This chapter is a condensation of a larger historical study: M. Watts, *Manufacturing Dissent: Production Politics and Rice in The Gambia,* forthcoming.

26 J. Scott, "Resistance Without Protest and Without Organization," *Comparative Studies in Society and History* 29 (1987): 434.

27 H. Moore, *Space, Text and Gender: An Anthropological Study on the Marakwet of Kenya* (Cambridge, 1986).

28 Ibid., 185.
29 O. Linares, "Cash Crops and Gender Constructs: The Jola of Senegal," *Ethnology* 24, 2 (1985): 83–94.
30 Rhodes House, Mss. Afr.s 945, Oxford University, n.d.
31 Public Records Office, London (PRO), CO 87/10, Rendall to Hay, 1834; see also D. Gamble, *Contributions to a Socio-Economic Survey of The Gambia* (London, 1949).
32 K. Swindell, *Strange Farmers of The Gambia: A Study of the Redistribution of an African Population* (Swansea, 1981), Centre for Development Studies, Monograph no. 15; A. F. Robertson, *The Dynamics of Productive Relationships: African Share Contracts in Comparative Perspective* (Cambridge, 1987).
33 "An alarming scarcity of foodstuffs have this year struck considerable parts of the river . . . on account of their neglect of the rice and corn fields": PRO 87/64, 1857.
34 This specialization occurred much earlier than Swindell suggests when he notes that foodstuffs were giving way to groundnuts "by the end of the nineteenth century": K. Swindell, "Searwoolies, Tillibunkas and Strange Farmers," *Journal of African History* XXI, 1 (1980): 102. In the 1861 *Annual Report,* Governor D'Arcy noted, "The Baddibu people . . . rarely . . . grow . . . sufficient food to feed themselves." PRO CO.
35 See Jeng, *An Economic History,* chap. 2.
36 Donelha observed women selling rice as early as 1585 at port markets along the Gambia River: A. Donehla, *An Account of Sierra Leone and the Rivers of Guinea of Cape Verde* (Lisbon: Junta de Investigaçoes Cientificasdo Ultimar, 1977): 149. Moore is explicit that in the early eighteenth century, rice was "their [women's] own property," sold after "they have set by a sufficient quantify for family use" (139–140). See F. Moore, *Travels in the Inland Parts of Africa* (London, 1738).
37 K. Blackburne et al., *Development and Welfare in The Gambia* (Dathurst. Government Printer, 1943): 4.
38 Robertson states that food imports began in The Gambia in 1867, whereas rice imports appear in the record in 1836; see Robertson, *The Dyamics,* 210. For observations on the food demands of strange farmers, see *Proceedings of the Third Conference of Protectorate Chiefs,* Sessional Paper no. 1, Bathurst, Government Printer (1946).
39 From 1835 to independence in 1965, the source of rice imports was never stable over the period 1835–1965. In the 1840s, a considerable quantity came from West Africa and thereafter from France, Germany, and Britain. During and after the First World War, the U.S. supply was dominant, superseded in the 1920s by France and in the 1930s by India and Burma. In the postwar period, Asian and U.S. rice has predominated.
40 PRO CO 87/69, D'Arcy to Newcastle, 1860.
41 PRO CO 87/220, Arbitrage Minute, 1921.
42 Through the 1920s, for example, strange farmers constituted on average 60% of the permanently resident adult population in Upper River Division,

accounting for roughly £18,000 of staple foodstuff imports per season. See Rhodes Houses Micr. Afr. 485 Confidential Diary, Travelling Commissioner, June 1925, and URD Annual Report, 1929.

43 PRO CO 87/45, MacDonnell to Grey, 1849.

44 "Nearly every person is in debt. . . . People who are in debt are running away. . . . I get more depressed every year over the [rice] debt." Rhodes House, Micr.Afr.485, Travelling Commissioner Whitehead, Southbank Diary, January 1921.

45 J. Carney, "The Social History of Gambian Rice Production: An Analysis of Food Security Strategies," (Ph.D. diss., University of California, Berkeley, 1986).

46 NAG 52:47/50, Department of Agriculture Files, Agriculture Extract (Banjul: National Archive, The Gambia, 1943).

47 J. E. Y. Hardcastle, *A Report on a Visit to The Gambia and Senegal,* Rokpur, Sierra Leone: West African Rice Research Station (1961); also, NAG 2/961, correspondence between Governor Denham to Lord Passfield, Secretary of State for the Colonies, Banjul: NAG, 10 October (1929).

48 G. M. Rodden, *A Report on Rice Cultivation in The Gambia,* Sessional Paper no. 2 (Banjul: NAG, 1943).

49 M. R. Haswell, *The Changing Patterns of Economic Activity in a Gambian Village,* Department of Technical Cooperation, Overseas Research Publication no. 2 (London, 1963); P. Weil, "Wet Rice, Women, and Adaptation in The Gambia," *Rural Africana* 19 (1973): 20–29.

50 "In view of the serious shortage of imported foodstuffs . . . which is likely to result from the spread of war, I have been considering the possibility of increased local production of food crops." NAG 2/3243 R/109 Report on Rice Cultivation, 1942.

51 Rae's report made a similar, and more sophisticated, argument. Roddan labored under the false assumption that rice production in The Gambia began in 1890 and that mangrove rice was only ten years old. *The Rae Report,* NAG 2/161445/29, "Irrigation" (1945).

52 The war transformed The Gambia from a parochial, forgotten place to a military and intelligence base; "it was the period when one went on tour with a brass band, and office messengers hidden in French commandant bedrooms, when one returned from an evening stroll to find a squadron of Polish air force officers on the verandah . . . when every wharftown rogue was on the payroll as a secret agent . . . when letters were concealed in pots of marmalade." D. Bayley, Diary, 315, Rhodes House Mss. Afr.s.47.

53 In central and lower Baddibu, peasants survived (?) on one meal per day between June and harvest. See Cohen Papers, Rhodes House, Mss. Afr.s.727, 1946, 14.

54 NAG 2/2527, F/76, 1947.

55 Including a bizarre local rice cup awarded to the chief and NA with most men in rice production. See "Report of the Department of Development and Agriculture" (Bathurst, Government Printer, 1953): 3–4.

56 C. van der Plas, *Report of a Survey of Rice Areas in the Central Division of the Gambian Protectorate* (Bathurst: Government Printer, 1957). NAG 9/331 SECOM NA 33 vol.1, 1945.
57 M. Haswell, *The Changing Pattern of Economic Activity in a Gambian Village* (London, 1963), Overseas Research Publication no. 2.
58 See van der Plas, *Report,* 14; also Rhodes House, 720.14.s., 1964, Rice Marketing, V. Nasta, 1964.
59 *The Rae Report,* 6.
60 Senior Agriculture Superintendent, February 1942, NAG 47/50 D230/1943, Rice Cultivation in The Gambia, 3. An ecstatic commissioner observed in September 1946 that he had spotted "the first Gambian rice farmer of the male sex" in Basse: NAG 47/40 A137/1940, Development of Irrigation Areas.
61 M. Cowen, "The Early Years of the Colonial Development Corporation," *African Affairs* 83, 330 (1984): 63–75; NAG 2/4342, R/108 Vol. II, 1947.
62 NAG 2/3240, 1948, Clark and Hutchinson, West Africa Rice Mission Report.
63 NAG 2/3250, Wright to Creech Jones, March 9, 1949.
64 NAG R108A 1950.
65 NAG 9/87 85C/11 CDC Rice Scheme at Willikunda, 1952. The £3,000 compensation came from the Fulladu West Treasury and the Farmers Fund.
66 NAG 9/87 85C/11 1951.
67 NAG 38/3 1958.
68 NAG R/393C 1958.
69 Gambia Rice Farm Annual Report, 1954, J. Gillespie, 3, Commonwealth Development Corporation, London.
70 Ibid., 3.
71 Ibid., 4.
72 NAG 2/3313 R/293a Vol.I, 1954.
73 See Watts, *Production Politics,* chap. 4.
74 Department of Agriculture, Banjul, File AD/POL 12, 1966.
75 This section draws on field research in The Gambia and on J. Dey, "Gambian Women and Rice in The Gambia" (Ph.D. diss., Reading University, 1980); J. Carney, "Social History"; A. Kargbo, "An Economic Analysis of Rice Production Systems and Production Organization of Rice Farmers in The Gambia" (Ph.D. diss., Michigan State University, 1983); and D. Brautigam, "Chinese Agricultural Aid to West Africa" (Ph.D. diss., Tufts University 1987).
76 Most of the perimeters that were double cropped every season over the 1980–1983 period were one- or two-man operations, i.e., belonged to wealthy "agrarian capitalists."
77 Walking through a Gambian perimeter, littered with pumps from Shanghai, rototillers from Bremen, threshers from Taipei, and combines from Britain is a mechanic's nightmare.
78 Over the period 1980–1983, 40% of the perimeters had been cropped for only one season or less.
79 Dey's study (1980:280) shows that more than two-thirds of rice land was designated as collective.

80 This section draws heavily on the published work of Judith Carney and Patrick Webb. See J. Carney, "Struggles over Land and Crops in an Irrigated Rice Scheme: The Gambia," in J. Davison (ed.), *Agriculture, Women and Land: The African Experience* (Boulder, 1988): 59–78; J. Carney, "Struggles over Crop Rights and Labor with Contract Farming Households in a Gambian Irrigated Rice Project," *Journal of Peasant Studies* 15 (1988): 334–349; Patrick Webb, "Intrahousehold Decision Making and Resource Control," IFRPI Working Paper no. 3 (Washington, D.C., 1989). Parts of this section of the paper appear in Carney and Watts, "Disciplining Women?" and Carney and Watts, "Manufacturing Dissent."

81 See Carney, "Struggles over Crop Rights," and Carney and Watts, "Manufacturing Dissent."

82 S. Sanderson, *The Transformation of Mexican Agriculture: International Structure and the Politics of Rural Change* (Princeton, 1986): 17. See also M. Storper and A. Scott (eds.), *Production, Work and Territory* (London, 1986); M. Watts, "Peasants under Contract," in H. Bernstein, et. al. (eds.), *The Food Question: Profits vs. People* (New York, 1990): 149–162.

83 K. Vergopolous, "The End of Agribusiness or the Emergence of Bio-technology?" *Journal of International Social Science* 37 (1985): 389–400. Contract farming is a form of vertical integration between growers and buyers/processors which directly shapes the production process. It has three aspects: a futures market, the linkage of factor and product markets, and the differential allocation of production and market risk. The formality of the contract varies widely, but contracting has been central to U.S. agriculture since the 1930s, especially for commodities with high perishability or high quality standards. See M. Watts, *Contract Farming in Africa,* Working Paper no. 1, Institute of Development Anthropology (Binghamton, N.Y., 1985).

84 D. Lehmann, "Sharecropping and Capitalist Transition in Agriculture," *Journal of Development Economics* 23 (1986): 333–354.

85 J. Davis, "Capitalist Agricultural Development and Exploitation of the Propertied Laborer," in F. Buttel and H. Newby (eds.), *The Rural Sociology of Advanced Societies: Critical Perspectives* (London, 1980).

86 Quoted by the project manager in the BBC film, *The Lost Harvest,* 1983.

87 The project plan underestimated the labor demands of their irrigation routines by almost one-third, which made nonsense of their claims that with the limited exception of November, all farm labor could be met easily from within the family household.

88 J. von Braun and P. Webb, "The Impact of New Crop Technology on the Agricultural Division of Labor in a West African Setting," *Economic Development and Cultural Change* 37, 3 (1989): 513–534. See also J. von Braun and K. Johm, *Trade-offs in the Rapid Commercialization of Smallholder Rice Production in The Gambia* (Washington, D.C., 1987), IFPRI; J. von Braun and P. Webb, *Effects of New Agricultural Technology and Commercialization on Women Farmers in a West African Setting* (Washington, D.C., 1987), IFPRI.

89 Von Braun and Webb, "The Impact," 524. Note that only 10% of project pump-irrigated plots were "under women's control."

90 Ibid., 525.

91 J. Carney, "Contracting a Food Staple in the Gambia," in P. Little and M. Watts (eds.), *Living Under Contract,* forthcoming.

92 The Jahaly-Pacharr project involved the improvement of traditional rice swamps whether tidal or rain-fed.

93 Von Braun and Webb argue that new male-controlled rice fields are "mainly used" for communal consumption and ignore the use of "communal" rice for individual accumulation. The decline in marketed surplus of rice (as percent of production) as women's share of rice land is reduced (529) is a spurious relation because the *volume* of rice sold from highly productive irrigated plots is very substantial (and accrues to the male head); see von Braun and Webb, "The Impact." For a discussion of male investable surpluses, see Carney and Watts, "Manufacturing Dissent."

94 H. Medick and D. Sabean, Introduction, in H. Medick and D. Sabean (eds.), *Interest and Emotion* (Cambridge, 1984): 4.

95 Von Braun and Webb see the household as a "mini-state" subject to rent seeking and taxation. In my view, this fundamentally misunderstands the dynamics of patriarchal and domestic power. They simply see an inevitable process of "centralization" (531) and captitulation, rather than regotiation, struggle, and multiple resolutions. See von Braun and Webb, "The Impact."

96 See J. Carney, "Contract Farming in Irrigated Rice Production," Working Paper no. 9, Institute of Development Anthropology (Binghamton, N.Y., 1987).

97 Ibid.

98 Von Braun and Webb "The Impact," 524.

99 In the ten villages studied by von Braun and Webb, 51% of on-farm labor in the irrigated plots was provided by men. See ibid., 518.

100 Twenty-six percent of all pump-irrigated labor was hired. Ibid., 518.

101 See Robertson, *The Dynamics,* 252–254.

102 See D. Gamble, *Economic Conditions in Two Mandinka Villages* (London, 1955); also J. Dey, *Gambian Women,* chap. 4.

103 P. Bourdieu, "The Social Space and the Genesis of Groups," *Theory and Society* 14 (1985): 731–732.

104 P. Willis, *Learning to Labor* (New York, 1981): 172.

105 E. M. Wood, "Capitalism and Human Emancipation," *New Left Review* 167 (1988): 1–21.

106 Ibid., 16.

107 K. Kautsky, *La Question Agraire* (Paris, 1906).

108 S. Berry, "Concentration without Privatization."

109 K. Hart, *The Political Economy,* 48.

110 See also J. Dey, "Gender Issues in Irrigation Project Design in Sub-Saharan Africa," in *Design for Sustainable Farmer Managed Irrigation Schemes in Sub-Saharan Africa,* vol. 1 (Wageningen: Department of Irrigation and Soil and Water Conservation, 1990), n.p.

7 *Fiona Mackenzie*

"A Piece of Land Never Shrinks": Reconceptualizing Land Tenure in a Smallholding District, Kenya

013 Q 15

Gicigo kia mugunda gitinyihaga
A piece of land never shrinks.
    —Kikuyu proverb

Kenya

Introduction

In the early 1980s, the Murang'a District Farmers' Cooperative Union decided to encourage its members to open joint accounts at its four Savings and Credit Sections. The move was a direct response to the declining quality of coffee production among smallholders[1] in the district.[2] Women farmers and, more recently, the union attribute this decline in high-quality coffee to the mode of remuneration[3] for the commodity.

Coffee was introduced in Murang'a during the "Emergency" of the 1950s when migrant men had been forcibly returned to the "reserve," and it was to them that the crop was directed. Despite this, the administrative record shows how production relied increasingly on women's labor. Shortly after independence, for example, the district agricultural officer estimated that of the 26,000 coffee growers in Murang'a in 1965, 16,000 were female, that is, were in sole charge of the crop.[4] In the present context of far higher levels of male out-migration, reaching over 60 percent of male household heads in some locations, the proportion of women solely responsible for coffee production has increased considerably.

As marketing for the crop is organized through sixteen local coffee societies of the union, payment is made to the shareholders, who are overwhelmingly male. In two societies for which data were collected in

194

1984, only 16.8 percent of the membership in Irati and 10.1 percent in Njora were female.[5] Evidence from interviews with women farmers in the district indicates widespread dissatisfaction as, responsible for the majority of the crop, they nevertheless depend on their husbands for remuneration for their labor. Such remuneration has frequently been unreliable and not commensurate with their labor input.

In many cases, women respond by withdrawing their labor from coffee production,[6] directing their energies elsewhere. Often, women sell their labor individually or in groups locally to other smallholders or travel daily to the coffee estates of Makuyu Division or Kandara Division. In both situations, they have immediate access to daily wages and thus greater control over their labor power. In recognition of this situation, the union has encouraged joint accounts as a significant step in facilitating women's control over the proceeds of their labor.

The link between agricultural productivity and mode of remuneration is clear as far as coffee production is concerned in Murang'a. The more general relationship between access to and control over land and productivity is less salient, although analysis elsewhere in Kenya alludes to this relationship.[7] Research into the question is embryonic, although Christine Jones, Jennie Dey, Judith Carney, and Michael Watts all cite evidence of the relationship between productivity and intrahousehold relations, thus connecting gender rights of access to and control over the means of production at the household level with the wider political economy.[8]

The lack of data from Murang'a does not allow me to address directly the relationship between agricultural productivity and security of access to land. But I propose as an initial step in this direction to explore the nature of insecurity of access to and control over rights to land, which Carney and Watts have shown to be closely linked to productivity in the case of rice.[9] Through the analysis of case histories collected from women and men in thirty-two households in Murang'a District, Central Province, in 1984, this chapter will, first, illustrate the nature of contemporary struggle vis-à-vis the land at the intrahousehold level; second, suggest a reconceptualization of rights to land in Kenya which gives visibility to the processes of both "class" and gender differentiation; and third, identify antecedents to the present struggle in order to place the instances of contemporary discourse over land in a historical context.

A key intention in the chapter is to challenge conceptualizations of gender and land tenure in Kenya that view "customary" rights to land as extinguished with the introduction of freehold tenure and the registration of individual title in the 1950s. Instead, I will suggest that an analytical framework based on the notion of legal pluralism, where both customary law and statutory law are conceived as arenas of struggle to which both men and women have access, is useful heuristically in untangling gender-differentiated rights of access to and control over land.

Instances of Contemporary Struggle

The first case concerns A.N.K.,[10] a professional nurse residing in Murang'a District. She concluded her discussion of her long struggle to obtain land with the words, "For a woman to be fully independent, she must understand the need to be strongly joined in [i.e., connected to] her family." She was referring to her natal family and the symbolic significance of her father's recent decision to register 0.4 hectare (1 acre) of his smallholding in the names of herself and her three sisters. The remainder of the holding, 4.5 hectares, would be inherited, following Kikuyu practice, by her two brothers. To her, the decision, which would guarantee "a refuge" in the event of marital breakdown, directly challenged an ideology of territorial control based on the patrilineally defined subclan, or *mbari,* the basic unit of Kikuyu society.

Her experience as a married woman who had given birth only to daughters and whose husband had on several occasions undermined her professional career had led her to recognize the insecurity of gaining access to land through her husband. On their marriage twenty-five years ago, her husband's father allocated 3.4 hectares of land that he subsequently registered in his name under the system of freehold tenure introduced in Murang'a in the 1950s. The later addition of 1.2 hectares to their holdings, purchased on the basis of their joint contributions, was similarly registered, at his insistence, in his name.

A.N.K. has managed to save money on her own, a difficult task carried out over a long period of time, and with this she has now purchased 0.6 hectares of her own. She relied on her father to negotiate the land for her. Her husband has now learned about this purchase and continues to express bitterness about it. Registration of land in her name, she contests, will allow her to pass land on to her daughters, which would otherwise not be guaranteed. On the death of her husband, failing a direct male heir, a brother of her husband could lay claim to the land on the basis of "customary practice," legitimating the claim in the *mbari* on grounds of territorial integrity.

The second case concerns W.G., an elderly woman who chose to "marry" a woman on her husband's death. Referring to this practice of a woman opting to become a female husband,[11] one elderly woman in Murang'a stated, "Some of these women are very cunning and they don't want their husband's brothers to inherit the land, and so they are forced to marry another woman."

W.G. acted with her husband's agreement to prevent his stepbrother from "snatching" their holding of 5.6 hectares. Of her seven children, four had died, leaving three daughters. Thus she faced the loss of land to a brother-in-law. On her marriage as a female husband, she prevented this action. She divided the land that was now registered in her name between herself and her wife, Wanjiku. This was entered as a mutation in the Land Registry. On the occasion of the marriages of two of Wanjiku's three sons, W.G. registered a portion of the land in their respective names.

Retaining title to much of the land in her name and her refusal to allow Wanjiku to give land to her daughter were among the reasons leading to disagreement between the two women. W.G. would like to give land to one of her own daughters, who although married, lacks it. But it has been an uphill battle to retain her husband's land in her own name even with a "wife" and sons, as her husband's brother has relentlessly and bitterly contested her rights to it. The latter had previously sold his inheritance and is now trying to regain land on the basis of *mbari* territorial solidarity.

In the two cases identified above, women with above average access[12] to what Claire Robertson and Iris Berger[13] have named "critical resources" have engaged in the struggle over land on the basis of sets of rights accorded under different legal regimes. A.N.K., through savings from salaried employment, has been able to purchase land. That such a move is relentlessly disputed was evident among several of the women interviewed. Land purchase, while not restricted to the salariat, is clearly more open as an option for this class. The compilation of data on land transactions from Presentation Books[14] dating from 1958 to 1984 in Murang'a suggests that since 1969 approximately 12 percent of land purchases have been made by women. The percentage of women who at present own land, in the sense of holding title deed, is unknown. Jean Davison's study involving 101 women in Mutira Location in Kirinyaga District, Central Province, indicates that the percentage remains very small (none of her sample indicated owning land).[15]

A very recent phenomenon, and again illustrative both of the degree of stress in this rural area and of intrahousehold conflict, is the recent purchase of land by two women's groups. For example, the Utheri wa Methi group in Makuyu, begun in 1981 with eighty members, purchased 16 hectares of land in this division, allotting 0.2 hectare per member for individual production. The land is registered in the group's name. The community development officer, Kandara Division, indicated (in 1984) that his office insisted on group ownership "in order to protect the women's interest."[16] Initiatives to purchase land have also been noted by Davison in the case of two women's groups in Chwele Sublocation, Bungoma District, Western Province.[17]

In part, legitimation of these actions on the part of women's groups is achieved through the recent idiom of the national ideology of *harambee* (literally, pull together). In part, women are drawing on previous modes of local sex-specific organizations such as *ngwatio,* a reciprocal labor arrangement. Membership in women's groups is drawn from all classes of rural society, but there is heavier representation from lower socioeconomic strata.[18] Women are acutely aware that while membership within a group allows them to achieve the necessary solidarity to address the economic and ideological contradictions they face as individuals,[19] they also need community support for their continued existence. Hence the groups engage in community activities such as the construction of cattle dips or nursery schools. There is a widespread concern among members, as pervasive as a consciousness of the contradictions that they face, not to destroy the fabric of society. A women's group leader in Mitero, Kiambu District, to the immediate south of Murang'a, quoted by Patricia Stamp, identifies the issue as follows:

How does a man exercise power as head of the home? So he has to try all means to suppress women's group activity, to make it not succeed. . . . We try not to be too aggressive, or to break the link with the family or even community. We can't expect to break that myth right away—it must be gradual. If you want to change it abruptly, you encounter a stronger resistance.[20]

In the cases of group land purchase in Murang'a, the land concerned entered the market after the subdivision of large farms in Makuyu Division, that is, from the estate sector. The different history of the area, its alienation as European land distinct from the Kikuyu Reserve[21] to which the rest of Murang'a belongs, means that there is more immediate territorial ambiguity in the purchase of land in Makuyu than in the other four divisions of Murang'a. Land in Makuyu does not belong to individual men with subclan, and thus territorial, affiliation. For this reason, land purchase may be easier here than elsewhere in the district.

In contrast to the case of A.N.K., W.G. fights for her rights to land on the basis of customary law. Although not common, manipulation of the practice of female husband has allowed some women to maintain autonomy vis-à-vis their husband's subclan, or *mbari*, in terms of rights to land, although the battle has been an ongoing one.

Other individuals illustrate a less successful outcome of struggle. For example, K.W.W., a widow, obtained title deed to the land she had cultivated in the coffee zone of Murang'a on the death of her husband. As she grew older and less able to work the smallholding, she divided it among her three married daughters, although retaining title herself. The married daughters do not live far away, and although they have land at their respective husband's places, until 1982 they also cultivated their mother's land.

In 1982, the daughters were forced off the land by K.W.W.'s deceased husband's elder brother who sold his own land shortly after consolidation in the 1950s and lacks any for his two sons. He has moved onto the land he considers his by right of customary inheritance practice and has divided it between his sons. K.W.W. has so far refused to give him title, but she does not have the "strength", that is, the financial resources, to go to court. Her husband's *mbari* is at least tacitly accepting a fait accompli. Without support of the *mbari* or access to legal council, she is unable to exercise the authority generally conferred to the holder of a title deed.

In a fourth case, the subclan or *mbari* has taken a more active role in preventing a woman from exercising authority over the land. This case, in 1984 before the High Court of Kenya in Nairobi, is between a woman who on her husband's death fourteen years ago assumed title to the 1.8 hectares she had farmed and a faction of her husband's clan which supports her brother-in-law's claim to the land on the basis of customary inheritance procedures. B.K., the widow, wishes to divide the holding between her two unmarried daughters. Fearing that on the possible future marriage of the daughters the land would pass to an outsider, a faction of the *mbari* is insisting that land be "returned to the *mbari*." In both this case and the third cited above, individual men have sought or assume *mbari* support in their claims on the basis of *mbari* territoriality and the customary practice of inheritance. And it may be argued that although *mbari* territoriality has been an integral component of *mbari* social and political organization since the Kikuyu moved into this part of the Kikuyu plateau in the 1600s,[22] land shortage has magnified its significance. Women's rights to dispose of land when they hold the title deed are clearly contested when they threaten loss of *mbari* territory. Where a woman, acting essentially as a "caretaker," holds title to the land until the marriage of sons, thus ensuring that patrilineal inheritance resumes, and *mbari* territorial control is not threatened, no dispute arises.

But women's customary rights to land, centering on usufruct, are also under threat from another source. Illustrative of a process of increasing polarization of land distribution, land sales increased dramatically between 1963 and 1982.[23] The courts of chiefs and subchiefs during the latter half of the 1970s and into the 1980s were, as a result, assailed by women unable to support themselves or their children, the land on which they had lived having been sold, often without their prior knowledge. In 1982, Charles Njonjo, in his capacity as attorney general, sent a directive to the land boards reminding them that all adult members of the household of the person selling the land were to be present at the hearing to indicate their agreement with the sale. The directive curbed the number of registered sales,[24] but the rapid increase in land transactions described as "gifts" in the Presentation Books had increased substantially by 1984. As "gifts" do not require the sanction of a land board, they may represent a circumvention of the directive.

Language, Laws, and Legitimation

The cases above suggest that women and men engage in a struggle over rights to land in two distinct legal spheres,[25] the one pertaining to "customary law," the other to statutory law. This conceptualization of tenure rights contrasts with that of Davison and Achola Pala Okeyo.[26] Both of the latter assume that customary rights under preexisting tenure systems were displaced with the "land reform" introduced under the Swynnerton Plan of 1954, which thereby reduced women to a state of dependency on their husbands. No longer were their usufruct rights guaranteed by the lineage. Okeyo, drawing on her survey of 135 lineage wives in Kisumu and South Nyanza, documents the "impact" of the registration of individual title to land on women. In practice, she writes,

these women would probably still enjoy their cultivation rights to land as lineage wives, but the status that guarantees their rights is being superseded by the new stipulation which gives individual men the right to alienate the land from which their female relatives (wives, mothers and sisters) expect to draw their livelihood for several years to come.[27]

Only 5.9 percent of the women in her sample had land registered in their own names.

Davison and Okeyo attribute women's insecurity to the institutionalization of freehold tenure, under which system previously allocative rights were equated with individual registerable ownership. Jean Hay notes that as a result of individual male control of the land, women perceive tenure reform as a threat rather than an opportunity.[28] But what I argue here is that insecurity results rather from the contradictions that arise from the contest of rights over land by individuals drawing on two different sets of legal rights, which interact with each other. In short, customary rights cannot be assumed to have been extinguished after 1954.

Soon after the completion of land registration in Kiambu, Central Province, Derek Homan questioned whether customary land rights were subsumed to the new legal system. He observed that the Land Register "was gradually ceasing to reflect the true state of affairs on the ground,"[29] a circumstance he attributed to the continuity of customary practices of patrilineal inheritance. More recently, Angelique Haugerud's study of two agroeconomic zones in Embu confirmed Homan's findings and illustrated further that the increasing contradiction between de jure and de facto rights to land was exacerbated by the fragmentation of holdings within and between ecological zones as households adopted risk-minimizing strategies.[30] In both areas, as in Murang'a, individualization of holdings had preceded land tenure reform by several decades, a circumstance that Gavin Kitching explores in depth as he relates how migrant males' differential access to nonfarm income was invested in land and led to increasing differentiation in rural society.[31]

But I would like to suggest that the "customary rights" to which writers such as Homan and Haugerud refer were not static, ahistorical, or autonomous, the product of a "self-contained particularity."[32] Nor are they purely an imperial construct, a "simulacrum" contained by the state or capitalist mode of production,[33] fixed or frozen through the colonial project as Francis Snyder and Martin Chanock portray.[34] Rather, to follow the conceptualization of David Parkin, Jack Glazier, and Sally Falk Moore, "customary law" and "customary rights" refer to a continuing domain of discourse or an arena of struggle.[35] In a situation of legal pluralism, customary law becomes one of the legal spheres to which disputants have recourse.[36]

Chanock's analysis in colonial Malawi and Zambia builds on Snyder's earlier observations of customary law in Sénégal which challenged notions of historical continuity.[37] Snyder argued that customary law "resulted from a particular conjunction of class forces and ideologies mediated through the colonial state, and that this law simultaneously masked and contributed to a struggle over power and over rural conditions of production."[38] It was an "ideology of colonial domination" achieved, in the land case of the 1950s cited, through the confluence of interests of the court's principal interpreter, a "chef de province traditional," and of the colonial administrators.

Chanock develops this perspective by focusing on the institutional processes through which customary law emerged, identifying the "legal mode" as a "weapon which could be used not only to define new relationships but to defend old ones, to fight a class rearguard action as well as to carve out new rights, and be used simultaneously to do both."[39] It was created through the confluence of interests of the colonial administration and chiefs to effect, in his study, an instrument, a "language of legitimation used primarily for the enforcement of new modes of authority."[40] Marriage laws were created to control female labor and access to productive resources at a time when men understood relations between men and women to be in "a state of crisis"[41] and when reliance on unpaid family labor was critical economically.[42] As Chanock shows, the manipulation of marriage laws was significant as men sought to exercise a greater degree of control over women, as access to land, the main means of production, and labor was defined through the social institution of marriage. Among matrilineages, on divorce, men forfeited rights to land. In the process, chiefs played an active and pivotal role as they drew on an "idealized version of traditional marriage," a "retroactive fantasy,"[43] in the creation of law with the British. Customary law became, to follow Chanock, frozen in time to reflect a particular historical moment. It was less a "survival" of a previous form than "a development of new tools of control to meet the needs of a new situation."[44] As his paper on land tenure makes clear, the value of the "resource" of custom varied not only by gender but also by socioeconomic stratum.[45]

Chanock's notion of customary law as fixed through the colonial project may be contrasted with research by Parkin, Glazier, and Moore. Although in the first two works women rarely enter the discussion except as objects in bridewealth transactions, the representation of customary law as an arena of struggle in all three provides a critical starting point for an understanding of gender relations to the land.

Parkin's discussion focuses on how land and palms, "the main indicators of social differentiation" in Giriama society in Kilifi District of coastal Kenya, are gained through the manipulation by a minority of "individual enterprising farmers"[46] of such customary practices as bridewealth transactions and reciprocal funerary obligations. The enterprising farmers, Parkin suggests, are "grappling with the problem of how to introduce new idioms to the common language of custom without going so far as to cut themselves off from the contacts needed in the competition for palms and land."[47] Such contacts, particularly elders, are needed as witnesses for transactions in property as these rights are not as yet officially recorded and to maintain a network of informants essential for knowledge of economic opportunity.

The language of custom is used, Parkin argues, to mystify the process of social differentiation, to conceal the contradictions between "the publicly manifest cultural justification for a role or activity . . . and the long-term, hidden or latent consequences for the society of this role or activity."[48] In the process, elders are portrayed as playing a paradoxical role. On the one hand, their authority is accentuated through their support of agnatic and gerontocratic principles in the allocation of property. But, on the other hand, "under the protection" of subscription to these ideals of a redistributional economy, "a new, more fundamental but initially illicit capitalist principle is smuggled in."[49] In this other capacity, elders, owing to their recognized legitimacy by the government, are valued as witnesses who sanction the individual sales of land and palms which undercut the ideology of sharing. In resolution of this paradox, elders may themselves manipulate definitions of agnation and clan membership.[50] The arbitration of clan membership, critical where rights to land are attained through clan adhesion, is the focus of more explicit attention in Glazier's study of the Mbeere of Embu District, Kenya, over the period 1969–1979, a time when a system of freehold rights to land was introduced. Customary law here becomes a "continuously evolving code"[51] informing the strategies that individuals or groups adopt to realize claims to large tracts of land to be registered under the freehold system of tenure.

One strategy adopted by individual members of a clan, or more commonly, by amalgamations of agnates in a context of increasing land scarcity, concerns the manipulation of clan membership, as this institution under customary law sanctions rights to land. Such groups, Glazier asserts, may represent a single descent group, or they may "fabricate" tradition using the "fiction of descent to define themselves in a customary idiom."[52] Membership may include affines, matrilateral kin, and other nonagnates who have made financial contributions to the group.[53] Descent ideology, one element of customary law, thus becomes the instrument of social differentiation while at the same time masking "the blatant maneuvers of selfseekers scrambling for land" through their emphasis of the "bonds of brotherhood and the legitimating function of now lengthy genealogical pedigrees."[54] As in Parkin's discussion, subscription to custom or tradition, while appearing to maintain the status quo, in fact "represents the very mechanism effecting social transformation."[55] Customary law becomes one of the legal spheres within which litigants frame their cases.

An analysis of law is the point of departure for Moore's longitudinal study of the Chagga in which she seeks to capture the iterative nature of the relationship between local struggle and large-scale process.[56] For Moore, customary law in precolonial times was a "complex system of political institutions, of semi-autonomous, organized social domains that controlled persons and resources, and of a system of ideas that ranged from the most materialistic sorts of cost accounting in cattle to the most mystical notions of the causes of misfortune."[57] Chagga law was

situated in ongoing arenas of action. It was a framework of organizations, relationships and cultural ideas, a mix of principles, guidelines, rules of preference and rules of prescription, together with conceptions of morality and causality, all of them completely intertwined in the web of ordinary activities.[58]

But Moore argues with reference to the beginning of colonial rule in the late nineteenth century, it was

attached to a political order quite differently constituted from that to which it was originally hitched, and operating in a framework of a different economy, residual "customary law" was an altered entity from the beginning.[59]

In her discussion of contemporary uses of customary law, Moore identifies the vulnerability of women vis-à-vis rights to land in the context of growing land shortage and its unequal distribution. Women, while having usufruct rights to land, do not inherit land under Chagga law.[60] Their vulnerability is based, in part, on the possibility of divorce and the degree to which a "discarded wife" may rely on the influence of her family to protect her rights to land. In part, the risks in a monogamous marriage relate to whether a woman has given birth to sons.[61]

The concept of territory, defined in terms of the patrilineage, emerges in Moore's work as central both to restrictions on female control of land and to conflict where "core" territory is alienated from the lineage without the sanction of lineage authorities. For example, Moore indicates that a man may not give land to his daughter, but, if he has land away from the "core lineage area," usually obtained by purchase, this may be given to a son-in-law.[62] Customary law in Moore's view may have been banished to the "private sphere" in contemporary Tanzania, but she concludes,

generations of lively and ingenious rural Chagga have in fact been using their traditions as one of a number of resources out of which to construct new arrangements to suit their ever-changing situations. The Chagga have neither broken with their past nor have they reproduced it.[63]

I will draw on strands of this debate to examine changes in relations between individuals and the subclan or *mbari* and between men and women as they pertain to land in the context of increasing social differentiation from circa 1910 to the tenure reform of the 1950s. Viewing customary law as an arena of struggle, I will emphasize elements of custom that enter this arena. For instance, I will argue that, as part of the process of social change, overall *mbari* authority vis-à-vis the individual has weakened, but where individual men, on the basis of customary rights, have claimed *mbari* territory, they have re-created territorial authority as an instrument of male solidarity and thus made it a powerful element in the discourse.

Territorial Definitions and Rights
Vis-À-Vis the Land: Murang'a District

The establishment of the colonial administration in the early 1900s, the delimitation of Kikuyu territory through the demarcation of "reserves" and the demands of the colonial economy all effected profound changes in the Kikuyu system of land tenure. This system was based on the *ng'undu,* the unit of land controlled by the *mbari.*[64] Previously, while the dialectic between the "two apparently antagonistic principles"[65] that determined rights to land in Kikuyu society, the *mbari* and the individual, had led to a certain degree of social differentiation, evidence specific to Murang'a District suggests that such differentiation is unlikely to have proceeded as far as in the district to the south, Kiambu.[66] Resolution of the tension implied by the two interwoven sets of rights could still be resolved through migration to Kiambu (then, Kabete), to a limited degree westward with the clearing of the forested slopes of the Nyandarua range, or through contractual relationships established outside the *mbari.*[67] That some degree of social stratification existed is certainly well documented, as references to *athamaki,* wealthy men, attest.[68] But in Murang'a, where the irredeemable sale of land was unknown, where inheritable allocative as well as usufruct rights to land were both subject to final *mbari* authority, relatively egalitarian productive relations pertained. This is not to imply that such rights were static; rather, they were the subject of ongoing negotiation and, at times, conflict.[69]

Under the *ng'undu* system, rules of inheritance, residence, and descent followed the male line. Within an *mbari,* the basic territorial and political unit, sons inherited cultivation rights to land, each son being allocated on marriage a portion of the land farmed by his mother for his wife's use.[70] Rights to uncultivated sections of the *mbari* were not inherited. Individual male rights to land were, under this system, less than absolute: tenancy and other contractual arrangements such as the redeemable "sale" or loan of land were always subject to veto by the *mbari* council.[71] At times, an individual was able to "circumvent" this authority by "selling" land outside the *mbari* on the grounds that it would then be easier to redeem later.[72] But the absolute sale of land was not practiced in the early 1900s in Murang'a.[73] Referring directly to land tenure in Fort Hall District (now Murang'a), M. R. R. Vidal, District Commissioner, giving testimony before the Land Commission in November 1932 stated, "Absolute sale without possibility of redemption is unknown, and as far as can be ascertained there is no such thing as unfettered individual control of land."[74] Elders from Gaki (now Nyeri), before the same commission, and in reply to a question as to whether land could be sold outright, replied, "All that is ever conveyed is a temporary and provisional right to reside, to cultivate and to keep stock on a given area or areas. There is always right of redemption."[75] Redeemable sale of land was arranged only in case of exceptional need, for example, to obtain sheep and goats for bridewealth payments.

Under the *ng'undu* system, women, while unable to inherit land, as wives in their husbands' *mbari* were allocated land for usufruct. Discussing this practice, women still speak of receiving land from their *mother-in-law,* a phrase that signifies the structurally significant position they held as head of a *nyumba* (literally, hut), the "matricentric unit" of a polygynous household.[76] Through a woman, her sons inherited individual rights to land. A woman's autonomy vis-à-vis the land of her husband's *mbari* could be significantly increased as a widow. While the system of rights is complex, reference to two practices illustrates this point. If of childbearing age, a widow had the option of entering a relationship of her choice, and any children resulting from the relationship inherited through her deceased husband.[77] Alternatively, if past childbearing age, as a female husband she could similarly increase the size of her household and reinforce her structural position in the *mbari.* Where no sons had resulted from her previous marriage, this practice was of considerable significance.

From 1903, Kikuyu territorial expansion was circumscribed. Kikuyu of Fort Hall District lost land on their eastern borders and to the west on the forested slopes of the Nyandaruas. Neither area had been "vacant."[78] One estimate indicated that one in three Kikuyu considered "he" had a claim to land outside the established reserve on the basis of inheritance practice. The Land Commission, collecting evidence in the early 1930s, received fifteen claims representing 38 *mbari* from the forest zone and twenty claims representing 102 *mbari* from claimed land either in the eastern zone or allocated to missions within the reserve.[79]

Since so much of the testimony brought before the Land Commission was politically motivated, it is difficult to evaluate. But the bitterness with which such organizations as the Kikuyu Central Association received the commission's recommendations indicates that the proposal to compensate the "tribe" rather than the individual was at variance with territorial claims as perceived by the *mbari.*[80] As Chanock has argued with reference to African land tenure, colonial administrators found it much easier politically and legally to expropriate and by extension, to compensate, what they perceived to be "communal" rather than individual rights.[81]

Yet, while spokespersons for the *mbari* voiced claims to land before the Land Commission set up by the colonial administration, it is evident that from the early 1900s, the *mbari* as an institution grew progressively weaker. By 1930, the increasing inequality in holding size had brought about considerable social differentiation. Few *mbari* had grazing land to open up for cultivation,[82] and increased pressure on the land caused both by the increasing inequality in its distribution and by population growth led to the migration of substantial numbers of Kikuyu to the Rift valley.[83] Buying and selling land, which was part of this process, was now well under way.[84]

The issue of the sale of land and its "redeemability" is critical in analyzing the balance of power between the individual and the *mbari*. Because previously "sales" had been redeemable, the *mbari* had retained its political and territorial integrity. Once redeemability came into question, the *mbari* was under siege from within and without the institution.

This issue came to the fore in 1944 in Fort Hall in such a way as to indicate a high degree of polarization. A meeting of the district Local Native Council (LNC) in that year passed by twelve votes to four a proposal to adopt three methods of land transaction that had been introduced in Nyeri: outright purchase, redeemable purchase, and tenancy. A later meeting changed this decision by eleven votes to four to meet Chief Njiiri's demands that *all* land sales, past, present, and future, where the purchase price had exceeded eight goats, should be considered "outright." The new decision met with "vociferous and determined" opposition in the local *barazas*[85] where discussion was subsequently held. The district comissioner commented as follows:

I believe that the protagonists of outright purchase (a minute proportion of the tribe) are entirely selfinterested; mainly they are persons who have "purchased" large areas of land which they are now unwilling to allow to be redeemed.[86]

Njiiri himself, by the time of land tenure reform in the 1950s, for example, had accumulated 207.9 hectares in 28 fragments.[87] Writing later in the 1940s, Coutts, district commissioner in 1948, maintained that "certain unscrupulous persons are using the redeemable custom to take back land which has been made fertile by a younger more progressive person." Manipulation of the custom of redeemability was also, in his view, leading to increased division between and within families as they engaged in "a mad individualistic race for more and more acres of eroded soil."[88] The vast increase in land litigation before the divisional tribunals is evidence of this. By 1949, the number of land cases had reached such proportions that the LNC enacted a bylaw stipulating that no land sold before the famine of 1898 could be redeemed. This bylaw and the increasing compensation that tribunals were giving for improvements to land in cases where the land was returned to the original owner decreased, in some measure, the insecurity of tenure, according to the district commissioner.[89]

This process of land accumulation on the part of "richer" Kikuyu, which many colonial officials condoned as not only in line with "Kikuyu individualism" but as "beneficial economically and agriculturally," took place within a context of more general social dislocation.[90] Elders, whom one district commissioner considered to have "sunk into obscurity" as far as influencing the younger generation was concerned, were yet necessary as witnesses in the process of litigation to which land accumulation gave rise.[91] But in the view of the district commissioner in 1951, elders "continue to abuse their position with respect to land cases, and extort exorbitant bribes from the parties concerned before giving evidence on the lines requested."[92]

Wealthy individuals such as Chief Njiiri, acting to increase their individual control or ownership of the land, were at the forefront of attempts to redefine the practice of redeemable land sales. However, this drive coexisted with a contradictory appeal to kinship ideology and final *mbari* authority to retain the practice of redeemability. A practice that in the past had ensured *mbari* integrity was now being used by more powerful members of society for purposes of effecting individual control over the land. Such individuals, under the guise of customary practice, sought to reaffirm control over holdings they had "loaned" to tenants. Their ability to regain control of such land through the idiom of redeemability or to substantiate their claim to land purchase (i.e., the irredeemable sale of land) rested on the degree of support they were able to obtain from customary sanctioning authority. Subscription in this context to the authority of elders indicated both recognition of the need to legitimate all land transactions through customary institutions where no written law yet existed and an undermining of the institution, as the process engaged in promoted individual control over the land.

For women, the success of individual men in controlling land through purchase is likely to have resulted in their relative loss of autonomy in its management, although this will have varied with economic stratum.[93] For the vast majority, rights to land have become less secure. However, women were not excluded from purchasing land, and Jeanne Fisher's data indicate that at least a small minority accumulated sufficient capital for this purpose:

Many women now buy gardens, although male relatives still conduct the transactions and mark the boundaries. One informant in Fort Hall, an intelligent, vivacious woman, summed up the position as follows: "In the past women did not buy gardens or cattle or *mburi* [sheep and goats], but in these days, when they have money, women buy gardens for cultivation, cattle and *mburi*." She concluded her remarks by saying that now women had "wisdom," and formerly they were fools of women (*irimu cia atumia*).[94]

The case studies presented above indicate the conflict to which such purchase gave rise. In a very real sense, they threatened the basis of *mbari* solidarity in patrilineal filiation.

Direct evidence of the relationship between land accumulation and size of nonfarm income, the "twin axes" around which social differentiation "revolved," can be gained from a survey of thirty farmers carried out by Kitching in Kangema Division in 1973 and from data collected in 1984 in Kigumo and Kandara divisions in Murang'a.[95] In both cases, respondents indicated that savings from nonfarm sources over the historical period of colonialism were directly related to the process of land accumulation, although the correlation is not, as Kitching observes, a simple one. It was related not only to the amount of income but also the time at which it was earned, the period over which capital was available for investment in land, and the price of the land. Data from the Economic Survey for Central Province 1963–64 provide circumstantial evidence of this relationship.[96]

Although some households obtained nonfarm income from business enterprises within the district, of far greater significance was income from wage and salaried labor off the reserve.[97] Kitching has estimated that by 1928, 41.7 percent of the adult males in Murang'a were involved in labor migration.[98] By 1943, 59 percent of the adult male labor force was in registered employment off the reserve.[99] While the majority of men migrated as unskilled labor with the objective of meeting the requirements of household survival, educated men from wealthier households acquired more highly paid positions, in which they accumulated capital for the purchase of land and hired labor to work it. As investment in land proceeded, men's agnatic links with the household were strengthened at the expense of wider *mbari* links, the latter's authority further weakening.

The colonial administration contributed to this process by ignoring existing political organizations and giving power to newly created chiefs. Some chiefs were *athamaki,* or local leaders; others were opportunists who had previously had contact with the British. Godfrey Muriuki considers Karuri, who became paramount chief in the early years of the century, to be one of the latter. Not only were chiefs unpopular because of their role in tax collection from 1902 onward, for their enforced recruitment of paid labor for settler farms and of unpaid labor for road construction and the building of *boma* (encampments), but also because of measures that led to their own enrichment.[100] Again, Muriuki cites the case of Karuri, who decreed that any potential initiate had to pay him a rupee before male initiation ceremonies could begin.[101] M. P. K. Sorrenson gives further evidence of chiefs' accumulation of land and association with British interests, a situation that led to great hostility to the institution of chieftaincy.[102]

One attempt was made to revive indigenous institutions through giving elders a role in local judicial proceedings by means of the establishment of native tribunals.[103] Native tribunals were established in 1913 by the colonial regime ostensibly to create a judicial institution more congruent with Kikuyu social order. Yet, although charged with the responsibility of judging cases of land dispute and minor criminal offenses, the tribunals were not *locally* based, as had been previous *kiama* (councils of male elders).[104] A native tribunal was located in each division of Fort Hall District. Prior to 1930, four divisional chiefs acted as their presidents, the vice-president and elders being chosen from a panel of elders for six months at a time.[105] Final authority lay with the district officer for each division who occasionally revised decisions.[106] Only after 1930, following the Native Tribunals Ordinance, were chiefs given a lesser role in the system and thus the elders a greater voice. Yet, the emasculation of the role of elders in both Nyeri and Fort Hall may at least in part be measured by the fact that the tribunals "were organized along the lines of British courts even to the extent of dressing up the elders in wigs and gowns."[107] There is clearly no guarantee that any customary law dispensed from this forum will have differed from that defined in other local institutions.

The administration created the Local Native Council in 1925 as a counter to Harry Thuku's Young Kikuyu Association's appeal for local representation. The government nominated 13 members and 12 were locally elected, although the government reserved the right to approve the latter.[108] Kitching argues that despite circumscribed powers, the LNC had a significant impact on local development.[109] With respect to increased rural stratification, two aspects of the LNC are worth noting.

First, from the 1930s onward, LNC members were increasingly drawn from an educated elite, and their definition of "progress" for Africans guided LNC action. Evidence suggests close links among LNC members, teachers, chiefs, headmen, clerks, and traders both because a man might fulfill several of these roles simultaneously and because of the close bond that united members of the small educated elite, many of whom would have attended the same schools.[110] To a very real extent, the LNC, together with other administrative structures, such as the chiefs, headmen, and native tribunals, created a cohesive group, which Sorrenson referred to as a "ruling class,"[111] far from representative of the mass of the population. This situation caused the district commissioner for 1944–45, P. C. Osborne, to note,

the fact that on occasions the LNC has shown itself patently out of touch with and sometimes even directly opposed to the views of the tribe clearly demonstrates that for all its success and achievements it is not by itself regarded as completely fulfilling the demand for political self-expression.[112]

Osborne's comment is a remarkable understatement in the light of subsequent Kikuyu organization in, for example, the Kenya African Union. The hostility shown to LNC action discussed earlier with respect to the issue of the redeemability of land sales in 1944 is one indicator of the extent to which elite and popular viewpoints diverged.

Second, as the sole source of capital loans until the 1950s, the LNC played a significant role in supporting the enterprises of the educated elite, not just in terms of the local businesses on which Kitching focuses but also, after 1942 and the introduction of the Agricultural Betterment Fund, in assistance to the so-called "better farmers." Although the loans were small (under K£50 each), through their support of enterprises of the rural elite they furthered the differentiation of this stratum from the rest of society.[113]

Land tenure reform, introduced under the Swynnerton Plan as a counterinsurgency move in Central Province in the mid-1950s,[114] accelerated the trend toward individual control over landholdings and provided a distinct legal sphere through which litigants could forward claims. The British intended this legal sphere to extinguish all previously existing rights under customary law.[115] At one level, therefore, tenure reform represented a further assault on *mbari* authority. Yet at another level, individuals had recourse to this same authority with considerable success in substantiating claims to land. Re-created, *mbari* authority has become a significant force in defining land rights. Customary rights sought under this guise rest on the notion of their claims on *mbari* territoriality, in contrast to registered individual ownership of particular parcels of land.

Land tenure reform began in Murang'a in 1954. First, it involved the adjudication of claims to land held under the ng'undu system by a committee comprised of a chief, or headman, a registrar, and local *mbari* elders.[116] Appeals were allowed within a period of sixty days.[117] Subsequently, the measurement of the frequently fragmented holdings took place. Holdings were consolidated and allocated on the basis of preexisting acreage, a small percentage being deducted for common use. By 1958, substantial errors in the process were noted despite the slow rate of implementation.[118] By 1960, the discrepancies had become major. Sorrenson considers part of the fault to have lain with the lack of survey expertise and inadequate supervision of the survey team.[119] But further inquiry, Lamb records, "revealed evidence of substantial corruption, of ficitious fragments of land being recorded, and of repeated contravention of the appeals procedure laid down in the Land Tenure Rules."[120] On demarcation, some landowners had managed to accumulate substantial additions to their land.[121] Reconsolidation, which involved repeating the entire previous measures of adjudication, measurement, and reallocation, began in 1961[122] and was completed in 1968.[123]

Registration of freehold title to the land followed under the Native Lands Registration Ordinance of 1959. The ordinance raises three issues pertinent to my argument. First, its final draft included no protection of "lesser rights." Sorrenson refers to "customary tenancy" practices to illustrate the issue. But his work has no reference to the loss of women's usufruct rights to land, which had previously been guaranteed by the *mbari* but which had become invisible with registration.[124] Rather, the ordinance regarded men's right to land, which had previously been allocative and subject to *mbari* authority, as the registerable interest. Possession of a title deed now gave to men virtually unbridled power over the land, the second point of relevance.[125]

Third, the practice of encouraging "join-ups" where holdings were under 1.22 hectares in size and the subsequent registration of the holding in the name of *one* owner meant that the rights of several holders went unregistered. As a result of this process, it was estimated that in Fort Hall, 3,000 to 4,000 rights holders were effectively "dispossessed." Although Sorrenson considers this matter to have been of little consequence, as only the "clever and unscrupulous" would have tried to turn their kin off the land, it would appear probable that the issue would be an ingredient for later dispute as pressure on the land mounted.[126] It certainly contributed to the situation, noted earlier, of the increasing discrepancy between de facto and de jure rights to land. At the basis of this discrepancy was the continued practice of customary inheritance along patrilineal lines.[127]

The reform did not intend to redistribute land more equitably. Rather, it cemented existing cleavages in Kikuyu society and furthered social differentiation through the increasing commercialization of land.[128] No quantitative data exist to indicate the degree of commercialization prior to "land reform." However, the rapid increase in land sales subsequent to the registration of land in freehold title suggests that polarization has deepened in Murang'a. While that individualization of tenure preceded the reform by several decades, it is also clear that the reform institutionalized such tenure and intensified the struggle among individuals for land.

Conclusion

In a very real sense, the research in Murang'a is exploratory. We need further work on dispute settlement both inside the courts during the colonial and postindependence eras and outside them. As Moore has shown with such acuity in chronicling the M___ lineage, an analysis of customary law and indeed of different modes of dispute resolution grounded in very different legal principles demands an investigation that relates what happens in the courts to day-to-day life outside.[129]

In particular, we need to learn how women and men use the court system at the level of the location (the chief's court) and the division (the land board) and the extent to which each gender formulates strategies in a complex situation of legal pluralism. Similarly, how such strategies vary according to class, in a situation of growing rural differentiation, needs assessment. In this context, Chanock has asked not only whose resource custom was but how different classes use the resource and portray customary law.[130] If customary law is conceptualized as continuing to be constructed and interactive with changes in political and economic relations, as I have argued in this chapter, then inquiry must also consider how actors' strategies affect the legal spheres themselves. As Sally Merry has pointed out, individuals choose among the legal spheres, according to the perceived relative costs and benefits of each. By their actions, they modify legal structure.[131]

Preliminary results from Murang'a illustrate that in the present situation of struggle over rights to land, both women and men legitimate claims to land through customary as well as statutory law. Neither of the spheres has watertight, impermeable boundaries. The case studies indicate that men have the upper edge in the contests located within them.

In large measure, men effect control over land through customary practices of succession and legitimate their rights where they do not hold title deed through claims to *mbari* territory. In one sense, inheritance rights are consistent with the *ng'undu* system of tenure. But, extracted from a context where inheritance of cultivation rights to land was only one element of an interlocking and multifaceted web of male/female, individual/*mbari* and intergenerational rights to land and did not confer outright ownership, I would argue that the practice of succession currently defined as "customary" fabricates or creates a social norm with little relationship to past practice. Similarly, territoriality may be perceived as one component of *mbari* social organization and function, but I would also argue that in the context of extensive land shortage, its role as a legitimating factor in male control of land has been exaggerated in the interest of individual material gain. The symbolic as well as the material reliance on land, whose value never shrinks, to paraphrase a Kikuyu proverb, remains a key motivating force in the discourse. In the process, solidarity based on kin relations in the *mbari* provides a potent instrument for collective action.

Appeals to *mbari* authority have been at the expense of individual women's rights under freehold tenure, as the case studies illustrate. But women themselves have evolved a discourse of resistance that they frame at least in part in terms of "custom." One instance of this is the woman who opted to become a female husband, manipulating this customary idiom in her own right to ensure her continued control over the land after her husband's death. Although faced with difficulty, she has successfully maintained autonomy vis-à-vis the *mbari* and her brother-in-law's efforts to seize the land.

In the more contemporary idiom of harambee, but drawing also on collective modes of labor organization such as *ngwatio,* women have managed as groups to effect more control over their access to resources. The shift in orientation of women's groups in the district over the last ten years, from a situation in 1978 where 90 percent of them were classified as non-income-generating savings and loans societies to the case in 1984 where 45 percent of the 550 groups were involved in an income-generating activity, is illustrative of women's awareness of male initiatives in controlling land and, through the land, labor.[132] The examples of land purchase by such groups are particularly interesting in this light.

The purchase of land by individual women may be explained similarly as indicative of a growing realization of vulnerability in terms of access to this resource. As a practice, men have bitterly contested this strategy. Further research is needed to identify the extent to which such land is put to immediate personal use or, when bought as an investment, is held for speculative purposes or rented out.[133]

The strategies used by women and men vis-à-vis rights to the land make it apparent that claims continue to be contested in both a legal sphere of customary law and one informed by statutory land law. In a situation where many women (but also men) do not have access to statutory law, claims contested in terms of property rights in people, legitimated through customary discourse, are frequently the only ones that are enforceable.

In turn, these sanctions are played out at the level of control over labor and its product. The recent action of the Murang'a District Farmers' Cooperative Union in the face of decreasing quality in coffee produced in the smallholder sector makes evident the degree of women's resistance to control over their labor exercised through the mode of remuneration for coffee, linked in turn to male control over the land, and its implications for increasing productivity. Further research is needed to assess not only how the operation of other agricultural institutions (e.g., those providing credit and extension) affect the productivity of women farmers but also how women's insecure rights to land in a situation of legal pluralism are related to agricultural productivity.

Notes

1 Smallholdings in Kenya are defined as under 12 ha (Kenya, Central Bureau of Statistics, *Statistical Abstract* [Nairobi: Government Printer, 1970]). Three of the five administrative divisions of the district are comprised solely of smallholdings. Kandara Division contains a few large farms, whereas Makuyu is still predominantly under large estates, although the latter are increasingly being subdivided.

2 For example, for the 1969–70 coffee season, 32.3% of Murang'a's coffee crop from the smallholder sector had been classified as grade 2 and 25.3% as grade 3 (Kenya, Central Province *Annual Report 1971*). In 1982–83, only 13.1% was classified as grade 2 and 27% as grade 3 (Kenya, Murang'a District Ministry of Agriculture and Livestock Development, *Annual Report 1983*). In neither case was any first grade coffee produced.

3 For a discussion of this concept, see L. Beneria and M. Roldan, *The Crossroads of Class and Gender: Industrial Homework, Subcontracting, and Household Dynamics in Mexico City* (Chicago, 1987).

4 Kenya, Murang'a District, Ministry of Agriculture, *Annual Report 1965*.

5 F. Mackenzie, "Land and Labor: Women and Men in Agricultural Change, Murang'a District, Kenya, 1880–1984" (Ph.D. diss., University of Ottawa, 1986): 416–417.

6 For comparable findings, see P. Stamp's research in Kiambu District to the south: P. Stamp, "Perceptions of Change and Economic Strategy among Kikuyu Women in Mitero, Kenya," *Rural Africana* 29 (1975–76): 19–44.

7 See, for example, M. J. Hay, "Women as Owners, Occupants, and Managers of Property in Colonial Western Kenya," in M. J. Hay and M. Wright (eds.), *African Women and the Law: Historical Perspectives* (Boston University Papers on Africa, VII, 1982): 110–123.

8 C. Jones, "Intra-Household Bargaining in Response to the Introduction of New Crops: A Case Study from North Cameroon," in J. L. Moock (ed.), *Understanding Africa's Rural Households and Farming Systems* (Boulder, 1986): 105–123; J. Dey, "Development Planning in the Gambia: The Gap Between Planners' and Farmers' Perceptions, Expectations and Objectives,"

World Development 10, 5 (1982): 377–396; J. A. Carney, "Struggles over Crop Rights and Labour within Contract Farming Households on a Gambian Irrigated Rice Project," *Journal of Peasant Studies* 15, 3 (1988): 334–349. See M. Watts, chap. 6, this vol., "Idioms of Land and Labor: Producing Politics and Rice in Senegambia."

9 Carney, "Struggles"; Watts, "Idioms."

10 Details in the case histories have been altered only insofar as it is necessary to ensure anonymity.

11 O'Brien distinguishes between surrogate and autonomous female husbands in "Female Husbands in Southern Bantu Societies," in A. Schlegel (ed.), *Sexual Stratification: A Cross-Cultural View* (New York, 1977): 109–126. Among the Kikuyu, when a widow was past childbearing age, she could opt to become a surrogate female husband. The option exercised by a woman who was childless or who had only daughters was intended to increase her husband's lineage, through her *nyumba* (literally, hut).

12 In Murang'a, 80% of the holdings in the small farm sector are under 2 ha in size; 46.5% are under 1 ha (Kenya, Central Bureau of Statistics, *Statistical Abstract* [Nairobi: Government Printer, 1970]: 81).

13 C. Robertson and I. Berger, "Introduction: Analyzing Class and Gender-African Perspectives," in C. Robertson and I. Berger (eds.), *Women and Class in Africa* (New York, 1986): 3–24.

14 The Presentation Books of the Land Registry, Murang'a District, list all land transactions. These include sales, mutations, successions, partitions, gifts, and morgages. No information is given as to the amount of land involved in each transaction.

15 J. Davison, " 'Without Land We are Nothing': The Effect of Land Tenure Policies and Practices upon Rural Women in Kenya," *Rural Africana* 27 (1987): 19–33.

16 Interview, December 1984.

17 Davison, " 'Without Land,' " 30.

18 See B. P. Thomas, "Cash, Credit, Cooperation and Community: Responses of Women's Groups to Socio-economic Change in Rural Kenya," paper presented at the Harvard/MIT Women in Development Group's Second Annual Workshop on Women, Work and Public Policy (1982).

19 See F. Mackenzie, "Local Organization: Confronting Contradiction in a Smallholding District of Kenya," *Cahiers de Géographie du Québec* 31, 83 (1987): 273–286; N. Mwaniki, "Against Many Odds: The Dilemma of Women's Self-Help Groups in Mbiri, Kenya," *Africa* 56, 2 (1986): 210–227; P. Stamp, "Kikuyu Women's Self-Help Groups: Toward an Understanding of the Relation Between Sex-Gender System and Mode of Production in Africa," in Robertson and Berger, *Women;* P. Stamp, "Matega: Manipulating Women's Cooperative Traditions for Material and Social Gain in Kenya," paper presented at the Canadian Association of African Studies Conference, University of Alberta, Edmonton (1987); B. P. Thomas, *Politics, Participation and Poverty: Development Through Self-Help in Kenya* (Boulder, 1986).

20 Stamp, "Kikuyu," 41.
21 Prior to the alienation of this land to white settlers, this area had been integral to the Kikuyu economy. See, for example, the evidence of Chief Kimani wa Thuo before the Kenya Land Commission, U.K., *Kenya Land Commission: Evidence and Memoranda* (H.M.S.O., 1934).
22 G. Muriuki, *A History of the Kikuyu 1500–1900* (Nairobi, 1974).
23 See Mackenzie, "Land and Labor."
24 Interview, Chief, Muthithi Location, November 1984.
25 S. E. Merry, "The Articulation of Legal Spheres," in M. J. Hay and M. Wright (eds.), *African Women and the Law: Historical Perspectives* (Boston: Boston University Papers on Africa, VII, 1982): 71. Merry defines a legal sphere as a set of rules defined by "custom" or "laws enacted by a political authority"; accepted procedures in the process of resolving disputes; "a political and economic context" from which the arbitrator derives authority to act; and "a structure of accessibility specifying economic, sex-linked, ethnic, and other requirements for access to the legal spheres.
26 Davison, " 'Without Land' "; A. P. Okeyo, "Daughters of the Lakes and Rivers: Colonization and the Land Rights of Luo Women," in M. Etienne and E. Leacock, *Women and Colonization: Anthropological Perspectives* (New York, 1980): 186–213.
27 Okeyo "Daughters," 206.
28 Hay, "Women," 117.
29 F. D. Homan, "Succession to Registered Land in African Areas in Kenya," *Journal of Local Administration Overseas* 1 (1963): 50.
30 A. Haugerud, "The Consequences of Land Tenure Reform among Smallholders in the Kenya Highlands," *Rural Africana* 15/16 (1983): 73–74.
31 G. Kitching, *Class and Economic Change in Kenya: The Making of an African Petite Bourgeoisie* (New Haven, 1980).
32 P. Fitzpatrick, "Custom as Imperialism," unpublished manuscript (1988): 1.
33 Ibid., 1.
34 F. C. Snyder, "Colonialism and Legal Form: The Creation of 'Customary Law' in Senegal," *Journal of Legal Pluralism* 19 (1981): 49–90; M. Chanock, *Law, Custom and Social Order: The Colonial Experience in Malawi and Zambia* (Cambridge, 1985); and M. Chanock, "A Peculiar Sharpness: Some Observations of Property in the History of Customary Law in Colonial Africa," paper presented at the Annual Symposium of the Center for African Studies, University of Illinois, Urbana–Champaign, 1987.
35 D. J. Parkin, *Palms, Wine and Witnesses: Public Spirit and Private Gain in an African Farming Community* (San Francisco, 1972); J. Glazier, *Land and the Uses of Tradition among the Mbeere of Kenya* (Lanham, Md., 1985); S. F. Moore, *Social Facts and Fabrications: "Customary" Law on Kilimanjaro, 1880–1980* (Cambridge, 1988).
36 Merry, "Articulation," 71.
37 Chanock, *Law;* Snyder, "Colonialism."
38 Snyder, "Colonialism," 52.

39 Chanock, *Law,* 67.

40 Ibid., 113.

41 Ibid., 192. Initially, the "crisis" had been caused by the abolition of slavery. Of this Chanock writes, "Slave marriage was a distinctive form of power over women in that it gave to men not only command of the labor of women but also control over the fruits of their reproductive capacity without any of the payments or reciprocal duties involved in ordinary marriage" (ibid., 165). Later the crisis and social disruption in general were explained by men in terms of changes in female behavior as women sought divorce in white men's courts or moved to urban areas rather than in terms of underlying economic change whose outward manifestations were conflicts between matrilineal and patrilineal social practice, migrancy, and urbanization (204).

42 Ibid., 236.

43 Ibid., 193–194.

44 Ibid., 145.

45 Chanock, "A Peculiar Sharpness."

46 Parkin, *Palms,* 1.

47 Ibid., 2.

48 Ibid., 98.

49 Ibid., 99.

50 Ibid., 21.

51 Glazier *Land,* 231.

52 Ibid., 190–191.

53 Ibid., 272.

54 Ibid., 281.

55 Chanock, *Law,* 282.

56 Moore, *Social Facts,* 9.

57 Ibid., 51.

58 Ibid., 90.

59 Ibid., 95.

60 Ibid., 200.

61 Ibid., 265. Here, Moore notes that under the "formal legal system," women can "hold land." No details are given, except in one case where registration of land in the name of a granddaughter was a front for male access to land.

62 Ibid., 242.

63 Ibid., 319.

64 The term *githaka* is more widely used in the literature to refer to the land controlled by the *mbari,* but, more accurately, it refers specifically only to the area of uncultivated land. Kenya, *Native Land Tenure in Kikuyu Province, Report of Committee and Appendix* (Chairman G.V. Maxwell) (Nairobi, 1929).

65 H. E. Lambert and W. Harris, *The Kikuyu Lands* (Nairobi, 1945), quoted in D. R. F. Taylor, "Fort Hall District, Kenya: A Geographical Consideration of the Problems and Potential of a Developing Area" (Ph.D. diss., University of Edinburgh, 1966).

66 C. M. Clark, "Land and Food, Women and Power, in Nineteenth-Century Kikuyu," *Africa* 50, 4 (1980): 357–370. Clark assumes in her argument that the territorial expansion of the Kikuyu in the nineteenth century would have affected social relations throughout their domain. But as land was available for "purchase" in Kiambu at this time, unlike the situation in Fort Hall (Murang'a), and as Kiambu was the frontier zone for migration, it is likely that social differentiation would have proceeded further here.

67 Taylor, *Fort Hall.*

68 For example, Muriuki, *A History,* 167.

69 See H. W. O. Okoth-Ogendo, "Some Issues of Theory in the Study of Tenure Relations in African Agriculture," *Africa* LIX, 1, p. 12.

70 Muriuki, *A History,* 76; M. P. K. Sorrenson, *Land Reform in Kikuyu County: A Study in Government Policy* (London, 1967): 10; J. Fisher, *The Anatomy of Kikuyu Domesticity and Husbandry* (Nairobi and London, 1954): 175; Kenya, *Native,* 33.

71 Sorrenson, *Land Reform,* 10; Muriuki, *A History,* 75.

72 Fisher, *The Anatomy,* 262.

73 M. W. Beech, "Kikuyu System of Land Tenure," *Journal of the African Society* 17, 65 (1917): 46–59; Fisher, *The Anatomy;* A. J. F. Simmance, "Land Redemption among the Fort Hall Kikuyu," *Journal of African Law* 5, 2 (1961): 75–81; U.K., *Kenya.*

74 U.K., *Kenya,* 578.

75 Ibid., Appendix 7.

76 The concept of "matricentric unit" is developed by C. Obbo in "Dominant Male Ideology and Female Options: Three East African Case Studies," *Africa* 46 (1976): 371–389.

77 The levirate was also practiced, but a woman was not obliged to accede to this relationship. See L. S. B. Leakey, *The Southern Kikuyu before 1903,* 3 vols. (London, 1977): 800.

78 U.K., *Kenya,* 120, 477.

79 Ibid., 370–371.

80 Sorrenson, *Land Reform,* 24–27. See, for example, Kenya, Fort Hall District (FHD), *Annual Report* (1934): 4–5.

81 Chanock, "A Peculiar Sharpness," 14–16.

82 Taylor, *Fort Hall,* 46.

83 T. Kanogo, *Squatters and the Roots of Mau Mau 1905–1963* (London: James Currey, 1987).

84 Kenya, Central Province, *Annual Report* (1938): 6.

85 A *baraza* is a local meeting, usually held at a chief's encampment.

86 Kenya, FHD, *Annual Report* (1944): 8–9.

87 Taylor, *Fort Hall,* 53.

88 Kenya, FHD, *Annual Report* (1948): 2.

89 Kenya, FHD *Annual Report* (1949): 4.

90 Kenya, Central Province, *Annual Report* (1947): 22.

91 Kenya, FHD *Annual Report* (1932): 2.

92 Kenya, FHD *Annual Report* (1951): 7.
93 For a discussion of this question, see Kitching, *Class,* 144–145; G. Kershaw, "The Changing Role of Men and Women in the Kikuyu Family by Socioeconomic Strata," *Rural Africana* 19 (1974–1975): 173–194; Mackenzie, "Land and Labor," chap. 6.
94 Fisher, *The Anatomy,* 187. My data from Murang'a call into question Fisher's suggestion concerning how frequently women purchased land.
95 Kitching, *Class,* 154, 367–361; Mackenzie, "Land and Labor."
96 Kenya, *Economic Survey for Central Province 1963/1964* (1968).
97 See Kitching, *Class,* 163; Fisher, *The Anatomy,* 138.
98 Kitching, *Class,* 250.
99 Kenya, FHD *Annual Report* (1943): 8.
100 Muriuki, *A History,* 167.
101 Ibid., 177–178.
102 Sorrenson, *Land Reform,* 45.
103 Kenya, Central Province, *Record Book* (1910). This move was made by Sir Percy Girouard following a meeting with the chiefs of Central Province in 1910.
104 Kenya, FHD *Annual Report* (1916): 10.
105 Kenya, FHD, *Annual Report* (1933).
106 Kenya, FHD, *Annual Report* (1924).
107 Kenya, FHD, *Annual Report* (1947): 45.
108 Kenya, FHD, *Annual Report* (1925): 5.
109 Kitching, *Class,* 188–190.
110 Ibid., 194.
111 Sorrenson, *Land Reform,* 47.
112 Kenya, FHD, *Annual Report* (1944): 3.
113 Kitching, *Class,* 195.
114 G. Lamb, *Peasant Politics* (Lewes, Sussex, 1974); Sorrenson, *Land Reform.*
115 E. Cotran, "The Development and Reform of the Law in Kenya," *Journal of African Law* 27, 1 (1983): 42–61.
116 Sorrenson, *Land Reform,* 168.
117 F. D. Homan, "Consolidation, Enclosure and Registration of Title in Kenya," *Journal of Local Administration Overseas* 1 (1962): 4–14.
118 Kenya, FHD, *Annual Report* (1958): 13. Sorrenson, *Land Reform,* 106–107, refers to the substantial opposition to land tenure reform, the result of the degree of allegiance to Mau Mau in the district.
119 Sorrenson, *Land Reform,* 171.
120 Lamb, *Peasant Politics,* 13.
121 Kenya, FHD, *Annual Report* (1960): 9.
122 Kenya, FHD, *Annual Report* (1961): 12.
123 Lamb, *Peasant Politics,* 14.
124 Sorrenson, *Land Reform,* 189.
125 Ibid., 191. Sorrenson notes that the Working Party on Land Tenure "stopped short of a complete abolition of native law and custom." In the

case of mortgages, for example, a complicated procedure was put in place to prevent the direct transfer of land to the mortgagee in the case of default.

126 Ibid., 214.
127 Homan, "Succession."
128 Redistribution did take place to an uncounted extent as the thousands of Kikuyu who migrated to settler farms for work lost in the process. See C. Leo, *Land and Class in Kenya,* (Toronto, 1984).
129 Moore, *Social Facts,* 209.
130 Chanock, "A Peculiar Sharpness," 18.
131 Merry, "The Articulation," 68.
132 These data are drawn from an unpublished Women's Bureau/Central Bureau of Statistics Survey, 1977, and data provided by the community development officer, Murang'a District, December 1984. Approximately 19 percent of adult women in the district belong to women's groups.
133 See Haugerud, "The Consequences."

8 *Peter C. Bloch*

An Egalitarian Development Project in a Stratified Society: Who Ends Up With the Land?

Introduction

This chapter explores the dynamics of access to land on a group of small-scale irrigation perimeters along the Senegal and Falémé rivers in the department of Bakel in eastern Senegal.[1] A principal motivation for the research was the impression, based on previous writings about the region, that the stratified societies whose members were the intended beneficiaries are extremely resistant to activities that threaten the relatively high status of traditional elites.[2] If this impression were justified, one would expect to observe either failure of the irrigation effort or continuous attempts on the part of elites to control the project or appropriate its benefits. The former is not the case; the latter may well be. Irrigation may be liberating for subordinate groups, however, and recent institutional changes may permit them to gain independent access to irrigable land in a way they were unable to accomplish before.

The perimeters were mostly established in the mid-1970s, when several factors favorable to irrigation were at work. The long Sahel drought had severely damaged the local economy, making rain-fed and flood-recession agriculture and livestock activities highly risky. The flow of remittance income from migrant workers in France was threatened by tightened immigration regulations and French unemployment. Population pressure had reduced the land surplus that many of the villages previously felt they had enjoyed. The government of Senegal was prepared to extent its development activities into the region for the first time. Foreign donors had become concerned about the preparedness of riverine populations for participation in grandiose future development plans for the Senegal River basin.

Most of these factors obtain to this day. The only one that may have changed is the climate: three good rainfall years in a row have convinced many that the drought cycle is over. If rain-fed and flood-recession agriculture is once again perceived as profitable, interest in irrigation may wane, especially among those groups who benefited from the prior situation through tithes and labor prestations in traditional agriculture.

The Context for the Study

Land Law

The *Loi sur le Domaine National* (Law on the National Domain), enacted in 1964, was an attempt to place the best aspects of customary African tenure systems on a modern egalitarian and democratic foundation. The law did not recognize the right of private ownership of land and made the state the manager of the national domain, which was virtually the entire land area of the country.[3] The state received the right to designate any part of this domain as being of public utility and thus to take it from its previous users. However, in the absence of the exercise of this power, farmers maintained their use rights without condition other than that they continue to cultivate the land actively. At the same time, the law made illegal the inegalitarian aspects of customary land tenure. It dispossessed traditional landowning nobilities, present in most of the nation's ethnic groups, of any claims such as tithes and rents which they had on farmers in return for access fo "their" land.

While the law made the state the guarantor of the national domain, it envisioned the establishment of a system of local government, one of whose major tasks was to manage rural land in a way that reflected local priorities and conditions. The administrative reform of 1972 established a system of *communautés rurales* (rural communities), organized according to geographic and ethnic concerns, with a locally chosen *conseil rural* (rural council) as the legislative body responsible for land distribution. Until the reform, Senegalese local government, like the French, was merely a manifestation of the central government, a quasi-military corps of governors and *préfets*. Under the old system, the lowest level was the arrondissement, administered by a *sous-préfet*. The new system established the communautés rurales as subdivisions of the arrondissements in order both to bring local government one tier further down and to increase local participation in it.[4]

The administrative reform was implemented region by region over the decade after 1972. Eastern Senegal, in which Bakel is located, was the last area to hold elections for the rural councils. These took place in 1982. The councils have done very little thus far, but it is clear that they will play a larger role in the future, assuming that the state continues its present policy of disengagement and decentralization. The rural councils may also serve as a modern means for traditional elites to maintain their dominance, legitimized by the trappings of democratic processes. In the department of Bakel, the same families who held the land in most of the villages firmly controlled the rural councils.

The Development of Irrigation in the Senegal River Valley

The Senegal River is one of the largest in Africa, second only to the Niger in the Sahel. Figure 8.1 shows the extent of its basin, which drains

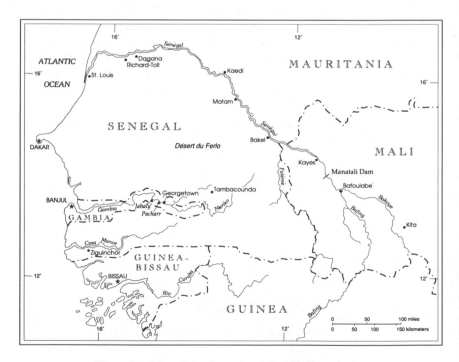

Figure 8.1. Map of the Senegal and Gambia River basins

289,000 square kilometers. The principal tributaries of the Senegal, the Bafing, the Bakoye, and the Falémé, rise in the moist uplands of the Fouta Djalon in Guinea. The river system is highly seasonal: at Bakel, which is considered the dividing line between the upper basin and the valley, the average flow in September, the height of the flood season, is 3,320 cubic meters per second (cumecs); in May and June, it drops to about 10 cumecs.[5] There is also substantial interannual variation in the river's flow. This century, the largest average rate over a year was 1,241 cumecs in 1924, and the lowest was 264 cumces in 1972. During the drought cycle that appears now to have ended, the average was rarely above 500 cumecs.

To regularize flow both within and between years, a dam has been built at Manantali in Mali. A complementary antisaltwater intrusion dam has been completed at Diama, near the mouth of the river. Together, these dams are to provide enough water for nearly one-half million hectares of mostly double-cropped irrigated land. In addition, Manantali will eventually generate hydropower and permit year-round navigation as far upstream as Kayes.

Most of the new irrigation development will take place on land that is now devoted to flood-recession farming during good years. This land, the so-called walo, is held by a minority of the population, mostly from the noble castes of both the Soninké who form the majority group in Bakel and the Toucoulcur who dominate the Middle Valley.[6]

Traditional Soninké Land Tenure Systems[7]

The Soninké concentrate in the region surrounding the three-way boundary of Senegal, Mauritania, and Mali. They are dominant along an 80-kilometer stretch of the Senegal Valley on the Senegal side, from Ballou to Waoundé. Bakel, the principal town, is roughly midway. Soninké social structure is rigidly stratified into three broad groups: nobles, subordinate castes, and descendants of slaves. (Table 8.1 presents a simplified schema of the caste system.) In the past, the nobles, clerics, and warriors did not themselves farm, instead relying on the labor services of slaves. This practice has disappeared now, and virtually everyone farms. Nobles, however, retain ultimate control over farmland. Members of the subordinate castes, descendants of slaves, and ethnic minorities gain access to farmland in return for one or more of a variety of payments, depending on the type of land and the relationship between its owner and the farmer. The principal payments for use of land are *diaka, ñiñagumankande, muso,* and *debigumankande*. Diaka is the Islamic *zakat,* generally 10 percent of the crop. Supposedly a religious tithe, this payment is more frequently a very secular land tax paid to landowners.

Table 8.1. Summary of the caste structure of the Soninké of the Gajaaga

Caste name	Description
Hooro	Nobles; the kingly Bacili are termed *tunka*
Moodini	Maraboutic (clerical) families
Mangu	Warriors and military advisers to the Bacili
Nyaxamala	Artisans; several subgroups are found, notably:
Saxo	woodworkers
Tégu	blacksmiths
Jaagarafu	Descendants of slaves attached to the royal family of the Bacilis who have been assigned responsibility to manage the Waalo, Falo, and Kollangal lands still retained by the Bacilis and to collect payments for use of those lands. Also called *kolyadio*.
Komo	Descendants of slaves without the above distinction.

Ñiñagumankande is a small crop share (literally, a basketful) paid to the landowner. Muso is the same as the Toucouleur *njoldi*, a variable crop share paid to the landowner, the amount depending on the relationship between landowner and user. Debigumankande is a small crop share (a basketful) paid to the village chief. Historically, these payments could add up to more than half the crop. According to Samba Traoré,[8] the system is breaking down now, so that everyone is becoming *maître de son champ* (master of his field).

The fundamental unit for production and consumption is the *ka,* a lineage segment that may consist of a father and his sons or several brothers. The oldest male, the *kagumme,* heads it and is responsible for land management. In dry-land agriculture, the ka farms a large part of its land as a common field (*té khoré*), with the kagumme organizing work and distributing its product. Individual men and women usually have their own, separate plots that they farm when the kagumme does not need them to work on the té khoré; the women's individual fields provide them with their only independent income.

Control of land is not the same in each village. The history of the relationship of each of them to the Bacili kings over the past 200 to 300 years dictates which families own, control access to, and collect use payments on the lands within its boundaries. Tables 8.2 and 8.3 summarize this situation for the six villages in the region downstream of Bakel.

Thus we see the complexity and diversity of traditional landholding arrangements within a very small geographic area. There are two types of villages, those (shown in table 8.2) where the Bacili have yielded their essential rights on all types of land,[9] and those (shown in table 8.3) where they have given a part of their rights, usufruct, on a part of the land (*jeeri*)[10] while retaining them on the valuable land. It is not only

Table 8.2. Families granted direct land rights by the Bacili

Village	Family name	Caste
Manael	Jallo (Diallo)	Mangu
Diawara	Saaxo[9] (Sakho)	Moodini
	Ba (Bâ)	Moodini
	Dukkure (Doucouré)	Moodini
	Bommu (Bomu)	Nyaxamala: tégué
	Koyita (Koïta)	Moodini
Yelingara	Sumaare (Soumaré)	Hooro
	Siibi (Sibi)	Mangu
	Dukkure (Doucouré)	Moodini
	Faadiga (Fadiga)	Nyaxamala: tégué

Table 8.3. Villages granted usufructuary rights to Jeeri land by the Bacili

Village	Land-administering family	Caste
Mouderi	Njaay (N'Diaye)	Hooro
	Sek (Seck)	Mangu
	Daraame (Dramé)	Moodini
Galladé	Bacili (Bathily)	Hooro
	Gunjam (Goundiam)	Mangu
	Daraame (Dramé)	Moodini
Gandé	Tuure (Touré)	Jaagarafu

nobles who control or administer land; families from all castes do so in one or more of the six villages. The Tuure of Gandé are the only descendants of slaves listed, and they are from a specialized subcaste appointed by the Bacili to deal with land administration, collecting payments from the users.

The Origins of the Irrigated Perimeters

The Bakel small irrigated perimeters (AID acronym, BSIP) were established as a result of local initiative. Migrants returning from years of work in France and the former French Empire, notably, Diabé Sow of the village of Kounghani and Seydou Nianghané of Ballou, wished to use the funds they had accumulated during their years abroad for some useful purpose at home, to prepare for the inevitable time when France's demand for African manual labor would dry up. A French nongovernmental organization (NGO) helped to develop small irrigation systems in several villages in 1975 and approached USAID to finance pumping equipment. Flush with Sahel drought-related funds,

USAID converted this small request into a $3.1 million project, which became $7 million by the time it was contracted out in 1977.[11] The project's purposes were to provide immediate drought relief and to permit learning by doing for an eventual expansion to medium- and even large-scale irrigation systems. Simultaneously, SAED, the parastatal agency created to execute the ambitious program of Senegal River Basin development, asserted its control of all irrigation in the department of Bakel, even that which had preceded its arrival. From a self-generated and modest effort, BSIP quickly became bureaucratized, capital intensive, and outward oriented. The Soniké, led by Sow and Nianghané, organized the Federation of Farmers to counter SAED's efforts to convert peasants into agricultural laborers. For a variety of reasons, the Senegalese government refused to recognize the federation as an official organization until 1984. Adrian Adams provides an insider's chronicle of this situation, eloquently telling the story from Sow's perspective.[12]

Sow's original idea was to generalize the family-wide té khoré to the entire village production group, approaching a socialist model of co-operative production. Thus, the earliest irrigated perimeters were collective in nature, with all participants equally contributing labor on a schedule determined by the head of the *groupement* (the production group), the analogue of the kagumme. The participants equally divided the produce as well. In contrast, SAED pushed for individualization of parcels, of farming decisions, and of distribution of rewards, though it would have left the groupement as a whole responsible for reimbursement of input loans. In practice, in most of the Soninké villages after the first two or three years, the perimeter extensions have consisted of the creation and expansion of family plots, frequently but not always managed as té khoré fields, with the village collective field becoming decreasingly important. The trend away from collective farming is primarily the result of the inability of the groupements to induce farmers to contribute their labor enthusiastically. Thus, production suffered and farmers began to lose interest in participating in irrigation.

It is important to note that both systems, the collective one espoused by Sow and the individualist one promoted by SAED and supported by USAID, are revolutionary; they are based on the principle of ignoring caste distinctions in granting access to irrigated land. By diverting attention from this fact, the struggle between SAED and the federation may have served the interests of the landholding elites, whose concern for ideological arguments about incentives is unlikely to be deep and whose desire to maintain or restore their authority over land and the revenues it generates remains strong. The drought made irrigation possible. As the head of a Soninké groupement was quoted as saying in 1983[13] and did say again in 1987: "A drowning man will grab onto any object you reach out to him to save his life, even if it is a knife; this is how we felt when we accepted SAED's help." In the past few years, people in the region have begun to believe that the drought is over. As this belief intensifies, irrigation's sharp edge may not be grasped as tightly by an elite whose fear of drowning has diminished. If the traditional agricultural system, combined with remittance flows, can once again provide a fairly reliable basis for the restoration of the nobles' control over land, nobles may prefer this to continued risky experimentation with innovations. Insofar as their power has not been broken yet, irrigation may therefore face eventual failure.

However, there is a new dynamic that works in the opposite direction. The inhabitants of the Senegal River valley have become very conscious of the implications of the *après-barrages,* the economic potential of the Manantali Dam. It will make water available for double-cropped irrigation in most of the Bakel region, and the nation will be under pressure to develop such systems rapidly to generate revenues to pay off the huge costs of river basin development. As we have seen, the land law allows the state to exercise eminent domain for development purposes, and villagers fear that if they do not respond to the opportunities for irrigation, the state will invite outsiders to do so. In the past three years, several individuals resident in the region have asked for land from the rural councils and have been given assistance with land preparation by SAED. They are invariably well connected politically, both locally and nationally. However, they are also members of the traditional landholding elite, nobles or their representatives. Thus, a part of the traditional elite is responding to the new opportunities and exercising a new type of control over economically valuable land.

Design of the Perimeters

SAED was well aware of the need to clarify landholding issues. While its technicians identified irrigable land according to technical considerations, it always consulted the village chief and always requested and usually received the agreement of the traditional landowners. In all cases, the owners ceded to the government the right to use the land, without relinquishing claims of ownership. There appears to be a consensus in the villages that if the groupement stops irrigating, the owners may take back their land, even though national law had invalidated all such traditional claims.

SAED imposed a condition of equal access in return for its assistance in developing the perimeter. In other words, the groupement was to be

open to all residents of the village who wished to join, regardless of caste
or gender. The only initial condition was participation in the land preparation that needed to be done before the works could be installed.[14] In
no village did all households participate, though at the outset the majority usually did. Nonparticipants are, according to participants, the most
conservative, xenophobic villagers, who feared that they would merely
be working for white people or other Senegalese.

At the outset, village groupements farmed the land collectively, as
Sow had envisioned. For one or two years, most succeeded quite well.
Then the universal problem of collective agriculture, the free rider,
raised its head, and many responded to SAED's recommendation to
individualize the perimeter and divide the available land among the
willing participants. On consultation with the villages, SAED instituted
a lottery system for plot choice, with no discrimination between castes.

Notwithstanding the condition of equal access, there is a great deal of
variation among villages in women's access to irrigated land. Married
women are almost always counted in the ka for the purposes of membership in the irrigation groupement. Sometimes, as in Ballou I, their participation awards the ka the same amount of land as men's participation
does. Sometimes, as in Aroundou, it counts only half as much. Sometimes, as in Diawara II, wives and other dependent women are not
permitted to participate at all, although female heads of households do.
Because households generally have more married adult women than
married men due to polygyny, the amount of irrigated land they can
have depends strongly on how women are treated.

Two other principles on which SAED and the village groupements
agreed were equality of plot size per participant and of land quality. This
too was to ensure equity of land distribution. These conditions appear to
have been observed, at least on paper. In a few cases, the groupement
leaders received extra land or the first choice of it, but most perimeters
were designed to minimize differences in quantity and quality as well as
in access to water. Figure 8.2 illustrates the typical design, using the
example of the Aroundou perimeter.

Two pumps lift water from the river over the high levee-like bank, and
the water spreads via the canal system shown. The plots are long, narrow strips extending from the high point of the system and descending
the gradual slope toward the marigot, or depression. The high land
tends to be sandy and permeable, which makes it not well suited for rice,
while the lower land near the marigot tends to have a higher clay content, which holds water better for paddy cultivation. Thus, all farmers
have land near the head of the irrigation system, sandy land, and clayey

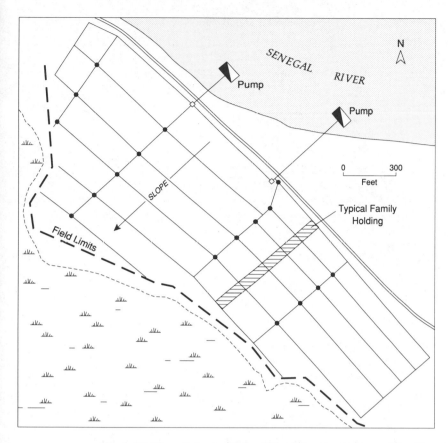

Figure 8.2. Plan of the Aroundou irrigation perimeter

land. In the particular case of Aroundou, each household is assigned land according to the number of participating adults: a strip 800 meters long (to the fifth parallel secondary canal) and 10 meters wide for each male and 5 meters wide for each female. A typical household with two adult male and seven adult females would therefore have a field of 800 by 55 meters, or over four hectares. Most perimeters have smaller individual holdings than Aroundou does, but the principle is the same.

Table 8.4 shows the current status of the Soninké perimeters. Each village had one perimeter as of the mid-1970s, and then in the mid-1980s, more perimeters began to be constructed as the old locations (such as in Diawara and Mouderi) reached the limits to expansion or schisms broke apart the groupement (as in Ballou). In every village

Table 8.4. Selected characteristics of irrigated perimeters, Soninké villages, department of Bakel

Perimeter	Year founded	Village popu- lation	Area (ha)	No. of mem- bers	Area/ member	% Area farmed in 1986	Percentage of nobles	slaves[a]	other
Ballou I	1976	2,499	120	476	0.25	88.1	90	4	6
Ballou II	1986	2,499	44	274	0.16	100.0	36	57	7
Aroundou	1976	1,436	76	187	0.41	99.3	57	23	20
Yafera	1976	1,271	102	211	0.48	62.7	n.a.[b]	n.a.	n.a.
Golmi Marabout[c]	1975	2,417	25	222	0.11	100.0	30	6	64
Kounghani	1975	1,415	37	160	0.23	98.6	n.a.	n.a.	n.a.
Bakel Kollangal	1982	8,015	178	539	0.33	96.1	20	71	9
Bakel Gassam- bilakhe	1976	8,015	42	220	0.19	68.8	17	78	5
Tuabou	1975	1,393	42	64	0.66	100.0	33	55	12
Manael	1976	1,212	25	267	0.09	100.0	51	19	30
Yelingara	1976	602	18	106	0.17	100.0	n.a.	n.a.	n.a.
Diawara I	1976	3,682	96	616	0.16	87.5	n.a.	n.a.	n.a.
Diawara II	1985	3,682	50	345	0.14	100.0	n.a.	n.a.	n.a.
Mouderi I	1976	3,547	68	135	0.50	100.0	29	63	8
Mouderi II	1985	3,547	62	118	0.52	100.0	14	73	13
Mouderi III	1987	3,547	50	58	0.86	—[d]	22	71	7
Mouderi femmes	1987	3,547	10	215	0.05	—[e]	29	57	14
Galladé	1976	698	38	192	0.20	12.5	48	50	2
Gandé	1976	585	19	89	0.21	26.3	45	36	19
Total/ Average		28,772	1,102	4,494	0.25		40	43	17[f]

Sources: Year, Population, Area, % Farmed in 1986: SAED and USAID data. No. of members and caste composition: Project census (SAED data on members for perimeters we could not visit).

Notes: [a]Includes *kome* and *jaagarafu*.

[b]n.a. means "data not available."

[c]Golmi Marabout was originally constructed for the sole benefit of the important religious leader (marabout) residing there. Golmi is the only Soninké village that does not have a villagewide groupement. Several people whose land borders the Marabout's have had their land included in the perimeter in recent years.

[d]For Yafera, Kounghani, Yelingara, and Diawara I, missing data are due to these groupements' unwillingness to participate in the study.

[e]For Diawara II, missing data are due to our inability to complete the census thus far.

[f]Overall average caste distribution calculated for those perimeters with available data.

there is an expressed demand for more land, both to expand the size of individual holdings and to increase the number of people with access to irrigated land.

There are several new groups in the process of formation, and there are also two other groups (Kounghani Marabout and Aroundou Emigrés, not shown in table 8.4) that are atypical in having been organized around a single individual or family and in having remained so.

There are substantial differences among perimeters along all the dimensions shown in the table. The villages are all large by Senegalese standards, reflecting the importance of access to the river. But excluding the administrative and market center, Bakel, they range in size from 600 persons to nearly 4,000.

There is a wide range in the size of the perimeters as well, although none is large. To give a scale of comparison, the Gezira scheme in Sudan has over one million hectares; the Office du Niger in Mali has 50,000; and a typical Middle Valley perimeter in Senegal has 1,000. The small size is a result of two factors: (1) the relative unavailability of irrigable land compared to downstream areas; and (2) the desire of SAED and USAID to begin on a pilot basis. The current USAID project intends to double the area irrigated, assuming an irrigable potential of at least 5,000 hectares.

Membership of the groupements ranges from tiny, Tuabou, to substantial, Ballou, Bakel, and Diawara. In the latter three, formal subgroups have been organized to cope with management on the tertiary systems. In spite of efforts by SAED to make the allocation of land equal within villages, substantial differences persist between them. This is generally because of differences in the availability of appropriate land. Manael, which has an abundance of dry land, has had to seek irrigation land within the village limits of Tuabou, which has limited dry land but more irrigable land than it presently uses. However, given the history of the region and the intervillage conflicts over land which are being played out currently, it is not likely that SAED will be able to equalize land per person across the villages in the project until the perimeters grow to transcend village boundaries.

Most of the irrigable land was farmed in 1986, with only two perimeters, Galladé and Gandé, showing substantial unused area. Both groupements attributed this to poor land clearing by SAED on new irrigated fields. Two others, Yafera and Bakel Gassambilakhe, farmed about two-thirds of the available land. There is no way of knowing from the data whether this was two-thirds of the farmers or two-thirds of the acreage of each farmer. The second year of good rains in the region was 1986, and by 1987, there were signs that farmers had gone back to dry-land farming at the expense of irrigation. In the 1987 rainy season (the principal season for irrigation), Aroundou did not irrigate at all, and during our field visit in August of that year, fewer than one-third of the parcels had been prepared for transplanting rice, one month later than usual. All groupements appeared to be unhappy with the lack of credit for purchase of inputs, and farmers began to think that the prospects for dry lands had returned to predrought levels. If we had 1987 data, the numbers in table 8.4 might look very different. However, in 1988, according to SAED, all groupements were irrigating again.

The caste composition of the perimeters varies considerably. In the absence of village census data, which are not available by caste, it is not possible to determine whether caste participation in the groupements reflects its proportion in the village population. However, the proportion of *komo* and *jaagarafu* (descendants of slaves) in the two Bakel groupements is substantially greater than in any of the other villages. We suspect, but have not yet been able to verify, that many of the members of these groupements are migrants into Bakel because they had inadequate access to land at home. There is one dramatic within-village difference to indicate as well: Ballou I has 90 percent nobles and 4 percent slaves, whereas Ballou II has 36 percent and 57 percent, respectively. Below, I tell the story of the Ballou schism.

Approach and Findings to Date of the Land Tenure Center Bakel Research Program

The introduction of small-scale smallholder irrigation systems into a stratified society can lead to a variety of outcomes with respect to the dynamics of land tenure. The project may survive and even grow over time. In this case, sons of the original beneficiaries may retain their land, while others lose it through abandonment or failure to pay debts to the groupement. Such losses can lead either to increasing concentration of holdings in the hands of elites and/or commercially minded farmers or to no change in land distribution among families or castes but merely a reshuffling to former nonparticipants and outsiders.

Alternatively, the project may fail, thereby eliminating all participants' access to irrigable land. Collapse may come from the unwillingness of elites to participate in irrigation; their inability to get dependent farmers to pay tribute and to farm irrigated plots for them; a successful takeover of the scheme by elites which causes casted people and captives to opt out of it; or other causes altogether. New perimeters may develop to allow a subset of the population to participate. In this case, new landholding elites may use their access to the rural councils to acquire irrigated land for themselves and their allies, or subordinate castes may break away from elite domination and strike out on their own.

In the early years of the perimeters, up to about 1980, it appeared that the original beneficiaries were retaining their land. Jean-Yves Weigel depicts an enthusiasm for irrigation that spread throughout Mouderi, though he found this strongest among the descendants of slaves, who even went to the extreme of hiring day labor from seasonal migrants to help them during peak periods.[15] In the early 1980s, renewed drought gave added impulse to the perimeters and motivated USAID to finance rehabilitation of much of the irrigated land and a doubling of the acreage of most of them. In more recent years, thanks both to a conviction that the drought is over and to a reduction of credit and of the government subsidies on inputs, the enthusiasm has diminished in many villages, though not in Mouderi, where seven perimeters exist and at least two more are in formation.

Our research program focuses on two closely related questions. Are there differences in access to irrigated land by gender and caste, and is this situation changing over time? How do households decide how to allocate their labor time between irrigated and dry-land farming, given that the two activities have overlapping peak periods?

The core data of the project are being collected by two graduate students, an agricultural economist, and an anthropologist. The anthropologist is addressing the first question in the turbulent and dynamic context of Mouderi, and the agricultural economist is addressing the second question by conducting comparative studies of several perimeters with both intensive interviews and surveys. This chapter concludes with a discussion of the first question. Subsequent articles will treat the second.

In the first year of the project, two brief visits were made to the study area to initiate contact, to secure local approval for the research, and to conduct key-informant interviews and the already-mentioned parcel census. In two subsequent visits, I have complemented the information then gathered. These visits have produced several discussion papers that have provided some of the data reported here.[16]

Here I give three indications of the dynamics at work. The first is the case of Ballou, one of the two villages where irrigation has been the most successful. The second, drawn from data from our groupement census, shows the striking differences between the original perimeters and the more recently organized ones. The third describes the complex situation in Mouderi.

The Ballou Schism

Ballou is a village of moderate size, 2,500 inhabitants, on the Falémé, just above its confluence with the Senegal, and is the farthest upstream of the Soninké villages. It is probably the most isolated during the rainy season, as it is the farthest away from the all-weather road. It has ample lands, both *fondé* (high river bank land, rarely inundated) and jeeri. It has a single dominant family, the Nianghané, many of whom have had successful migration experiences not only in Europe but in North and Central Africa as well. While its location is relatively southerly, implying more rainfall than at the northern, downstream end of the department of Bakel, there does not appear to be any more reluctance to irrigate in Ballou than in, say, Gandé, at the other extreme of the department.

Ballou has the largest irrigated area and, with 720 members as of 1985, the largest number of group members of any of the villages affiliated with the BSIP except Bakel itself. In 1985, an election of the leadership of the groupement led to a schism. The former president, Seydou Nianghané, was defeated by his half-brother, led the schismatics in forming a second groupement, Ballou II, and sought land for a perimeter and help from SAED in preparing it. The second task was quickly accomplished. SAED offered help with a grader, as they intermittently had during previous extensions of the original perimeter. But getting land was not as easy.

The procedure envisioned by the law is to apply to the rural council for use rights. This is a simple matter, involving no more than a brief written request, and does not entail the payment of fees. In principle, under the provisions of the Law on the National Domain, the rural council should not refuse to allocate land to local inhabitants who wish to use land productively. But the schismatics instead began by following the procedures of customary law and applied first to the village chief. The chief, another member of the Nianghané family, refused them. They then went to the village's representative to the rural council, also a Nianghané. He refused to intervene. So finally, as the third step, Ballou II took its request to the rural council itself. The principle became fact: the rural council granted the groupement the land it requested.

There are several possible explanations for these developments. First and most simply, a defeated president may have opted for exit after losing the relatively complete control of the perimeter he had enjoyed since its inception. The chief and the village rural council representative then punished him for splitting up the groupement. However, the split may have become inevitable because of the large size of the membership. Such a total, 720, 190 of them men grouped in fifty-nine kas, is a large number to maintain under a single leadership. Yet another factor leading to the split was increasing social tension brought about by the equalization of incomes and status which irrigation introduced. The Ballou II membership list shows that 57 percent of its members are komo, descendants of slaves, whereas only 4 percent of the Ballou I members are. Hooro, or nobles, comprise 90 percent of Ballou I, while they comprise only 36 percent of Ballou II. These numbers suggest that caste issues were beginning to be raised. When the irrigated perimeter was finally judged to be a success, the traditional leaders decided they wanted to control it, which meant reducing the role of the casted people and slaves. Seydou Nianghané legitimized the original perimeter at a time when the village leadership was unwilling to commit itself to irrigation. The komo may have asked him to serve a similar role in getting them out from under the dominance of the traditional leadership in Ballou I. Whatever the legal status of the rural council and the equality before the law of all Senegalese, it is inconceivable that a group of komo could have succeeded in persuading the rural council to grant them land without a leader from the hooro or moodini classes.

The new president of Ballou I uttered the words quoted above: "A drowning man will grab onto any object you reach out to him to save his life, even if it is a knife; this is how we felt when we accepted SAED's help." In this case, the drowning person represents the elite. The knife is slicing away at their grasp on the local economy, a grasp maintained by their control over land. Once irrigation succeeded, their ownership of large areas of dry and flood-recession land would become irrelevant because irrigation would be the principal source of farm income. Thus, irrigation threatens the livelihood only of the elite. The dispossessed view it as their way out. To the extent that this explains the schism, Ballou II exemplifies the threat to elite domination that irrigation has brought; members of subordinate castes with independent access to land are no longer forced by either economic necessity or customary patron-client relationships to farm and to pay tithes on elite-owned land. Meanwhile, Ballou I, as long as it continues to thrive, is an example of increasing concentration of holdings in the hands of the elite. However, it remains to be seen to what extent this perimeter depended on the descendants of slaves for its successful operation.

Caste Distribution on Recent Versus Original Perimeters

The numbers in table 8.4 indicate that the newer perimeters appear to have larger numbers of *komo* than the older ones. This is demonstrated systematically in table 8.5, which divides the Soninké perimeters into

Table 8.5. Caste structure on recent versus old perimeters

	Xoore	Moodi	Mangué	Castes	Komo	Jaagarafu	Miscel-laneous	Missing	Total
Total	1,281	176	39	126	1,303	78	55	66	3,124
Mouderi II	16	2	5	5	67	19	4	0	118
Mouderi III	13	1	0	1	17	24	2	0	58
Mouderi femmes	63	5	9	15	105	18	0	0	215
Bakel-Collengal	110	14	0	16	379	0	20	0	539
Ballou II	99	6	0	12	157	0	0	0	274
Total Recent	301	28	14	49	725	61	26	0	1,204
Total - Recent = Original	980	148	25	77	588	17	29	66	1,920
% Recent	25.0	2.3	1.1	4.1	60.3	5.1	2.1	0	100
% Original*	52.8	8.0	1.3	4.1	31.6	0.8	1.4	*	100
% Total*	41.9	5.8	1.2	4.1	42.6	2.6	1.8	*	100

*The percentage distribution on the original perimeters and for the total is calculated excluding the "missing" category. The missing are in Golmy and are likely, given the perimeter's organization, to be nobles. If they were included as such, the contrast between recent and original perimeters would be somewhat greater.

two categories, the originals established during the 1970s and the more recently created ones for which we have information. The caste distribution is markedly different. Over half of the membership of the originals is noble (xoore and moodi), compared to only one-fourth on the new perimeters. The share of former slaves is one-third on the former and three-fifths on the latter. The intermediate groups, mangué, castes, and miscellaneous, have roughly the same share of membership in the two categories. This suggests that the impulse to expand irrigation is disproportionately found among the former slaves, who have less access to flood-recession agriculture and therefore benefit relatively more than nobles from irrigation.

This conclusion should be made with some caution. As noted above, Ballou II is composed primarily of people who left Ballou I. They were members of the original groupement from the beginning. This is also true, to a lesser extent, of Mouderi II. In the absence of comparable census information from the early years of the BSIP project, we cannot make a definitive argument that *new irrigators* are primarily from the dispossessed castes. The information does show, however, that the latter group is exiting from the original perimeters to form new ones, perhaps as a declaration of independence from their traditional masters. But it is necessary to look somewhat more closely at the data. In spite of their quite similar caste structure, the three new Mouderi perimeters shown in table 8.5 have very different histories. Below, I describe the Mouderi situation in more detail.

Mouderi

The village of Mouderi is unique in that virtually all of its irrigable land is controlled by people from the neighboring village of Diawara, the Saaxo family, who as we have seen purchased it from the Bacili kings for a *muud* (8–9 pounds) of gold. This has meant that the creation or extension of each perimeter has required long negotiations and litigation. In spite of this, Mouderi is now the most dynamic village with respect to irrigation.

Mouderi has at least eight groupements, of which seven had begun operations by early 1989. Mouderi I was an original perimeter, founded in the mid-1970s. Its membership was open to the entire village, and it started with approximately 500 participants, who farmed collectively on fewer than thirty hectares. The returns per participant were low, and members began drifting away, so that by 1980, only about thirty families remained. Since then, the perimeter has performed quite well with its more reasonable amount of land per participant (0.5 ha per participant in 1986).

With the return of the drought in the early 1980s and the impending completion of the Senegal River dams with their promise of year-round water, many of those who had dropped out of Mouderi I wished to resume irrigation. Unable to return to the original perimeter, they obtained sixty-two hectares of land and formed Mouderi II. This groupement allocated its land to heads of household only, thereby excluding women and junior men from participation. The women reacted by forming their own groupement and requesting land for themselves. Their case was strengthened by the fact that many of them had been farming, in traditional fashion, on the land taken for Mouderi II. The rural council allocated them a small, distant perimeter that is labeled "Mouderi femmes," with individual plots one-tenth the size of those on Mouderi I and II.

In the past five years, the pace of irrigation development has quickened, with a new twist. The dynamic situation in Mouderi can be largely attributed to two men, the president of the rural council and the local deputy to the National Assembly, who have been active in promoting the creation of perimeters in Mouderi. In addition to their contributions to the development of irrigation for others, however, they have also done very well for themselves. The *député,* a member of the jaagarafu caste that administered and collected taxes on land for nobles, has strong political connections in Dakar and has ambitions to develop a substantial commercial farming operation on his thirty hectares. The president, a xoore and a member of a minor branch of the chiefly family of Mouderi, has been responsible for the creation of all the perimeters except for I and III (the deputy's) and for the allocation of land to women's and youth groups in all the villages of the rural community. He has also, however, created a fifty-hectare perimeter for himself, V, on which he has exclusive control of ten hectares.

Mouderi III was formed by the National Assembly deputy, a jaagarafu; Mouderi V by the president of the rural council, a noble who is also the power in Mouderi II; and Mouderi VI by an absentee member of the same noble family as Mouderi V. All three of these owe their success to their influence in the rural council. All three are members of the traditional landholding or land-administering elite. These perimeters represent a continuation of elite control in spite of the numerical predominance of descendants of slaves that table 8.4 shows. In these cases, the slave-caste members were all formerly the slaves of the elite members who found the groupements.

In addition, four other groupements are in various stages of formation, one by a Muslim brotherhood (VI), one by a youth group (VII), one by a women's group (VIII, a superset of the one that has been farming Mouderi femmes), and one to include farmers with little previous participation in irrigation (IX). While we have no quantitative information on the caste structure of these four groupements, our key informants suggest that they are composed essentially of nonelite people. They are also, with the exception of the women's group, all-male. All were granted land (with individual holdings substantially smaller than on the other perimeters) at the initiative of the president of the rural council—after he had obtained land for himself and his allies.

The Mouderi groupements fit into three categories. Mouderi I stands by itself as a rejuvenated version of the original model of a villagewide, nonexclusionary perimeter. Mouderi II, III, IV, and V all have membership limited to a subset of the population: family heads, the traditional gerontocracy, in Mouderi II; and the allies of politically connected people in III, IV, and V. Mouderi femmes and Mouderi VI–IX also represent subsets of the population—but traditionally subordinate ones. The idealism of the early years, that the entire village could work together with a common purpose, has clearly not survived. While elites have managed to control some of the new development, they have not been successful in controlling all of it. In fact, a part of the elite, as represented by the president of the rural council himself, has recognized the need to extend access to irrigated land to all segments of the population. The basis of access has changed, however, from the original "universal access" to "separate but more or less equal."

The lesson to be learned from Mouderi is that control over the land allocation process is no longer strictly in the hands of the traditional elite, but all those who now have this control are members of the traditional elite. Being a noble or a jaagarafu is a necessary, but not a sufficient, condition for control of land in the new institutional situation; one must also have access to power in its modern form: the rural council.

Conclusion

In this chapter, I have presented some evidence of changes in access to land on the Bakel small irrigated perimeters. The dynamic is clearly related to caste structure and gender. Dispossessed groups have exited from the original perimeters in some villages, forming new ones in Ballou, Mouderi, and Diawara but not yet elsewhere. Women have attempted, with limited success in Mouderi but not elsewhere, to secure access rights of their own. These facts suggest that elite control over land allocation has been weakened. However, the most striking development works in the other direction. In Mouderi, for example, a new land-controlling elite, with national political connections as well as membership in the traditional local elite, dominates the rural council. It has appropriated substantial amounts of irrigable land for itself and has chosen the members of its own groupements. To its credit, it has also begun to ensure that subordinary groups have access to irrigable land, and it has done this over the objections of the traditional elite. Other parts of the Bakel zone have not yet participated in Mouderi's reinvigorated irrigation boom, but the Ballou schism is a forerunner of things to come. Thus, although all segments of the population are able to participate in irrigation, the original hope of universal and egalitarian access to irrigated land, shared by both Diabé Sow and SAED, has evaporated.

Notes

1 This chapter is based in part on analysis contained in P. Bloch, "The Dynamics of Land Tenure: The Case of the Bakel Small Irrigated Perimeters," Bakel Discussion Paper no. 1 (Land Tenure Center, University of Wisconsin–Madison, 1987); S. Traoré, "Le système foncier Soninké du Gajaaga," Bakel Discussion Paper no. 4-F (1987); M. Sella, "An Exploration of Alternative Land Tenure and Organizational Arrangements for the Bakel Small Irrigated

Perimeters," Bakel Discussion Paper no. 2 (1987); M. Bloch, "The Role of Women in the Bakel Small Irrigated Perimeters," Bakel Discussion Paper no. 3 (1987); and P. Bloch, "The Dynamics of Land Tenure on the Bakel Small Irrigated Perimeters: Final Report on the Land Tenure Center Research Program" (1989).

2 A. Adams, *Le long voyage des gens du fleuve* (Paris, 1977); A. Adams, *La terre et les gens du fleuve* (Paris, 1985); J.-Y. Weigel, *Migration et production domestique des Soninké du Sénégal,* Travaux et Documents de l'ORSTOM, no. 116 (Paris, 1982).

3 Individuals were given a grace period of six months following the enactment of the law to register their holdings and receive title. Virtually all of the land so registered was urban.

4 However, the independence of the communautés rurales from the central government is far from complete. Rural councils' decisions must be approved by the sous-préfet, who in turn is closely supervised by his superiors, the Ministry of the Interior in Dakar. See G. Hesseling, *Le droit foncier au Sénégal: L'impact de la réforme foncière en Basse Casamance* (Leiden, 1982).

5 P. Platon, "The OMVS program," *Marchés Tropicaux et Méditéranéens,* special issue (Paris, 1981).

6 For a description of the Toucouleur land tenure system, see J.-P. Minvielle, *La structure foncière du Waalo Fuutanké* (Dakar, 1977); and T. Ngaido, "Socio-Economic Implications of Irrigation Systems in Mauritania: The Boghé and Foum-Gleita Irrigation Projects" (M.S. thesis, Department of Agricultural Economics, University of Wisconsin–Madison, 1986).

7 This is a very brief summary of a complex system. For more detail on the Soninké, see E. Pollet and G. Winter, *La société Soninké* (Dyahunu, Mali) (Bruxelles, 1971); Weigel, *Migration;* and Traoré, "Le système foncier."

8 Traoré, "Le système foncier," 34.

9 The Saaxo in fact *bought* the lands of Diawara from the Bacili (for one *muud* (8–9 pounds) of gold, according to Traoré, "Le système foncier"). They then ceded land to their allies, the other listed families, who had participated with them in the negotiations for it.

10 Jeeri land is dry farmland. As Traoré, "Le système foncier," notes, "in ceding the dry land to these families, the Bacili retained the totality of their land tenure rights on 'all lands where water flows'; in other words, on all the inundatable lands, i.e., the floodplains, riverbanks and estuaries."

11 USAID, "Bakel Crop Production: Senegal, Project Paper" (Dakar, 1977).

12 Adams, *Le long voyage* and *La terre.*

13 P. Bloch, "Senegal: Senegal River Basin," in *Land Tenure Issues in River Basin Development in Sub-Saharan Africa,* P. Bloch et al., LTC Research Paper no. 90 (Land Tenure Center, University of Wisconsin–Madison, 1986).

14 Most villages accept men as new members without the clearing prerequisite if they pay a small membership fee; women are not always given the same opportunity. See M. Bloch, "The Role of Women."

15 Weigel, *Migration*.

16 Those cited in n. 1, plus P. Bloch, "Land Tenure Structure of the Bakel Small Irrigated Perimeters: Base Line Survey Report, Part I," Bakel Discussion Paper no. 5 (1987); and P. Bloch, "Land Tenure Structure of the Bakel Small Irrigated Perimeters, Part II," Bakel Discussion Paper no. 7 (1988). An earlier version of this paper was printed as Bakel Discussion Paper no. 6. All are available by request from the author at LTC.

PART 3

RADICAL AGRARIAN REFORM AND AGRICULTURAL PERFORMANCE

9 *H. W. O. Okoth-Ogendo*

Agrarian Reform in Sub-Saharan Africa: An Assessment of State Responses to the African Agrarian Crisis and Their Implications for Agricultural Development

O 13 Q 15

Sub-Saharan Africa

Perspectives

That sub-Saharan Africa is in the throes of an agrarian crisis is now conceded.[1] Indeed, with a food sufficiency ratio of less than 85 percent, sub-Saharan Africa is the only region in the world that does not produce enough food for its own people. Although a large and diversified body of literature is already accumulating on the nature and dimensions of that crisis, an equal amount of effort is not going into an evaluation of state responses in terms of the specific measures taken to try and resolve it.

This chapter discusses some of those measures in relation to what states in eastern and southern Africa have come to see as the *primary causes* of that crisis. Specifically, it discusses agrarian reform policies, plans, and programs for increasing agricultural productivity through interventions directed at improving access to and control of land, production processes, and support services infrastructure. As a precursor to the discussion, a general review of the nature and "presumed" causes of the crisis is necessary.

The Dimensions of the Crisis

Manifestations

It is generally agreed that the African agrarian crisis is essentially a crisis about land. Its condition, availability, and productivity are functions of the organization of labor, the state of agricultural technology, and the resilience of social ideologies that reinforce modes of access to and control of it. It is the negative manifestations of the crisis, namely, extreme population (or land) pressure, stagnation in agricultural productivity, severe food shortages, and general deterioration in living conditions especially in the rural areas, that have become its most quantifiable and visible symptoms.[2] The question to ask is, what is the reason for the crisis? For what it suggests is the existence of normative confusion, if not total anomie; structural contradiction, if not collapse; and basic systemic instability, if not disintegration in African agrarian relations.

Causes

Scholars are deeply divided on the issue of how the crisis is to be explained. Some of the explanations that have been proffered include the persistent effects of colonial exploitation, too high a rate of population growth, inefficient (or obsolete) production technologies, chaotic tenure regimes, market distortions, inherent or fundamental deficiencies in African social structure, the presumed inability of Africans to manage their own economies, and domestic (or state) policies that tend to discriminate against the rural, food-producing sectors of the economy.[3] Those explanations can be divided into diametrically opposed arguments. On the one side are explanations that see external social forces as the criminal that is answerable for the predicament; on the other are those that focus primarily on the victim, that is, African agrarian systems, as the villain of the piece. Because these two arguments are not merely a distillation of the dispassionate intellect of Africanists but also reflect, in no small measure, the policy positions on which most African states have founded their agrarian reform plans and programs, it is important to examine them in some detail.

The Argument That the Crisis Is Externally Induced
The argument that the African agrarian crisis is primarily the product of external forces has been made in a variety of ways. The one most often heard among progressive scholars states that it is the inherently exploitative international context in which sub-Saharan African economies op-

erate which explains that crisis. The way out, it is argued, is for Africa to make the "correct" ideological choices and/or insist on the establishment of a new international economic order.[4]

As a global and comparative heuristic designed to explain Africa's underdevelopment in a historical trends scenario, there is great merit in this perspective. It needs, however, to be taken down to the micro-level before it can yield explanations that are of immediate value to the present discussion. At that level, the most important aspect of the argument is that much of the African agrarian crisis has to do with the system of resource management and exploitation that was erected and pursued by colonial capitalism throughout sub-Saharan Africa for nearly a century and that survived, and in most cases was reentrenched, by the decolonization process in the 1960s.[5] Nowhere was this more ruthlessly executed than in terms of land (including minerals) and labor resources in British Colonial Africa.

It was understood quite early in British colonial policy that an efficient process of exploitation required that land be effectively controlled. That control was usually achieved through the extension of legal ideologies and mechanisms that varied with purpose, geopolity, and amount of deceit and intrigue necessary to obtain it. What was important was that *control* was achieved; the *means* by which this was done, often, was a mere rationalization.[6] In Swaziland, South Africa, Southern Rhodesia (now Zimbabwe), and Kenya, the relevant means involved a series of military and juridical exercises of varying intensity, duration, complexity, and absurdity depending on the manner in which colonial conquest itself was achieved.

Swaziland, which was first invaded in the mid-nineteenth century by the Boer concession hunters, is perhaps the most interesting in this respect. According to a report issued by British colonial authorities in 1907, "practically the whole area of the country was [by the turn of the century] covered two, three and even four deep by concessions of all sizes for different purposes and for greatly varying periods. In but very few cases were even the boundaries defined; many of the areas had been sub-divided and sold several times and seldom were the boundaries of the super-imposed areas even co-terminous."[7]

Therefore, when the British superseded the Boers in Swaziland following the Anglo-Boer war of 1899 and the country began to assume the style of a settler colony, the first thing that was done was to confirm the validity of most of those concessions and then force the concessionaires to surrender at least one-third of the land covered by their respective concessions for "the use and occupation" by the Swazis (Acts no. 3 of 1904, no. 28 of 1907, and no. 41 of 1916). The effect of that "partition," which the Swazis never accepted, was that the Boer concessionaires retained more than 63 percent of Swazi territory. A system of deeds registration enacted soon after allowed them to record these as absolute estates in accordance with the principles of Roman-Dutch law, which the British had extended to Swaziland.

Land expropriation in South Africa was more brutal and protracted. The Boer invasion and settlement of South Africa was based (as indeed all British settlements were) on the supposition that the land was ownerless and therefore open to acquisition by right of conquest of first settlement. According to a noted colonial scholar and administrator,

when towards the end of the eighteenth century the Boers advancing northwards first met the southward movement of the Bantu, neither Boer nor Bantu could justifiably claim to have any superior title to the land.[8]

What was crucial, however, was that with the advantage of superior military power, the Boers were able by the middle of the nineteenth century to dismantle most of the political and social organizations of the African peoples, especially the Zulu and the Sotho, who had mounted great resistance to colonization. The Boers then worked out a system of "native" control, which the British later perfected and legislated in the form of the 1910 Act of Union and the Natives' Land Act of 1913. This latter Act, Lord Hailey explains, was meant to settle once and for all the issue of where the precise boundaries of native land were. It did that by enabling the regrouping of African populations in "reserves" sited along rivers or streams or in rugged and arid regions. The result of this exercise was that approximately 87 percent of South African territory was put beyond the reach of Africans.

The processes of land expropriation in Zimbabwe and Kenya were somewhat similar. They were interlaced with a juridical wrangle that ran from about 1890 to 1930 in the one case and 1939 in the other. The pattern of land distribution and organization of settlements between indigenous communities and the colonizers at the end of that wrangle, however, bore, in both cases, all the characteristics of those developed in Swaziland and South Africa several decades earlier. In the case of Southern Rhodesia, a land commission chaired by Morris Carter recommended in 1926 that the separation of Africans and Europeans was both expedient and practicable. Said the commission,

However desirable it may be that members of the two races should live together side by side with equal rights as regards the holding of land, we are convinced that in practice, probably for generations to come, such a policy is not practicable nor in the best interests of the two races, and that until the native has advanced much farther in the paths of civilization, it is better that points of contact between the two races should be reduced.[9]

Those views were incorporated in the Land Apportionment Act of 1930, which became the cornerstone of land policy in Southern Rhodesia throughout the colonial period. During that period, nearly 70 percent of Southern Rhodesia territory was either exclusively reserved for the colonizers or otherwise unavailable for use by Africans.

Nearly ten years later, in 1934, the same Morris Carter was to recommend a similar system of legalized segregation for Kenya as well. The Kenya Land Commission, which had been appointed to review colonial land practices including instances of "compensation" for expropriated Africans, recommended, after affirming those expropriations, that a final and secure assurance be made to Europeans through an Order-in-Council holding that the land they had seized would remain inviolable. This was done in 1939 through two Orders-in-Council, one for the European highlands and the other for the "native" areas. Approximately 75 percent of all the high-potential land in the country was expropriated to the colonizers.[10]

British land policy in other parts of East and Southern Africa varied only in degree, not in kind. In Northern Rhodesia (now Zambia), that difference lay, at least from the 1940s onward, merely in the language in which legislation was couched rather than in its essence. As early as 1928, a "native" reserve had been created in the East Luangwa District for the purpose not of "protecting" the rights of indigenous peoples but of clarifying what areas could be expropriated by the North Chartered Exploration Company.[11] Later, the colonial government created two new categories of land, namely, Crown land and native trust lands, as mechanisms, in the one case, of excluding Africans from land suitable for European settlement or earmarked for mining development, and, in the other, of enabling Europeans to acquire rights in African areas as and when the colonial government thought this desirable. In either case, the land rights of Africans were clearly insecure. Indeed, as colonial development progressed into the 1940s and 1950s, it was the latter category that was expanded as an instrument of continued expropriation.

In Nyasaland (now Malawi), where the establishment of "reserves" by that name was rejected early in 1921 on the ostensibly laudable ground that it would "seriously prejudice the welfare of communities who are obliged, owing to shortage of water and other local circumstances to live in scattered villages,"[12] the colonial government was nonetheless able to exclude Africans from some 5 percent (probably more) of the best land by merely manipulating the concepts of "crown" ownership and trust holding. In Tanganyika (now mainland Tanzania) and Uganda where settlement was a secondary issue, the expropriation of such land as was required was conducted on the basis of the supposed residual proprietary power of the colonial sovereign, and the separation of the races, which was nonetheless considered necessary, was achieved through legislation prohibiting the sale of land to and by Africans.[13]

The uniformity of land control mechanisms in force in East and southern Africa, particularly the theory that the colonial power had acquired radical (or ultimate) title, and the legal doctrines that were derived from it (i.e., trusteeship, rights of occupancy, reserves, etc.) had for their rationality concerns that went beyond agricultural settlement to include control of mineral resources as well. Indeed in *all* of these countries, such mechanisms were buttressed by legislation that vested in the colonial power all minerals whenever these might be found. The reservation of land for use of Africans or, as in the case of Tanzania after 1923, the prohibition of alienation of freehold or absolute title to land did not in any way derogate from colonial appropriation of mineral resources. In that sense, therefore, no indigenous communities were ever immune from expropriation, relocation, or physical destabilization in colonial Africa. Indeed studies of French, Belgian, and Portuguese land policies in Africa indicate that the British were not unique in this respect.[14]

Next to land, the need to secure a continuous supply of cheap and dependable labor was central to the dynamics of colonial capital. This was particularly important in the settler economies of Kenya and Zimbabwe where the colonizers generally lacked the technical capability and financial resources necessary to make agriculture pay. In the context of Zambia and South Africa, African labor was clearly indispensable to the success of the mineral industry there. A complex system of legislative and administrative controls were therefore developed to facilitate the extraction of sufficient labor on an efficient delivery basis. Those controls included the following mechanisms and processes:

(i)   a series of what were often referred to as "humane pressures" such as employment registration (through the *Kipande,* or native passes), progressive taxes levied on adult males, their huts, widows, or even wives, and "vagrancy" laws;

(ii)   administrative coercion of able-bodied males of the "apparent" age of sixteen or over onto the farms or mines;

(iii) resident (or "kaffir") labor contracts involving, among other things, heavily exploitative share-tenancy arrangements; and

(iv)   of course, progressive reduction of available land within the reserves so as to marginalize indigenous agriculture and hence speed up out-migration.[15]

As a general principle, the legal organization of these mechanisms and processes was designed to keep the laborer constantly on the farm or mine, and coupled with the fact that wages were generally fixed at a level *below* the tax rate, the effect was almost permanent loss to the reserves.[16]

The linkages between the historical scenario outlined above and the primary matrices forming part of the agrarian crisis are not difficult to see. These may be summarized as follows:

(i) First, in all cases examined, the boundary between areas reserved for the indigenous people and the colonizers was invariably coterminous with the division between productive and unproductive land, ecologically endowed land and hostile environments. Indeed the shares of various land use zones between the races were always in inverse correlation to one another: the more suitable the zone was, the larger was the share of it allocated to the colonizers (or the crown) and the smaller to the African and vice versa.[17]

(ii) Second, the notion, as expressed in the "reserves" or "bantustans" policy, that African populations were expected to conform to "ethnic control maps" ran counter to economic and production forces operating in the reserved areas at the time. With time, it was this policy, especially the fact that in addition to excluding Africans as a group from expropriated areas or Crown land, it also forbade access by individuals to land reserved for the use of communities not their own, that became a major disequilibriating factor as population began to mount and technologies of production to stagnate within the reserves.[18]

(iii) Third, the labor policies, mechanisms, and processes outlined above ensured such serious depletion of productive forces in the reserves that food production was often lower than the subsistence demand in those areas. As a result, shortages interspersed with severe famines was a commonplace occurrence under colonialism.[19] As one researcher on South Africa and Zimbabwe commented,

By making relentless demands for labor, it was the mineral revolution (in the one case) which ultimately led to the impoverishment of the African peasantry . . . paradoxically, it was the absence of such a revolution (in the other) which had much the same effect.[20]

(iv) Fourth, the dismantling, especially in South Africa, of indigenous political and social institutions had important consequences for the stability of production relations. Attempts to replace these through the imposition of arrangements founded on the theory that the African had not yet arrived at a level of sophistication that would enable him to plan his own economy only served to aggravate the situation.

The agrarian crisis in Africa, on this analysis, has more than just an intimate linkage with the past. The policies, institutions, and practices that precipitated that crisis and facilitated its perpetuation remain in evidence in most of sub-Saharan Africa. It is a crisis born of a long history of social stagnation, resource plunder, and service deprivation, compounded as we shall see, by more contemporary factors.

The Argument That the Victim Is the Culprit

Whereas the overwhelming majority of scholars will readily admit to the relevance of the colonial experience as a factor in Africa's current predicament, there are a significant number who will still deny that that experience is its fundamental or even major cause. These are the scholars who direct their attention primarily at the victim and argue that the cause(s) of that predicament is to be found in the very nature and constitution of African agrarian organizations. Their enquiry typically proceeds on the assumption that there must be and usually is a single normative or institutional problematique that must be isolated, diagnosed, and cured if Africa is to extricate itself from the burden of underdevelopment. Quite often, that problematique is identified a priori and its pathology conducted within a broad spectrum of epistemology to which the particular scholar subscribes. A number of such positions are examined briefly here.

The first draws together scholars or policy advisers who believe that the crisis is but a historically determined epoch in the evolution of social institutions from a premodern, precapitalist, and status-bound stratum to a fully individualized and contractarian one. Little concession is usually made, on this analysis, to discrete social or cultural settings. Colonial anthropologists, who were some of the earliest to propagate this argument, drew their inspiration from theories developed by a number of ninteenth-century Western European scholars such as Sir Henry Main, Paul Vinogradoff, and Max Weber who thought such progression was inevitable.[21] Having slotted the African at the status end of that continuum, the conclusion that followed was that he was not expected to be a good agriculturalist. A report issued in the 1920s in Zimbabwe commented as follows:

It cannot be said that the native of Mashonaland is a good agriculturalist, his methods are wasteful and in a way ruinous to the future interests of the country. . . . As a rule bush country is selected for gardens, generally in the granite formation where the soil is easy to dig and cultivate. . . . No attempt is made to manure the ground, except with wood, ash and weeds which are dug in. . . . It takes about ten to fifteen years for gardens to recover and be again fit for cultivation.[22]

And yet a mere decade or so earlier, it had been the Shona who were producing the cereals that the colonizers were expropriating for speculative resale to South African mining populations.[23]

Although this assessment of African agricultural behavior was, as we indicate below, sometimes couched in terms of lack of "modern technology," its *cultural* dimensions were and remain distinct. Montague Yudelman reports that this dimension was often based on "divergent attitudes [between African and Europeans] towards increasing productivity." Drawing on the theory of Dr. J. H. Boeke, who studied economic policy in Indonesia in the 1950s, Yudelman argued, as indeed many still do, that since the indigenous economy was either precapitalist or noncapitalist,

its patterns of behavior, attitudes and value systems are the antithesis of the capitalist ethic. Typically, the non-capitalist sector is rural; producers are not materialistic; incentives to increase production such as higher prices have little effect; the indigenous population is not interested in production for profit but is concerned only with satisfying a limited range of wants that is almost static in character.[24]

In short, the agrarian crisis in Africa is often reduced, on this analysis, to the persistence of "innate" forces or a total absence of economic or environmental rationality.

The second position runs in the same vein but is more specific. It argues that the crisis is firmly rooted in defective tenure arrangements that have no place in twentieth-century agriculture. Tenure systems were often painted in terms that not only set them apart from other social organizations but also gave them a mystique of collectivism and inflexibility that was not always easy to decipher. The fact that these systems were considered a major drawback to agriculture, however, was usually not in doubt. As a recent analysis of land tenure in Lesotho notes,

A succession of overseas economic missions . . . have without exception stated categorically that the traditional system of land tenure is quite unsuited to modern economic development and that it was a man-made obstacle whose removal was a pre-condition to economic growth.[25]

The author notes that these missions were merely echoing a large body of literature "invariably written by expatriates generally addressed to the British colonial administration, and [which] almost always found traditional tenure practices to be an impediment."[26] An important contribution in that literature and one that has gained much prominence (or is it notoriety?) in African reform circles is Kenya's *Plan to Intensify African Agriculture* (1954) and Southern Rhodesia's *What the Native Land Husbandry Act Means to the Rural African in Southern Rhodesia: A Five*

Year Plan which will Revolutionize African Agriculture (1955) about which a vast amount of commentary already exists.[27]

The defective elements in African land tenure were normally identified in the following manner. The primary defect, it was argued, was the fact that these tenure systems were communal, meaning that all the attributes of "ownership" were thought to reside in the "tribe," the "lineage," the "clan," or similar units. From this flowed certain inherent problems, namely, that African tenure systems were (a) incapable of providing security for land development since, among other things, title could not be marketed or otherwise negotiated; (b) generators of fragmentation and eventually subeconomic parcelation by reason of the fact that every adult member of a given unit was always entitled to some land; conditions that led to diseconomies of time, labor utilization, and scale; (c) the source of incessant disputes by reason of diffuseness of rights and lack of clear title and thus a disincentive to long-term investments; and (d) by reason of thus being "communal," so fraught with externalities that land deterioration was inevitable.[28]

In the matrilineal societies of Central Africa, one study adds, colonial agricultural experts sometimes added another inherent problem: that a man would have no incentive to improve land over which he had tenuous and transitory tenure and no prospect of handing it on to his son.[29]

These two positions represent but a small sample of the argument that the causes of the African agrarian crisis are fundamentally internal to and inherent in African agrarian systems. The basic point to remember, however, is that since it was (and still is) usually made in refutation of the "dangerous heresies" of the earlier argument, it always was and in a number of countries still remains the official explanation of that crisis. Indeed, with the entry into African economic decision making of international agencies and multinational corporations, that position has become *the* explanation. Julius Nyerere laments,

the Third World is now blamed for its own poverty. Each country is analyzed separately (by the agencies). Its problems are then explained in terms of its socialism, its corruption, the laziness of its people and such-like alleged national attributes.[30]

Agrarian Reform in Sub-Saharan Africa

State Responses to the Crisis

There is no doubt that the manifestations of the agrarian crisis— population pressure, stagnation in agriculture, food shortages—were in evidence long before the decolonization process started in the late 1950s.[31] But when colonial authorities decided to do something about the situation, they did so in terms that suggested that their own policies and exploitation mechanisms had nothing whatsoever to do with it. Consequently, they proceeded to formulate reform policies and devise plans and programs that were essentially diversionary.

Colonial Responses to the Crisis

The timing of colonial responses to the deteriorating agrarian condition in the African areas throughout East and Southern Africa is revealing. In most cases, concern turned to those areas either when demand for migrant labor was low, as was the case in the depression years of the 1920s and 1930s, or when it became clear that immigrant agriculture alone could not sustain the empire, as was suddenly discovered during and after the trauma of the second imperialist war of 1939–1944.[32] It was always in those circumstances that colonial authorities thought that improvement in the agrarian condition in the African areas might complement colonial agriculture and thus help to perpetuate colonial relations of production. However, the specific approaches taken were extremely fragmentary.

The first of the vast number of ills that were identified, especially after 1945, was excessive population in the African areas. In 1946, Phillip Mitchell, then governor of Kenya, sent a dispatch to the colonial office on the general agrarian situation as it affected the African population in Kenya in which he argued that the primary cause of deterioration of the physical environment was overpopulation compounded by bad land management practices.[33] By way of solution, a policy paper issued the previous year prescribed schemes of land settlement and redevelopment programs. As I have had occasion to explain elsewhere,[34] these schemes and programs involved, in the one case, population movements into "empty" spaces *within* the reserves, and, in the other, terracing, bush clearing, strip cropping, water furrows, and stock reduction in settled areas in the reserves.

Robert Chambers, who has studied settlement schemes in tropical Africa, observes, not unexpectedly, that "it was not until the decade following the Second War that settlement schemes in anglophone Africa enjoyed their first heyday."[35] He notes that those that were implemented during this period fell mainly into three streams. The first stream had its source in attitudes of conservation and was seen "as one means of attack on the combined problems of erosion and over-population" (24). Among the schemes falling into this stream, he lists the Sukumaland Development Scheme in Tanganyika (now mainland Tanzania), the Shendam Resettlement Scheme in northern Nigeria, the Kigezi Resettlements in Uganda, the resettlement schemes of the Eastern Province of Northern Rhodesia (now Zambia), and the Makueni Settlement Scheme in Kenya. Similar schemes were also mounted in Swaziland following the promulgation of the Swazi Settlement Act of 1945 (no. 2 of 1946; see also the Swaziland Native Land Settlement Proclamation and the Swaziland Native Land Settlement Rules, 1946). Attempts to organize schemes along similar lines in Southern Rhodesia, however, led to violence and had to be abandoned.[36] The second and third streams of postwar settlement, which Chambers attributes to experiences outside Africa, ideology, vision, interests, faith, and capital, were not so much attempts at solving the population or land utilization problem as at introducing new systems and technologies of resource use.

The land reconditioning and redevelopment programs that followed the collapse of settlement schemes involved a modest infusion of capital and the introduction of government-controlled land use structures. In general, the capital was obtained from the colonial Development and Welfare Office, which in 1945 increased the United Kingdom contribution to such expenditure in the colonies to £120 million for a ten-year period.[37] The utilization of that capital was entrusted, in most cases, to new institutions directly supervised by the colonial government.

In Kenya, the utilization of a share of that money, amounting to approximately £4 million over the ten-year period, was entrusted to a nonstatutory body called the Development and Reconstruction Authority working through the African Land Utilisation and Settlement Board (later African Land Development Board, or ALDEV). In Southern Rhodesia, this was entrusted to the Natural Resources Board set up by legislative instrument in 1941.[38] In both cases, the administration was given wide powers over the African population, including those of compulsory removal, relocation, and stock reduction.[39] That these programs, like the settlement and resettlement schemes before them, did not succeed was a great puzzle to colonial administrators. ALDEV complained in 1956, "The question of how best to enlist the full and continuing energy and co-operation of African peasants in the betterment of their own lands has yet to be conclusively answered."[40] Two years earlier, the Natural Resources Board had sounded a stern warning to the Southern Rhodesia government in the following words:

The time for plain speaking has now arrived, and it is not exaggeration to say that at the moment we are heading for disaster. We have on the one hand a rapid increase taking place in the African population and on the other a rapid deterioration of the very land on which these people depend for their existence and upon which so much of the future prosperity of the country depends.[41]

All schemes and programs meant for the resolution of the population and land deterioration problems were designed to operate within the framework of existing land relations. The failure of these schemes led colonial authorities to the alternative position that it was those relations, in particular, tenure arrangements, that were the problematic factor toward which reform measures should be directed.

Although only in Kenya did this alternative receive a full dress rehearsal, experimentation was carried out in Uganda[42] and, of course, Southern Rhodesia.[43] In Swaziland, where a movement had started almost immediately after the 1907 "partition" to expand the pool of Swazi Nation Land by buying back expropriated land, colonial authorities were unable to progress beyond the settlement phase of response. Indeed, Swazi suspicion of colonial intentions with regard to land was always and remains quite strong. Hence, rather than accept further experiments with Swazi Nation Land, the Ngwenyama (traditional ruler) set up an organization called Tibiyo Taka Ngwane to speed up repurchase of expropriated land.

Experimentation with tenure reform in Uganda was limited to a few pilot schemes, mainly in Kigezi, Ankole, and Bugisu districts. According to a publication issued in 1955 by the colonial government in Uganda, the objectives of reform were to "encourage individual land ownership in such a manner as not to annihilate the goodwill of traditional authorities, nor to prejudice good husbandry; nor to abandon such safeguards as are essential for future progress of the people."[44] In this respect, therefore, the government of Uganda had, as did that of Kenya, accepted the essence of the recommendations of the East African Royal Commission of 1953–1955,[45] recommendations that, it might be added, were vigorously opposed in Tanganyika.[46]

Experimentation in Southern Rhodesia was rather different in that as theirs was a system of property law rooted in Roman-Dutch precepts, it was not easy to shift to the Torrens systems of registration that tenure reform à la the East Africa Royal Commission required. Consequently, what the colonial government came up with in the Native Land Husbandry Act of 1948 was a "land centralization" program involving the resiting of homesteads, standardization of landholdings, limitation of stock, and greater control of husbandry. The homestead resiting and standardization of holdings aspects of the program involved the granting of farming rights to individuals and of grazing rights to specified communities based not on land area but on a rated carrying capacity basis and the imposition of good husbandry practices. In other words, unlike the Kenya and Uganda experiments, the Southern Rhodesia program

continued much of the "conservation bias" of the Natural Resources Act [but also] in one fell swoop . . . proposed to replace the tribal-communistic system of allocating land according to need with a hybrid tribal-capitalistic system of individual holdings and communal grazing.[47]

Yudelman's assessment of the impact of Southern Rhodesia's program sums up better than any the impact of tenure reform, wherever attempted under colonialism.

The implementation of [the Native Land Husbandry Act] . . . had high human costs. Alien concepts [were] introduced but not understood; traditional authority over land rights . . . usurped by the market place. The whole basis of society . . . threatened, and security . . . undermined rather than enhanced. . . . Perhaps more importantly, implementation . . . [did] not produce tangible benefits. It . . . [took] away something which, though intangible [was] important, and [did not] replace it with anything meaningful to most producers.[48]

That may appear severe, but as tenure reform programs survived decolonization in a number of these countries, a further look at Yudelman's assessment is deserved.

A general observation may now be made on the various reform policies and programs outlined above. Clearly, they offered only partial solutions to the problem, were pursued in a most half-hearted manner, and, most unfortunately, were born of a great deal of misconception of what the nature and characteristics of African agrarian systems were. Almost to a scheme, the settlements were sited in areas most unsuitable for human habitation, and the land development and reconditioning programs often led not to expansion but to the physical reduction of cultivable land. The tenure reform programs appear to have been seen as capable of inducing agricultural change on a "broad-spectrum" basis. Not only were the normative constraints of tenure arrangements expected to be removed but production structures were expected to change because new production units were being introduced through land "concentration" (Southern Rhodesia) or "consolidation" (Kenya and Uganda) and the organization of supporting services such as credit, cooperatives, and marketing facilitated through improved security of tenure and better farm planning.

Contemporary Responses to the Crisis

Although the transition to independence was, for most of sub-Saharan Africa, relatively smooth and constitutional, land issues remained potentially explosive. This was particularly the case with regard to plantation colonies such as Kenya, Zimbabwe, and Mozambique where massive displacement of indigenous populations had occurred in the course of colonial rule. In yet others such as Guinea, Guinea-Bissau, and Angola where the transfer of power was more or less chaotic, the issue of access to land was no less important in postindependence economic reconstruction.

Besides, in nearly all of these countries, the agrarian crisis grew worse instead of better. Where the colonial government had been able through coercion and systematic implementation of numerous sanctions-oriented legislations to hold the lid on indigenous demands and conflicts over land rights, particularly within the so-called reserves (or bantustans), postcolonial governments found themselves no longer able or morally constrained to do the same. Where colonial governments would have been satisfied with policies and programs designed merely to intensify agricultural practices in areas already under severe land pressure, postcolonial governments now needed to respond to ever-increasing demands for instant land redistribution. And, where it had been possible—at least on an experimental basis—to settle landless people on unoccupied land contiguous to or surrounded by populations dominated by ethnic persuasions not their own, interethnic land conflicts arising from the resurrection of historical claims after independence made this option unavailable.

From this highly simplifed background, it is tempting to posit a scenario of normative and institutional change representing radical discontinuity from colonial land policies and program options evidenced by a comprehensive reconstruction of the agrarian system as a whole. In the event, however, the complexities and paradoxes of managing the independence enterprise made it impossible or even impolitic for many African countries to introduce radical change. Indeed, an examination of the manner in which struggles over land have been treated in postcolonial Africa suggests that independence did not stimulate any fundamental reappraisal of the true nature, extent, and severity of the crisis. Two explanations for this apparent impasse are offered here.

In the first instance, far from creating an enabling environment for novelty and experimentation, independence in many of these countries in fact altered the environment of state power in such a manner as to weaken the capacity of governments to initiate new, let alone radical, policies. The independence constitutions of most of these countries stipulated that the institutions extant at the end of colonialism should survive the transfer of power.[49] In any event, the very heavy investments by metropolitan capital concerns in African economies yet to be liquidated at independence ensured that very little, if any, radical changes could be

untries such as Kenya, Swaziland, and more recently, Zimba-
the manner of resolving land issues was specifically written
truments of power transfer, radical reforms were ruled out.
cond instance, excessive concern with foreign exchange gen-
the primary means of economic sustainability usually meant
that the status quo ante was to be preferred. For plantation economies,
this usually meant that the large-scale farming sector was to be preserved. Indeed, in countries such as Mozambique where the large-scale
farmers had fled the country before independence, the immediate concern of the postcolonial government, as indicated later, was nonetheless
how best to preserve large-scale farming.

Irrespective of the ideological and other preferences or predilections
of independence elites, therefore, the normative and institutional parameters defined by colonialism did not change. Continuity was the rule
rather than the exception. As a result, postcolonial responses to the
agrarian crisis were generally in the nature of consolidation and expansion of colonial policies and programs, on the one hand, and limited
experimentation with new but not altogether novel strategies within the
framework of inherited structures, institutions, and bureaucracies, on
the other.

Consolidation and Expansion of Colonial Responses
Perhaps the best-known and most systematic consolidation and expansion of colonial policies and programs was and remains in Kenya. Despite the change in the political environment of power, the independent
government in Kenya perpetuated, with even greater zeal, the tenure
reform and settlement schemes initiated in the colonial era, and for
much the same reasons.

The tenure reform program, which is currently estimated to have
brought over 90 percent of all registerable land in Nyanza, Western, Rift
Valley, Central, and Coast provinces on to a Torrens register, continued
to draw its economic and political rationale from the 1954 plan referred
to above. Despite misgivings by scholars and some administrators both
during the colonial era and after independence, the program remains
top priority in the government's land policy.

An interesting variation in tenure reform, but one that nonetheless
has its inspiration in colonial theories about African tenure systems, is in
process in Malawi. There, the process of individualization is coupled
with the adjudication and registration, in appropriate cases, of customary rights qua customary rights. As was the case in Kenya and Zimbabwe, the program was first conceived of in the early 1950s and took the

form, initially, of land improvement or village reorganization schemes. According to a recent study,

The project basically involved the reorganization of the land-holding pattern of an area in such a way that each household ended up with one consolidated plot equal in size and quality to the total area of its former collection of pieces and fragments. The entire village was then geared to an overall land utilization plan.[50]

Although village reorganization schemes had collapsed by 1960, the independent Malawi government revived and strengthened their tenure reform aspects by vesting absolute proprietorships in respect of consolidated holdings in individuals rather than villages. The only difference between this version and that in force in Kenya is that community rights over villages, burial grounds, and grazing lands were reserved and registered as such.

The expected "broad-spectrum effect" of tenure reform notwithstanding, the Kenyan government could not entirely avoid land redistribution programs after independence. But such programs when they came were, so far as the peasantry was concerned, mounted essentially on the settlement principles of the colonial era. In that respect, therefore, they took the form mainly of attempts, first, to ease off pressure from the reserves, and second, to resolve the problem of chaotic tenure arrangements arising from large squatter settlements in the "highlands." In the one case, a series of settlements in what was known as "the Million-Acre Scheme"[51] were hived off the highlands and assigned to ethnic groups in specified reserves. In the other, a number of similar schemes were organized for the settlement of registered squatters mainly from the Central and Rift Valley provinces.

Security of tenure was available to settlers of the first scheme only on full discharge of their loan and husbandry obligations. None whatsoever was promised or even contemplated for settlers of the second scheme. In either case, the argument against immediate grant of security of tenure was essentially colonial, namely, that careful tutelage was necessary before the African could be entrusted with absolute property rights. Consequently, tenure relations were based, in the one case, on conditional freehods, and, in the other, on temporary occupation licenses (TOLS). In this respect, therefore, the organization of the latter settlement took the form of the post-1945 schemes that were, in any event, also maintained and extended by the Kenyan government.

Malawi, Zimbabwe, and Swaziland are other examples of countries that also found it necessary to build on colonial settlement principles as a

ensibly, of attacking the problem of land distribution. In Ma-
schemes, whether established on public or private land, were,
etion, declared government property. Settlers on such schemes
were then granted TOLS to enable them to cultivate the land initially for five years.[52] Although, as I have noted, colonial settlements did not take off in Southern Rhodesia, the Zimbabwe government was quick to set up similar schemes to accommodate "refugees, the destitute . . . and people without land in the over-crowded Tribal Trust Lands."[53] However, these were rather ad hoc measures awaiting the formulation of a comprehensive land policy. In Swaziland, where the settlements had their origins in a land purchase program very similar to Kenya's Million Acre Scheme, the administrative organization was similarly ad hoc, and the schemes remained without clear tenure principles.[54]

However, colonial settlement principles were not restricted only to conventional, that is, redistributive or conservation, programs. They were, at least in Kenya and Swaziland, extended to permanent or experimental irrigation schemes. In Kenya, for example, tenure relations based on TOLS which had been used in colonial schemes in Mwea-Tebere and Yatta were extended to the Ahero Pilot and Bura schemes. It is interesting that despite the very clear contradiction in the colonial mind with respect to the abstract curative properties of individual title and tenure practice in settlement schemes, the TOLS was always vigorously defended by independent African governments who relied on it.

Alternative Policies and Programs
Although continuity has generally been the rule in sub-Saharan Africa, other and more "radical" agrarian reform options have been tried in several countries. Some of these were of the classic Latin American land distribution variety, while others were directed mainly at changes in production structures. In the former category may be placed Ethiopia and Mozambique; in the latter, Tanzania and Benin. A number of pilot programs in the latter category were also carried out in Kenya, Nigeria, Côte d'Ivoire, and Cameroon.

The Ethiopian reforms, which are the most recent and revolutionary in sub-Saharan Africa, have their origins in historical circumstances not essentially different from that of many Latin American countries or, to come nearer home, Egypt before the Land Reform Law of 1952.[55] Indeed, the agrarian structure that was in existence at the time of the overthrow of Emperor Haile Selassie I in 1974 was virtually identical with that in Egypt, except that it was more backward and wholly feudal. The reforms that were introduced in a proclamation issued in 1975 argued that in order to increase agricultural production and to make the tiller the owner of the fruits of his labour; it [was] necessary to release the productive forces of the rural economy by liquidating the feudal system under which the nobility, aristocracy and a small number of other persons with adequate means of livelihood have prospered by the toil and sweat of the masses.[56]

The proclamation then proceeded, first, to declare all rural land to be the collective property of the Ethiopian people; second, to distribute land to any person willing to personally cultivate rural land sufficient for his maintenance and that of his family; third, to prohibit alienation of land other than of use rights by way of succession only; and fourth, to set up peasant associations for its implementation. It was perhaps in the establishment of peasant associations that the proclamation had its greatest impact. For these were not merely new production units in the agrarian structure, they were in every respect vehicles for the repoliticization of the Ethiopian masses along the new socialist line. Indeed, the public education campaign that followed—called *Zemecha*—made such use of these associations.

Whereas in Ethiopia it was necessary to nationalize land to distribute it to the peasantry, in Mozambique, no such steps were necessary since many of the large estates formerly owned by Portuguese settlers were, at independence, largely abandoned. The most developed land therefore came under state ownership "not by virtue of nationalization, but through abandonment and rescue."[57] The choice facing the independent government of Mozambique, therefore, was not whether or not to nationalize the large farms but whether or not to denationalize them.

The government chose in these circumstances to preserve the large estates as state farms and to consolidate smallholdings into cooperative enterprises to be worked by the peasants living on them. But while the new property structure established by the Land Law of 1979 was decidedly *collective* in nature, limited private property rights in the form of registered licenses were reserved to enable a certain amount of semi-capitalist investments to come in. But such rights were clearly stated to be subject to the overriding power of the state and the social interest of the Mozambican people. However, irrespective of its proprietary basis, the law subjected all agricultural land to an overall use plan sanctioned and administered by the state.

The reforms that have been undertaken in Ethiopia and Mozambique have been concerned mainly with changes in land tenure structures, for, in the historical circumstances of those countries, tenure and distribution were the most problematic elements in the agrarian system. In Tanzania and Benin, the thrust of reform has been mainly in the direction of reorganization of production structures.

In Tanzania, where the land had always been vested in the state, even under colonialism, whatever reforms in tenure relations that were found necessary after independence were relatively easy to accomplish. These were mainly concerned with the removal of residual forms of English property regimes such as leaseholds and a limited number of freeholds granted before 1921, the date of British assumption of jurisdiction, and their conversion into rights of occupancies: the basis of property relations after that date. Further, a number of "feudal" customary tenures were in existence in parts of the country which the independent government sought to abolish. Hence tenure reform per se, in Tanzania, was over by 1969.

Attention turned, in the 1970s, to an attack on production structures. These the government sought to radicalize through the introduction of collective farming based on *Ujamaa,* or socialist, villages. The primary objective of Ujamaa villages was first, equitable distribution of resources to rural communities; second, the democratization of community leadership; third, self-reliant and endogenously propelled development; fourth, the achievement of higher levels of productivity of land per unit factor input; and fifth, a more efficient service distribution to village communities. The villages were therefore seen not only as production units but also as foci for the distribution and management of basic services such as water, electricity, education, and health.

Although the political phase of the Ujamaa program preceded and in most respects overshadowed its primary legal organs, by 1975, the latter were firmly in place. The Villages and Ujamaa Villages (Registry Design and Administration) Act (no. 21 of 1975) provided not only for the registration of villages as corporate entities but for machinery enabling the commissioner of lands to issue them with rights of occupancy in the same way as individuals desiring to use agricultural land. The villages were then expected to use and manage the land as a collective asset along socialist principles. By 1982, over 80 percent of Tanzania's population had been resettled in such villages.

The establishment of collective farms in Benin in the 1960s was in no way as comprehensive as the Ujamaa program in Tanzania. What was done there was the establishment of "supervised" collectives in which each participant was expected to contribute a certain amount of land in exchange for a proportionate share in the enterprise. The collectives were administered by an elected board in which the government had representation. The government also provided supporting services, to facilitate the operations of the collectives.[58]

Observers have drawn attention to the fact that the countries that chose to try alternatives not based on colonial formulas were also experimenting with new ideologies. However, we know from Latin American experiences that extremely conservative regimes have also been able to push through equally radical programs. It is not surprising, therefore, that independent regimes as conservative as those in Kenya, Nigeria, Ivory Coast, and Cameroon were also able at one point or another to experiment with collective farms, plantation cooperatives, and rural and land banking institutions. A more important explanation is that the political exigencies of the time in those countries were clearly conducive to such reforms.

Implications for Agricultural Development

Some Preliminary Issues

It was earlier indicated that one of the more important raison d'être for mounting programs of reform by colonial and postcolonial governments was, in the words of the Ethiopian proclamation, to increase agricultural productivity by releasing "the productive forces of the rural economy." It may be useful, therefore, to first inquire into the way in which that end was expected to be achieved. Essentially, what agronomic experts and planners expected were structural adjustments along one or more of the following lines. First, it was expected that agrarian relations would be restructured in such a way as to afford the tiller greater control over the land itself. In the context of the tenure reform programs such as were mounted in Kenya and Malawi, that control was seen as conditional on the emergence (or imposition) of a principle or rule of absolute proprietorship in favor of individual cultivators. In Ethiopia and Tanzania, that control was thought to lie in social solidarity and the basic principles of egalitarianism that kept indigenous social relations stable. In other words, appeal was being made to some concept of security in both cases even though the tenure arrangements necessary for obtaining it in either case were clearly at variance with one another. But control, however obtained, was seen as fundamental to agricultural development, for only in this way could access to land resources be guaranteed.

Second, it was expected that with appropriate changes in land tenure, production units, that is, the decision-making spheres defined by social cohesion, a specific quantum of property rights, and a defined area of land,[59] would operate more rationally and efficiently. According to both reform strategies, this should be an inevitable development, the one arguing that their particular form of tenure reform will have removed a number of important externalities and the other that equilibrium will have been restored in the agricultural enterprise. Consequently, the production process was expected to function in such a manner as to ensure continuity of output and the development of external management linkages with the larger socioeconomic network of which the individual or community was a part.

It is important to further clarify the scientific basis on which the latter argument rests. It is the acknowledged fact that at least before colonial intrusion, production cycles in African agrarian systems were highly developed. A recent study of the effects of apartheid on poverty in South Africa makes the point forcefully.[60] It explains, for example, that apart from simply enabling agrarian communities to produce enough food on a self-sustainable basis, production structures performed extremely important social functions.

As in almost all societies whose economy is based on subsistence grain-farming, social organization is dominated by the *family farming system*. In order to ensure the continuity of an activity of a seasoned nature, which requires in particular the transmission of food resources over a period of time, the organic and functional reproduction of the production units is regulated by careful management of the grain reserves, the redistribution of food supplies and the strict control of reproduction relations particularly through marriage and filiation.[61]

The agrarian reforms in Tanzania and the movement back to traditional control of land in Swaziland were essentially fired by the need to recapture this complementarity between social needs, production efficiency, and tenure arrangements.

Third, it was expected that supporting services infrastructure necessary for a healthy agricultural industry would develop. The components of this infrastructure would include credit facilities, marketing arrangements, and new (appropriate) technologies of production. Although the tenure reforms were based on the assumption that these infrastructural facilities would be automatically attracted to agriculture, their necessity was never in doubt, so was the fact that they were capable of productive management under any reform program. The issue of technology was always of particular interest to policymakers, planners, and program administrators. For whereas some saw technological absorption as the variable assisting the state in the restructuring of agrarian relations, others saw this as an antecedent process and one that is possible only if structural reorganization had already paved the way for it.[62] Indeed, there are many countries in which infrastructural services were set up in anticipation of changes in land relations either through tenure reform or land redistribution programs. As an infrastructural service, the availability and absorption of new farming technologies were always seen as an important agrarian reform package.

An Assessment of Development Implications

To what extent have these expectations been realized? The collective wisdom of those who have studied agrarian transformation programs throughout Africa does not bear out that optimism. An assessment of Kenya's own tenure reform program suggests that it has not progressed beyond the situation observed by Yudelman with respect to Southern Rhodesia, to which reference was made above. My own recent assessment notes that whereas no evidence exists that agricultural production has increased by virtue of that program, there are plenty of data to indicate that it has resulted, in general, in inequalities both structural and political-economic within the agrarian sector. Indeed, it has led to the emergence of a relatively rich middle peasantry that enjoys much useful linkages with central bureaucracies. As a result, that elite is able to draw substantial social and production advantages from the state.

The corollary to this has been the emergence of significant instances of landlessness, especially in areas of high land pressure. In a country that does not have a dynamic agroindustrial sector, this means that the "liberated" peasant has little alternative but to drift into the cities. In the pastoral/nomadic areas where tenure reform took the form of "group" registration, the problem became not one of landlessness but of the imminent collapse of the pastoral economy itself. Finally, the expected broad-spectrum effect of tenure reform, especially in the area of credit, did not really materialize. Far from generating credit for agriculture, the reforms led mainly to the impoverishment of this sector and the capitalization, at its expense, of industry and other service sectors.

An assessment of the Tanzania and, more recently, Ethiopian reforms are not encouraging either.[63] The problem in both these countries would seem to have been their excessive reliance on political as opposed to socioeconomic tools in circumstances where conventional wisdom would have dictated a more comprehensive attack on rural underdevelopment. A common thread of failure to integrate what is politically desirable with what is economically feasible therefore seems to run right through agrarian reform programs in these two countrie. Ethiopia, in particular, might well find itself in the company of Egypt. There, a recent evaluation suggests, first, that because of relatively high ceilings, her land distribution program, while succeeding in removing the very large landowners, only served to consolidate the middle class. The result was that they were able to regroup and to frustrate more radical reforms. Second, the cooperatives that were expected to help the lower peasantry by redirecting resource transfers to them did little of the kind. Many of these institutions were in fact hijacked by the middle elites for their own purposes. And, third, any absolute increases in production growth generated by the reform were wiped out by a runaway population. Thus, Egypt relapsed into the classic food deficiency syndrome in which sub-Saharan countries now find themselves.[64]

A more obvious fault is that the engines, that is, the institutions, that were being relied on to drive reform efforts were themselves fundamentally inappropriate. Somehow it was always assumed that agrarian bureaucracies, particularly those inherited at independence, were fully equipped at all times to handle any program, whatever its complexities and ideological parameters. That may well be the clue to the apparent failure of most of these programs.

Concluding Remarks

This essay suggests that while the African agrarian crisis continues to deepen, the agrarian reform policies and programs now being pursued in sub-Saharan Africa are unlikely to provide the turnaround the region is desperate for. It will be necessary, therefore, to not only reassess the wisdom of investing such staggering amounts of resources in those programs but also to investigate more productive alternatives. This is particularly urgent in the case of reforms that are directed at tenure changes per se, rather than at the agrarian structures and conditions under which production relations operate. It is public knowledge, of course, that dramatic increases in production have been recorded at one time or another in a number of countries where these reforms are in process. The yeoman farmers of Kenya and Malawi, and more recently the community peasants of Zimbabwe, have been known to produce significant surpluses. The doubt this essay raises is with respect to the sustainability and replicability of these experiences and their long-term social and political costs.

Notes

1 S. Berry, "The Food Crisis and Agrarian Change in Africa," *African Studies Review* XXVII, 2 (1984); R. Chambers, "The Crisis of Africa's Rural Poor: Perceptions and Priorities," *Discussion Paper* no. 201 (University of Sussex, Institute of Development Studies, 1985); S. K. Cummins et al., *African Agrarian Crisis: The Roots of Famine* (Boulder, 1986); H. W. O. Okoth-Ogendo, "The Perils of Land Tenure Reform: The Case of Kenya," in J. Arntzen, L. Ngcongco, and S. Turner (eds.), *Land Policy and Agriculture in Eastern and Southern Africa* (Tokyo, 1986); United Nations Food and Agricultural Organization, *Apartheid, Poverty and Malnutrition* (Rome, 1982).

2 United Nations Economic Commission for Africa, *ECA and Africa's Economic Development, 1983–2008: A Preliminary Perspective Study* (Addis Ababa, 1983); R. Faruqee and R. Gulhati, *Rapid Population Growth in Sub-Saharan Africa: Issues and Policies* (Washington, D.C., 1983).

3 M. Yudelman, *Africans on the Land* (Cambridge, Mass., 1964); R. McNamara, *One Hundred Countries, Two Billion People* (London, 1973); R. van Zwanenberg, *Colonial Capitalism and Labour in Kenya* (Nairobi, 1974); A. Hill, *The Demographic Situation in Sub-Saharan Africa: A Background Paper* (Washington, D.C., 1981); D. Hunt, *The Impending Crisis in Kenya: The Case for Land Reform* (Aldershot, 1984).

4 R. Dumont, *False Start in Africa* (London, 1966); M. Bedjaoui, *Towards a New International Economic Order* (Paris, 1979).

5 R. D. Wolff, *The Economics of Colonialism: Britain and Kenya, 1870–1930* (New Haven, 1976); W. G. Hynes, *The Economics of Empire: Britain, Africa and the New Imperialism, 1870–1895* (London, 1979).

6 H. W. O. Okoth-Ogendo, "African Land Tenure Reform," in J. Heyer, J. K. Maitha, and W. M. Senga (eds.), *Agricultural Development in Kenya: An Economic Assessment* (Nairobi, 1976).

7 A. J. B. Hughes, "Land Tenure, Land Rights and Land Communities on Swazi Nation Land in Swaziland," (Ph.D. diss., University of Natal, 1971).

8 Lord Hailey, *An African Survey* (London, 1957): 689.

9 Sir M. Carter, *Report of the Land Commission of 1925* (Salisbury, 1926): 4.

10 Sir M. Carter, *Report of the Kenya Land Commission of 1933* (London, 1934).

11 P. M. Mvunga, "The Colonial Foundation of Zambia's Land Tenure System," (Lusaka, 1980).

12 Hailey, *An African Survey,* 710.

13 G. F. A. Sawyer, "Discriminatory Restrictions on Private Dispositions of Land in Tanganyika: A Second Look," *Journal of African Law* XIII, 1–2 (1969); R. Noronha, *A Review of the Literature on Land Tenure Systems in Sub-Saharan Africa,* Report no. ARU 43, Research Unit, Agriculture and Rural Development Department, the World Bank (Washington, D.C., 1985)

14 Noronha, *A Review;* B. Isaacman and J. S. Isaacman, *Mozambique: Women, the Law and Agrarian Reform* (Addis Ababa, 1980).

15 Yudelman, *Africans;* R. Palmer and N. Parsons (eds.), *The Roots of Rural Poverty in Central and Southern Africa* (London, 1977); G. Arrighi, "Labour Supplies in a Historical Perspective: A Study of the Proletarianization of the African Peasantry in Rhodesia," *Journal of Development Studies* VI (1970).

16 van Zwanenberg, *Colonial.*

17 Yudelman, *Africans,* 77; Hailey, *An African Survey,* 680.

18 Okoth-Ogendo, "African Land."

19 J. Heyer, "The Origins of Regional Inequalities in Small-Holder Agriculture in Kenya, 1920–1973," *East African Journal of Rural Development* VIII, 1–2 (1975).

20 Palmer and Parsons, *The Roots,* 230.

21 R. S. Rattray, *Ashanti Law and Constitution* (London, 1929).
22 Yudelman, *Africans,* Appendix A.
23 Palmer and Parsons, *The Roots.*
24 Ibid., 91.
25 J. Eckert, *Lesotho's Land Tenure: An Analysis and Annotated Bibliography* (Masara, 1980): 1.
26 Ibid.
27 J. Heyer, et al. (eds)., *Agricultural Development in Kenya: An Economic Assessment* (Nairobi, 1976); Yudelman, *Africans;* E. Clayton, *Agrarian Development in Peasant Economies* (Oxford, 1964); A. Killick, *Readings in the Political Economy of Kenya* (Nairobi, 1981).
28 Okoth-Ogendo, "Property Theory and Land Use Analysis: An Essay in the Political Economy of Ideas," *Journal of Eastern African Research and Development* V, 1 (1976).
29 Palmer and Parsons, *The Roots.*
30 J. Nyerere, "Africa and the Debt Crisis," *African Affairs* LXXXIV, 337 (1985).
31 Okoth-Ogendo, "Property Theory"; Arrighi, "Labour Supplies"; Palmer and Parsons, *The Roots;* P. Mitchell, "General Aspects of the Agrarian Situation in Kenya as It Affects the African Population," Dispatch no. 44, April 7, 1946.
32 See, for example, Heyer, "The Origins."
33 Mitchell, "General Aspects."
34 Okoth-Ogendo, "Property Theory."
35 R. Chambers, *Settlement Schemes in Tropical Africa: A Study of Organizations and Development* (London, 1969): 23.
36 Yudelman, *Africans.*
37 Chambers, *Settlement.*
38 Southern Rhodesia, *The Laws of Southern Rhodesia* (Salisbury, 1964); see especially Cap. 264.
39 See, for example, Kenya's Native Authorities Ordinance no. 2 of 1937.
40 Kenya, African Land Development Board, *Annual Report* (1956).
41 Southern Rhodesia, Natural Resources Board, *Annual Report* (1954).
42 J. Obol-Ocholla (ed.), *Land Law Reform in East Africa* (Kampala, 1986).
43 Yudelman, *Africans.*
44 Government of the Protectorate of Uganda (1955).
45 East African Royal Commission, Command paper 9475 (1956).
46 J. Nyerere, *Freedom and Unity* (Dar-es-Salaam, 1966).
47 Yudelman, *Africans.*
48 Ibid., 126.
49 H. W. O. Okoth-Ogendo, "Constitutions without Constitutionalism: An African Political Paradox," American Council of Learned Societies, mimeo. (1987).
50 D. W. Nothale, "Land Tenure Systems and Agricultural Production in Malawi," in Arntzen et al., *Land Policy.*

51 H. W. O. Okoth-Ogendo, "Land Ownership and Land Distribution in Kenya's Large-Farm Areas," in Tom Killick (ed.), *Papers on the Kenyan Economy* (Nairobi, 1981): 329–337.

52 Nothale, "Land Tenure."

53 J. M. Mungoshi, "Land Settlement in Zimbabwe: A Case Study of Chisumbanje," unpublished paper (1982).

54 Government of the Royal Kingdom of Swaziland (1983).

55 S. Radwan, *Agrarian Reform and Rural Poverty: Egypt, 1951–1975* (Geneva, 1977).

56 H. W. Michael, "Zemacha: An Attempt at Rural Transformation in Ethiopia," in H. W. O. Okoth-Ogendo (ed.), *Approaches to Rural Transformation in Eastern Africa* (Nairobi, 1981).

57 A. Sachs, "Liberating the Land, Liberating the Law," in A. Sachs and G. H. Welch (eds.), *Liberating the Law: Creating Popular Justice in Mozambique* (London, 1990): 39.

58 E. Jacoby, *Man and Land: The Fundamental Issue in Development* (London, 1971).

59 D. R. Denman and S. Prodano, *Land Use: An Introduction to Proprietary Land Use Analysis* (London, 1972).

60 FAO, *Apartheid*.

61 FAO, *Apartheid*. See also S. Radwan, *Agrarian Reform and Rural Poverty: Egypt, 1951–1975* (Geneva, 1977).

62 R. W. Cummings, "Land Tenure and Agricultural Development" (Madison, 1978); A. Pearse, *Seeds of Plenty, Seeds of Want: Social and Economic Implications of the Green Revolution* (Geneva, 1980).

63 G. Hyden, *Beyond Ujamaa in Tanzania: Under-Development and an Uncaptured Peasantry* (London, 1980); Dessalegn Rahmato, *Agrarian Reform in Ethiopia* (Uppsala, 1984).

64 Radwan, *Agrarian Reform*.

10   *Dessalegn Rahmato*

Land, Peasants, and the Drive for Collectivization in Ethiopia

Ō 13

ρ 3∨   Q 15

Ethiopia

Introduction

Initially, the agrarian policies of postrevolution Ethiopia were fairly
populist and pro-peasant, but they became increasingly "statist" as the
revolution began to harden and the anticipated opposition from rural-
based counterrevolutionary forces proved much less threatening than
had been feared. However, the shift toward statism was accompanied by
a deepening agricultural crisis that forced the country into increasing
dependence on Western food aid. This statist tendency persisted until
March 1990, virtually the eve of the collapse of the first postrevolution-
ary state.

Statist agrarian policies consisted of collectivization and a host of
other agricultural and fiscal arrangements that, in whole or in part,
helped to extend the frontiers of the state in the countryside. These
included villagization, resettlement, grain procurement, and control of
grain marketing and pricing. What the political and planning authorities
called the promotion and expansion of "socialist relations of production" in the rural areas was thus a grand package of disparate and
sometimes complementary programs that were in force in one form or
another for over a decade. This discussion mainly concerns the complex
issues of access to land in a social setting dominated by old Soviet-style

socialist reforms and the interplay between peasant agriculture and collectivization. I use the term "collectivization" loosely to refer to group-based large-scale agricultural operations initiated or influenced by the state. In our case, this includes both rural producer cooperatives and state farms. Because of space limitations, I shall not discuss the rest of the "socialist" package of programs noted here. I will also not be able to treat the recurrence of devastating famines in the last ten or more years, rural insurgency, or the intensification of rural poverty.

The agrarian question in postrevolution Ethiopia has had as many political ramifications as economic ones and forms an important element in the political history of the country. In the initial period of the revolution, between 1974, when the military authorities assumed power, and 1978, land and peasants became significant factors in the course of state power consolidation. In the second period, from 1978 to 1990, both peasants and land were the object of state policy, which increasingly sought to solve the acute food problems of the country, on the one hand, and to promote the newly defined goals of the revolution along mainly Stalinist lines, on the other. Let us examine this a little more closely.

The dynamics of state-society relations in the early years of the revolution were unclear. The response of the peasantry, which had greater "royalist" sympathies than the other popular classes, to the overthrow of the monarchy and the landed classes by an unknown band of petty and middle-level officers was uncertain and hence of great concern. The new authorities (the Provisional Military Administrative Council, PMAC, or Derg) understood that the decisive battle between the revolution and counterrevolution would take place in the rural areas and that the peasantry's decision to support one side or the other would largely determine the outcome. In consequence, the men who masterminded the downfall of the *ancien régime* were eager to dislodge the landed classes from their rural base of power and to win the loyalty of the peasantry. This was one of the major rationales of the land reform of 1975, which at one stroke stripped the aristocracy and landed gentry of all their wealth and possession in the countryside. In July of the same year, another piece of radical legislation nationalized all urban land and rented houses, thereby depriving these same classes of any source of independent wealth or income. This virtually sealed the fate of what would have been the opposition from the right.

It is worth noting that even before the Derg deposed the monarchy in September 1974, it was aware of the power of the threat of dispossession and of the great fear the propertied classes had of losing their holdings. In a relatively frank speech delivered by Major Fisseha Desta, a senior member of the PMAC,[1] on the tenth anniversary of the establishment of the Derg, he points out that all through July and August 1974, the military authorities cautioned notables wanted for arrest to either give themselves up peacefully or lose their property. This tactic, he noted, effectively garnered a large number of "feudal" elements who eagerly came forward to be detained.

Moreover, while the armed forces, which came to look on the revolution as their own handiwork, could provide some essential services, mainly military in character, the enormous politicoadministrative void created by the revolution could only be filled by a professional or political organization that did not exist at the time. The new authorities looked on the state burearcracy, which was for the most part closely tied to the old order, with suspicion and even loathing. The task of running the country, of extending the authority of the state to the village level, and of dismantling the older order required a new administrative or political apparatus staffed, according to the early views of the Derg, with young, educated, nationalist, and incorruptible elements. However, such an apparatus would not be available for quite some time.

With one of its most important provisions, the 1975 land reform set up Peasant Associations (PAs) in each *kebbelle,* or locality. These organizations of peasants had an elected leadership and a legally defined set of responsibilities including the maintenance of law and order, adjudication of conflicts, and later, collection of state revenues. Subsequently, PAs were established on district, provincial, and national levels. Here was a new organizational chain stretching down to the peasant village, paralleling that of the old state bureaucracy, one that would serve as an instrument of basic administration. Right from the beginning, in opposition to some of its civilian advisers, the PMAC insisted that it should establish PAs immediately, before launching land redistribution. In effect, this decision undercut the authority of the old apparatus of local administration in the rural areas. Eventually, the PAs came to perform tasks usually associated with a peasant-based political party, particularly at the grass-roots level.

Land redistribution and peasant organization served the PMAC well, particularly because in the early years the new government was virtually absent from the rural areas, the peasantry was in a state of uncertainty or agitation as a result of the revolution, and armed disturbances were taking place or imminent in various parts of the country. Land reform and peasant power—and it seemed at the outset that the PAs were to be the self-governing arm of the peasantry—now came to be regarded by the peasantry as the new symbol of authority, thus easing the transfer of their loyalty to the Derg. This was no mean achievement considering how poorly the new government projected its image, thanks to its habitually secretive practices, its poor communications, and its lack of such high-profile symbols as crown, royalty, and "blue blood," which had served the old authorities so well. Without their radical agrarian policies, the new authorities would have faced serious challenges from rural-based counter-revolutionary forces. As it turned out, the right opposition fielded a limited force in what could only be described as token resistance.[2]

The second period witnessed the hardening of the revolution and a shift of policy in favor of rapid collectivization. The programs that were initiated at this time required that the peasantry change from an active force of the revolution to a passive recipient of government directives. The objective now was to promote "socialist production and socialist relations" in the countryside as rapidly as possible. The new authorities believed that collectivization would solve the problems of agricultural backwardness and food shortages and prevent the emergence of capitalist forces in the rural areas. They would have accomplished these twin goals, and the overarching ideological objective, sooner but for the backwardness of peasant consciousness. They persuaded themselves that had this consciousness not been so low, the transition to socialism would have been achieved much faster. At the outset, therefore, they would have to guide, goad, or push the peasantry into new collective ventures and new forms of production.

The new policies came to sour state-peasant relations, an unnecessary outcome and one that they could have avoided had the authorities toned down the highly doctrinal content of rural programs and been more flexible and innovative in their approach to rural transformation. A partnership between state and peasantry would have been the best course under the given circumstances, but the Derg chose instead a hard line, and it did so at a time when the rural economy was on the verge of a serious crisis and the price of the policies in question was likely to be high.

Most readers of this volume will be familar with the arguments in favor of socialist agriculture. These arguments have changed little since they were first elaborated some one hundred years ago.[3] It is not clear to what extent Ethiopian policymakers were knowledgeable about socialist economic theory in general and socialist agriculture in particular, and certainly no public debate was conducted on the relevance and suitability to the country of this approach. However, policy planners were familiar with some elements, discussed briefly below, of the orthodox socialist theory of agriculture, and a good many of them formed the cornerstone of Ethiopian collectivization.

As the literature presents it, the orthodox socialist theory of agriculture contains a number of contradictory elements. Its conception of the peasant is the first such element. It believes the peasant to be the backbone of Third World revolutions and expects him to become one of the main beneficiaries of ensuing social transformation. And yet it thinks that peasant production is incompatible with socialist development. Moreover, it says that the peasant harbors capitalist aspirations and that peasant agriculture, left to its own devices, will give rise to social differentiation, and the emergent *kulaks,* or rural capitalists, will exploit and dominate the rural population.

Further, this case for socialist agriculture rests on the proposition that peasant-based, smallholder enterprises are inefficient, that progress moves inevitably toward large-scale production that is more dynamic and more conducive to modernization, and that socialism promotes the real interests of rural society and provides a source for domestic capital accumulation. Moreover, socialization will inhibit rural differentiation or class exploitation and, through the rapid development it stimulates, will bring quick improvements in living standards. Since it views peasants and rural producers in general as strongly attached to their old ways and slow to achieve socialist consciousness, it justifies "imposed" collectivization as an option, since the benefits will eventually justify the means. Rural, and often imposed, collectivization has thus become synonymous with socialization and has remained the model for socialist agrarian transformation since the 1930s.

The experiences of the last half century have called into question the validity of most of these arguments as collective agriculture has fared poorly in one country after another and as the expected rapid development in rural production failed to materialize. In the African case, some have attributed the failure to the bureaucratic institutions of the "state-class" or the ruling "bureaucratic bougeoisie,"[4] but this is not very convincing and at best provides a partial answer to a complex problem.

There is no reason why a thorough but carefully crafted land reform should inevitably give rise to antagonistic rural classes, to rural capitalism, or to interrural class exploitation. For example, recent Marxist and non-Marxist studies of Soviet collectivization now agree that there is no evidence that an indigenous rural capitalism was emerging in the 1920s when collectivization was imposed on the Soviet peasantry.[5] Moreover, too much has been made of the rural differentiation argument, as if the desired alternative is complete social homogeneity, something that borders on utopian thinking, and is practically impossible to achieve. China took the most stringent measures to promote rural egalitarianism in the 1960s and 1970s but was unable to achieve it, as the evidence from two sympathetic observers shows.[6] Finally, this may sound heretical, but, within bounds, rural differentiation is a healthy development and may promote, among other things, the faster diffusion of new ideas and techniques through the fruitful competition it creates.

The expected rapid development in rural production after collectivization did not materialize either in the Soviet Union or China, two examples that are often cited. The last famine in the Soviet Union was in 1946–47, but all through the period 1931–1952, Soviet people were dying in large number from starvation and/or food deficiency diseases.[7] In China, Western observers estimate that more than six million persons died in 1958–1961 of famine, which information was withheld from the Chinese people as well as the world,[8] although this did happen before collectivization was launched in full.

It is now commonly accepted that Soviet agriculture has not yet recovered from the ravages of Stalin's collectivization, and the country continues to import large quantities of grain to feed its population. Further, there is consensus among contemporary students of Soviet economic development that collectivization failed to meet the objectives set for it outside the sphere of food production. As one keen observer has pointed out, collectivization "provided the crucible with which many of the most anachronistic elements of Soviet state socialism took shape, including the antagonistic relationship between the state and the peasantry [and] the emergence of the cult of personality. . . . Collectivization, moreover, not only set back rural development by decades, but it also may have drained rather than stimulated overall development, including industrialization."[9]

Chinese agriculture has had a mixed record. Given the scarcity of cultivable land relative to population and exploitation by imperialist powers in the prerevolution period, the attainment of food security in the 1970s is a considerable achievement. Nevertheless, the record is not a glowing one, and as Elisabeth Croll has shown, there are still pockets of malnutrition and localized chronic hunger. Per capita food production reached a peak in 1958 but declined with the onset of collectivization. Indeed, China did not surpass the 1958 figures for both this and per capita grain availability even by the end of the 1970s,[10] despite the huge investments it poured into collective agriculture and rural infrastructure.

The weakness of orthodox socialist agriculture theory, at least in the African context, is that it openly promotes the subordination of the interests of the peasantry in pursuit of illusory objectives and for the benefit of nonrural classes. This is hard to justify either in class terms, as the peasantry makes up the great majority of African societies, or in economic terms, as the one resource that these societies cannot afford to do without, namely, food, is produced by peasants. The double subordination of the rural production arises when smallholder production is suppressed in favor of collective operations and the interests of rural society are sacrificed to promote those of the urban classes. There is no conclusive evidence that large-scale production is inherently superior to peasant production in Third World conditions, nor is smallholder agriculture inherently incapable of evolving to modernity given the appropriate stimulus and encouragement. As I will try to show in below, peasant production in postrevolution Ethiopia actually performed better than the collective sector despite having been battered by such factors as unfavorable environmental conditions and prejudicial state policies.

Land Reform and Collectivization

The land reform of 1975 was the basis on which all subsequent rural policies, including those promoting collectivization, were formulated. I have dealt with the subject at length elsewhere, and the discussion of it here will have to be brief.[11]

The old agrarian system was a complex one, which cannot be fully discussed here. However, for present purposes, some aspects of the system are worth mentioning, since they provide a framework for comparative analysis. Broadly speaking, the two main tenurial arrangements in the country before land reform were "communal" ownership (the *rist* system), where consanguineous descent controlled access to land, and tenant holdings (or sharecropper arrangements) in which the landlord determined, in the final instance, the distribution of plots and the security of holdings. There were a considerable number of small owner-operators, but the sector they formed was largely subordinated to the two others in terms of the parameters of economic and political power.

Of the two, the sharecropper arrangement by far predominated. The Ethiopian landlord was a traditional one. He was not himself a working farmer and had only a limited input in the production activity of his tenants, but he appropriated their surplus through rent and other customary exactions. While in many instances the landlord had extensive possessions, the general practice was to divide up the lands to rent out to tenant cultivators. Except for a small, capitalist, mechanized sector, there were no large-scale land operations, primarily because neither the economic culture of the landed classes nor the available, indigenous agrotechnology allowed or favored plantation-type farming enterprises.

Thus, to a large extent, the old system did not deny the peasantry access to land within the constraints set by availability and population growth. What made the system stagnant and a serious impediment to progress was rather the exploitive property relations involved and the siphoning of the peasant surplus to meet the consumption needs of the dominant classes. We shall later see that in terms purely of access to land, the postrevolution reforms did not improve matters much, at least after the initial phase of redistribution. The reforms' chief accomplishments were the abolition of what I wish to call social landlordism and of the subordination and exploitation of the peasantry by both absentee and rural-based social classes.

It is not clear how the legislation of 1975 was formulated or took its final shape. Land reform was a popular subject with the concerned public in the prerevolution period, and the radical youth movement adopted it as a major political demand as early as the mid-1960s. There is no convincing evidence that the military men, who masterminded the overthrow of the old regime and whose opposition activities began in June 1974, had seriously considered the redistribution of rural property prior to September of that year, when they finally deposed the aging emperor. It is quite likely, although the evidence is only circumstantial, that the Derg began to consider the issue of land reform and its legislation in earnest at about the end of January of the following year.

In one of the first policy documents issued shortly after their seizure of power, the new authorities referred briefly to the land system and promised a tenure reform to benefit the peasantry and to improve production. But this was only a passing comment, and the nature of the reform envisaged remained unclear for about half a year. Whether the expected reform would provide the rural population greater access to land, or merely tinker with existing property relations, or introduce a more equitable tenurial arrangement for the peasantry at large was then a burning question, but policymakers refused to deal with it for quite some time.

However, the early policy documents contained general references to "state control" of natural resources. For example, one pointed out that since "land belongs to the entire Ethiopian community, the government is the trustee of this important national resource. And it is the responsibility of the government to determine land tenure policy in an appropriate manner; in a manner that promotes productivity."[12] But the government held no public debate on the subject, nor did it actively seek the opinions of specialists, academics, interest groups, or concerned individuals. It was only with the public announcement of the legislation on March 4, 1975, that it revealed the real content of the reform. Thus, one of the most radical and historic measures of rural reconstitution ever carried out in Ethiopia was initiated and legislated in nearly complete secrecy.

At the same time, the land reform is generally considered the most widely acclaimed social reform measure of the military government. About half a million people turned out in Addis Ababa for a huge rally the day after the legislation was announced. Similarly, spontaneous demonstrations involving thousands of people occurred in many of the major provincial towns. However, most urban supporters of the new legislation were celebrating not so much the benefits gained by the peasantry but rather the dispossession of the landed classes, particularly the feudal nobility. Moreover, very few people at the time had the occasion to study the legislation, or realized the full implications of the reform. The peasantry, which was to be the main beneficiary, remained largely ignorant of developments until, several months later, students and extension agents descended on the rural areas to organize them into PAs and to help in the redistribution of land.

The reform[13] is probably one of the most radical attempted in the Third World in the last three decades and compares in thoroughness and social impact with the Chinese and Vietnamese reforms of the 1950s. It made no concessions to landed property or the landed classes and severed the link between the landlord and the laboring peasant, thereby clearing a way for a direct and unmediated access to the peasantry. Quite apart from its benefits in terms of property redistribution, land reform also served as a means of "capturing" (in the sense employed by Hyden)[14] what hitherto had been a relatively "uncaptured" rural population. By completely dispossessing the owning classes, redefining the right of ownership and of usufruct, and promoting the equalization of holdings and of labor, land reform, more than any other measure before or since, succeeded in bringing about the peasantization of rural society.

The core of the legislation is the provision that states that land is "the collective property of the Ethiopian people" and that private ownership in land is prohibited. Under the law, the peasant household has only usufructuary right over the land it cultivates and cannot transfer this right by sale, mortgage, lease, or any other means. Thus, at one stroke, the reform deprived all individual owners, including smallholder owner-cultivators, of their property and turned all rural households willing to live by their own labor into mere possessors of usufruct. In brief, what we have is a mode of property ownership in which the state, as the "trustee" of the people, acts as the real landlord, with the right, in the last instance, of redisposing of land. This involves the separation of the cultivator from his means of production and the vesting of the right of ownership in the state and has similarities with the Asiatic mode of production discussed in some of Marx's works. Extension agents and local officials routinely alienated land belonging to peasants or their PAs for a variety of purposes, including cooperatives and state farms. The "nationalization" of land, not specifically stated in the legislation but nonetheless real in practice, became the cornerstone of the country's new agrarian system.

The second most important aspect of the reform is the treatment that it meted out to the landed classes. It swept both the landed nobility and the local gentry from the rural world and did so simply by confiscating their property without compensation and denying them access to land. This was truly a purgative act, and it transformed rural Ethiopia into a mono-class society of self-laboring peasants. However, the dispossession of the landed classes did not significantly enlarge the "land fund" for redistribution, as the property of these classes was already being worked by the peasantry under a variety of customary arrangements. This limited the redistributive impact of the reform since there were no large reserves of unutilized land and no latifundia-style plantations, and in the majority of cases, peasants simply retained the land they were cultivating. However, the economic and political elimination of the landed classes must be considered the most important achievement of the reform, and, unless a radical counterrevolution occurs in the future, rural Ethiopia has nothing to fear from landlordism or other traditional exploiting classes.

The third aspect of the reform is that it empowered local peasant communities to set up what are known as Peasant Associations to oversee the redistribution of land, to maintain common assets, to resolve conflicts, and to serve as law enforcement agents in the community. However, PAs also had a variety of other functions, such as collecting taxes and other state exactions, channeling government directives to the peasantry, and mobilizing peasants for community-oriented or political purposes, which increasingly tied them to the apparatus of the state. The chances for popular participation in local government and for peasant self-management, which the legislation promised, were lost when these rural organizations were quickly subordinated to the interests of state administration at the local level.

One positive outcome that both policymakers and the informed public largely ignored is that the reform swept away many of the root causes of land-related ethnic discontent. Relations among the various nationalities in the country have never reached the explosive level found in some African countries, but neither were they exactly harmonious. The strains and low-level conflicts, especially between the people of southern origin and those of the north, were a legacy of the agrarian history of the country and centered around the issue of land rights and landlord-peasant relationships. In particular, in the southern regions, the dominant landlords were all northerners, and the peasantry here regarded itself as virtually an outcast in its own homeland and culturally subordinated as well. By dispossessing the landlord class and restoring land rights to each community, reform removed the causes of ethnic conflict associated with rural property. Each PA community now became socially and ethnically homogeneous because all previously dominant social elements, who often were outsiders, were excluded from participating in the reform process.

The reform had a good number of positive elements, but its weaknesses and negative elements seriously undermined its overall benefits to the peasantry. Of the latter, we shall look briefly at three major examples: the selective impact of the reform; the diminution of holdings; and the dynamic leveling down it brought about. The reform gave rise to a uniformity of tenure throughout rural Ethiopia (barring, of course, areas where pastoralism or shifting cultivation is practiced). All peasants came to have usufruct right over the land they cultivated. This was an achievement in itself.

Not all peasants benefited equally from the reform. Indeed, some were actually hurt, and others gained little or nothing. For the landless peasants, the reform provided access to land; for the tenants, it removed the burden of exploitation by landlords. But the small owner-cultivators, which I estimate to have made up a quarter of rural households, were dispossessed of their right of ownership. The reform provided access to *land use* for all, and in this it has remained true to the principles of social equity. In almost all cases, peasants themselves carried out the actual task of land allocation through chosen PAs or what were called land allotment committees, which consisted of respected peasants in each community. For this reason, the principle of "equal share for equal households" was fairly and uniformly adhered to. In most instances, land was allotted on the basis of households and household size.

The reform does not guarantee either sufficiency or security of holdings. Under existing conditions, the average rural Ethiopian household of 4.5 members required about three to four hectares of good-quality land (1 hectare is equal to 2.47 acres) to meet all its basic needs and outside obligations and to have a modest marketable surplus. While the reform permits holdings up to a maximum size of 10 hectares per household, in practice average plots are minuscule, ranging from 0.25 to 0.5 hectare in the high population density, permanent crop regions to 1.5 to 2.0 hectares in the cereal complex zone. Thus, for a large majority of peasants, social equity has meant below-subsistence or even below-threshold holdings. Often enough, the redistribution process involved land grading that offered each household strips of plots from several grades of land in the community, a method of ensuring a fair and equitable distribution. The unfortunate outcome was that land fragmentation became a central aspect of the new system, and there is no prospect of resolving the problem within the framework of the reform.

However, the most damaging aspect of the reform remains the insecurity of holding to which it has given rise. Two factors further aggravated insecurity. First, the peasant household does not actually own the plots to which it is entitled, and the state or its agents can alienate the land from the user. Second, the reform has involved a leveling down effect. A rural household has access to land only within its own PA, which is supposed to have jurisdiction over a legally and spatially defined land area of 800 hectares (1,976 acres). But such is the settlement pattern in the rural areas that some PAs possess more and some less land than that set by the law. Moreover, not all the land in a PA may be fit for cultivation: some of it may be wetland, stony ground, pasture, or woodland. Young peasants who become eligible for land cannot acquire it because all of it has already been distributed. As a consequence, standard practice for many years has alienated land from peasants in the community who are considered to possess "large plots" for redistribution to new members. What "large" means varies from place to place and depends not just on the physical size of the land in question but on the size of the family using it. This progressive leveling down of individual possessions, quite common in the first decade of the land reform, has created deep uncertainty and resentment among peasants and is one of the chief factors for the poor performance of smallholder agriculture.[15]

The reform put great emphasis on the self-laboring peasant household and prohibited tenancy, the leasing or renting of land, and the hiring of labor. However, all three practices were widely resorted to in many parts of the country with the tacit approval of rural organizations. This was an attempt on the part of the peasantry to overcome the weaknesses of the land reform, particularly its unintended but nonetheless real tendency to exacerbate rural poverty. For the peasant who rented land from another, it was a means of supplementing his income, while for the peasant who leased his plot to another, it is a survival strategy. In the latter case, the land would not have been worked because the family concerned does not have access to draft animals and/or other essential resources.

In the short run, the reform also blocked rural out-migration because a peasant's holding was conditional on his or her continuing membership in a PA and any extended personal absence or nonutilization jeopardized the person's right to the land. Further, the chances for off-farm employment were minimal since land reform abolished the privately operated farm enterprises that gave seasonal employment to many peasants. Moreover, landlessness, which a variety of customary support arrangements made less painful in the past, will become an increasingly serious problem. The new system has not been able to accommodate the high rate of population growth, particularly in the northern regions, and this will eventually lead to high rates of rural unemployment and of rural to urban migration and may further provoke social tension and civil conflict.

Land reform was not accompanied by impressive growth rates in food production, although the initial results were not discouraging. Given the uncertainties of the rural population in the wake of the reform and the sporadic unrest that then took place, the modest crop gains that were recorded at the time revealed that the reform had had a positive impact on peasant production. The harvest year 1979–80 registered the best results, but this was the year when peasant producer cooperatives were launched and the collectivization drive actively promoted. If we look closely at the available crop production figures from 1979 to 1987, we can detect clear indications of a declining trend in per capita food production, a general stagnation in agricultural growth, and a decline in per capita grain availability in the rural areas. This poor record may be due in part to the structural weakness of the reform and the shift it brought in resource allocation from the individual to the collective sector.

Further, the reform did not effectively address the long-term malaise of Ethiopian agriculture, which had been undergoing a slow process of involution since the end of the 1940s. This involution was a legacy of the archaic tenure system that stifled personal endeavor and suppressed rural differentiation in the form of competitive social groups that could have played a dynamic role; of the growing burden that the peasantry had to bear because of increasing exactions by the state and the landlord; of the transfer of its surplus and resources out of the rural world; and of the loss of natural resources arising from poor land use practices and environmental stress. In the 1950s and 1960s, agrarian decline occasioned a great out-migration of peasants from the provinces in the north and northeast and the settlement of "underutilized" lands in the forested areas of the southwest and southeast.[16] What the rural economy needed most was a judicious land reform to which the old regime was not receptive and large investments in agriculture to benefit peasant production which the pre- and postrevolution authorities were unwilling to commit.

At the time of the shift to collectivization, there were no clear signs that peasant agriculture, though in poor condition, was in crisis or that individual production as a system was about to exhaust, or had exhausted, its full potential. However, it was obvious that peasant agriculture was deeply starved of investments, of technical support and service, and of innovative ideas. Furthermore, there was no significant class opposition to the new agrarian system since landlord resistance had been crushed earlier, and there was no emergent kulak class active in the rural areas. Indeed, as I have argued in the work cited earlier, the reform inhibits rural class formation and encourages small-scale enterprises. At the time, the chances for rural capitalism outside of petty trade were quite slim, and this continues to be the case. In brief, the major reason for the shift to collective agriculture was political and doctrinal rather than economic.

Following the land reform, the most serious difficulties that arose were temporary food shortages in the major urban areas and sharp rises in grain prices. Initially, this was due mainly to higher consumption of grain by the producers themselves, some speculative hoarding and trading by peasants, and shortages of trucking capacity. The harvest in the first year of the reform was estimated to be relatively good, but nevertheless basic grain prices jumped by more than 30 percent in 1976 and continued to rise in the following years.[17]

Matters were worsened because trucking capacity was seriously reduced by the government's decision to commandeer all transport vehicles for the offensive against insurgency in the north of the country and the war effort against Somalia in the east. Further, the state found it necessary to intervene in grain marketing, and this involved not only procurement by the Agricultural Marketing Corporation (AMC), the state purchasing agency, but also the fixing of price levels for marketed crops.

The government wagered on collectivization soon after carrying out land reform, first by heavily investing in state agriculture and later by launching cooperatives. According to the country's ten-year plan issued in 1984 and targeted to run to 1993, the transition to "socialist agriculture" was to have been completed in the main by the end of the plan period, by which time the "socialist" sector of rural production would have become dominant, as shown in table 10.1. As the table indicates, planners placed high hopes on cooperative endeavor, which they believed would be most cost-effective and the main engine of rural transformation.

By mid-plan, the evidence suggested that fulfillment of the collectivization plans of the government by the end of the period would require some drastic steps. The formation of cooperatives had progressed only moderately, and the peasant sector stood just as preponderant as at the beginning. At the same time, there were indications that policy planners were then more concerned with consolidating existing enterprises than

Table 10.1. "Socialist" agriculture in the ten-year plan (%)

Sector	1984–85		1987–88		1993–94	
	Area	production	Area	production	Area	production
Peasant	95.4	94.8	89.8	87.5	39.6	36.6
Cooperative	1.4	1.4	6.6	6.2	52.2	51.9
State	2.8	3.6	2.9	5.9	6.4	10.0
Other*	0.4	0.2	0.7	0.4	1.8	1.5

Source: National Committee for Central Planning, *The Ten-Year Guiding Plan* (Addis Ababa, 1984), and *Assessment of Annual Plan Implementation* [Amharic] (Addis Ababa, 1988); Ministry of Agriculture, *Annual Report.*
*Collective farms in settlement schemes, Ministry of Agriculture-run projects, etc.

encouraging accelerated collectivization. In March 1990, the government formally abandoned certain key elements of its strategy, and in June 1991, it was overthrown by military insurgents.

Let us now turn to peasant producer cooperatives (PPCs) and state farms. The policy guidelines for PPCs were issued in June 1979, and implementation began soon after. Cooperatives were to be undertaken in three stages. At the lowest level were "primary" cooperatives, called *malba,* in which there was common ownership of land but individual ownership of livestock and farm equipment, similar to a traditional joint cultivation scheme. Malbas were to give birth to "secondary" cooperatives, called *welba,* where all agricultural resources including livestock and work tools were owned in common. At the highest level were *weland,* which would be formed of two or more welbas and which would involve complete collectivization. At least on paper, the weland resembles the Soviet *kolkhoz* of the 1930s. Peasants involved in the primary and secondary cooperatives kept individual garden plots.[18] Information on PPCs showed that in the agricultural year 1987–88, of the total of 3,723 enterprises in the country, 69 percent were malbas and the rest welbas. Up to this time, there were no welands, although Ministry of Agriculture specialists were preparing plans to establish such enterprises in the near future.[19]

Theoretically, as few as three persons living in the same PA may form a PPC, but the authorities needed a minimum of thirty persons formally to register the organization, and the process might take anywhere between two and four years, sometimes more. As of 1988, not more than 13 percent of the PPCs had received their registration, a status that was necessary to obtain credit services from the banks, to enter into contractual agreements with state enterprises, and to attract more extension services and investment aid from government sources.

The establishment of the State Farms Development Authority, later renamed the Ministry of State Farms Development (MSFD), formally launched state agriculture in May 1977. Among the major objectives of state agriculture were alleviation of the country's food problems, the provision of raw materials for domestic industry along with the expansion of agroindustries, the expansion of output for export purposes, and the creation of employment opportunities. State farms were also to be a reliable source of food for state procurement agencies.

The Private and the Collective

Private peasants continued to outperform the collective sector as a whole and the state farms in particular. The collective sector benefited from preferential treatment and a multiciplicity of state measures that were largely unavailable to smallholder agriculture. We shall return to this later.

The evidence for the relative superiority of peasant agriculture came from a wide variety of official and independent sources. The best measure of efficiency available to us is crop yield. According to the Central Statistical Authority's (CSA) reports on crop production for the years 1979–80 to 1986–87, yield in the private sector was consistently higher than in cooperatives for all crops surveyed. Further, in the same period, average yields of peasant farms exceeded those of state farms for such basic crops as *teff* (*Eragrostis abyssinica,* the staple crop of northern Ethiopia), sorghum, and all varieties of pulse and oil crops. They were nearly comparable for wheat but relatively poor for barley and maize.[20] The CSA's annual crop production surveys are considered the most reliable in the country. Several reports prepared by the Central Planning Office and the Ministry of Agriculture also reveal that productivity of PPCs was lower than on private farms, sometimes by as much as one-third.[21] Studies prepared by the regional planning office for northeast Ethiopia show that cooperatives in the famine-prone province of Wollo have been less efficient than peasant farms for the years for which information is available.[22]

The Swedish International Development Agency (SIDA) independently assessed the performance of the peasant and cooperative sectors in a 1985 report. The study, which covered the provinces of Arssi and Bale, found that crop yield on peasant farms was consistently higher than on cooperatives. The study included several showcase cooperatives in both provinces, but the finding was that peasant farms make more efficient use of resources than do cooperatives.[23] A 1987 World Bank report also concurred that in general, peasant agriculture performed much better than either cooperatives or state farms.[24] A number of individual researchers similarly arrived at the same conclusion based on micro case studies in various parts of the country.[25]

A team of Soviet economic advisers attached to the country's planning agency affirmed that collectivization had poor prospects and was an unprofitable policy, though in a roundabout way. In a report prepared for the government, the Soviet specialists strongly backed private peasant agriculture and criticized the wastefulness and inefficiency of state agriculture. The authors, all top experts from the Soviet planning agency, GOSPLAN, emphasized that the government should direct its major effort toward stimulating production in the private sector. Large-scale, mechanized operations, they argued, were best run as private enterprises, and they recommended the promotion of private endeavor in this area.[26] It should be noted that they prepared and submitted their report to the Ethiopian authorities before Gorbachev launched his new economic initiatives in Russia. As a general rule, Soviet bloc economic advisers do not recommend collectivization to Third World countries.

Peasant Producer Cooperatives

Ethiopian cooperatives were large-scale enterprises in the formal sense of the term. In a majority of them, the man/land ratio was very low, frequently lower than on peasant farms. For example, in many cooperatives in Wollo, the average amount of land worked by each cooperator was 1 hectare; in Arssi, it ranged from 1.5 to 2.0 hectares; and in Bale, it was about 1.8. The national average for the crop year 1987–88 was about 1.7 hectares. According to a report of the Ministry of Agriculture, the typical cooperative enterprise had a holding of 136 hectares, of which about a third was uncultivated for various reasons, and a membership of about eighty family heads, of which some 6 percent were women.[27] On the average, each cooperator worked about 1.1 hectares of land, which was below the optimal level in terms of efficiency of labor or of land use. In brief, PPCs did not benefit from scale of operations or from a more efficient deployment of labor.

Moreover, PPCs, just as much as individual cultivators, were constrained by a shortage of draft animals, their main traction power. On the average, a household in a cooperative had access to 1.2 draft animals, which was a little lower than the national average for peasant cultivators, while 2 animals are necessary for plowing. A few enterprises had access to modern tractors through purchase or rental arrangements. Cooperative labor was organized on a "work gang" basis, but these work gangs were rarely selected on the basis of performance, capability, or compatibility. Thus, the net result was less intensive labor, delays in completing necessary tasks, and lower quality of output. The system of evaluation and remuneration, which was modeled on the Chinese point system, was not well received by peasants who complained that it encouraged the lazy or the incompetent and was subject to abuse; a considerable number of local extension agents also complained loudly about the system. Both these practices gave rise to low morale among peasants in many cooperatives.

The Ministry of Agriculture's report on PPCs, noted above, attributed their poor performance to shortage of draft animal power, the "individualistic" orientation of cooperators, embezzlement of enterprise funds by elected officials, and low turnout during peak labor periods.[28] One ought to add to this, poor deployment of labor, inefficient use of resources, and poor management practices. Further, local state agencies frequently interfered in the work of the enterprises either directly by dictating cropping and work plans or indirectly by organizing frequent meetings and rallies that required the participation of the enterprise work staff or officials.

However, cooperatives had privileges not available to private cultivators or even to state agriculture. Cooperators paid less income tax per head than individual peasants and received modern inputs such as fertilizers, pesticides, and improved seeds at subsidized prices. Bank interest rates for the enterprises were also comparatively low. Further, extension work gave priority to the enterprises: since before the famine most extension agents were instructed to give priority to cooperatives in their activities.

In the agricultural year 1987–88, the registered cooperative enterprises obtained 64 percent of their soft loans from government banks and the rest from other sources, including peasant service cooperatives. In a number of cases, PPCs defaulted on payment of the loans, which they obtained from the service cooperatives. Most of the credit went to buy equipment and farm animals and to pay for a variety of services such as tractor rental. But some of the larger enterprises obtained free grants, in cash or in kind, for infrastructural investments as well for schools and clinics, mostly from the government but on occasion from donor agencies.

Further, rural extension agents quite frequently alienated farmland and common pasture belonging to peasants and PAs and allocated it to cooperatives whenever the latter complained of shortage of land. This practice was fairly widespread and aroused resentment. Eviction of peasants from their land to make way for cooperatives also became routine. Poor peasants who had insufficient or mostly marginal land often formed cooperatives to have access to higher-grade land. The government provided this by evicting other peasants, who, in turn, were frequently offered the poor or marginal lands abandoned by the former. This, too, created resentment and insecurity among peasants.

Moreover, during the peak seasons, PPCs drew additional labor from the PA within which they were located. Their PA or extension agents often obliged indivdual peasants in the vicinity of PPCs to work several days per season for the enterprises without pay, a form of socialist corvée labor that was gaining ground in areas where there was low availability of seasonal labor. Similarly, members of rural youth associations, an arm of the PA, provided labor, again free of payment, during land preparation, weeding, and other demanding periods.[29]

State Farms

The story of state agriculture was one of mismanagement, of wasted resources and financial loss on a large scale. Since 1977 when the government formally gave its blessing to state farm development, the enterprise incurred a total accumulated loss of 613 million Birr (about US 296 million). In the same period, the enterprise received, on the average, 64 percent of the annual state capital expenditure allocated to agriculture.[30] The peasant sector, which provided more than 95 percent of the country's food needs, received an annual investment of less than half of this.

In the first decade of its formation, the Ministry of State Farms carried out large expansion schemes in many parts of the country. Generous government grants and liberal bank loans encouraged it in this endeavor. At the beginning, its holdings measured a mere 55,000 hectares, but five years later, this had expanded fourfold and the regions it was operating in had increased considerably. This feverish expansion turned out later to have been poorly planned and in some cases, environmentally damaging. At this time, the cultivated area under state control measures over 210,000 hectares, of which 86 percent is rain-fed farmland, some of which was taken from peasant associations. At the height of its expansion activities, some peasants were evicted from their land to make way for mechanized state agriculture, particularly in Arssi and Bale provinces and also on a smaller scale in the Mettekel area of Gojjam Province.

State Farms' contribution to the country's exports and its share of foreign currency earnings declined through much of the 1980s. In this period, its annual exports, which consisted mainly of live animals, horticultural produce, and oil crops, averaged 6 percent of the country's total exports. The enterprise used up large amounts of foreign exchange because its operations were highly capital intensive, and it had to purchase all its chemical inputs (fertilizers, pesticides, etc.) and spare parts from outside with hard currency. It was now estimated that State Farms could only cover about 40 percent of its foreign currency requirements from the export of its own products. Thus, far from earning the nation the hard currency it desperately needed, as the planners had hoped, state agriculture continued to drain the country's foreign earnings.

Over the years, state agriculture greatly abused the technology it employed, and its equipment handling and stock management methods were atrocious. There were frequent breakdowns of machinery and equipment, and repairs took a long time to complete because of the difficulty of obtaining needed spare parts. Similarly, the enterprise's cropping and land use practices were abusive and environmentally damaging.

Most of the farms rarely practiced crop rotation. As a result, continuous monocropping led to the build-up of crop diseases, pests, and noxious weeds causing deterioration in crop yield and quality.[31] For several years, AMC refused to purchase wheat from the enterprise because of the poor quality of the crop that the latter offered. To counter the ill effects of monocropping, many farms employed fertilizers on a large scale. However, it often carried out fertilization without prior investigation of soil types, of crop requirements, and of residual effects. Similarly, the enterprise's water control and management practices were highly inadequate. Faulty irrigation works, the absence of proper water control schemes, and lack of sufficient drainage systems led to the build-up of high levels of salinity in soils.

Some large-scale projects were abandoned partially or in full due to the above reasons as well as to mismanagement and reckless labor deployment practices. The Humera sesame estates, which had once been thriving private operations, are now in poor condition because for several years after the revolution they were worked by commandeered labor. Soil erosion is widespread and, according to official sources, affected three out of every four farms operated by the Ministry of State Farms Development. The individual peasant was often much better at protecting the soil and fighting the ill effects of erosion than either state agriculture or cooperatives.

These poor practices, coupled with low morale among staff and workers and poor planning and management, contributed considerably to the poor record of State Farms. In brief, state agriculture drained the country's scarce resources and failed miserably to meet the objectives that state planners set for it.

In the latter 1980s, the drive for collectivization slowed down, suggesting that collectivization was not easy for the government. The "socialist" offensive was blunted mainly because (a) the state was engaged on far too many fronts, among them, villagization, resettlement, and state grain marketing; (b) the resources of the state were limited, and the high cost of collectivization was slowing down the program; and (c) there was a divergence of views on collectivization between officials in the party hierarchy, who wished to accelerate the drive, and those in the planning and implementing agencies, who tended to be more cautious and more economic-minded.

Conclusion

The distinctive aspect of the rural policy of postrevolution Ethiopia was that it provided rural producers access to land use, on the one hand, but denied them the opportunity to take advantage of its benefits, on the other. The central flaw of the land reform of 1975, which subsequent legislation did not attempt to correct, was its failure to provide peasant households with individual ownership and title deeds. All the other weaknesses of the reform, which in the aggregate negated the real benefits of the new land system, arose from this basic mistake. The "nationalization" of land was a poor substitute for the exploitive land system of the prerevolution period, because the state was a more burdensome and more intolerant landlord and because ownership rights provide greater motivation and, above all, more security than usufructuary rights.

However, smallholder agriculture, cooperatives, and large-scale farming can play a useful role in agricultural development if given the right conditions and proper incentives and if guided by judicious policies. I do not have space to debate the issue here, but I believe that some form of what may be called "agricultural pluralism" provides a more flexible alternative to hard-line policies that insist on placing all eggs either in the smallholder or in the collective agricultural basket.[32] Just as collective agriculture, even under the best of circumstances, has severe limitations, so too does peasant production whose long-term developmental prospects are not as bright as its admirers make out. In particular, independent cooperative enterprises can be effective in certain areas of specialized agriculture that require capital investment and group labor and where production is geared largely to the market.

In conclusion, one ought to conceive of an equitable and vigorous economic system in the rural areas as consisting in the main of individual peasant production and associated production, articulated in a way beneficial to both. Associated production involves free and equal producers who come together voluntarily and for their own purposes to carry on economic activity in concert. For free association to be possible, there must first be forms of landownership compatible with an independent peasantry. Real, participatory socialism will have to await the transformation of the peasant and his social environment and the rationalization of production through the agency of modern technology.

Notes

1 The full text is reproduced in *Addis Zemen,* 29 June 1984.
2 See my "The Political Economy of Development in Ethiopia," in E. Keller and D. Rothchild (eds.), *Afro-Marxist Regimes: Ideology and Public Policy* (Boulder, 1987).
3 Some of the recent literature on the subject includes R. R. Fagen et al. (eds.), *Transition and Development: Problems of Third World Socialism* (New York, 1986); A. Hussain and K. Tribe, *Marxism and the Agrarian Question* (London, 1983); A. Saith (ed.), *The Agrarian Question in Socialist Transition* (London, 1985); C. White and G. White (eds.), *Agriculture, the Peasantry and Socialist Development,* IDS Bulletin Special Issue (Brighton, 1982); G. White and E. Croll (eds.), *Agriculture in Socialist Development* (Oxford, 1985); G. White et al. (eds.), *Revolutionary Socialist Development in the Third World* (Brighton, 1983).

   For the Soviet experience, see R. W. Davies, *The Socialist Offensive: The Collectivisation of Soviet Agriculture 1929–1930* (London, 1980); M. Ellman, *Socialist Planning* (Cambridge, 1979). For Eastern Europe: R. Francisco et al. (eds.), *The Political Economy of Collectivized Agriculture* (New York, 1979); K. E. Wadekin, *Agrarian Policies in Communist Europe* (The Hague, 1982). For problems in Third World socialist countries: F. Colburn, *Post-Revolutionary Nicaragua: State, Class and the Dilemmas of Agrarian Policy* (Berkeley, 1986); G. Gunn, "The Angolan Economy: A History of Contradictions," in E. Keller and D. Rothchild (eds.), *Afro-Marxist Regimes;* O. Ruesch, "Peasants and Collective Agriculture in Mozambique," in J. Barker (ed.), *The Politics of Agriculture in Tropical Africa* (Beverly Hills, 1985).

   I am writing as a sympathizer of an "open" Marxism, that is, nondoctrinaire and nondogmatic.
4 See H. Bernstein and B. Campbell (eds.), *Contradictions of Accumulation in Africa* (Beverly Hills, 1985).
5 Hussain and Tribe, *Marxism,* 137.
6 P. Nolan and G. White, "Socialist Development and Rural Inequality: The Chinese Countryside in the 1970s," *Journal of Peasant Studies* VII, 1 (1979): 3–48.
7 Ellman, *Socialist Planning,* 97.
8 B. Ashton et al., "Famine in China, 1958–61," *Population and Developmental Review* X, 4 (1984): 613–645.
9 M. Selden, "The Crisis of Collectivisation: Socialist Development and the Peasantry," in C. White and G. White (eds.), *Agriculture,* 10. See also Hussain and Tribe, *Marxism,* 274. The orthodox thesis that collectivization provided the Soviet Union with the surplus for rapid accumulation and rapid

industrialization has been demolished by J. R. Millar, "Soviet Rapid Development and the Agricultural Surplus Hypothesis," *Soviet Studies* XXII, 1 (1970): 77–93; and M. Ellman, "Did the Agricultural Surplus Provide the Resources for the Increase in Investment in the USSR during the First Five Year Plan?" *Economic Journal* 85 (1975): 844–864. The latter work argues that collectivization did not increase the net agricultural surplus or gross output in this period.

10 E. Croll, *The Family Rice Bowl: Food and the Domestic Economy in China* (Geneva, 1982): 6, 62.

11 Dessalegn Rahmato, *Agrarian Reform in Ethiopia* (Uppsala and Trenton, N.J., 1984).

12 Provisional Military Government of Ethiopia, *Declarations of the Provisional Government of Ethiopia* (Addis Ababa, 1974): 10.

13 The discussion that follows is based mainly on my work noted above, on the sources cited in footnote 10. In the latter half of 1991, as this work went to press, the legislation of 1975 remained the legal basis of agrarian property relations in the Ethiopian countryside.

14 G. Hyden, *Beyond Ujamaa in Tanzania: Underdevelopment and the Uncaptured Peasantry* (Berkeley, 1980).

15 A recent World Bank report argues that many of the government's rural policies, including land reform, are responsible for the stagnation in agricultural production. World Bank, *Ethiopia: Agriculture-A Strategy for Growth, A Sector Review* (Washington, D.C., 1987): 13–20, 52–56.

16 A. P. Wood, "Spontaneous Agricultural Resettlement in Ethiopia, 1959–1974," in J. I. Clarke and L. A. Kosinski (eds.), *Redistribution of Population in Africa* (London, 1982); "Population Redistribution and Agricultural Settlement Schemes in Ethiopia 1958–80," in J. I. Clarke et al. (eds.), *Population and Development Projects in Africa* (Cambridge, 1985).

17 See the retail price data for food in Central Statistical Office, *Statistical Abstracts 1972 to 1980* (Addis Ababa, 1973–1981).

18 Provisional Military Government of Ethiopia, *Peasant Producer Cooperatives* (Addis Ababa, 1979).

19 Ministry of Agriculture, *Annual Report of the Cooperative Department* (Addis Ababa, 1988): 1–14. Unless otherwise noted, information about PPCs in the pages that follow is taken from this document, 26–28. See also, Ministry of Agriculture, *Report on the Fulfillment of Production Plans of Peasant Producer Cooperatives for the Year 1982/83* [Amharic] (Addis Ababa, 1983); *Gibrinnachin* [Amharic] (Addis Ababa, 1984); *General Agriculture Survey, Producers Cooperatives Preliminary Report 1983/84* (Addis Ababa, 1985). Tegegn Teka, "Rural Institutions in Post-Revolution Ethiopia: A Survey of Developments with a Focus on Agricultural Producers' Cooperatives," paper prepared for the Oxford Centre for African Studies (Oxford, 1988).

Since this work is about collective production, I have left out Peasant Service Cooperatives, which as the name implies, provide marketing and credit services to the peasantry.

20 For details, see Dessalegn, "The Peasants and the Comrades Problems and Prospects of Socialist Transition in Rural Ethiopia," paper prepared for the African Studies Association (Denver, 1987).

21 Hyden, *Beyond Ujamaa.*

22 Regional Planning Office for Northeast Ethiopia, *A Preliminary Survey of Agricultural Production in Wollo in 1985/86* [Amharic] (Dessie, 1986); *A General Report on the 1986/87 Agricultural Production Sample Survey of Wollo Region* (Dessie, 1987).

23 Swedish International Development Agency, *Proposal for SIDA Support to Rural Development in Arssi and Bale 1986/87–1988/89* (Stockholm, 1985).

24 World Bank, *Ethiopia* (Washington, D.C., 1987).

25 Alemneh Dejene, *Peasants, Agrarian Socialism and Rural Development in Ethiopia* (Boulder, 1987); Tegegne Teka, *Rural Institutions*, 25. See also J. M. Cohen and N.-I. Isakson, *Smallholder vs. Agricultural Collectivization: Agricultural Debates in Ethiopia since the Revolution; Paper for the Conference on Problems of the Horn of Africa* (Washington, D.C., 1987). This is a poor work based on a brief visit to the country and on secondary sources. It has since been published in *World Development* XVI, 3 (1988): 323–348.

26 National Committee for Central Planning (NCCP), "Considerations on the Economic Policy of Ethiopia for the Next Few Years," report prepared by a team of Soviet consulting advisers attached to the NCCP; unpublished manuscript (Addis Ababa, 1985): 23–24. See also, Paul B. Henze, *Ethiopia: Crisis of a Marxist Economy, Analysis and Text of a Soviet Report* (Santa Monica, Calif., The Rand Corporation, April 1983). Henze published the report as an Appendix, A.1-A.3.

27 Ministry of Agriculture, *General Agricultural*, 5; *Annual Report*, 14–15.

28 Some of these practices are reported in two studies prepared for the Institute of Agricultural Research. Aleligne Kefyalew and S. Franzel, *Initial Results of Informal Survey: Adet Mixed Farming Systems Zone* (Addis Ababa, 1987); Alemayehu Mamo and S. Franzel, *Initial Results of Informal Survey: Sinana Mixed Farming System Zone* (Addis Ababa, 1987).

29 Ministry of Agriculture, *General Agricultural; Annual Report.*

30 Ministry of State Farms Development, *Towards a Strategy for the Development of State Farms*, Vol. I, *Main Report* (Addis Ababa, 1986): 385; Vol. II, *Production of Crops;* Vol. III, *Livestock Production;* Vol. IV, *Soils, Land Use, Irrigation and Mechanization;* Vol. V, *Agro-Industries*. These volumes are my main source of information. See also the same agency's *State Farm Development* [Amharic] (Addis Ababa, 1984); *Ministry of State Farms, Its Rule, Organization, Present and Future Activities* (Addis Ababa, 1984).

31 The discussion that follows is based on ibid., Vol. I, chaps. 8–10, and Vol. IV.

32 I have argued for a such a position in my "The Peasants and the Comrades." Cohen and Isakson's "Smallholder" is a full defense of peasant agriculture, and I call this approach just as hard-line as its opposite.

11   *Michael Roth*

Somalia Land Policies and Tenure Impacts: The Case of the Lower Shebelle

$$\overline{O}\,13$$

$$Q\,15$$

Somalia

Introduction

Land tenure in Somalia is in a state of transition. Customary land tenure arrangements govern most cultivated land and nearly all pastoral land. But, state leasehold tenure based on statutory law is becoming more widespread, particularly in Somalia's two main river valleys, the Shebelle and the Jubba (fig. 11.1). Land legislation passed in 1975 officially transferred control of tenure rights on all Somali land from traditional authorities to the Government of Somalia Democratic Republic (GSDR). Landholders are permitted to register limited amounts of land as state leaseholds or concessions, with usufructuary rights for fifty years which are renewable.

Land registration in early years was closely linked with GSDR programs aimed at establishing a modern corporate agriculture. In the 1970s, the GSDR passed various laws and programs to promote the establishment of state farms, cooperatives, and large private plantations. Such policies have increased land concentration, displaced some landholders, and in some instances, decreased the tenure security of landholders wihout leasehold rights. In more recent years, the strongest demand for state leaseholds has come from private landholders, both large and small. Despite strong demand, limited government resources for administering titles and complicated registration procedures have resulted in high costs of leasehold acquisition, giving wealthier and better-connected individuals a comparative advantage in acquiring concessions.

Compared with customary tenure systems, land rights under state leasehold tenure are more restrictive. The land law limits landholdings to only one parcel, imposes high administrative costs on transfers, discourages fallowing and other land-resting strategies, and biases land allocation toward large corporate agriculture. Landholders not registering land face the risk of government expropriation, and farmers are reluctant to lend or rent out land for fear that the renter may permanently claim it.

Conflicts between state leasehold tenure and customary tenure were relatively innocuous as long as demand for land remained low and land resources remained relatively abundant. However, demand for land, particularly for high-quality land in Somalia's river valleys, has been rapidly rising because of four external factors: rampant price inflation, foreign assistance and capital development programs, foreign barriers to Somalia's livestock exports, and increasing real crop prices. While demand has been strong, supply has become more inelastic, as cultivation pushes nearer the limits of potential irrigable land in the river valleys.

In this chapter, I describe and evaluate the impacts of government land policy on tenure security and land allocation. I first analyze the institutional and macroeconomic forces that are increasing demand for land in Somalia's riverine areas. I then evaluate Somalia's land policy and land legislation that promoted the corporatization of agriculture in the 1970s and established the basis for state leasehold tenure and land registration. I then use results from a study on security of tenure and land registration in the Lower Shebelle as a case study of the impacts of the registration process on land allocation and tenure security.

Agricultural Economy

Prior to its major land reforms in 1975, Somalia was experiencing stagnant economic growth and rising food imports. Measured by gross domestic product (GDP), the economy grew at an average annual rate of 1.0 percent during the decade 1960–1970, while agriculture declined at an average annual rate of 1.5 percent.[1] The average index of food production per capita in 1977–1979 was only 85 percent of base 1969–1971 productivity.[2] Food imports, largely aid, represented 27 percent of merchandise imported value in 1960 and 25 percent in 1978. Food aid imports alone averaged 21.4 kilograms per capita in 1977–1979.[3]

After a decade of reforms and economic adjustments in the 1970s,

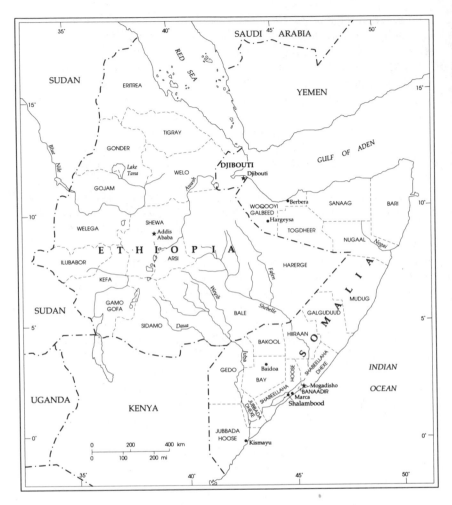

Figure 11.1. Map of the Shebelle and Jubba River basins

agriculture reversed its decline in the early 1980s. Between 1980 and 1985, food production per capita increased marginally, while GDP in agriculture grew at an inflation adjusted annual rate of 8 percent.[4] Conversely, GDP in manufacturing and industry declined at average annual rates of 3 to 5 percent, while the service sector grew 4 percent annually. Food aid imports of cereals still averaged 248 thousand tons or about 45 kilograms per capita in 1984–85,[5] but donors have sharply reduced aid in recent years.

Crop agriculture has traditionally been a secondary activity in a primarily pastoral economy. Livestock production as a percentage of GDP averaged 32 percent over the 1982–1986 period, compared with 15 percent for crop agriculture.[6] However, growth in crop cultivation appears to be outpacing growth in the livestock sector. Total area cultivated grew at an average annualized rate of around 4.5 percent between 1973–1975 and 1982–1984, while the size of cattle, sheep, and goat herds grew around 1 to 2 percent per annum.[7] Nevertheless, capital investment outside the commercial irrigated areas is limited. As illustrated by World Bank data, Somalia has one of the lowest fertilizer use rates in the world.[8]

Demand for Land Resources

With average annual rainfall of less than 430 millimeters and poor soils outside of the riverine areas, there is a high economic premium on land with good access to irrigation water. The supply of irrigable land, however, is limited and highly inelastic at present levels of land use. Of Somalia's 866,000 hectares of arable land in 1986, 11 percent was irrigated either by pump or gravity irrigation.

Demand for higher-quality land in the river valleys has continued to strengthen despite growing scarcity. Government policies, described below, provide outside investors, often urbanites, with the means to acquire land. But five external factors have increased effective demand for land and are driving up land value: price inflation, insecure deposits in the formal banking sector, international trade restrictions on livestock exports, foreign assistance and capital investment, and improved grain-to-nongrain price ratios.

High price inflation discourages investors from holding financial assets and increases the incentive for holding land or commodities (e.g., gold). As measured by the GDP deflator, price levels rose at an average annual rate of 10 percent over the period 1965–1980 and in excess of 45 percent annually between 1980 and 1985.[9] Based on the 14 percent nominal rate of interest received on bank deposits in 1985,[10] financial assets in real terms would have yielded a 31 percent negative annual return. The financial collapse of banks in late 1987 further increased investors' concerns about the safety of bank deposits. The GSDR's cancellation of the foreign exchange auction in that year led to cash hoarding and illiquidity of the banking system. As a result, investors experienced high transaction costs on withdrawals and financial transfers.

Saudi Arabia's 1983 import embargo on livestock from Somalia, pending GSDR implementation of appropriate vaccination and quarantine measures, has severely curtailed exports and foreign exchange earnings.

Livestock exports, which averaged 83 percent of total export earnings between 1981 and 1983, fell from $106 million in 1982 to $35 million by 1984.[11] The fact that Saudi Arabia was by far the dominant buyer of Somali cattle exacerbated the losses. Somalia has since found other trading partners (e.g., Egypt), but exports have not yet regained preembargo levels. Assessing the overall economic impacts of the embargo is difficult because of poor and limited data. But, in the long run, quarantine and export restrictions will reduce demand for livestock, lower prices and returns to livestock producers, and encourage some shift in human and capital resources away from the livestock sector to crop agriculture.

Public investment in river basin development and land-intensive technology has increased the supply of irrigated land and increased investors' expectations of economic returns. Official development assistance, consisting of loans and grants received from donors on a concessionary basis, amounted to $354 million in 1985 ($65 per capita), or 14.5 percent of GNP.[12] About 132,000 hectares of land on the Shebelle River are now under irrigation. Two-thirds of this area is irrigated by canals from 7 barrages (3 of which have been constructed since 1980) and one-third from an estimated 330 pumps that draw water from the river.[13]

A rise in the relative price ratio of grain-to-nongrain commodities in the early 1980s improved economic returns to cereal agriculture and, in turn, increased the derived demand for arable land. Prior to 1982, farmers were required to sell their crops to the official cereals marketing agency (Agricultural Development Corporation, ADC) at artificially regulated prices that were six to eight times lower than parallel market prices.[14] In 1981, the official prices of sorghum and maize were increased 50 percent, and ADC's monopoly powers were eliminated. Between 1980 and 1985, official maize prices increased over 100 percent in real terms.

Cropped area has expanded rapidly as an outcome of these factors. During the five-year period spanning 1979–1981 to 1984–1986, total area harvested grew at an annualized rate of 3.6 percent (on a base of 798,000 ha). For individual crops, sorghum area declined at an annualized rate of 1.3 percent (478,000 ha), while maize area grew 15.8 percent (151,000 ha) per annum. Area under bananas (325,000 ha), Somalia's most important export crop behind livestock, rose at an annualized rate of 9.8 percent. Yet, in 1986, the area under cultivation still represented only 1.4 percent of Somalia's total land, compared with 13 percent considered to be potentially arable.[15]

With price liberalization has come a gradual shift of human and capital resources into crop agriculture. Existing farmers, lacking inputs and land-intensive technology, have tried to expand their holdings, while businessmen and state officials claimed land in less-developed areas along the Shebelle.[16] Investment opportunities in other sectors, such as banking, agribusiness, and industry, declined as a result of excessive government regulation and control. Somalia's burgeoning urban population turned to farming for income and farmland for investment, giving rise to a large absentee class of landholders. Thomas Labahn observed a considerable increase in absentee landlords in two villages on the Lower Shebelle, many being traders investing their profits in farmland.[17]

These structural adjustments raise two key questions with respect to land policy and legislation. First, to what extent has statutory law provided for secure individual or community property rights in land? Second, how has government policy exacerbated or facilitated land use planning and resource management in agriculture?

Land Policy

Somalia established its first formal land tenure policies under the colonial regimes of the British in the north and the Italians in the south. Britain established its protectorate in northern Somalia between 1884 and 1886. The Italians consolidated their control in southern Somalia between 1889 and 1905. Two decrees under the Italian regime formulated the first official land tenure policies in the south. Royal Decree 695 of June 8, 1911, and the Governor's Decree 815 of January 19, 1912, collectively established the Italian state's right of sovereignty over vacant lands (i.e., those in excess of the current population's present and future needs) and its right to issue agricultural concessions out of state domain for Italian citizens or others of foreign nationality. From the early 1900s until independence in 1960, large tracts of land along the Shebelle were appropriated for concessionary development and large-scale private production of bananas and sugar. Land tenure reforms were later drafted by a special commission in 1965 but were never passed by Parliament.

Following the socialist revolution of October 1969, the new government announced a series of agrarian reforms aimed at stimulating growth and economic development. Between 1970 and 1976, it passed as many as twenty-two laws regulating the agricultural sector.[18] Among the more important developments were the Law on Cooperative Development of 1973, which established the legal basis for farm cooperatives; the Agricultural Crash Program of 1974, which established a program for temporarily allocating land to government employees and students from agricultural training colleges; the Agricultural Land Law of 1975, which created the state leasehold system; and the creation of the Agency for Resettlement and Community Projects in 1976, which gave the government authority to settle nomads and refugees in riverine areas.

According to Yusuf Robleh and Yassin Hussen, the reforms were intended to enhance agriculture's growth and prominence in the economy, tap Somalia's underexploited base of land resources, increase resource use efficiency, and reduce the country's dependence on food imports.[19] David Laitin saw the purpose of the land reform as replacing an archaic system of communal tenure and nomadic pastoralism with one more economically productive and less destructive of the land.[20] Susan Gunn points out that GSDR planners at the time believed that common ownership was environmentally degrading, that nomadic pastoralism was unproductive, and that traditional institutions were inefficient and outmoded. The reforms were thus intended to (a) place control of land in the hands of the state; (b) draw population into new occupations (settled farming); and (c) substitute modern institutions of production and marketing for traditional forms.[21]

Policymakers saw modern corporate structures as the solution for Somalia's agricultural decline. The GSDR openly promoted the establishment of state farms, cooperatives, and large private farms under the rubric of agricultural modernization. By 1979, there were 233 group cooperatives controlling an area of nearly 35,000 hectares and 48 multipurpose cooperatives with over 32,000 hectares. In 1984, government state farms controlled over 45,000 hectares in the Shebelle valley and nearly 25,000 hectares in the Jubba Valley.[22] Areas reserved for the Crash program contained 20,000 hectares and for resettlement schemes, another 27,000 hectares. State farms and cooperatives, through the agricultural land legislation, were granted exemption from land size restrictions and given preferential access in leasehold acquisition.

Agricultural Land Law

The Agricultural Land Law of 1975 and subsequent decrees are the principal statutes that determine land rights associated with state leasehold tenure (Appendix 1). The law asserts state ownership of all agricultural land but provides for the issuing of concessions to cooperatives, state farms, autonomous agencies, municipal governments, and private farmers, whether an individual, family, or company. Responsibility for administering land in accordance with the law is vested in the minister of agriculture. Those holding concessions prior to this law were given six months from the date of enactment to reregister the land as a new concession. Any concession not reregistered within this six-month period was terminated (excluding cooperatives established under Law no. 10, April 10, 1973).

Concessions are limited to one per family or individual; no concessions can be granted to absent persons. The duration of a concession for private farmers is fifty years (renewable), but cooperatives, state farms, autonomous agencies, and local governments have no time limits. Land "ceilings" on concessions are also imposed. An individual or family can obtain a concession of up to 30 hectares of irrigated land and 60 hectares of rain-fed land. The ceiling increases to 100 hectares for an individual or family with a banana plantation. State farms, cooperatives, autonomous agencies, municipal governments, and private companies are exempted from these ceilings. Concessions cannot be bought, sold, leased, or rented (rights may be transferred if the lessee is incapacitated or dies), although these restrictions have been relaxed in recent GSDR circulars.[23] The government may revoke a concession that exceeds size restrictions, is used for nonagricultural purposes, is not used productively, is unnecessarily fragmented, is transferred to another, or is not farmed for two successive years. However, weak enforcement of these provisions results in wide disparities in land use and allocation under state leasehold tenure and customary tenure arrangements.

A 1987 circular from the Ministry of Agriculture (MOA) revised the registration process.[24] An individual wishing to register a parcel must write an application letter to the district agricultural officer (DAO) of the MOA. The DAO is then supposed to post a notice of the application at the district party secretary's office, the district commissioner's office, the police station, the district MOA, and the village center. After thirty days, a committee made up of the Department of Land and Water Resources (DLWR) district officer, a district policeman, the chairman of the local village committee, the applicant, and a draftsman should adjudicate the claim, delineate boundaries, and draft a map. The DLWR officer and the policeman must each then write a report to their superiors stating farm location, area, soil type, present use, and tenure status. The DAO sends a report to the party secretary for approval.

A district registration number is assigned and all previous reports, the map, and the original application are supposed to be forwarded to the regional agricultural officer (RAO) for approval and issuance of a regional registration number. The RAO is responsible for taking the documents to the director of DLWR of the MOA in Mogadishu. The director is responsible for checking the application for conflicting claims before sending the file to the minister of agriculture for signing. All leaseholds must then be approved by the minister. Once signed, the registration procedure is complete, and copies are returned to the landholder and various

DLWR offices. In practice, however, the registration process sometimes starts at the national level by an individual or cooperative seeking land. In this case, a letter is written to district or regional agricultural coordinators, directing them to find unregistered land for the applicant.

One of the land law's most striking features is that it does not recognize the customary rules and procedures of the indigenous institutions that still govern access to land and pasture.[25] Pastoralists are given no tenure rights. Noncompliance with the provision requiring immediate registration has resulted in a large class of landholders without legal rights to land. The two-year provision on idle land, resulting in state expropriation, is strongly biased toward permanent cultivation and against conservation. A number of studies mention an increase in unnecessary forest clearing in the Jubba valley by registered landholders.[26] Further, cooperatives and state farms receive preferential access to land in the registration process, particularly in terms of size of leaseholds, number of leaseholds, and duration of lease.

Manipulation of registration procedures is common.[27] It is generally accepted that personal connections and unofficial gratuities are essential to obtain a lease. Farmers sometimes register different landholdings in different kin members' names to circumvent the one parcel per household provision. Groups of farmers sometimes pool money and register a block of land under one farmer's name, despite the risk of that farmer claiming their land. Individual(s) sometimes form a company that is not subject to size restrictions and use the registration system to claim unregistered land. The MOA, however, is not equipped to detect multiple leaseholds registered under different family members' names or to prevent a speculative land market.

State Leasehold Tenure

By 1986, eleven years after passage of the Agricultural Land Law, GSDR registry offices had cumulatively issued 12,561 titles for concessions, covering 256,000 hectares nationwide (Appendix 2), roughly 0.5 percent of Somalia's total land area. Land registration has been quite active in rain-fed areas in the north, measured by number of leaseholds. But in area terms, registration has been most active in the river valleys. Over 75 percent of all registered land is listed as irrigable, meaning it is within close proximity to a river but is not necessarily irrigated.

Districts along the Shebelle River, with the closest access to the capital city, Mogadishu, have the highest proportion of registered land. In the Middle Shabelle, 2.7 percent of total land area was registered in 1986, including 1,474 farms averaging 38.1 hectares per farm. Farther downstream in the more commercially developed Lower Shebelle, 5.3 percent of the total surface area was registered, including 3,361 farms averaging 43.5 hectares per farm. However, these averages are deceiving. As will be seen shortly, landholdings vary from a few hectares to several hundred in size.

Registered farms tend to be large units, usually with state or cooperative affiliation. Leaseholds averaged 27 hectares per farm nationally in 1986, compared with an average of 3 hectares for all farms, registered and unregistered. Registered farms in the Upper Shebelle (Hiraan), Middle and Lower Shebelle, and Middle and Lower Jubba districts average between 30 and 50 hectares. M. O. Fadal, Amina Shego, and Yassin Ali estimate that state farms controlled 18 percent of the registered area in 1984, the Crash program 5 percent, resettlement schemes 7 percent, cooperatives 19 percent, medium-scale private farms (20 to 200 ha) 5 percent, and small-scale farms 46 percent.[28]

In June 1989, a random sample of 722 entries was drawn from the central land registry in Mogadishu (10% sampling frame) covering the period from about 1981 to May 1989.[29] The survey revealed several interesting characteristics about the profile of registered farms:

1. A large proportion of concessions are registered by private companies. Land may be registered by an individual, private company (*Shirkadda*), cooperative (*Iskaashatadda*), or religious commune (*Xerta*). Results from the survey show that 76.3 percent of concessions had been registered by individuals and 23.5 percent by private companies. Land registered in an individual's name may either indicate an individual holding or a company. Thus, the percentage reported for private companies is underestimated.

2. Sizes of concessions for private companies are considerably larger than for individual concessions. Private companies in the sample average 194.0 hectares per concession compared with 26.4 hectares for individual concessions. Both of these mean farm sizes are considerably in excess of 3.8 hectares, the average farm size in Somalia.[30]

3. A large proportion of the concessions recorded in the land registry are round figures of 30, 60, or 100 hectares. Measurement of a parcel during adjudication would generally result in an odd fraction for area recorded in the register unless land is delineated by survey prior to acquisition, as in the case of opening new lands. But, as noted earlier, the registration process can be reversed. A directive from Mogadishu may be issued to find land for an applicant, an area of land equal to the ceiling is requested, and that area is mapped out by field survey and recorded in the register. While not a precise measure of land registered in this manner, the data suggest widespread use of land registration as a

means to gain access to land. Out of the 722 entries, 23.3 percent are precisely 30, 60, or 100 hectares in size. When broken down by type of ownership, 35.8 percent of private companies registered land in round lots compared with 19.4 percent for individual concessions.

4. A number of concessions greatly exceed the 100-hectare ceiling in the land law. Out of the total of approximately 7,200 registrations, 54 concessions exceeded 500 hectares in size. Of this total, 40 concessions fell in the range of 500 to 1,000 hectares, 8 in the range of 1,001 to 2,500 hectares, 5 in the range of 2,501 to 5,000 hectares, and 1 farm was 7,000 hectares. Further, 50 of these 54 concessions were registered as private companies, 1 as a cooperative, 1 as a religious organization, and 2 as individual concessions. With the possible exception of the individual concessions (an individual name can either mean a company or a personal holding), all the above are exempt from land ceilings in the law.

5. The vast majority of concession holders are men. Out of the total number of individual concessions, 92.7 percent are registered in the name of men and 7.3 percent in the name of women.

The Agricultural Land Law and the Law on Cooperative Development have provided local officials, private traders, and urban-based speculators with the official credentials to acquire land. Immediately after liberalization, a large number of companies applied for leaseholds on unregistered irrigable land. Establishment of state and cooperative farms has increased the area under corporate agriculture. However, it is less clear to what extent these entities have actually increased cultivated area. Since the most fertile areas were already settled, the establishment of state and cooperative farms on the best land in many cases resulted in the displacement of existing landholders and crop cultivators, principally small farmers, who lacked financial resources, who were unfamiliar with land registration procedures, or who were unaware that their customary rights were no longer valid.[31]

The GSDR has moderated its support for state and corporate farming in recent years. Despite preferential access to machinery, fertilizer, seed, and labor, state farms have not proven to be more efficient or productive.[32] Research in the Lower Shebelle has shown that state and cooperative farms are often undercapitalized, severely lacking in human and technical resources, and poorly managed.[33] Lack of capital and poor management are now forcing many corporate enterprises to revert to private holdings. Most of the land in the Crash program and some in resettlement areas and cooperatives have now been redistributed to private farmers. In the more densely settled Lower Shebelle, labor scarcity has motivated large corporate enterprises to offer small areas of land to permanent workers (0.25–0.5 ha per worker) to ensure a stable labor supply.[34]

Land Tenure in the Lower Shebelle

The Shalambood research site (SRS) consists of an 8,500-hectare rectangle on the Lower Shebelle River near Merca at the heart of Somalia's most important food and export crop producing region. The Genale dam, constructed by the Italians in 1926, rests at one corner of the site. The town of Shalambood, with a population of 22,240, is located at the opposite corner. Its boundaries enclose sixty-three formerly Italian-owned aziendas. Since the departure of their owners, landholdings have been transferred to smallholders, state-owned farms, state cooperatives, or large private farms. Water for irrigation comes from the Genale reservoir and flows by gravity through a web of primary (Dhamme Yassin), secondary, and tertiary canals. (See fig. 11.2.) The irrigation scheme has fallen into a poor state of disrepair and is badly in need of rehabilitation. The research site contains a complex matrix of farms with different tenure rights and widely varying access to land and water resources. Larger private, state, and cooperative farms, growing mainly bananas for export, tend to be located adjacent to the Dhamme Yassin primary canal and river. These farms tend to be larger-scale enterprises that are normally registered, are commercially oriented, have the best access to irrigation water, and provide an important source of employment for permanent and temporary workers from surrounding areas. Extending outward from the Dhamme Yassin canal and large plantations are the smaller holdings. Parcels in smallholder areas adjacent to the secondary canals have relatively good access to water, while those on the scheme's outer periphery have little or no access. Registration by these smallholder households is less frequent, and registration of parcels is spottier.

An in-depth study of tenure security and access to land and water resources was undertaken in the SRS in early 1987 prior to the design of a USAID irrigation rehabilitation project. Institutional profiles were developed for large state, cooperative, and private farms through structured informal interviews with plantation managers. A one-round structured questionnaire was administered to a randomly selected sample of fifty-six small farmers on the scheme to obtain detailed information on resource access and use. Smallholders received priority focus in the study because of their greater vulnerability to land grabbing and because they stood to be the principal beneficiaries of improved irrigation. Interviews were also held with large and small farmers, local authorities, and

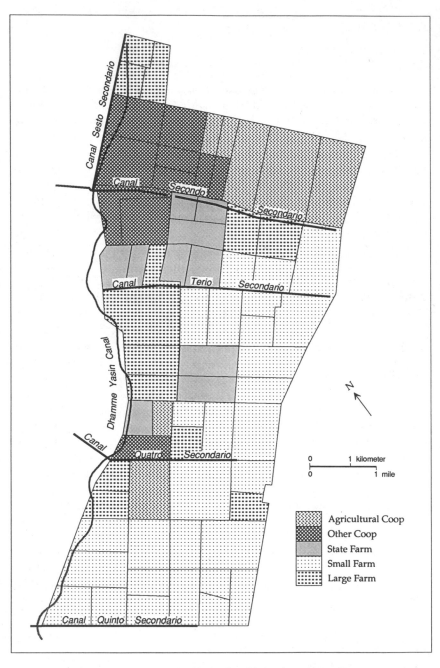

Figure 11.2. The Shalambood irrigation scheme

310

other key informants to develop a broader perspective of resource access, use, and allocation in the SRS.[35]

Land Concentration

As table 11.1 illustrates, land distribution is skewed toward large state, cooperative, and private farms. Of approximately 8,500 hectares com-

Table 11.1. Land concentration and average landholdings, land tenure profile, Shalambood study area

	Number of farms	Total area controlled (ha)	Average area per farm (ha/farm)
Independent smallholders[a]			
Surveyed areas with complete data	1,386	1,390	1.0
Areas with incomplete farm data		290	
Smallholder agricultural cooperatives			
Ispahaysi cooperative	800	950	1.2
Dayax cooperative	48	60	1.3
Matrico cooperative	159	158	1.0
Large group cooperatives			
National Petroleum Cooperative	2	690	
Charcoal Cooperative	2	458	
Building and Public Transport Cooperative	1	50	
Sample average			239.6
Crash program areas[b]		2,285	
State farms			
AFMET Demonstration Farm	1	400	
Kamiro, MOA Agriculture Strengthening Farm	1	100	
Prison farm	1	310	
Police farm	1	60	
Sample average			217.5
Large Private Farms	14	1,342	95.9
Total		8,543	

Source: Michael Roth, Harry Lemel, John Bruce, and Jon Unruh, *An Analysis of Land Tenure and Water Allocation Issues in the Shalambood Irrigation Zone, Somalia* (Madison: Land Tenure Center, University of Wisconsin, March 1987).
[a]"Surveyed" means that land areas were verified by data collected by either (1) the Land Tenure Center; (2) Tippetts, Abbett, McCarthy, and Stratton, "Genale Irrigation Rehabilitation Project: Feasibility Study, Annex I, Natural and Human Resources" (Washington, D.C., September 1986); or (3) Richard McGowan, Larry Johnston, Alfred S. Waldstein, Gus Tillman, and John Speed, "Irrigation Water Lifting in the Shebelle Water Management Project," Associates in Rural Development (Burlington, Vt., 1986). Remaining areas were inferred from maps of the area, but number of farms are unknown.
[b]No estimates were available or could be obtained for the number of farms in Crash program areas.

prising the scheme, independent smallholders controlled 20 percent, agricultural cooperatives 14 percent, large group cooperatives 14 percent, Crash program farms 26 percent, state farms 10 percent, and large private farms (in excess of 30 ha) 16 percent. Large private farms, including one belonging to the Palestinian Liberation Organization, range in size from 30 to 300 hectares, with average landholdings of 96 hectares per farm. Group cooperatives average 240 hectares and state farms 218 hectares. Small-farmer holdings, including independent farmers and members of agricultural cooperatives, average 1.0 to 1.3 hectares.

The term "cooperative," implying a group of individuals taking collective action on input procurements, selling, or cropping decisions, is misleading in the SRS context. The National Petroleum Cooperative operates as a firm without members. Profits go to the National Union of Cooperatives (NUC). The Charcoal Cooperative operates as a limited partnership. Its 114 members invested equal contributions of capital to finance the development of the farm and equally share profits, with a fixed percentage going to the NUC. The Public Transport and Building Cooperative operates similarly with members from the building and trade professions. Starting with 1,000 hectares, this cooperative has since shrunk to 50 hectares because of poor management and inadequate capital. The remaining land has recently been transferred to the 800 smallholders comprising the Ispahaysi agricultural cooperative.

Agricultural cooperatives are distinguishable from other cooperatives by their small-farmer membership. They are mandated to assist their members with fertilizers, pesticides, seeds, and mechanized services, but input distribution is severely constrained in practice. Many farmers in such cooperatives believe that the land is theirs. However, management maintains the opposite. Farmers with cooperative land have security against outsiders' claims and are spared the costs and inconveniences of individual registration. Some farmers have expressed their preference for individual leaseholds to control their own destiny and preclude the possibility of being expelled and losing their land, even though expulsion is quite rare in the SRS.

Large commercial farms, state and private, normally reserve land for the personal use of permanent and seasonal farm workers. Although laborers lack individual leasehold rights, evictions are rare. The prevalence of land sharing and the high premiums large farms are willing to pay to recruit and keep good workers suggest a strongly competitive labor market. While the amount of land given as payment varies from farm to farm, laborers generally receive between 0.25 and 1.0 hectare each. Altogether, they cultivate approximately 16 percent of the 3,410 hectares held by large commercial farms.

Smallholder Land Tenure

Smallholders in the sample include both individual landholders and those from the agricultural cooperatives. Holdings average 2.2 hectares (table 11.2), about twice the average for the SRS (table 11.1), and are fairly uniform, although women tend to hold fewer parcels and less land. Despite provisions in the land law allowing only one parcel per household, multiple parcel ownership is common. Twenty-five percent of respondents held two parcels of land, while 7 percent held three or more.

Table 11.2. Land tenure characteristics, smallholder sample, Shalambood study area

	Male respondents	Female respondents	Total respondents
Number of respondents	44	12	56
Total family size	9.0	6.5	8.3
Farm size distribution (farms):[a]			
0.0 to 0.99 ha	6 (14)	5 (42)	11 (20)
1.0 to 1.99 ha	19 (43)	6 (50)	25 (45)
2.0 to 4.99 ha	11 (25)	1 (8)	12 (21)
5.0 ha plus	8 (18)	0 (0)	8 (14)
Mean average farm size (hectares)	2.61	0.87	2.24
Number of farms with:[a]			
1 parcel	27 (61)	11 (92)	38 (68)
2 parcels	13 (30)	1 (8)	14 (25)
3 or more parcels	4 (9)	0 (0)	4 (7)
Average parcels per household	1.5	1.2	1.4
Average years parcel has been held[b]	18.2	13.8	16.0
Main parcel was acquired by:[a,b]			
Inheritance	6 (14)	4 (34)	10 (18)
Settled from unclaimed land	8 (18)	3 (25)	11 (20)
Bought	5 (11)	1 (8)	6 (11)
Allocated by the government following failure of the Crash program	4 (9)	3 (25)	7 (12)
Allocated by the government after departure of Italian owners	21 (48)	1 (8)	22 (39)

Source: Michael Roth, Harry Lemel, John Bruce, and Jon Unruh, *An Analysis of Land Tenure and Water Allocation Issues in the Shalambood Irrigation Zone, Somalia* (Madison: Land Tenure Center, University of Wisconsin, March 1987).
[a]Figures in parentheses are percentages of total respondents in each category.
[b]Figures for parcel acquisition refer to the main parcel only, thus data may underestimate the incidence of acquisition by transactions.

Several factors help to explain multiple parcel ownership: (1) land fragmentation has reduced holdings below subsistence needs, requiring land
acquisition; (2) farmers acquire parcels along several canals as a risk
management strategy to ensure access to scarce water supplies; (3) inheritance; (4) speculation; and (5) investment motives.[36]

Restrictions in the land law on multiple parcels appear to be aimed at
curbing fragmentation and excessive land accumulation. While fragmentation is a problem, there is no empirical evidence in the SRS that
productivity has declined as a result. Worries about land accumulation,
among smallholders, are unfounded. With an average of 2.2 hectares,
farm sizes are far below the law's 30-hectare ceiling.

Farmers are very reluctant to disclose parcel information. Subsequent
research has revealed that one-third of the respondents interviewed
falsely reported their number of parcels. Landholders face a dilemma.
Not registering a parcel can result in loss of land to outsiders through the
registration process. Conversely, registering means increased government scrutiny and risks of losing remaining parcels, although expropriation has been rare. Some farmers circumvent this restriction by registering land in the names of family members or close kin.

Land Transactions

Land settlement patterns in the SRS are relatively long-standing (table
11.2). Nearly 45 percent of the sample had cultivated their main parcel
for twenty or more years; the average is sixteen years. Of the fifty-six
respondents in the survey, 39 percent had been allocated the land by the
government after the Italians left, 20 percent claimed it from unused
areas, 18 percent acquired their main parcel through inheritance, 12
percent were allocated it after the demise of the Crash program, and 11
percent bought it (table 11.2).

Although some farmers admit to renting, purchasing, and selling land,
there is no way of knowing precisely the extent of land transactions
among families, neighbors, and friends. Land sales are universally acknowledged. Thirteen percent of respondents at some time acquired
land through direct purchase (table 11.3). One land sale was reported.
Results also show that while none of the respondents said they rented
out land in 1986, four farmers rented in land. Since land disputes and
land grabbing often stem from rental arrangements, farmers, particularly those who rent out land, are generally reluctant to fully disclose
them.

As demand for land resources has grown, land access has become
more restrictive for farmers and their children. All unused areas of the

Table 11.3. Land transactions, smallholder sample, Shalambood study area

	Male respondents		Female respondents		Total respondents	
	n	%[a]	n	%	n	%
Number of respondents	44	(79)	12	(21)	56	(100)
Number of respondents who have ever sold or given away land	1	(2)	0	(0)	1	(2)
Number of respondents renting out land	0	(0)	0	(0)	0	(0)
Number of respondents renting in land:	3	(7)	1	(8)	4	(7)
Payment in cash	3	(7)	1	(8)	4	(7)
Payment in kind	0	(0)	0	(0)	0	(0)
Number of respondents who have ever bought land	6	(14)	1	(8)	7	(13)
Principal motive for buying land:						
Land was a good investment	6	(14)	0	(0)	6	(86)
Wanted better-quality land	0	(0)	0	(0)	0	(0)
Wanted to control own farm	0	(0)	0	(0)	0	(0)
Previous land was inadequate	0	(0)	0	(0)	0	(0)
Not able to respond	0	(0)	1	(8)	1	(14)

Source: Michael Roth, Harry Lemel, John Bruce, and Jon Unruh, *An Analysis of Land Tenure and Water Allocation Issues in the Shalambood Irrigation Zone, Somalia* (Madison: Land Tenure Center, University of Wisconsin, March 1987).
[a]Figures in parentheses indicate percent of respective sample size except for the category "principal motive for buying land," in which case the figures are the percent of those who bought land.

scheme are now claimed. Permanent cropping is pervasive. Farmers would like to buy land, but according to one respondent, prices have soared, rising from SoSh 2,000 per hectare ten years ago, to SoSh 60,000 today (SoSh 100 = $1). In such an inflationary environment, it is not surprising that six out of seven respondents who had ever bought land did so because it was a good investment (table 11.3). Children of some settled smallholders are reportedly leaving farming in the area because of land scarcity. Sometimes land is found in more land-abundant areas outside the scheme, although prices are rapidly growing beyond the means of younger farmers. Acute land scarcity, limited financial resources for its acquisition, and succession leading to uneconomical size of holdings combine to force offspring more and more to seek nonfarm employment or to return to nomadic life.

Tenure Security

Based largely on theoretical propositions of neoclassical economics, two important economic benefits are obtainable from increased tenure security: increased incentives for land investment as landholders perceive greater probability of reaping the rewards from the investment; and reduced uncertainties in land transfers, thereby lowering transactions costs and facilitating the transfer of land from less efficient to more efficient uses and users.[37] The presence of tenure security does not automatically increase investment if labor or capital market imperfections constrain the supply of investment inputs or increase transfers if the land market restricts them. Conversely, in the presence of well-functioning labor and capital markets, inadequate tenure security can diminish investment incentives and decrease land transactions. Enhanced tenure security, then, is a necessary but not a sufficient condition for development.

Landholders' perceptions of tenure security are not directly observable in a research setting and thus require the use of proxies. On the basis of one such proxy—presence or absence of land rights—the security of state leasehold tenure is mixed. The registration process appears to increase the ownership security of those landholders making efficient use of their land. Yet restrictions in the land law on land transfers increase transaction costs in the land market, and the two-year provision on development increases the insecurity of landholders adopting conservation practices (fallow, forestation).

Past or present disputes over landholdings are another proxy. Disputes are a good indicator of tenure insecurity if weak tenure rights result in conflicts over land. However, if disputes result in a case being taken to the courts and to rights being defined more clearly and recorded, the court records themselves can be used to verify claims to land.

Based on the Shalambood survey, unregistered land is more often involved in disputes than registered land, and disputes over ownership rights are more common than over boundaries. While only 9 percent of farmers in the sample reported ever having had a land dispute, 25 percent perceive that such disputes are becoming more common in the SRS. The most serious disputes are in frontier areas.

Land disputes normally originate from three sources. First, they frequently arise from rental arrangements in which a renter refuses to hand back unregistered land to the rightful landholder at the end of the agreed term. Since idle land is perceived to be unproductive and/or not needed by the landholder, the legal provision that bans both transactions and leaving land idle increases the risk of renting out land. Farmers are particularly wary of renting out for periods longer than a year, believing that the risk of losing land increases with the rental term.

Second, disputes arise as a result of legal provisions declaring that land left unused for two years is considered abandoned. While James

Riddell maintains that this provision will reduce land speculation by absentee investors, Gunn questions the adverse impacts of such policies on fragile soils due to permanent cropping.[38] In the absence of manure or fertilizers, arid zone farming requires fallow to maintain fertility. Unless "land use" is redefined to encompass fallow and fodder crops, long-term dependence on costly inputs or a decline in agricultural productivity is imminent.

A third class of disputes involves official documents issued in Mogadishu which either assign leaseholds directly to individuals or serve as directives to regional officials to locate unregistered land for someone. Urban land speculators acting individually or as part of a group cooperative are displacing long-term landholders from their land. Local small farmer representatives rank land grabbing as the most serious problem small farmers face, even above water scarcity.

Tenure insecurity is a serious concern on more productive lands, usually those with better access to irrigation water. In a scheme where canals reach all lands, 11 percent of respondents received no irrigation, 46 percent received one irrigation, and 35 percent received two or more, while 9 percent did not cultivate in the 1987 *Gu* (heavy rains) season. In the 1987 *Deyr* (light rains) season, 53 percent of farmers in the sample received no irrigation and therefore could not plant, 40 percent received one, and only 7 percent received two or more. Substantial disparities in yields exist between those parcels with good access and those with poor access to irrigation water. Maize yields on land receiving two or more irrigations during the 1985 Gu season averaged 13.6 quintals per hectare, compared with 7.0 quintals per hectare on land with one or less.

The largest farms, usually registered, have land closest to the primary canal with the best access to water. Flows are not metered or priced according to usage. However, farmers indirectly contribute labor or cash for clearing irrigation ditches (water is free by Islamic custom, although levying charges for such services as drawing or delivering water is permissible). Water users associations ration water on smallholder lands, but these groups have only limited control over water taken by larger commercial enterprises.

Since the economic costs of water are low, the largest farms use as much as they wish, operating near or at the top of their yield response function to water. Although these larger plantations have the best access to water, tenure security is relatively high as nearly all large farms are registered. Smallholders with farms on the periphery, with poor access to irrigation, often express no insecurity because the value of land to outsiders, and thus the expected loss of land, is low. Farmers with the least secure landholdings tend to be located in areas with moderate access to water and with the largest potential production response if irrigation capacity were improved. These farmers generally lack the financial resources to register their land as a concession, yet the land is most vulnerable to land grabbing because of its higher value and more insecure status.

Land Registration

Despite the appearance of high tenure insecurity, few independent farmers have registered their land. Of farmers in the sample, 29 percent had land registered through membership in an agricultural cooperative. Sixteen percent claimed to have individual title to their primary parcels. On closer inspection, fewer than 5 percent of the farmers claiming to have title actually held leases. Farmers claimed that land was registered on the basis of paid land tax receipts or court summaries of disputes decided in their favor. An additional 7 percent were in the process of registration.

If tenure security is so important to small farmers, why haven't more registered their lands? Among survey respondents who were not registered or were in the process of registering, 33 percent cited high costs, 21 percent mentioned complicated procedures, 17 percent mentioned lack of familiarity with registration procedures, and 9 percent said the parcel was simply too small. Only 6 percent felt there was no need to register land.

Costs of registration are a sticky problem. Registration in Somalia is based on a sporadic system. The government has established a local and regional registry office in Genale within relatively close distance of most farmers in the area, but landholders must bear the transaction costs of acquiring title. Registry operations are hampered by tight budget constraints and lack of facilities. Shortages of paper, filing cabinets, and fuel and low salaries place severe constraints on registry operations. While registration is in principle free, applicants in reality must pay the costs of site visits, surveys, maps, and so forth, to obtain title. Although the registration procedure only requires a farmer to go to the district office, farmers report making countless trips to various regional and national offices to ascertain the status of their file, incurring expenses for transportation and lodging. Charges for a formal map of the site reportedly can cost as high as SoSh 10,000, due to limited drafting services in rural areas. Low government pay scales are problematic. At salary levels of $20 to $30 per month, there is an incentive for civil servants to extract a portion of the high economic rent associated with leasehold title.

There does not appear to be systematic exclusion of landholders from the registry. Rather, price seems to provide the main rationing mechanism, and high costs appear to determine the low volume of registration activity among smallholders. High costs, in turn, have biased the acquisition of title toward larger farmers, the wealthy, or well-connected individuals who possess superior knowledge of government bureaucracy and procedures. Substantial improvements in the efficiency of the registration process and cost reductions will thus be necessary if registration is to be brought within the means of smallholders. And until costs of registration are made more affordable, nonconcession holders will continue to face risks of land grabbing and weakened security of tenure.

Conclusions

The Agricultural Land Law of 1975 officially brought all Somalia's land resources under state domain. Individual landholders and organizations could obtain usufructuary rights to a parcel for fifty years, renewable thereafter. Initially, government programs to modernize agriculture through corporate forms of management spurred the spread of state leasehold land. Such policies encouraged higher land concentration ratios. But it is questionable whether they expanded the area cultivated or improved productivity. Since many of the most fertile areas were already settled, the establishment of state and cooperative farms on the best land in many cases resulted in the displacement of existing landholders and crop cultivators.

As long as demand for land remained low, conflicts between state leasehold and customary tenure remained at a minimum, confined primarily to the most fertile and accessible areas in the river valleys. However, four factors have increased the utility of holding land and the effective demand for land resources: rampant price inflation, international trade restrictions on livestock exports, foreign development assistance and capital investment, and higher grain-to-nongrain price ratios.

The state leasehold process has provided investors and speculators alike with the means to obtain currently untitled land. Statutory tenure remained relatively innocuous, as long as land was abundant. But irrigation development on the Shebelle is rapidly reaching full potential, while demand for land continues to strengthen. Land prices have soared, land speculation and land grabbing have become prevalent, and the tenure security of nonleaseholders has weakened. Development of the valley has presented landholders with increased investment opportunities, but it has also exposed them to market fluctuations and resource dislocations.

The land law, despite its best intentions, has alienated farmers from their lands and left them with little legal recourse for securing their tenure rights. Some farmers have not registered their lands because the quality of land resources does not justify leasehold acquisition or because the modern world and state leasehold tenure have not yet encroached on the domain of customary tenure. Others have not sought title because costs are high, procedures are too time-consuming, or multiple parcels restrict registration. However, by failing to register, farmers face the risk of expropriation or outsiders claiming the land. While many small farmers perceive the registration process as too expensive, bureaucratic, and cumbersome, urban land seekers more accustomed to bureaucracy or well-connected individuals turn these procedures to their advantage. They have been able to legally acquire state leasehold land in prime agricultural areas under the auspices of progressive reform.

Government implementation of land registration is responsible for permitting land grabbing to take place. Policymakers bear some blame for not foreseeing the land conflicts that would arise and for failing to enforce tenure rights based on long-term use. However, the GSDR cannot be entirely faulted. Running a system of land registry offices at district, regional, and national levels imposes high recurrent costs on its budget and strains the capabilities of its skilled manpower. Compliance with registration programs is thus voluntary, relying on individual participation to bear the high costs of implementation. Because of limited resources, registration is expensive, explaining why smallholders wanting to register land are unable to do so while wealthier and better-connected farmers are able to pay the higher rents.

However, one must question whether the state leasehold system has longer-term benefits to offer, or even whether the country would be better off without it. This point is debatable. Certainly, the state leasehold process has led to landholder displacement and increased tenure insecurity in some instances. But one cannot ignore the market changes that are occurring in the Somalia economy; tenure insecurity might result even without GSDR intervention. In an Africa affected by debt crises, tariff and nontariff trade interventions, structural adjustment programs, price reforms, foreign development assistance, and capital investment programs, one can no longer assume that the long-term adaptability and resiliency of customary tenure will automatically withstand such change.

Does legislation provide the necessary legal criteria for sound land use planning? Modernization has entailed significant economic and social costs in terms of resource dislocation. Restrictions on number of parcels overly constrain the number and area of state leaseholdings of private individuals. One leasehold per household is an onerous restriction. The law imposes further restrictions on land transfer and use rights. It provides disincentives for cultivating fodder and fallow crops while encouraging permanent cultivation and deforestation. The law does not accommodate property rights issues on rangeland; nor does it allow for land reserves, either for parks or conservation. The number of concerns raised here and the economic and structural changes taking place in Somalia today indicate that the time may now be right for a reform of land policy and legislation.

Appendix 1: Key Provisions of the Somalia 1975 Agricultural Land Law

I. *Mandatory Registration:* Articles 5 and 19 of the 1975 land law make land registration compulsory. Permission to use land that is not registered ceases six months following implementation of the law.

II. *Duration of Title:* Usufructuary (leasehold) rights to land are granted to users by the state on the basis of variable-term leases that vary in length and degree of restrictiveness, depending on whether the lessee is an individual, family, or corporate body. Leasehold titles for individuals or families are fifty years in duration and renewable. Titles for cooperatives, state farms, or other autonomous agencies have no time limits imposed on the duration of the lease (Article 7).

III. *Parcel Restrictions:* An individual or family may obtain only one leasehold title irrespective of farm size; granting of leasehold titles to absentee persons is prohibited (Article 6).

IV. *Land Area:* Land ceilings on leaseholds are 30 hectares of irrigated land or 60 hectares of rain-fed land for individuals or families. Special provisions allow this ceiling to be raised to 100 hectares for banana plantations leased by a family or individual. Cooperatives, local government bodies, state farms, autonomous agencies, and private companies are excluded from these size restrictions (Article 8).

V. *Land Transactions:* Registered leaseholds cannot be leased, sold, or otherwise transferred to other parties, although the law provides for right of transfer to the state or heirs in the case where the leaseholder becomes unable to farm the land for health or other reasons (Article 12). Title is allowed to transfer to rightful heirs on the death of the leaseholder. If the heirs do not wish to farm the land, it may be redistributed by the state, with the heirs receiving compensation from the new holders based on the costs of investments that may have been made in the land, not the land per se.

VI. *Use Rights:* The lessee has the right to use the land for agricultural purposes; construct farmhouses for the purpose of managing the farm; keep a reasonable number of livestock on the farm; construct necessary facilities for rearing of the livestock; join a cooperative society; and contribute land to a cooperative society.

VII. *Responsibilities of the Landholder:* Provisions in Article 14 require the lessee (a) not to use the land for any purpose other than that for which it was allocated (i.e., for agricultural purposes); (b) to cultivate the land in the best possible manner, to raise fertility, and to achieve the highest possible yields; (c) not to transfer, mortgage, sell, lease, or in any way transfer the land to another party; (d) not to unnecessarily fragment the land; (e) to fairly compensate employees; (f) to pay the land tax levied by the government.

VIII.   *State Nationalization:* The state reserves the right to nationalize lands in excess of the area restrictions in Article 8 and to repossess land of a current user who fails to meet the conditions set forth on a lease or fails to cultivate the land for a successive two-year period (Article 15). Article 10 establishes public domain rights of the state to nationalize lands for the public good. The state, by Article 11, has the right to allocate nationalized lands to landless individuals, cooperatives, state farms, or other autonomous agencies.

Law no. 23 of 1976 reemphasized certain provisions in the law regarding agricultural land:

IX.   *National and Special Agencies:* Land controlled by national agencies (presumably state farms) are not bound by size restrictions imposed by the 1975 law. "Special agencies," defined as agencies in which the government is part owner, may have size restrictions imposed by the minister of agriculture.

X.   *Repossession/Nationalization of Land:* Any land that is not used for farming or livestock rearing for a period of two years will be given to someone else. Repossessed lands will be reallocated to those persons (a) who are adult and Somali by birth; (b) who have no other agricultural land; and (c) who have the economic capacity to pay compensation to the previous owner.

XI.   *Taxes:* Tax rates are SoSh 5 ($0.05) per hectare per year on rain-fed lands and SoSh 10 ($0.10) per hectare per year on irrigated land. Tax revenues go to the municipal treasury.

Source: This Appendix is summarized from a translation of the Somali Land Law, translated by Abdirahman Beileh, "Somali Legislation Relating to Land" (Madison: Land Tenure Center, University of Wisconsin, February 1985).

Appendix 2: Land Characteristics Including Total Land Area, Area Cultivated, Irrigated and Rain-Fed, Registered and Unregistered, Somalia, 1986

	Total land area (thousands of ha)	Cultivated[a] area under rain-fed agriculture (thousands of ha)	Cultivated[a] area under irrigation (thousands of ha)	Rain-fed land registered (thousands of ha)	Irrigable[b] land registered (thousands of ha)	Number of registered farms	Area (ha) per farm registered	Area (ha) per farm unregistered[c]
Northwest regions[d]	4,480	90.5	—	24.3	8.5	2,927	11.2	6.4
Central and Northeast regions[e]	32,260	32.5	—	22.3	2.2	2,651	9.2	1.0
Hiraan	3,400	15.3	13.0	0.5	15.8	355	45.8	2.5
Middle Shebelle	2,080	86.8	26.9	—	56.1	1,474	38.0	5.0
Banadir	80	—	—	—	—	—	—	—
Lower Shebelle	2,770	167.2	29.8	16.4	129.6	3,361	43.5	3.0
Lower Jubba	4,900	10.3	16.2	4.4	12.6	501	33.8	1.3
Middle Jubba	1,870	49.7	4.9	3.9	15.9	375	52.6	4.0
Gedo	4,470	37.8	1.6	—	10.5	540	19.4	2.2
Bay	4,120	244.4	—	12.3	5.4	377	46.7	4.3
Bakool	2,630	38.9	—	—	—	—	—	7.7
Total	63,060	773.2	92.4	84.1	256.4	12,561	27.1	3.3

Source: Ministry of Agriculture, Department of Planning and Statistics, "Yearbook of Agricultural Statistics 1986/87" (Mogadishu, 1987).

[a]Cultivated land is distinguished from cropped land in that it includes arable land, perennial crops, and fallow land.

[b]Includes land irrigated by pump irrigation and controlled and uncontrolled gravity irrigation.

[c]Cultivated area divided by total number of farms (MOA, 1987, 5), registered and unregistered.

[d]Includes the districts of Awdal and West Galbeed.

[e]Includes the districts of Togdheer, Sanaag, Sool, Bari, Nugaal, Muduug, and Galgaduud.

Notes

1 World Bank, *Accelerated Development in Sub-Saharan Africa, An Agenda for Action* (Washington, D.C., 1981): 144.

2 Ibid., 143.

3 Ibid., 151, 166.

4 World Bank, *World Development Report 1987* (Washington, D.C., 1987): 204.

5 Ibid., 212.

6 Government of Somali Democratic Republic, Ministry of Agriculture, *Yearbook of Agricultural Statistics 1986/87* (Mogadishu, Somalia, June 1987): 33.

7 P. Conze and T. Labahn (eds.), *Somalia: Agriculture in the Winds of Change* (Saarbrucken-Schafbrucke, Germany, 1986): 32, 33, 59.

8 World Bank, *Development Report,* 212.

9 Ibid., 202.

10 Ibid., 250.

11 *The Europa Yearbook* (London, 1986): 2321.

12 Ibid., 244.

13 United States Agency for International Development, "Shebelle Water Management I Project Paper and Annexes" (Mogadishu, Somalia, May 1987).

14 Ibid., Annex, 142.

15 Conze and Labahn, *Somalia.*

16 Ibid.

17 T. Labahn, "The Development of the Cultivated Areas of the Shebelle River and the Relationship between Smallholders and the State," in P. Conze and T. Labahn (eds.), *Somalia: Agriculture in the Winds of Change* (Saarbrücken, 1986): 127–146.

18 Y. E. Robleh and Y. H. Hussen, "The Agrarian Laws of Somalia," *The Half-Yearly Law Review* 5, no. 11 (1977): 34–40.

19 Ibid., 34–40.

20 D. Laitin, "The Political Economy of Military Rule in Somalia," *Journal of Modern African Studies* 14, no. 3 (1976): 449–468.

21 S. Gunn, "Land Reform in Somalia," in J. P. Powelson and Richard Stack (eds.), *The Peasant Betrayed* (Lincoln Institute of Land Policy, Cambridge, Mass., 1986).

22 M. O. Fadal, A. Shego, and A. Sheikh Ali, "Land Resource, Farm Size and Structure, Land Tenure and Taxation" (USAID/Somalia, January 1985).

23 Point 16 of the May 24, 1987, circular from the Ministry of Agriculture on *Guidelines for the Giving of Farm Land,* says, "The changing of farmland and certificate will be executed by the ministry after the two parties reach an agreement between themselves and bring a notarized agreement" (English translation).

24 See *Guidelines for the Giving of Farm Land,* Ministry of Agriculture, May 24, 1987.

25 A. Hoben, "The political economy of land tenure in Somalia," in R. Downs and S. Reyna (eds.), *Land and Society in Contemporary Africa* (Hanover, N.H., 1988): 192–220.

26 See J. C. Riddell and M. S. Samatar, "Land Tenure Dynamics in the Jubba Valley," Associates for Rural Development (Burlington, Vt., 1988); and C. Besteman and M. Roth, "Land Tenure in the Middle Jubba: Issues and Policy Recommendations" (Madison: Land Tenure Center, University of Wisconsin–Madison, August 1988).

27 See A. Hoben, "The Political Economy of Land Tenure in Somalia," in R. E. Downs and S. P. Reyna (eds.), *Land and Society in Contemporary Africa* (Hanover, N.H., 1988): 192–220; and M. Roth, H. Lemel, J. Bruce, and J. Unruh, *An Analysis of Land Tenure and Water Allocation Issues in the Shalambood Irrigation Zone, Somalia* (Land Tenure Center, University of Wisconsin–Madison, March 1987).

28 Fadal, Shego, and Sheikh Ali, "Land Resource."

29 M. Roth, J. Lawrance, A. S. Mohamood and J. Bruce, *Land Tenure Policy and Registration in Somalia: An Action Plan for Legislative and Administrative Reforms* (Madison: Land Tenure Center, University of Wisconsin, June 1989).

30 Ministry of Agriculture, Department of Planning and Statistics, "Yearbook of Agricultural Statistics 1986/87" (Mogadishu, 1987).

31 See Riddell and Samatar, "Land Tenure Dynamics"; Besteman and Roth, "Land Tenure in the Middle Jubba"; and Munzinger et al., "Support to Smallholder Irrigation."

32 "The Somalia Social and Institutional Profile: An Executive Summary" (African Studies Center, Boston University, Working Papers #79, 1983).

33 Roth et al., *An Analysis of Land Tenure.*

34 Ibid.

35 Detailed research results are reported in Roth et al., *An Analysis of Land Tenure.*

36 Besteman and Roth, in "Land Tenure in the Middle Jubba," describe the value of multiple parcel holdings (each consisting of one or more land types) as a strategy for managing production risk under different climatic situations. *Dhasheegs,* or inland low-lying depressions, collect and hold flood- and rainwater for long periods of time and thus are important during droughts. Inland higher ground, called *doonk,* is preferred after floods, because the floodwaters drain more quickly from higher ground, enabling early cultivation. However, doonk land produces poorly during droughts. Riverbank land, called *jiimo,* is valued for its underground water that percolates up through the soil. It will usually produce something during droughts, although not as well as dhasheeg land, and is the best land for fruit trees.

37 See D. Ault and G. Rutman, "The Development of Individual Rights to Property in Tribal Africa," *Journal of Law and Economics* 22, 1 (1979): 163–182; and O. Johnson, "Economic Analysis: The Legal Framework and Land Tenure Systems," *Journal of Law and Economics* XV (Chicago, 1972): 259–276.

38 See Riddell and Samatar, "Land Tenure Dynamics"; and S. Gunn, "Land Reform in Somalia," in J. P. Powelson and Richard Stack (eds.), *The Peasant Betrayed.* 1986.

Merle L. Bowen

Socialist Transitions: Policy Reforms and Peasant Producers in Mozambique

HD
O13
Q15
Mozambique
p21

Introduction

Many Third World revolutionary states have abandoned their programs of rapid collectivization. Governments realized that it was not a primary requirement of socialist agricultural development. In general, rapid collectivization led to disappointing results: state farm, cooperative, and peasant agricultural production declined. For these reasons, Third World socialist countries have altered their original agrarian strategy of development, placing greater emphasis on peasant farming production.[1]

Mozambique has been no exception. The Frelimo[2] government pursued large-scale collectivization at the expense of peasant farming production. From independence in 1975 to the Fourth Congress in 1983, the government established large-scale state farms, giving them the preponderant share of agricultural investment. Most cooperatives and peasant farmers had to rely on their own resources. Frelimo also limited the growth of private capitalist farmers. After the congress, the state implemented significant agricultural reforms: it dismantled many of the country's state farms, distributing land to peasant and private farmers and providing them with services, inputs, and consumer goods.

In this chapter, I consider the effects and implications of Frelimo's reforms from 1983 to 1987, the years between the Fourth and Fifth Party congresses. A detailed case study of Chokwe, an agriculturally important area located in the country's southern province of Gaza (see fig. 12.1), describes the opportunities and constraints facing different groups following state distribution of irrigated land. Emphasis is placed on the capacity of peasant farmers to increase production when they have access to means of production and labor. I also highlight three areas of the peasant economy affecting production in the Chokwe irrigation scheme: subsistence needs, consumer goods availability, and marketing and transportation systems.

Mozambique's Agricultural Development Strategy

Prior to the Fourth Party Congress in 1983, Frelimo pursued an ambitious socialist strategy of development. In agriculture, this strategy was based on organizing the dispersed peasant population into communal villages and restructuring their productive activities along collective lines through cooperatives and state farms. Clear priority was given to the state farms. It was decided to develop and extend the state farm sector, using high technology to increase the urban food supply as soon as possible and to provide export crops to bring in foreign exchange.[3] The Frelimo government's policy to place most of its agricultural investment in the state farm sector starved the peasant family, private and cooperative sectors of resources, markets for products and infrastructure. The large investments in the state farm sector, moreover, had disappointing results. In 1981, the Ministry of Agriculture admitted that not one state farm was profitable.[4]

The most serious omission of Frelimo's agricultural policy from 1975 to 1983 was its relative neglect of the peasant family sector. Problems in encouraging peasant marketed production arose from the pricing policy. Low fixed prices acted as a disincentive to produce for the official market and fueled the growth of parallel outlets. Perhaps the greatest problem was the lack of consumer and producer goods in the rural stores for peasants to purchase with cash. Overall, insufficient attention was paid to either producing domestically or importing those goods that peasants needed for farming and for which they should have wanted to market their surplus.

Beginning in 1980, Mozambique's economic difficulties were intensified by escalating South African military destabilization. Under South African sponsorship, the Mozambique National Resistance (Renamo), a surrogate force, became a major instrument of economic sabotage and terror, especially in the countryside.[5] By 1983, the war had become an increasingly serious drain on the country's limited economic resources.

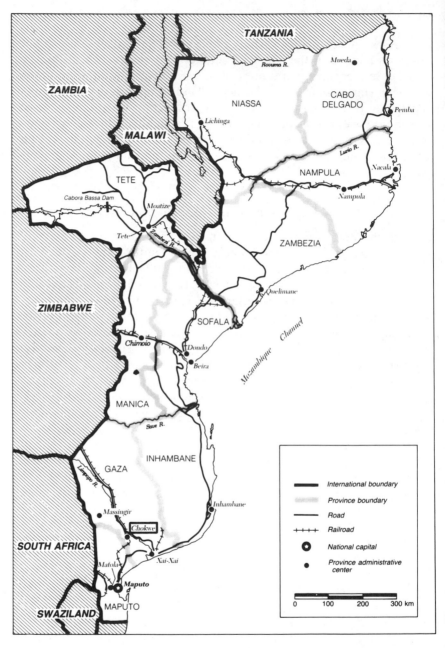

Figure 12.1. Map of Mozambique
Source: Mocambique-Vias de comunicacao. Atlas Geografico (Vol. 1), Ministerio da Educacao e Cultura, Republica Popular de Mocambique, 1979.

Frelimo's Fourth Party Congress reforms were an attempt to correct the mistakes and shortcomings of previous government economic policies. Frelimo called for a general shift away from large-scale, centrally planned, capital-intensive development projects, which had dominated the government policy in the 1975 to 1983 period. A new emphasis was accordingly placed on more decentralized, market-oriented, small-scale projects. The congress concluded that large-scale, capital-intensive agriculture was beyond the technical and organizational capacity of the country's labor force. The state sector was not to be expanded but rather reorganized and consolidated. The congress further directed state structures to provide much greater assistance to the family cooperative and private sectors. The new emphasis on the family and private sectors was an admission that the recuperation and growth of agricultural production could not be achieved solely through collective forms of production.

In response to the Fourth Party Congress decision, the Mozambican government began to implement a program of reforms predicated on four main policy and institutional changes: regional prioritization, administrative decentralization, liberalization of commercial activity, and allocation of resources on the basis of economic pragmatism rather than ideology.[6] First, in the context of South African destabilization and continuing adverse climatic conditions, the government began channeling scarce resources to priority regions. These were regions where economic, military, and climatic situations presented the best opportunity for positive results. Second, a comprehensive process of administrative reorganization and decentralization of state structures responsible for implementing economic policy was undertaken to obtain the best return on the investments made. Third, in view of the acute shortage of investment resources available to the Mozambican government, scarce economic inputs began to be channeled to those sectors that had the capacity to use them most efficiently, whether these were state enterprises, cooperatives, or private or peasant farmers. Fourth, the government initiated a general liberalization of commercial activity: prices were freed for many agricultural and manufactured goods in an attempt to stimulate production by private and peasant farmers. Prices for many other products that continued to be subject to official control—for example, staple food crops such as cereals including rice, maize, sorghum, and wheat—were increased substantially. By turning to a more market-oriented economic strategy, Frelimo hoped to correct the economic imbalance that had resulted from past policy mistakes.

In the years following the Fourth Party Congress, however, South African destabilization undermined Frelimo's attempts to implement these reforms. South Africa continued to support Renamo in spite of the 1984

Nkomati Accord that required both countries to prevent their territories from being used as bases for attacks on the other. By 1986, the war threatened the subsistence and security of millions of Mozambicans.[7]

Rural Development in the Chokwe Irrigation Scheme

According to the 1980 general population census, the district of Limpopo, including the town of Chokwe, had an area of 2,706 square kilometers and a population of 117,128.[8] It is one of ten districts situated in Mozambique's southern province of Gaza. In 1986, most of the 23,657 families in the district were involved in agriculture, and more than 14,000 of these had a small landholding in the irrigation scheme.

The irrigation scheme in Chokwe (fig. 12.2) is the largest in the country; a total of 25,000 hectares were under irrigation in 1987. An additional 2,000 hectares within the scheme were out of production, primar-

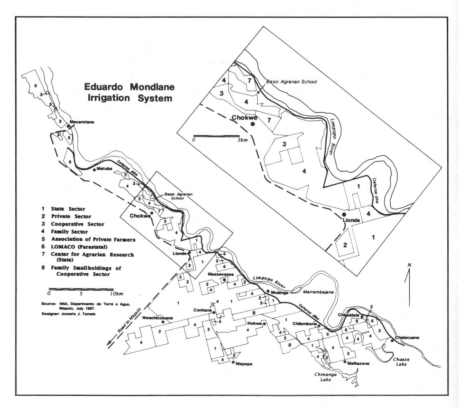

Figure 12.2. The Eduardo Mondlane irrigation system

ily because of salinity. Outside the jurisdiction of the Sistema de Regadio Eduardo Mondlane (SIREMO) scheme, there was an area of about 4,000 hectares irrigated by water pumped directly from the Limpopo River to Macaretane, Matuba, and the Bolsa de Chilembene. SIREMO is the state service enterprise responsible for the management and maintenance of the entire irrigation scheme.

Since its installation in the early 1950s, the Chokwe irrigation scheme has been crucial to the provision of food for the southern region of Mozambique. In 1954, the Portuguese expropriated fertile valley land from the local peasantry and established the Colonato do Limpopo, a settlement scheme that set up Portuguese settlers, and later a small number of *assimilados,* with enormous state-financed infrastructural investment in irrigation. Assimilados—those few Mozambicans who, by virtue of their education and their adoption of Portuguese language and customs qualified for a specially designed second-class Portuguese citizenship—were permitted on a probationary basis to cultivate two hectares each of inferior land.

The development of peasant agriculture in Chokwe, as in all of southern Mozambique, has been dependent on migrant work in South Africa since the turn of the century. By the 1940s, an average of 20 percent of the economically active male population of Gaza Province was away in wage employment in South Africa.[9] Over an extended period, peasant agricultural production became dependent on migrant wage labor. The wage became not merely a means of supplementing income from agriculture but also a source of finance for the purchase of agricultural equipment such as plows as well as cattle.[10]

At independence, thousands of Mozambican peasants entered the colonato, replacing the departing Portuguese settlers. From 2,600 individuals at the end of 1974, the number of peasants grew to 3,175 in 1975 and then to approximately 6,000 in 1976. By then, 10,000 more peasants were demanding access to landholdings in the Chokwe irrigation scheme.[11] In 1977, the Limpopo River overflowed, and large areas of the valley were inundated. The government evacuated the threatened population from the flooded areas, resettling them on high lands in newly established communal villages. Subsequently, Frelimo prohibited those peasants who were cultivating land in the Limpopo Valley to return to their farms. Most of the irrigable area (92%) was incorporated into a huge industrial complex, the Complexo Agro-industrial do Limpopo (CAIL), which was to integrate farming, livestock breeding, processing plants, and warehousing and marketing facilities. The agroindustrial complex was to provide an economic base for the communal villages in the area. The remaining area (8%) was given to cooperatives.[12] Both the state farms and cooperatives produced mostly rice, essentially following the colonial monoculture cropping pattern.

From 1977 to 1983, peasant household survival strategies in Chokwe were limited to wage employment at CAIL, participation in agricultural producer cooperatives, and agricultural production on family farms in the rain-fed areas. Few peasants depended solely on family farming in the rain-fed areas, where the sandy soils did not hold water. With the reduction of Mozambican miners in South Africa in early 1977, men searched for wage employment at state farms and in the urban areas. Women's labor on state farms was limited to seasonal peak periods such as weeding and harvesting time, when they were employed as temporary, unskilled, casual workers.

The CAIL state farm was not able to guarantee the subsistence and reproduction of workers and their families for two main reasons. First, since CAIL practiced rice monoculture, it required only seasonal labor, which meant that state farm wage labor could not provide a regular income for the peasant families of the communal villages supplying labor to it. Seasonal labor—just as during the colonial period—implied that family subsistence depended not only on wage income but also on sale of cash crops and on production for consumption. This situation in part accounted for the chronic labor shortages that plagued CAIL and the state sector everywhere, especially during crucial periods of the agricultural season.[13]

Second, there were shortages of basic consumer goods in the countryside. From the peasantry's point of view, there was not much incentive to sell labor if there was nothing to be bought with the wages earned. State farms sought to resolve this problem by establishing special shops for their workers. But given the limited quantities of food and consumer goods available in such stores, their value in promoting the formation of a stable labor force was limited.[14] Outside the state farm stores, workers' salaries did not permit them to buy the basic consumer goods, such as cooking oil, sugar, soap, and cloth, because these goods increasingly were available only at speculative prices in the parallel market.

Similarly, peasants neglected cooperative farms, giving priority to their own farms as well as other economic activities. From the outset, all cooperatives struggled with basic technical and organizational problems, stemming from illiteracy, inexperience, and low level of technical expertise and from insufficient inputs and assistance from the state. Serious deficiencies in planning, administration, and credit prevented the early consolidation and development of the cooperative movement in Chokwe.[15]

By the end of 1982, it was becoming increasingly apparent to the government that its state farm strategy of development was not having the desired economic effects. The official reasons given to explain the state sector's poor performance were technical ones. In the case of CAIL, social and political factors also played a significant role. According to one analysis, Mozambican peasants were bitter about not receiving land in the irrigation scheme after independence.[16] Peasants were not prepared to be workers on state farm land that they had originally occupied and were expelled from, first by the colonial government and then later by Frelimo. Hence, they resisted the government's collectivization efforts.

Following the decisions taken at the Fourth Party Congress, the Secretariat de Estado a Reconstrução do Vale do Limpopo e Incomati (SERLI), including the CAIL state farm, was dismantled and a number of smaller state farms were established. Additionally, a substantial quantity of state farm land was distributed for use by the family and private sectors. In 1983, the government chose the district of Chokwe as one of the country's thirty priority regions to receive development resources.[17] Subsequently, an agricultural directorate, the Gabinete de Dirreção e Coordenação das Empresas Agrarias do Chokwe (GDCEAC) was established in the town of Chokwe. This directorate was the center of administration, planning, and coordination for the four agricultural sectors—state, private, family and cooperative. In the Chokwe-GDCEAC area of influence, more than 26,000 hectares of irrigable land were distributed among these sectors, as shown in table 12.1.

In the Chokwe irrigation scheme, the category "peasant sector" was

Table 12.1. Land occupation by sector, Chokwe irrigation scheme

Sectors	1985			1986-87		
	Units	Ha	%	Units	Ha	%
State	10	11,000	45.8	7[a]	8,500	32.0
LOMACO[b]	—	—	—	3	2,500	9.0
Family	12,000	9,000	37.5	14,371	9,650	36.0
Private	300	2,500	10.4	436	4,600	17.0
Cooperative	14	1,500	6.3	14[c]	1,500	6.0
Total		24,000	100.0		26,750	100.0

Source: GDCEAC, Chokwe, August 1987.
[a]The seven state farms were in Lionde, Massavasse, Conhane, Nwachicoluane, Mapapa, Hokwe, and Chilembene.
[b]Lonhro-Mozambique Agricultural Company, LOMACO, is an enterprise jointly owned by the Mozambican government and LONRHO, the British multinational corporation based in London. It took over the territory formerly controlled by three state farms in Chilembene-Hortil, Matuba, and Macaretane.
[c]In 1987, there was a total of 2,583 cooperative members.

understood to include those peasants with two hectares. It did not take into consideration cumulative hectarage for a family household, although it was common that more than one member had received a landholding. There were many instances in which one household actually cultivated four or five hectares. Number and size of rain-fed farms, means of production such as work oxen and plows, and available labor force per peasant household were not seen as relevant factors.

Among the family and private sectors, there were a significant number of rural households who did not meet all the general characteristics of either of these sectors. For example, there were rural producers classified as private farmers who did not own their means of production but rented oxen and plows or state-owned tractors and hired wage labor. Both officials and local people considered these individuals to be private farmers because they were middle farmers during the colonial period. It was believed that these farmers had the potential to be "productive farmers" again with some assistance. In Chokwe, the definition of peasant and private farmers included local considerations.

According to a 1986 survey of private farmers in Chokwe, approximately 436 private farmers occupied 4,600 hectares with great land size differences ranging from 4 hectares to 200 hectares. The average land size was 8.48 hectares per individual in the irrigated area only.[18] Private farmers were obliged, as were peasants, to comply with the agricultural calendar imposed by the irrigation system. In addition, private farmers had individual contracts with the government, stating what crops they should grow and what yields should be obtained. Of the total production, a fixed percentage was sold to the state: this share varied, depending on the area of each private farmer, from 40 percent for 4 hectares up to 95 percent for 150 to 200 hectares.[19]

The private farmers were chosen according to several criteria, including agricultural capacity, experience, and ownership of means of production (draft animals, plows, tractors, water pumps). Many of those peasants who had been *colonos* or on probation in the colonato were considered to be private farmers. In addition, a number of Portuguese farmers who remained after independence received land. In 1980, there was a total of 34 private farmers with 215 hectares in the irrigated area. By 1986, the number had increased to 435 private farmers, of whom 391 (90%) were Mozambicans and 45 (10%) were noncitizens.[20] In comparison to the other sectors, the private sector had the most significant growth—2,500 hectares in 1985 to 4,600 hectares in 1986, an increase of 84 percent.

Part of the new area was former state farm land within the irrigation scheme, and part was new territory outside the SIREMO scheme, made irrigable with the use of imported water tubes, pumps, and other hydraulic equipment financed by USAID and other external donors. Since 1984, the United States has contributed a small amount of high-profile aid to the private farming sector, especially in Maputo and Gaza provinces. The cumulative total of U.S. assistance to private farmers was US$44.73 million in early 1987.[21] This aid consisted of equipment including tractors, trucks, and fuel as well as other materials. The United States frequently channels its aid to private farmers, those most likely to accumulate, reinforcing social differentiation in the countryside.

Systematic records of private farmers, their land size, means of production, labor force, and inputs, were not kept. It was, therefore, impossible to determine if some private farmers were expanding their hectarage substantially or if the total number of private farmers was increasing. According to the head of the private sector at GDCEAC, both of these factors accounted for the increase in hectares during this period.

Between 1985 and 1986, there was a further distribution and expansion of irrigated land. The state sector reduced its hectarage from 11,000 to 8,500 hectares, with the difference of 2,500 hectares going to LOMACO, a consortium owned by the Mozambican government and the British multinational corporation, LONHRO. In part, the reduction of state farm land reflected government policy and, in part, a decrease in external assistance from socialist countries.

From 1985 to 1987, the family sector increased from 9,000 to 9,650 hectares, or 7 percent. By 1986, more than 14,000 peasants had received landholdings in the irrigation scheme ranging from 0.5 to 1 hectare each. But the average hectare per unit, as shown in table 12.1, fell from 0.75 in 1985 to 0.67 in 1987. In other words, there was a decline in the percentage of land held by families. The Nordic countries provided most of the external assistance to the peasant sector in the form of extension services and supply of agricultural inputs. This issue of support to the peasant sector is elaborated below.

In 1983, the cooperative sector was reduced from an estimated 3,200 hectares to 2,500 hectares.[22] In 1987, the cooperative sector retained the same area. Of the 2,500 hectares, however, only 1,500 were cultivated collectively. The remaining 1,000 hectares were lent to cooperative members who cultivated small landholdings individually. This land was administered by GDCEAC's cooperative department, although in practice it was used for family farming. According to the president of the agricultural cooperatives in Chokwe, small plots ranging from 0.4 to 0.5 hectare were given to each cooperative member to farm individually—using the cooperative's resources and inputs—as an incentive to work on the collective farm.[23] This policy was initiated in 1979 following the decision to end advanced monthly salaries to cooperative members. Initially, when cooperatives were established in Chokwe, the bank lent large sums of money to cooperatives to pay its members monthly salaries in advance for their agricultural production. This monthly payment was considered an added incentive to participate in collective work. In most cases, production results did not cover the salaries and production costs.[24]

With the redistribution of land, marketed rice production in the irrigation scheme increased to 12,000 tons in 1982-83, 16,000 tons in 1983-84, 28,000 tons in 1984-85, 42,000 tons in 1985-86, and an estimated 50,000 tons in 1986-87.[25] According to João Mosca, the director of GDCEAC, there were three main reasons to account for the increases in production:

The dismantling of CAIL had dramatic consequences. First, the number of state farms was reduced, and smaller farms were established. The system of management changed for the better. With a reduced area, the state was able to provide adequate resources, both technical and material. Also, the capacity to control and direct the state farms improved. Second, the distribution of irrigated small landholdings to peasant farmers resulted in gradual yield increases. The family sector yield, averaging 3.0 tons per hectare, was better than the yields attained at CAIL which ranged from 1.9 to 2.5 tons per hectare. In CAIL's seven-year history, in only one year did it produce 2.7 tons per hectare. A third factor was the distribution of farmland to private farmers. In general, the state's land distribution policy unleashed a new attitude for all agricultural producers. It introduced a new dynamic that was accompanied by resources and supplies such as seeds, fertilizer, and herbicide which arrived with more or less certainty at the required times.[26] (Author's translation of interview.)

At GDCEAC, a department was established to specifically assist and manage the peasant family sector in the Chokwe area. Approximately 150 personnel worked with the family sector department, including foreign experts, national technicians, and extension workers. The department also was given the responsibility to coordinate the donor-sponsored "peasant projects." In 1987, there were three projects assisting the family sector in Chokwe: the Mozambique and Nordic Agricultural Program (MONAP) Project 7, the French Project to Support Family Agriculture, and the World Lutheran Federation Project to Support the Family Sector. The two main objectives of each project were to provide extension services (limited to education and training) and to supply agricultural inputs.

But by 1987, the impact of these projects on peasant farming was minimal, owing to a number of organizational and technical problems. First, these projects, like other donor-sponsored peasant projects found in neighboring Tanzania,[27] depended mainly on imported producer (seed, fertilizer, plows, hoes, and sickles) and consumer goods (motorcycles, bicycles, rubber boots) that arrived from months to years after the projects were initiated officially. To make matters worse, equipment and vehicles usually arrived without spare parts, so that when they broke down, they were permanently out of circulation. The Chokwe projects increased import requirements and overloaded already strained administrative structures and distributive systems. Given that system breakdown was a continuing postindependence problem in Mozambique, a project-oriented approach had rather serious consequences.

Second, competition rather than genuine interest in development often prevailed among these projects. During the 1986-87 agricultural season, the leaders of the projects competed for village areas as well as for trained national agricultural technicians.

Third, the projects were designed and implemented by administrative officials—both foreign and national—without technical training and knowledge of rural conditions in Mozambique. In the case of MONAP Project 7, the greater part of its attention was given to organizational and administrative issues at the Ministry of Agriculture, at the expense of fieldwork. Consequently, the project was left without technical assistance and without directives for more than two years.[28]

Fourth, education and training courses for peasants were slow to get off the ground for lack of trained personnel. Recruitment of foreign agricultural experts was a problem, largely due to the war situation, which made it difficult to work in the countryside. The MONAP Project 7, for example, was in Chokwe for more than two and a half years, yet it had not offered basic courses on water management and drainage systems to peasant farmers because it had not been successful in hiring a foreign expert. Only since the middle of 1987 has the Chokwe project been operating with two expatriate specialists in livestock and agriculture and in irrigation, respectively.

Fifth, most of the national extension agents assigned to the projects were former state farm workers who were transferred to the family sector when CAIL was dismantled. They had practical experience in rice cultivation, but few, if any, had formal technical training on agricultural production in irrigation schemes. By the end of 1987, the project still had not given due attention to the training of its own staff or to the elaboration of an appropriate method to support extension activities in the field. The extension agents were limited mostly to administrative tasks, which they performed inadequately, largely because of lack of experience and poor organization and planning skills. During peak agricultural periods, some extension agents worked their own farms, at the expense of the project.

Because of their own training limitations, the extension agents preferred to work with middle peasants who owned or had access to means of production, showed initiative, and therefore were easier to assist. Furthermore, there was an overwhelming gender bias among extension staff. The majority of extension agents were men, and they preferred to contact male farmers, who with their confidence and organizational skills gained from experience in wage labor and greater exposure to the official education system, were better equipped to take advantage of the extension services.

Changes at the local level illustrate that a more market-oriented agricultural strategy and land distribution to peasants and private farmers have increased both marketed production and social differentiation. Greater output has been achieved at the expense of greater inequality in the countryside.

Peasant Agriculture in Lionde Village, Chokwe District

The peasants and private farmers of Lionde were the first rural producers in the area to receive land in the irrigation scheme. This rural community offered an opportunity to analyze Mozambique's agricultural policy reforms under relatively favorable conditions. Lionde, located about eight kilometers from the town of Chokwe, was one of MONAP Project 7's activity areas and, consequently, received substantial technical and material assistance.

In 1986, Lionde, consisting of five neighborhoods, had a population of approximately 8,500 inhabitants, or 1,776 families.[29] According to 1980 census data, the majority of the active population in Gaza Province, including Lionde, was engaged in agrarian activities, approximately 83 percent and 70 percent, respectively. The French project's 1986 survey of the family sector in Lionde which sampled 500 peasants in the irrigation scheme (approximately 17% of the total peasant population with irrigated plots) revealed that less than half of them cultivated rain-fed farms. For those 213 peasants who cultivated rain-fed farms, approximately 50 percent had less than one hectare.[30] Since the 1983-84 agricultural season, Lionde peasants, like most farmers in the Chokwe area, had had little or no agricultural production on their rain-fed farms. With these dry-land areas out of production, the importance of having a landholding in the irrigation scheme increased.

The drought thus affected peasant differentiation directly, separating those peasants who had access to irrigated fields and those who cultivated rain-fed farms only. Evidence of the severity of the prolonged drought was the increasing number of peasants who were farming landholdings in the *zona morte,* or pirate zones, which were irrigable areas outside

SIREMO's jurisdiction. Peasant farmers often pirated the water of the irrigation scheme using water tubes connected to a secondary canal.

From 1983 to 1987, the government distributed state farm land to the family sector gradually. By November 1986, a total of 1,592 hectares were distributed to 2,900 peasants in Lionde, an average of 0.5 hectare per individual. According to the president of Lionde's Executive Council, there were approximately 440 persons—of whom some were state farm workers—still waiting to receive a landholding in 1987.[31] Other individuals on the waiting list were displaced people from distant areas who had left their homes because of drought and war.

The land distribution procedure was directed and coordinated by the Lionde Frelimo Party and government officials in collaboration with neighborhood secretaries. They organized meetings with the population in each of the neighborhoods to discuss and choose who would receive a landholding in the irrigation scheme. The peasants who received land were chosen according to priorities established at both national and local levels. First priority was given to peasants who lived exclusively from agriculture. Residents born in the area, with or without other economic activities, received second priority. Third priority was given to residents born in other areas but who wanted to farm and owned their means of production to work. Agricultural workers at state farms received fourth priority. The government's objective was to give workers land to prevent them from abandoning entirely the state farms for individual economic activities, in other words, to stabilize a permanent labor force on the state farms.

In 1987, peasants had not received land titles to their assigned plots in the irrigation scheme.[32] In theory, if a plot was not cultivated, it was to be given to someone who had the capacity to use it. This decision was to be made jointly by the family sector and local political structures. In Lionde, there were no cases where land had been reassigned.

In addition to the official distribution criteria, there were other factors considered in deciding who received land in Lionde. Some of the influential factors included a complex combination of kinship relations, political linkages, and economic and social status in the community. According to the president of the Executive Council, widows and other single female-headed households were give priority. Single men, in contrast, were not eligible to receive a landholding.[33] Special consideration was also given to households that had had farms in the colonato.

The capacity of peasant households to take advantage of the small landholdings in the irrigation scheme depended primarily on two factors: ownership or access to cattle and an organized labor force. Both of these factors are examined below.

Cattle had two main functions in the Chokwe irrigated farming system. First, they supplied draft power and were the primary means available to the family sector for plowing as well as for other agricultural operations, and they were also used for transport. Second, they were a means of storing capital obtained from mine work or years of good harvests and likewise could be sold in poor years to obtain food or credit for other agricultural inputs. This was particularly important in a climatically fluctuating area like Chokwe.[34]

The heavy clay loam soils, spread out over the irrigation scheme, required the use of oxen and plows and thus could not be cultivated easily by those peasants who owned only hoes. In some zones, it was too difficult to plow even with oxen. Given Mozambique's desperate economic situation, mechanization was not a solution for the family sector. According to the director of GDCEAC, the strategy to improve family farming production was to introduce better animal traction including improved plows and quality of work oxen. In 1987, however, there were not sufficient draft animals to plow peasant landholdings in the irrigation scheme.

Although the largest number of cattle in Mozambique was found in Gaza Province, they were unevenly distributed among peasant families. The 1980 general census showed that 76 percent of family households did not own cattle. The number was higher in Lionde, where 82 percent of peasant families were without cattle.[35] It should be noted that these figures did not take into account the effects of the severe drought that began in 1982 and the war against Renamo, which accelerated after 1981. These two factors reduced significantly the total number of cattle in Gaza.

The Instituto Nacional de Investigação Agronómica's (INIA) 1986 pasture and soil survey of Chokwe found between 61 percent and 100 percent (mean 83%) of family sector farmers were using animal draft power for plowing, depending on the locality and the crop.[36] In Lionde, it found that 86 percent of peasant farmers used animal draft power to prepare their landholding for maize production. The percentage dropped significantly for rice production because peasants often broadcasted rice seed while maize was still in the field, eliminating the need to plow their land again.

Most peasant farmers were forced to rent oxen and plows. A 1986 survey on the costs of production for rice and maize for the state, private, and family sectors estimated that it cost 12,000 meticais (mt) a hectare (equivalent to US$300 at the official exchange rate) to hire draft animals for plowing.[37] During the periods when there was a high demand for draft animals (August–October and April–July), Lionde peasant farmers paid competitive prices ranging from 6,000 mt (US$150) to 8,000 mt (US$200) per 0.5 hectare.

Some farmers paid in kind to rent draft animals and plows, generally food for small animals. Following the 1986-87 rice harvest, for example, peasants paid one hundred kilos of husked rice, having a value of 15,000 mt in the parallel market, in exchange for six days (four hours per labor day) of draft animal use to plow 0.5 hectare.[38] It was also common for poor peasants in Lionde to pay in labor power. At the start of the agricultural season, a poor peasant hired himself out to a farmer with oxen and a plow to form a production team. He then worked full-time plowing the fields of the cattle owner, as well as the farms of other peasants who hired the owner's animals. In return for his labor, the peasant plowed his own farm. This arrangement enabled a poor peasant to gain access to means of production.[39] In some cases, an agreement was reached between those peasants who owned oxen and plows but did not have a landholding in the irrigation scheme and those peasants with irrigated plots but who owned no means of production to prepare the land. The oxen plowed the field, and then the two households shared the small landholding, often growing two different crops simultaneously. In other cases, state farm workers whose fixed salaries of 4,500 mt (officially, US$112.50) per month in 1986 did not permit them to pay competitive ox-rental prices shared their landholding with peasants who owned oxen and plows.

The local government showed some flexibility, permitting different forms of association between those peasant households with irrigated landholdings and those households with means of production. But it did not allow peasants to rent or lend their entire plots to other individuals. Similarly, the state decided not to intervene in regulating prices for oxen and plow rental. According to the director of the peasant sector at GDCEAC, government interference would result in fewer draft animal owners renting their oxen.[40]

The dependence on draft animals for plowing both in the irrigation scheme and in rain-fed areas was thus very marked, and any attempt to increase agricultural productivity had to take this factor into account. In the last few years, with the rapid increase in productive land available to the family sector, the demand for work oxen has not been met. In Lionde, fields were often plowed late and crops were sown after the optimal time period because peasants waited to hire work oxen and plows. The restriction of available work oxen for hire also meant that the farms prepared by animal traction were plowed poorly. Lionde peasant farmers frequently complained that rented draft animals only plowed their fields once instead of the necessary two plowings and harrowing, and in some cases, the oxen owner never returned to complete the job.

Livestock production in the district had some serious problems, as seen from the animals dying from weakness at watering points in the dry season. There were also conflicts between crop and livestock production, with destruction of crops by cattle and destruction of irrigation canal banks by cattle coming to drink. Often animals lost their balance and drowned in the canal. According to the above-mentioned pasture survey, the main causes of these problems were excessive cattle concentrations in certain areas due to the poor security situation in surrounding districts, which led to many cattle moving into the Chokwe district in recent years; the fear of grazing animals in underpopulated areas some distance from the villages due to cattle thieving; the uneven distribution of communal villages, which often had more cattle associated with them than the surrounding area could support; and the poor distribution of drinking points, which led to cattle having to travel excessive distances from grazing to drinking to the night kraal.[41]

In Lionde, many oxen were fed maize stover either standing in the fields after harvest or carted to the kraals. A large number of cattle owners in Lionde explained, however, that they did not rent their work oxen because of food shortage. This shortage reflected both a lack of access to grazing areas beyond the periphery of the irrigation scheme and low maize production in the hot season, reducing the availability of stover for feed.

The principal source of labor on peasant landholdings in Lionde was the family. The most visible active family members on these farms were women—wives, mothers, daughters, sisters, nieces, and other women members of the extended family. In many cases, these women lived together in the same family compound. Daughters-in-law, for example, who lived with their husbands' families were expected to work long hours on the family farm because of a nexus of affective relations and customs in which the lever of *lobolo,* bride price payment, played an important role. Frequently, parents-in-law exploited their son's wives because they had contributed toward the bride payment.

In Lionde, the majority of men were salaried workers employed either at one of the six state companies that operated in the village or at an enterprise in the nearby town of Chokwe. As the administrative, commercial, and industrial center for the district, Chokwe was also the home of many local state enterprises such as Boror (a seed, agrochemicals, and fertilizer distribution firm), Agricom (an agricultural marketing parastatal), Hortofruticola (an agricultural parastatal marketing mainly fruits and vegetables), GDCEAC, and Mecanagro (a state machinery park). The railway was also a major employer of men from Lionde.

Men's agricultural work in Lionde was limited to plowing the fields with draft animals, irrigation, and other seasonal duties that they integrated with wage work. The other communal villages in the irrigation scheme had a higher percentage of men working regularly on family farms because they had fewer possibilities of wage employment. In comparison to Lionde, the other communal villages each had only one state enterprise.

With the redistribution of landholdings to the family and private sectors in Chokwe, there was an increasing use of peasant wage labor on these farms. The general categories listed below provide a profile of this peasant labor force.

The first category included a significant number of poor peasant households—usually consisting of single mothers, widows, and the elderly—that were failing to increase production or productivity because they did not have a sufficient labor force and lacked the means of production, in particular, draft animals and plows, at critical periods in the agricultural season. Their fields were plowed late, if at all, and many were forced to prepare their farms with a hoe, compromising agricultural production at the beginning of the season. Although a family member or members might have worked seasonally or part-time in the wage economy—usually at a state enterprise—the cash contribution to household expenses was very little in relation to the high cost of consumer goods following the implementation of Mozambique's Economic Recovery Program (PRE) and speculative prices in the parallel market.[42]

These poor peasant households did not have food reserves or cash accumulated to pay agricultural laborers who frequently demanded food or other consumer goods such as soap, sugar, and cooking oil in exchange for labor. Because of a general situation of good shortages from the combined effects of war and drought, workers preferred food to cash.

During the 1986-87 rice season, some of these families failed to produce rice on their landholdings, while others managed to farm less than 0.25 hectare. In many cases, family members worked as agricultural laborers for other peasant farmers in the irrigation scheme, for private farmers, or at the state farms, leaving their own landholding uncultivated in return for payment in food. An increasing number of families were "too poor to farm"; they were able to keep farming only if much of their time was devoted to paid labor.

The quantity of husked rice received for agricultural work varied with the task: for weeding rice, an individual received six or seven kilos per day, at six hours per labor day; for harvesting the crop, five or six kilos per labor day; and for threshing rice, ten kilos per labor day. These were the going rates per labor day for agricultural tasks on both family and private farms during the 1986-87 agricultural season But other pay arrangements existed, too: twenty kilos of husked rice for four days of harvesting and threshing rice or a quantity of rice at the end of the harvest, usually two or three sacks, each weighing seventy-five kilos. Peasants, unlike private farmers, combined systems of payment, often paying some laborers per day and others per task. Many found it difficult to pay workers per day over an extended period.

The second category was made up of those households that depended solely on family labor, usually using both immediate and extended family members. In cases where extended family members assisted in the peak labor periods, for example, weeding and harvesting of rice, they were paid a quantity of food, determined by production results, at the end of the harvest. In Lionde, payment ranged from two to four sacks (seventy-five kilos each) per individual.

There were a growing number of households using extended family members through the entire rice season. Many of these individuals were displaced people, uprooted from their homes because of the war and drought. They became permanent workers on Lionde family farms, although peasant farmers attempted to mask the relations of production, identifying these workers as "family" members.

For households with men still working in South Africa, the migrant worker's wage played an important role in recruiting seasonal family laborers. Peasants explained that these households usually offered soap and other consumer goods purchased in South Africa with miners' earnings in exchange for family labor power during the peak labor periods.

The third category was made up of peasant households that hired seasonal wage laborers (usually one to three persons) during the peak labor periods for rice and to a lesser extent for maize, in addition to family labor. Usually, this labor force was part-time, working only two to five days consecutively. Because payment was nearly always in kind—approximately six kilos of husked rice or five kilos of maize per day per worker—these families could not afford to hire workers for more than a few days at a time. The farm laborers were usually peasants from Caniçado, an area on the other side of the river, who had left their rain-fed farms in search of food for family consumption and for maize seed for the next planting season. The selling of labor power in exchange for food is one aspect of *ku thekela* (literally, "to take from somebody else"), a general strategy that agrarian populations in southern Mozambique adopt in their defense against drought and famine.[43]

Again, those peasant families with migrant workers in South Africa had advantages in hiring seasonal laborers. They often received consumer goods, including food and, to a lesser extent, South Africa's currency, the rand. Most of the goods were for the miner's family: goods that they needed for day-to-day survival such as production implements, material to repair houses, and other consumer goods. In some cases, families set aside a part of the consumer goods to exchange for agricultural labor power. Consumer goods like sacks of maize and flour were exchanged for labor, giving these goods a production use.

The fourth category included a growing number of family households who employed regular wage laborers on the small landholdings in return for payment in food and/or cash. These families usually had a regular wage earner (e.g., a husband or son employed full-time at a state enterprise) or they had a fairly stable income based on agricultural marketed production. In the latter case, these families had more than one field in the irrigation scheme. An example best illustrates this category of family households that was representative of an increasing number but still a minority of families in Lionde.

The Sitoe family cultivated 5 hectares in the irrigation scheme, of which 0.5 hectare was managed by the wife who was considered a member of the family sector. She also farmed 0.5 hectare in the pirate zone. The husband, classified as a private farmer, cultivated 4 hectares. This family, like many households in the Chokwe area, did not own cattle, a plow, or other means of production to prepare its farms. Prior to independence, however, the family had farmed a small landholding in the colonato, employing seasonal workers. With one foot in the family sector and the other foot in the private sector, this household paid a permanent agricultural wage labor force both in food and in cash to work on all the farms. In addition, it hired seasonal workers during the peak labor periods. The number of seasonal workers varied according to the task: ten persons to weed and twenty individuals to harvest the rice. The labor force consisted of women and men, both young and old, from outside the locality but usually within the districts of Limpopo and neighboring Caniçado. These workers were usually paid the minimum wage per month and received food as well as accommodations during the rice season.

From the early 1980s, the rising influx of people to the Chokwe area from regions suffering from drought and war provided the necessary labor force for those family households who had food reserves and cash to increase agricultural output and to accumulate further. By 1987, there were 19,000 displaced people in the Chokwe district, 4,600 of whom were in the town.[44]

This category of peasant households who employed regular agricultural laborers benefited from the inputs and resources of both the family and the private sectors. These relatively wealthy peasants were the major recipients of the family sector's extension services. In Chokwe, Frelimo's agricultural strategy has led to increased output and social differentiation between peasants and private farmers and within the peasant sector. Since the situation of poor peasants, the majority of rural producers, has not improved, the government's land reform policies could lead to smallholders' discontent instead of "releasing peasant energies."

The Peasant Economy: Other Considerations

Although peasant farmers' access to means of production and labor was critical for improving agricultural production in the irrigation scheme, there were other considerations that affected rice output. Three areas of the peasant economy that influenced production were subsistence needs versus the market, consumer goods availability, and transport and marketing facilities. All of these issues are examined below.

A crucial factor in determining a peasant's marketed production was whether the small landholding in the irrigation scheme could produce one or two crops during the agricultural season. Some zones only had one cycle because the soils, suffering mainly from slow drainage or high salinity, could not sustain two-crop seasons. In Lionde, the principal family cropping system was rice in the hot season (September-March) followed by maize, beans, and vegetables in the cool season (April-August). Only a very small area in Lionde was not suitable for rice. In that area, peasant farmers grew maize and cow peas in the hot season followed by maize, beans, and vegetables in the cool season.

For the middle peasants who owned or had access to tractors, draft animals, plows, and other instruments of production, the small landholdings in the irrigation scheme permitted expansion of their survival strategy. In Lionde, for example, during the hot season, middle peasants grew rice to consume and sold or exchanged a small quantity for maize and consumer goods to the state. During the cool season, they grew maize for family consumption and some produced vegetables for market. For the middle peasantry, access to resources and assistance from aid projects were important incentives.

Marketed vegetable production played an increasingly important role in the peasant economy. One Lionde farmer explained to me that he bought a team of draft animals largely with his earnings from the 1985-86 vegetable production that he sold to Hortofruticola, the state marketing enterprise.[45] Vegetables as a cash crop appeared to be crucial to the survival of peasant households without any other regular source of wage income. In Lionde, families without any regular wage earners tended to be female-headed households. With the income earned by selling vegetables, these families purchased day-to-day necessities and put aside an amount of cash to pay for land preparation, seed, and other expenses.

During the 1986-87 agricultural season, of the total 1,592 hectares in Lionde, peasant farmers sowed 600 hectares of rice (38%) and 793 hectares (50%) of maize.[46] Approximately 88 percent of available farmland was cultivated. The agricultural data suggested that peasant farmers still preferred to produce maize in the hot season for family consumption rather than rice. Although they were aware of the technical problems of cultivating maize in the hot season, peasants continued to grow it for a variety of reasons.

First, maize was the preferred food crop. The negligible production on rain-fed farms had aggravated the local shortage. As long as the state could not provide sufficient quantities of maize, peasants were determined to grow it, even if production was low.

Second, peasants still had not been given land titles to the irrigated plots. They were very aware that their land could be redistributed at any time to private farmers or taken back by the state. Without any guarantees, they pursued individual family strategies, giving priority to maize production.

Third, maize did not require as much labor power as rice cultivation. Poor peasants explained that they lacked the labor force to produce rice. Their households did not have sufficient immediate family members to assist in the necessary agricultural operations, especially weeding, and they could not afford to pay wage laborers. In the cases where poor peasants felt obliged to sow rice in a small area of their field, the rice was poorly weeded or not weeded at all.

Fourth, peasants doubted that SIREMO would allocate water to the family sector when it was well known that there was not sufficient water at the Massingir Dam to irrigate family, cooperative, private, and state farms. During the 1986-87 rice season, rainfall was inadequate, and there was not sufficient water in the dam during October and November (the optimal time to sow rice) for the entire irrigation scheme. The total rice area lost inside the irrigation scheme was approximately 2,500 hectares.[47] Although all sectors experienced losses, some were affected more than others. Priority was given to the state sector, followed by the private sector and then family and cooperative farms. The government's decision was based on investment and potential output.

Another factor accounting for production losses in all sectors was the poor state of the irrigation scheme's infrastructure. A major limitation was the poor or nonexistent third drainage system, which resulted in very low slow drainage of the fields before the rice harvest. This led to difficulties in transporting the harvest out of the fields and delays in plowing and planting the following maize crops.[48] SIREMO lacked the resources—equipment and technical assistance—to repair and maintain the infrastructure.

After 1983, the Mozambican government and the donor projects established in Chokwe made serious efforts to supply rural producers with seeds and other agricultural inputs. They also tried to guarantee transport and marketing of surplus crops in exchange for consumer goods. Since the 1985-86 agricultural season, the government has offered peasants maize in exchange for rice. Rural stores that served as Agricom outlets and state farms also supplied other basic consumer goods in exchange for rice. These efforts have only been partially successful, because the maize quantities have not been sufficient to meet the demand. Although the quantity of consumer goods in the countryside has increased substantially, the government still was unable to provide the high-quality and incentive goods to encourage the sale of peasant surpluses at official prices.[49]

In 1987, there existed a local parallel market in rice. According to most peasants I interviewed, the rice sold in the parallel market was mainly for local consumption, although some found its way to Maputo where it was resold and husked by hand. In 1986, for example, a sack of rice (50 kilos) sold for 10,000 mt (US$250)in the parallel market in Lionde. Following the rice harvest in 1987, a sack of rice sold for 15,000 mt (US$37.50) in Maputo.[50] In June 1987, the meticais, the national currency, was devalued from US$1 = 40 mt to US$1 = 400 mt.

In 1987, the main obstacle to the development of smallholder vegetable production was the lack of an organized system of collection and marketing of fresh vegetables. Neither Hortofruticola nor Agricom purchased directly from peasant farms. In Lionde, it was common to observe peasants selling their tomatoes and onions at the local market or along the roadside in small quantities transported in ox carts rather than selling their products to state firms. Some peasants explained that they preferred to sell their vegetables at their field to reduce rotting and transport cost. Frequently, individual buyers handpicked their own vegetables, and then the owner weighed and sold the produce to them.

The relatively few peasant households who were able to market their vegetables were those who owned or rented oxen and carts and could transport their production to Hortofruticola, located in the town Chokwe. Even when peasants managed to transport their production to the state marketing enterprise, the crops were not guaranteed transport to Maputo on the same day, largely for reasons of economies of scale. The result was that crops rotted waiting in warehouses to be transported. Hortofruticola gave priority to commercial farmers who had significantly larger quantities of vegetables to market. In some instances, peasant farmers who had direct contacts with urban buyers were able to ensure transport of their crop to Maputo. In 1987, the produce from Chokwe was being transported to Maputo in daily military convoys because of the security situation on the main road.

One of the effects of both government and donor policy in Chokwe was that the large private farmers were succeeding in acquiring the technical assistance and marketing resources available, while the majority of peasant farmers were being left out. One way in which private farmers benefited over peasant producers was through control and ownership of means of transport. The small pickups distributed by donors such as USAID have been sold mainly to private farmers.

Conclusion

In the early 1980s, the general climate of insecurity and the extreme scarcity of goods and revenue limited the Mozambican government's ability to supply inputs and services to all rural producers. These factors, in addition to Frelimo's bias toward state farms, were responsible for low agricultural production in all sectors. After 1984, changes in the government's·agricultural policy favoring peasant producers and private farmers, regional prioritization, administrative decentralization, liberalization of commercial activity, and provision of consumer and producer goods made possible through concessionary financing from the international community contributed to agricultural growth in the Chokwe district. The Mozambican government has improved rice production in the Chokwe irrigation scheme by implementing an agricultural strategy that includes both land reform (distribution of state farm land to peasants and private capitalist farmers) and agrarian reform (provision of services, inputs, consumer goods, markets, and improved infrastructure).

Although Mozambique's agricultural policy has led to greater output, it has been at the expense of greater inequality at the local level in the countryside. In Chokwe, wealthy middle peasants and large private farmers have been the major beneficiaries of agrarian changes—as well as foreign aid—leading to and consolidating a process of socioeconomic differentiation among rural producers. The state has tolerated the growth of social differentiation because the primary objective of its current policy has been production maximization. Yet rural differentiation will be a formidable political and economic problem in the long run. As in the past, poor peasants, the majority of rural producers, have not been the main concern or beneficiaries of state agricultural policy. Mozambique's reforms that have favored middle peasants and private farmers could fuel the poor peasants' dissatisfaction with Frelimo's agricultural reform policies. At the national level, it remains to be seen whether increased agricultural output can be sustained. Given the absence of any significant state or foreign aid assistance to poor peasants, it is not clear how privatization, price liberalization, and other market strategies implemented in a context of war will stimulate further increases in production.

Notes

The data for this article are based on extensive research over a period of one year in the district of Chokwe. From July 1986 to August 1987, I lived and worked in that rural area observing and concluding multiple follow-up interviews with peasants and private farmers. A shorter version of this chapter has already appeared in the *Canadian Journal of African Studies* 23, 2 (1990). I wish to thank the Social Science and Humanities Research Council of Canada for providing the financial assistance that made the research possible. A Minority Supplementary Research Grant at the University of Illinois provided additional support. I am grateful to Thomas Bassett, William Martin, and Firmino Pinto for their thoughtful comments. A special word of thanks is due to my friends, colleagues, and informants in Mozambique.

1 The case studies of Cuba, China, Vietnam, Ethiopia, and Tanzania are examined in "Agriculture, the Peasantry and Socialist Development," *International Development Studies Bulletin* 13, 4 (1982); G. White, R. Murray, and C. White, *Revolutionary Socialist Development in the Third World* (Sussex, 1983); and T. Ranger, *Peasant Consciousness and Guerrilla War in Zimbabwe* (London and Berkeley, 1985).

2 Frelimo is the Portuguese acronym for the Frente de Libertação de Moçambique (Front for the Liberation of Mozambique), the ruling party in Mozambique since independence in 1975.

3 P. Raikes, "Food Policy and Production in Mozambique Since Independence," *Review of African Political Economy* 29 (1984): 95–107.

4 J. Hanlon, *Mozambique: The Revolution under Fire* (London, 1984): 101.

5 For historical background on Renamo, see P. Fauvet, "Roots of Counter-Revolution: The Mozambique National Resistance," *Review of African Political Economy* 41 (1984): 108–121. From 1981 to 1983, Renamo destroyed 140 villages, 840 schools, 200 health posts, and 900 rural shops and caused thou-

sands of deaths and hundreds of millions of dollars of damage to the Mozambican economy. O. Roesch, "Economic Reform in Mozambique: Notes on Stabilization, War and Class Formation," *Taamuli* (forthcoming).

6 The principal source for the remainder of this discussion is Roesch, "Economic Reform in Mozambique."

7 South African aggression through the Renamo rebels forced more than 2.9 million Mozambicans off their land. About 1.7 million of these were displaced inside the country, while the remainder fled across the borders. The government estimated that the number of those in need of emergency aid, because of the war and natural disasters, was 4.5 million, or about a third of the entire population. Mozambique Information Office, "Prime Minister's Report on Economic Recovery," no. 114, September 24 (1987): 5.

8 In the 1980 census, the district of Limpopo is separate from the town of Chokwe. For this chapter, the two areas are considered as one region. Republic Popular de Moçambique, *Primeiro Recenseamento Geral da População* (Maputo, 1983).

9 Centro de Estudos Africanos, *The Mozambican Miner: A Study in the Export of Labour* (Maputo, 1980): 85.

10 R. First, *Black Gold: The Mozambican Miner, Proletarian and Peasant* (Brighton, Sussex, 1983): 183–185.

11 K. Hermele, *Contemporary Land Struggles on the Limpopo* (Uppsala, 1986): 18.

12 P. Woodhouse, H. Jimenez, W. Heemskerk, M. Spittel, and W. Slobbe, *Smallholder Farming Systems Research in the Chokwe Irrigation Area* (Maputo, 1986): 1.

13 B. O'Laughlin, "A Questão Agrária em Moçambique," *Estudos Moçambicanos* 3 (1981): 9–32.

14 Ibid.

15 A. Wardman, "The Co-operative Movement in Chokwe, Mozambique," *Journal of Southern African Studies* 11, 2 (1985): 294–304.

16 K. Hermele, *Land Struggles and Social Differentiation in Southern Mozambique: A Case Study of Chokwe, Limpopo 1950–1987* (Uppsala, 1988).

17 K. Hermele, "Reorganization and Interdependence: The Agricultural Setup in Chokwe, Gaza Province," mimeo. (Maputo, 1986).

18 Projecto Français de Apoio Agricultura Familiar, "Inquérito: Sector Privado" (Chokwe, 1986).

19 Hermele, *Contemporary Land Struggles*, 17–18.

20 Ibid.

21 Agencia de Informação dc Moçambique, "Cooperation, Trade and Agreements," Bulletin no. 129 (April 1987): 15.

22 União das Cooperativas Agrícolas do Chokwe, "Dados Estatísticas das Cooperativas" (Chokwe, 1987).

23 Interview with Fundamo Chauque, president of the Chokwe Agricultural Cooperatives, on April 16, 1987, in Chokwe, Gaza Province.

24 Wardman, "The Co-operative Movement."

25 Interview with João Mosca, Director of GDCEAC, on April 20, 1987, in Chokwe, Gaza Province.

26 Ibid.

27 A. Coulson, "Agricultural Policies in Mainland Tanzania," *Review of African Political Economy* 10 (1977): 74–100; and Raikes, "Food Policy."

28 B. Fret, K. Hermele, and G. Akesson, *Assessment and Proposals for Reorientation: MONAP Project 7* (Maputo, 1987): 5.

29 Interview with Americo Jalane, president of the Executive Council of Lionde, on February 16, 1987, in Lionde, Gaza Province.

30 Projecto Français de Apoio Agricultura Familiar, "Inquérito: Sector Familiar em Lionde" (Chokwe, 1986).

31 Interview with Americo Jalane, president of the Executive Council of Lionde, on February 16, 1987, in Lionde, Gaza Province.

32 President Joaquim Chissano gave out the first land use titles to peasant farmers on April 27, 1988, in the district of Marracuene in Maputo Province. He explained the importance and the value of the land use titles: "The title gives its owner the right to make correct use of the land given to him or her; the land can be used individually or collectively; the land can be passed on to the owner's descendants; and the titles given to the family sector are free. In contrast, private farmers are charged for the use of the land over a determined period." The government planned in the near future to distribute land use titles to peasants in all provinces, districts, and localities. Agência de Informação de Moçambique, "Land Use Titles Given Out in Marracuene, Maputo" Bulletin no. 142 (May 1988): 9–10.

33 Interview with Americo Jalane, president of the Executive Council of Lionde, on February 16, 1987, in Lionde, Gaza Province.

34 J. Timberlake, C. Jordão, and G. Serno, *Pasture and Soil Survey of Chokwe* (Maputo, 1986): 1.

35 Republic Popular de Moçambique, *Primeiro Recenseamento.*

36 Timberlake et al., *Pasture and Soil Survey,* 2.

37 Projecto Français de Apoio Agricultura Familiar, "Inquérito: Sector Privado" (Chokwe, 1986), n.p. At the official exchange rate, US$1 = 40 mt; at the unofficial rate, it was approximately US$1 = 1,500 mt.

38 Interview with Lionde peasant on April 10, 1987, in Lionde, Gaza Province.

39 Interview with Alpheus Manghezi, researcher at the Centro de Estudos Africanos, Universidade Eduardo Mondlane, on February 25, 1987, in Maputo.

40 Interview with Ernesto Mausse, director of the Family Sector in Chokwe, on December 16, 1986, in Maputo.

41 Timberlake et al., *Pasture and Soil Survey,* 2–3.

42 In January 1987, the Mozambican government introduced a comprehensive economic recovery program to reverse the country's economic decline.

43 A. Manghezi, "Ku Thekela: Estratégia de sobrevivência contra a fome no sul de Moçambique," *Estudos Moçambicanos* 4 (1983).

44 Agencia de Informação de Moçambique, "Hunger Worsens in Four Provinces," Bulletin no. 136 (November 1987): 6.

45 Interview with Silva Baloi, peasant farmer, on November 10, 1986, in Lionde, Gaza Province.

46 These statistics were provided by Franciso Tivane, head of the Family Sector at GDCEAC, on May 25, 1987, in Chokwe, Gaza Province.

47 Interview with João Mosca, director of GDCEAC, on April 20, 1987, in Chokwe, Gaza Province.

48 Woodhouse et al., *Smallholder,* 47.

49 In 1985, the value of goods was approximately 20,000,000 mt (US$500,000); in 1986, it was 100,000,000 mt (US$2,500,000); and in 1987, it was 500,000,000 mt (US$1,250,000). In 1985 and 1986, the official exchange rate was US$1 = 40 mt; and in 1987, US$1 = 400 mt. Interview with João Mosca, director of GDCEAC, April 20, 1987, in Chokwe, Gaza Province.

50 Interview with an informant on June 15, 1987, in Maputo.

13 *Terence Ranger*

The Communal Areas of Zimbabwe

Introduction

Since independence, the lands on which the great majority of Zimbabwean cultivators live have been officially designated as the communal areas. Certainly, they could not have gone on being called by either of their two colonial names—first, the reserves, and then, after the 1967 Land Act, the tribal trust lands. Both were altogether too redolent of successive stages of colonial ideology, the term "reserve" implying an area held back from a general process of modernization and the term "tribal trust land" carrying with it all the anachronistic flavor of Rhodesia Front Indirect Rule. (As one of chief Makoni's councillors asked me in 1981, "Who were we to trust?") Nevertheless, the term "Communal Areas" has its own ironies.

The first irony is that the term has been adopted in independent Zimbabwe because it is thought to reflect an African attitude to land rather than a European one. The initially positive attitude to communal tenure comes out clearly enough from one of the earliest official reflections on landholding, the rather rambling parliamentary response of Moven Mahachi, Deputy Minister of Lands, Resettlement and Rural Development, in January 1981, when asked what forms of ownership would prevail on the new resettlement schemes:

At the moment nobody owns land. It is vested in the President. We are thinking seriously whether to transfer ownership to the farmers or to leave it as it is. We are inclined to think communal ownership is better. . . . The existing land in the T.T.L.s is communally owned. We are applying communal ownership on the land we are acquiring. None of us has a right to justifiably profit from it. In fact, I would regard it as God's land.[1]

Yet the whole notion of "communal tenure" is preeminently a European construct. Hans Holleman remarked in 1969 that many "persistent fallacies" had arisen in the minds of white colonial administrators and technocrats from the use of "such pert but obscure phrases as 'communal tenure,' 'communal use,' and land being 'vested in the chief.' "[2] More recently, Archie Mafeje has also stressed the externality of the notion of "communal tenure" but this time in relation to white radical and left-wing thought. He emphasizes the distance between white South African Communist analytical categories and the realities of black rural life: "Their imported notions of 'tribal economy'" 'communal land tenure,' 'feudal landlords,' and 'peasants,' were like semantic categories abstracted from another language."[3]

The classic European notion of communal tenure, whether of the right or of the left, was based on a false history. The chief, it was held, had been "a territorial ruler."[4] He held all the land. As the acting provincial commissioner, Manicaland, wrote in 1971 with particular reference to Chief Makoni:

There is no individual ownership of land. All the land vests in the chief. . . . He is the "muridzi we nyika," the owner of the land. The tribesmen may use the land for dwellings, for cultivation, and for depasturing stock, but only with the permission of Makoni. . . . For good and sufficient reasons (in the tribal context) he may and does withdraw not only permission to cultivate or depasture stock, but even permission to reside in the Makoni area. He is entitled to destroy crops grown without his authority or in the incorrect area, or seize cattle depastured without his consent.[5]

The acting provincial commissioner was emphasizing Makoni's power because he wanted the chief to impose agricultural and conservation rules on his people. But he would have agreed with the colonial version of "tradition," which insisted that the chief held the land and employed his powers over it only as the "trustee" of the tribe. Everyone, it was insisted, had "an inalienable right to a reasonable share according to his requirements, a right as secure as is a person's membership of the community."[6] In the left-wing version of the African past, this situation represented a transitional stage between "primitive communalism" and full-blown "feudalism."

Like almost all other theories about precolonial "tradition," however, this one founders on the rough and ready realities of nineteenth-century Zimbabwean life. David Beach has recently suggested that there were *no* rules of succession in Shona chiefships in the nineteenth century and that successful contenders depended on force and fraud and the backing of a powerful faction in a constant competition with other contenders and factions for power and spoils. Land was part of the spoils of the victor in these competitions, along with cattle and women and other captives of war; the members of the losing faction lost their lands and fled to the shelter or a rival chiefdom. Under these circumstances, a land right as "secure as is a person's membership of the community" was not very secure.

Moreover, in a situation of constant conflict, people lived clustered together in large villages controlled by chiefs or a few powerful headmen. Chiefs commanded the services of slave wives and of young men who were prepared to give labor and service in return for war-captive brides; large fields were cultivated for the chiefs by these subordinates, and labor was also given by "free" men and women. These also paid tribute in kind from their harvests. Powerful newcomers, who could offer the chief military or economic support, were allocated advantageous lands in preference to long-established but less influential residents. There was little carryover of "traditions" of communal tenure from this precolonial period to the very different realities of early colonial Rhodesia, in which the large chiefly villages gave way to settlements scattered all over the territory; in which chiefs were undercut in power by the colonial administration but at the same time supported against contenders for office. Yet if the idea of chiefly "trusteeship" was largely a myth, so too was the idea of chiefly "ownership" of land. In early colonial Rhodesia, full private ownership of cattle herds *was* granted to Ndebele chiefs, but no such transfer from "communal" to private property took place so far as land was concerned. It was not possible in Rhodesia, as it was in some parts of Kenya, for a chief to accumulate title to large holdings and to develop entrepreneurial farming. Power rather than entitlement had been the key to nineteenth-century chiefship; when military power lapsed, so too did economic possibility. Stripped of their slave wives and dependent bride-service young men, the chiefs no longer cultivated great fields. Their "free" subjects, anxious to develop the peasant option, soon ceased to offer labor or to pay tribute. Chiefs had to rely on fees and bribes but were unable in early colonial Rhodesia to demand either in return for allocating land.

The idea—and to some extent, the practice—of "traditional communal tenure" grew up in a sort of rural power vacuum during early colonialism. Chiefs had lost power over land, and no one else had assumed it; the colonial authorities were content to leave emergent peasant production to itself; there was no shortage of land, as people spread out from the old centralized villages; and people essentially allocated land to themselves by moving into it during the great process of peasant resettlement of the countryside. Thereafter, in these new peasant communities, land allocation was basically local and consensual, at least until the interventions of the colonial state from the 1920s onward. In 1985, an interministerial draft plan for reform in the communal areas described the "traditional" operation of communal tenure in terms that probably *did* apply to the early colonial years but not to the period before or after.

"Right of avail" includes rights (i) to cultivate land (historically as much as could be managed); (ii) to graze livestock (traditionally where one pleased except on land actually under *growing* crops and traditionally as many cattle as owned); (iii) to take timber for building and firewood; (iv) the use of water (no person or group could preempt to themselves a water supply); (v) to the use of sand, stones and other minerals; and (vi) to a site on which to build a house. . . .

Nominally, the Clan Chief or, through delegation, the Ward Head, or Kraal Head will make the specific grants of rights of avail. However these leaders do not have autocratic powers; they are essentially spokesmen, representing a group interest after consensual decision making has taken place. Only after extensive investigations and discussions will the Kraal Head make an official ruling, by which time almost all the local population knows what it will be and agrees with it.[7]

It follows from this all-too-brief historical sketch that it is a mistake to suppose—as both white and black commentators have done—that a return to traditional communal tenure necessarily involves a restoration of effective chiefly control over land and rights of avail. During the brief decades in which the traditional system worked, chiefs had little power over land. Nor is there any evidence to suggest that Zimbabwean chiefs and headmen are any likelier now than they were in the precolonial past to act merely as trustees for their people in the management of land. When powers over land allocation *were* given to chiefs under the 1967 Tribal Trust Land Act, they could not use them, it is true, to regain a nineteenth-century arbitrary power. But many chiefs used them instead to extract fees and gifts, often bringing aliens onto the land. A. K. H. Weinrich provides an example in her study of old and new peasant communities in Karangaland. Thus, in Shoko Tribal Trust Land in the late 1960s,

Chief Shoko made extensive use of this new right and indiscriminately allocated land in grazing areas, even on steep slopes which were seen marred by erosion.

People who received land, "thanked" their chief through gifts of money, ranging between £2 and £5. . . . No land was given out in the grazing area where the chief herded his own cattle. . . . This large-scale land allocation drastically reduced the common pasture. . . . Chief Shoko ordered one cultivator . . . to hand over his field to a friend of the chief because it yielded good crops.[8]

If the notion of chief as trustee is fallacious, so too are many other assumptions about the operation of communal tenure. The word "communal" has been particularly misleading. Modernizers have lamented and romantic socialists have rejoiced in the supposedly collective and anti-individual qualities of a communal tenure system. During the colonial period, many native commissioners strove to perpetuate what they held to be the essential and traditional egalitarianism of communal tenure. "The writer's views are purely communistic," wrote one native commissioner in 1944. "The thought of creating a capitalist native class is too appalling to contemplate."[9] He and other administrators strove to enforce traditional collectivity. Even in the 1970s, such administrators tried to turn the supported inheritance of "traditional communalism" to account. Thus, in 1974, the peasants of Chiweshe Tribal Trust Land, among whom were numbers of successful entrepreneurial tobacco growers as well as many relatively large-scale producers of maize, were concentrated into so-called protected villages. The main aim of these concentrations was to deny food to the guerrillas. But the local district commissioner told visitors that he regarded the new arrangements as permanent:

Land Husbandry would now be carried out as "collective farming." Referring to *nhimbe,* the traditional work party, he said that "collective farming" had been a traditional feature of Shona culture.[10]

Ironically enough, not long after this pronouncement, position papers were being prepared for ZANU/PF on the "agricultural reconstruction of Zimbabwe" which took something of the same position. The author argued that nhimbe "were similar" to the "seasonal mutual aid teams" that were a feature of Chinese collectivization. In her recommendations for change after AANU/PF came to power, she wrote,

I therefore suggest that villages, which even today consist predominantly of kinsmen and have retained some forms of communal work, such as the *nhimbe* parties, be regarded for production purposes as corporate bodies. . . . Each of these units could then, for agricultural purposes, be treated as one large farm. . . . All arable land should, wherever possible, be comprised in one large block so that at a later stage communal cultivation becomes possible. During the first stage peasants may retain rights to the land they have cultivated until then, but efforts should be made to persuade them to cultivate it in common; that is, the *nhimbe* practice should be extended.[11]

Since 1980, assertions have often been made that "rural socialism" of a simple sort was "traditional" to communal cultivators. Notions of this kind led Nelson Mawema, ZANU/PF chairman of Masvingo Province, to claim in August 1984 that "while there may have been a drought in the form of rain . . . there was no ideological drought in Masvingo. . . . Our people have the kind of orientation suitable for a socialist set-up."[12]

All this represents a persistent misconception. As Hans Holleman rightly says, "Communal tenure does *not* mean that all land is used (let alone cultivated) in common by the community; or that the rights of individuals are therefore—so runs the fallacy—rendered insecure."[13] A Zimbabwean historian, the late Richard Mtetwa, remarked in his doctoral thesis on the Duma people of Masvingo Province that many colonial development schemes had failed precisely because they had been based on this mistaken assumption about traditional collectivism. In practice, as he demonstrated for the precolonial period, communal tenure allowed for very considerable disparities in the size of family landholdings, and the nhimbe system very greatly advantaged the large farmer, who could brew more beer and attract his poorer neighbors. The observer from the Catholic Commission for Justice and Peace who heard the Chiweshe district commissioner propound his theory of the nhimbe work party as the forerunner of collective production, commented, "I was dismayed to hear the District Commissioner and to note that he was preparing to solve the crucial land problem on the basis of this incorrect assumption."[14] As Esau Chiviya shows in his thesis, peasants since 1980 have amply displayed their suspicion of collectivization. He describes this scene:

A delegation of five rural old men that had returned from visiting a model collective farm came into the office. The group had purchased a farm and they wanted some advice on how best they could settle the members. On behalf of the group, the spokesman rejected the idea of collective ownership of land, and the idea of communal living and eating. The spokesman stressed that "our group does not want what we saw. . . . We want individual plots, individual living."[15]

Chiviya was told by officials that this sort of reaction was "due to propaganda against socialism by previous regimes" and to "peasant ignorance." In fact, it seems likely to be due to the individualism of communal tenure.

The obverse of the "collectivism" fallacy, of course, has been the idea that communal tenure penalizes individual endeavor. The 1985 draft report for reform of the communal areas, whose discussion of traditional rights of avail I cited above, goes on to stress that the whole operation of communal tenure presupposes a "subsistence" economy rather than one producing for the market:

The right to cultivate is based on the need for food for survival, it is not based on the concept of growing crops for sale or profit. Thus for survival purposes, the right to grow food crops takes precedence over grazing rights of society at large; but the reverse may hold in the case of crops grown for profit or trade, which could be sacrificed to grazing or damage therefrom if the survival of cattle is at risk. . . . Although the above rights are not included in the nation's written laws they are enforced through consensual society pressure. . . . Within this setting innovation and individualism tend to evolve slowly. . . . The present land tenure system in the Communal Areas cannot cater for land pressure and a fair land distribution in general and the development needs of the individual holding in particular. Instead, the present land tenure system is hampering to a large extent rural development.[16]

The report proceeds to make "an impact analysis" of communal tenure, finding that it has negative effects on increasing yields, marketing surplus, technological innovation, capital investment, and protection of natural resources, and concludes that it has "severe disadvantages with respect to growth stimulation."

This emphasis on the "subsistence" implications of communal tenure in Zimbabwe seems very odd in view of the twentieth-century history of the areas in which it has operated. I have argued above that classical communal tenure throve in the period when Zimbabwe's peasant economy was emerging and that its operation was not only consonant with but favorable to the choice of the peasant option. Since 1980, the production and marketing achievements of the "communal" peasant sector have been striking enough to throw some doubt on the report's conclusions. Moreover, during the 1920s and 1930s, communal tenure facilitated the emergence of significant numbers of large-scale, plow-using entrepreneurs *in* the Reserves. These men opened up large areas of land, which was allocated to them or which they managed to clear for themselves. They preferred to farm land in the Reserves rather than to seek individual title because in the latter there was no rent to pay, because after a period the land farmed could be abandoned to fallow and fresh land claimed, and because they could use the nhimbe institution to draw on the labor of their neighbors.[17]

There was plainly nothing in the operation of communal tenure to prevent the emergence of differentiation in the reserves (or of grossly unequal cattle holdings on the common grazing lands) or to prevent the emergence of enterprise. What prevented any further differentiation and repressed the inegalitarian enterprise of the reserves entrepreneurs was repeated intervention by the colonial state. Native commissioners whose views were "purely communistic" greatly disliked the reserves' entrepreneurs and used every opportunity of land redistribution to undercut them. The so-called centralization schemes of the 1930s and 1940s, which involved separation of grazing and arable land, the resiting of houses and villages, and the reallocation of plots, were exploited so as to attempt equalization of holdings. The Land Husbandry Act of 1951—often regarded as introducing the potential of capitalist accumulation in the Reserves—in fact had the general effect of another equalization of holdings. Hence, the egalitarianism of Zimbabwean communal tenure owed nothing to its intrinsic character and everything to interventions from outside it.

The final fallacy of the external model of communal tenure is the idea of its traditionality and archaism. Under it, commentators assume, Zimbabwean cultivators go on doing what they have done for centuries. Thus, the Chavunduka Commission of Inquiry into the Agricultural Industry found in 1982 that "in many communal areas, farming systems remain limited to practices evolved under traditional shifting cultivation. . . . The current overgrazing of most communal areas appears to be the result of the absence, under traditional tenure, of a reasonable reward for reducing stock numbers."[18] Such a comment ignores the fact that almost all cultivators of maize now make use of fertilizer and that planned sale of cattle to finance the acquisition of plows has long been a feature of Zimbabwean peasant strategies. Whatever may be wrong with contemporary Zimbabwean peasant farming is certainly *not* due to its unchanging character. Nor can communal tenure in itself be criticized on the grounds of archaic irrelevance to modernity. It has been used, as we have seen, to enable choice of the peasant option; it has been exploited by entrepreneurs. It has also been used to allow for engagement with the industrial economy. Communal tenure has enabled a pattern of expansion and contraction of the cultivated area so as to correspond with the household's strategies of labor export and retention.

Because the whole model of communal tenure is a colonial construct, then, and carries with it so many misconceptions, it is ironic that the new Zimbabwean regime should have established the term "communal areas." But there remains another irony. Just at the moment when the term itself has been officially invoked, so determination of land allocation and use has been removed from all the parties who have been engaged in it over the last hundred years. In 1981, the District Councils

Act set up elected councils as the key institution of rural local government. In 1982, the government introduced the Communal Land Act, which gave the district councils power to allocate land. It was announced that "existing land rights would be preserved, but new permits to occupy land would have to be given by the District Council. . . . District Councils granting land for residential or agricultural use would have to have regard for customary law and grant land only to those people who have a customary right to it." The determination of customary law had already been transferred from chiefs' courts to new local bodies appointed by the Ministry of Justice under the Customary Law and Primary Courts Act of 1981. Not only chiefs and headmen but also villages and households were replaced by the new institutions of district councils and primary courts.

The 1985 draft report on communal area reform commented,

The combined effect of these two legislative measures has the potential for profound changes in the land tenure situation in the long term, but, it is thought, will not result in any significant changes in the short and medium term. If successful, the measure will leave the traditional leaders with little more than a conservative function and will allow substantive innovation provided that matters are not forced too quickly, i.e., provided that the new courts' early interpretation of customary law reflects to a large degree the present consensual decision making process, and that the new district councillors similarly respect and represent the fundamental wishes of their constituencies.[19]

These are large provisos. The district councils began with little popular support or credibility and have more recently been given a major role in enforcing planned changes in the farming and residential patterns of communal areas which will transform landholding and land use far beyond the remedy of an appeal to customary law. As the Zimbabwean sociologist, Angela Cheater, remarked in a conversation in 1987, the term "communal areas" is now something of a misnomer. If anything they have become "conciliar areas."[20] At least one law case has been taken against a council allocation of land, when a civil servant in Harare sued a council for requisitioning his unused family land in a communal area to build a school. He lost the case, though he was awarded compensation. Indeed, the legal position remains very unclear. A promised land tenure bill, which, it was said in 1983, would provide "a single tenure system with non-discriminatory rights and obligations" has never, in fact, been introduced.[21] It seems likely that most recent allocations of land in the communal areas have little legal basis. They certainly have little to do with communal tenure, however defined.

The Communal Areas Since Independence

The history of the communal areas since 1980 falls into two phases. In the first, there was an absence of effective central control. Despite the enactments of the district councils, the primary courts, and the Communal Land Acts of 1981 and 1982, the new structures took time to become at all effective. In practice, what was experienced was a relaxation of central control for the first time for decades. In these years there was a revival of all the old possibilities of action within flexible communal tenure. Chiefs and headmen and entrepreneurs and village committees and peasant households were all involved in the processes of land allocation, appropriation, and use in the communal areas during these years. Meanwhile, despite these renewed flexibilities, a series of official inquiries were repeating the old colonial fallacies of communalism, traditionalism, and archaism. The state became convinced that it had to move away from communal tenure but not because it knew what was occurring on the ground. The state's conviction derived from the old illusions of the inflexibility of communal tenure rather than from renewed flexibility. At any rate, these official convictions, though they have not yet led to formal tenurial reform, *have* resulted in renewed statist intervention in the rural areas, determining patterns of settlement, landholding, and land use. By the mid-1980s, land reform has ceased to mean the redistribution of land from white to black through the Resettlement process and has come to mean the reshaping of the communal areas.

None of these processes have so far been illuminated by scholarly research and publication. The many works that have been produced on the Zimbabwean rural areas have focused on the Resettlement programs and to a lesser extent on squatters on commercial farms. Few have focused on land tenure and land use in the communal areas. Hence, in what follows, I draw heavily on scattered reports in the Zimbabwean press and on official reports. I begin by documenting the activities of chiefs, headmen, committees, entrepreneurs, and peasant households.

Chiefs and the Communal Areas Since 1980

Three themes emerge from press reports on the action of chiefs since 1980. One of these is that chiefs have been able to represent themselves as spokesmen for popular defense of "tradition" against unpopular state policies. Another is that chiefs and headmen have been allocating land in return for fees and bribes. A third is that there has been increasing conflict between chiefs and councils over land allocation.

It was widely thought at the end of the guerrilla war that chiefs had been discredited in Zimbabwe's rural areas. Many were killed by guerrillas. David Lan, in his influential book and articles, argued that authority had passed from the chiefs to spirit mediums and from the mediums to elected village committees.[22] Many people thought chiefship could never again recover credibility. This view has turned out to be mistaken, or at least premature. And one of the reasons for the persisting popular support for chiefs is that they *seem* to be so closely associated with the notion of communal tenure. I have argued above that this is inaccurate historically, and I shall argue below that a popularly adminstered form of communal tenure is both possible and desirable. But in Zimbabwe since 1980, the state has managed to give the impression to many rural people that it is against "tradition," not only invented and oppressive tradition but also flexible custom in which "the people" have a crucial interest. In one of his brilliant essays about peasant politics in the Transkei, William Beinart has shown how even peasant progressives and women who were disadvantaged by patriarchal traditionalism rallied round the chiefs to protect communal tenure.[23] Something of the same thing may have been happening in Zimbabwe.

It was first manifested not in defense of the communal areas but in criticism of the government's plans for Resettlement. Government and party have strongly repudiated any idea that resettlement areas should be in any sense an extension of communal areas. Thus in August 1984, Nelson Mawema, ZANU/PF chairman for Masvingo Province, urged that only those with master farmers' certificates should be resettled and within an overall plan drawn up by agricultural experts: "We would hate to see the whole of Masvingo turned into a communal area."[24] Yet to many peasant producers in the communal areas, the ideal has been the addition of land to them; land that would ease shortage of grazing and that would allow for the expansion of the possibilities of communal tenure. Chiefs often expressed this ideal. In July 1982, for instance, Senator Chief Kayisa Ndiweni chaired a meeting between peasant farmers in Ntabazinduna District and government resettlement officers:

The Government's resettlement policies are "un-African" and against the wishes of the people, Senator Chief Kayisa Ndiweni said. The people do not want resettlement. All they want is an extension of the communal lands. The Government should buy adjacent farms and add them to the communal lands. . . . Many of the farmers and councillors present vigorously supported the chief.

Cde Simon Pavakavambwa, chief irrigation officer in the Department of Rural Development, faced a barrage of questions when he explained Government resettlement policy . . . he said the Government did not want to extend the former tribal trust lands. It wanted to transform resettlement areas into productive land. . . . Even if a farm purchased was adjacent to a communal area, it would be resettled according to the Government philosophy. "It will not be added to the communal land," he said, amid murmurs of disapproval from the peasants, a few of whom left the meeting.[25]

By the time of the 1985 elections, chiefs had emerged not only as advocates for the addition of land to the communal areas but also as symbols of communal tenure within them. Bishop Abel Muzorewa disturbed government by accusing it of planning widespread collectivization of land and also of disrespect for the chiefs. To undercut such criticism and to reassure rural opinion, Mugabe held an *indaba* with over two hundred chiefs in March 1985:

Represented by Senator Chief Kayisa Ndiweni (Matabeleland), Senator Chief Charumbira (Masvingo), Chief Mutasa (Manicaland), and Chief Mangwende (Mashonaland East) they expressed their grievances frankly. They complained in strong language that they felt they had been stripped of their traditional powers. They said they did not understand new Government legislation such as . . . policy on land distribution and the function of primary village courts.

Elected councillors, said Chief Mutasa, "wanted to destroy the chieftancy and take over their powers." The chiefs demanded the right to appoint councillors and thus to regain the power to allocated land. Mugabe made the concession that if they would undergo training "to understand the new laws governing the country," chiefs would be given the presidency of primary courts. But he made no concession over council membership or land allocation.[26]

As well as championing tradition, however, chiefs and headmen in many areas were getting on with the business of allocating land in return for fees. In September 1985, for instance, the *Herald* reported that

traditional leaders in Goromonzi have been criticized for bringing squatters into the district. The Goromonzi-Kubitana District Council found there was a great influx of aliens into the district. The Council, at its meeting, blamed this influx on greedy headmen who were either bribed or demanded fees from people wishing to settle in the district.[27]

As late as October 1987, the *Herald* reported the local government minister, Enos Chikowore, as attacking chiefs and headmen on similar grounds:

A touchy issue was that of Mozambicans now coming into Zimbabwe who were being given land by headmen and chiefs. Once they were found they would be fished out and resettled in refugee camps where they would become part of the displaced people. We hear stories that headmen and chiefs are resettling

Mozambicans. Wherever this happens we urge peasants to inform the Government. . . . There were cases where headmen and chiefs had resettled Mozambicans for a fee or for the purpose of increasing the number of people under them. If we find such cases . . . the headmen and chiefs will be criminally prosecuted because they will have violated the Communal Land Act. . . . Headmen and chiefs were not allowed to resettle people directly but only as a council.[28]

By 1987, indeed, the contestation between chiefs and councils was acute. Some councils appointed chiefs and headmen to their land allocation committees, but most claimed the exclusive right to distribute land. In November 1987, Chikowore visited Murehwa to settle "a wrangle between chiefs, kraal heads and councillors who had the right to allocate land," declaring, of course, that "District Councils are the only organs entitled" to do so.[29] In February 1988, Mudhomeni Chivende, governor of Mashonaland West, ordered

an immediate end to the haphazard allocation of land in some district council areas of the province. . . . District Councils were the only local authorities charged with the responsibility of allocating land in the communal areas. "The grabbing of land, stream-bank cultivation and wanton destruction of the country's natural resorces should cease forthwith." . . . The governor said the reorganization of the communal lands should be be viewed as a means of establishing an efficient and economic way of providing services to the rural communities. Local authorities should therefore aim at minimizing conflicts between traditional leaders, party cadres, village and ward development committee leadership, as such tendencies hampered development projects.[30]

Despite all this, chiefs remained unrepentant. Senator Chief Mangwende told the Senate on February 16, 1988,

Zimbabwean chiefs will continue fighting for powers to allocate lands. We will keep on talking until we are heard just like we did when we wanted the power to administer justice. You cannot be a chief without land. The power to administer justice and allocate land, these two go hand in hand. . . . People should not think that the powers to allocate land were taken away from chiefs forever.[31]

It is little wonder that Beach has recently commented on the vigor with which contenders now contest for chiefships:

Chieftanship remains big business and it may get even bigger if current proposals to return to them some of their old powers take effect . . . in practice, as opposed to theory, Chiefs may well be able to ensure that their followers get such benefits as land. Since Independence, therefore, claims to chiefly titles have if anything increased.[32]

Committees, Entrepreneurs, and Households Since 1980

It is clear from some of the citations above that chiefs and councils have not been the only contestants over allocation of communal land. Governor Chivende described "party cadres" and "village and ward development committee leadership" as also involved in conflicts over land. Party and other village-level committees predate councils; such committees were the effective authorities at the end of the war, and many of them have been reluctant to submit to fitting into the newly erected hierarchy of decision making and enforcing. It is clear that some of the village development committees (VIDCOs) still represent radical local interest. In January 1988, for example, the *Herald* carried a letter from a proud son of Chiweshe District, attacking the work of the district's VIDCOs.

Places where we used to graze cattle and go puddle-swimming have been turned into ploughing land and dwellings. Rivers from which we used to catch fish have become receptacles of eroded soil, and hills that once boasted thick bushes and trees have now degenerated into passage ways. The aim behind the VIDCOs is no doubt noble but they have been grossly misdirected in their efforts. More often than not these VIDCOs are staffed by land-hungry youngsters who will not show any restraint.[33]

On other occasions, the struggle to control the VIDCOs has taken on the character of a proto-class war. Thus, in December 1985, the National Farmers Association (NFA) of Zimbabwe—a body representing the Master Farmers of the Communal Areas and scornful of the alleged inefficiency of the large majority of peasants—demanded that only "good farmers" be considered as members of VIDCOs. The NFA backed a call for tenurial changes so that its members could be given individual titles to their land and thus be able to offer collateral for Agricultural Finance Corporation loans.[34] Even larger-scale entrepreneurship has also been possible in at least some communal areas since 1980. Figures reminiscent of the interwar reserves entrepreneurs have emerged. A press story to which I have mislaid the reference but which I remember vividly dealt with an urban dweller who had found after years of vain striving that fortune really lay in the rural areas. The man, who was being held out as an example, had returned to his home communal area where he was farming some two hundred acres of land with great success. There was no indication of how he obtained this land, whether by fee or bribe or merely by occupying and working it.

There have also been instances of more popular exploitation and extension of communal tenure. The *Herald* carried an unusual story in October 1984 in which communal tenure was reestablished on a stretch of land by popular action. The land was Majoro, declared a European area under the Land Apportionment Act, from which peasant families had been evicted:

> After the eviction of the original Majaro residents from their land in 1931, for reasons best known to themselves, no white farmers ever settled in or tried to develop properties in Majaro. Some of the evicted Majaro residents sought and found homesteads in the eastern district of Nyanga, others settled in districts to the north of Mutoko. . . . At independence, most of the scattered original Majoro residents were too old to go back and rebuild their homes, while some had died. But their offspring started to move back—as they are still doing today—with the blessings of Chief Chimoyo and the Mutoko District Council.[35]

More generally, Zimbabwean households have continued to exploit the flexibility of communal tenure to combine rural and urban incomes. In a valuable paper, Deborah Potts has recently shown the continuation in independent Zimbabwe of migrant labor flows to and from the towns. She sees these as no longer the result of colonial capitalist coercion but of household choice:

> The existence of communal land tenure is the major factor which allows migrants to have the option of re-entry into the rural sector. Any attempt to alter this factor would have wide-ranging implications for Zimbabwean rural-urban migrants. . . . The option of circular migration acts as a security net.

She notes that Zimbabwean policymakers dislike circular migration and that a "15-year blueprint for Zimbabwe's future rural development contained guidelines which, if implemented will result in many non-farming urban dwellers losing their traditional rights to land." She comments that "this policy . . . would be fantastically unpopular" and that "without compensatory legislation on pension and welfare rights for the urban population, implementation of such a policy would be disastrous for a section of the population."[36]

In some cases of acute land shortage, however, collective defenses of "communal tenure" are giving way to fierce contestations for land within communal areas. In March 1989, for instance, the member of parliament for Chiweshe, Chen Chimutengwende, lamented that in Chiweshe Communal Area, "a serious shortage of land . . . has led to conflicts among the peasants." There had been no resettlement schemes in the area, and "a typical peasant family holds less than 2 ha of mostly sandy soil." In these circumstances, peasant factions who *had* influence with the district council were using it to achieve the eviction of those who did not.[37] The

Herald of March 6, 1989, recorded just such a case, in which Chiweshe District Council had evicted Samuel Dendemera of Nyakudya village. According to Dendemera,

The land he occupied had been given to him in 1969 by the ex-chief Makope of Mazowe district. This had been approved by the then District Commissioner. When the liberation war broke out he and his family had been moved to a protected village until 1980 when he returned to his place but to his surprise, the council claimed that he was a squatter. "In 1985 they burned my huts and property which police estimated at about 2000 dollars." . . . Cde Dendemera, who is the village head, said he was the only one being evicted "because I suspect they have earmarked someone else to take my place." . . . Even now there were some of his rivals who were growing their crops in his fields.[38]

Finally, in this complex and contested scene, there have been abuses of influence by more powerful men. In March 1988, for example, "a row over land" broke out in Hwedza Communal Area between an elderly woman and Senator Stanlake Marwodzi. Marwodzi claimed that he had bought the field in question for $160 in the early 1970s from the late village head. He also claimed that the district council supported him in his claim thus derived from land purchase. The woman claimed that she had inherited the land from her mother-in-law and that the village head had had no right to sell it. Local village elders backed her version of the story, but the senator was able to call in the police to evict her.[39] And in April 1989, the press broke the story of the relations between Binga District Council, in northern Matabeleland, and the governor of that province, Jacob Mudenda. Mudenda had often reminded the council of its obligations and powers with regard to land allocation, had warned them about "the consequences of abusing power vested in them," and had urged them "to rid the Sinamagonde area of squatters." Yet the governor had himself forced one of the councillors to allocate him a plot in the communal area "ideal for cotton and sunflower." As the outraged council pointed out, this was "in contravention of the Communal Lands Act."[40]

An Academic Case Study

It is clear, then, that the actualities of land allocation, title, and holding vary greatly from place to place in Zimbabwe's communal areas, according to the balance of power between chiefs, headmen, councillors, "squatters," and politicians. I know of only one academic study that illuminates a particular case. This is Donna Pankhurst's excellent study of Murasi village near Musami in what used to be Chief Mangwende's area. Her account shows the extraordinary mixture of factors that have brought about the present situation of highly modified "communal tenure."

Murasi was established in 1959 on land hitherto thought suitable only for grazing and used exclusively up to that time by a subchief. His use of the land contravened the regulations of the Land Husbandry Act, then theoretically in force. So also did the foundation of Murasi, which took place entirely without the knowledge or consent of the native commissioner. "A local wealthy man" bribed the subchief to allow him to control the use of the land and to allocate it to others. This entrepreneur then proceeded to give out the land in return for payments, first to his own clients and then to people from other tribal trust lands. The first settlers, and the friends of the subchief, got the largest plots of arable land and of wetland gardens. From its inception, the village was a very unequal community, with incomes from agriculture varying greatly.

During the liberation war, the founding entrepreneur left the area and did not return after 1980. He has ceased to be in any sense the controller of the land. But the new land-allocating authorities also have no effective control over it. The original land allocations have become frozen. After the first payments there have been no further sales.

It is generally the case that wealth has not enabled households to gain more access to land. This is because the rights developed through custom and practice with regard to land dictate that land cannot be sold . . . it also may not be requisitioned by any locally-recognised authority in the event of disuse.[41]

Land originally allocated to men who are now absent in the towns is still regarded as theirs and has not been reallocated.

Land holdings remain "frozen" and there is great reluctance to subdivide arable plots between children, or to give up any while the landholder is still alive. . . . The elected Village Development Committee is not able to allocate land in an absolute sense, but has effectively intervened after the deaths of several men in the village to ensure that widows are not made landless. . . . The Village Development Committee's intervention is, strictly speaking, illegal under national law.[42]

It will be seen that landholding in Murasi has not become commercialized, despite the origins of the village. "Custom" has rapidly grown up to protect effective tenure. But this custom does not operate in a "traditionally" communal way. Until the death of the household head, his sons are virtually landless. And there is no reallocation of land according to need and the capacity to use.[43]

The Zimbabwean Government and Land Reform
in the Communal Areas

We have seen that before 1980, ZANU/PF consultants were advocating the exploitation of communal tenure so as to develop first communal and then collective farming. Since then, there have been many calls for a socialist transformation of the countryside. In November 1983, for example, a correspondent writing in the monthly magazine, *Moto,* gave his prescription for land reform under the heading, "Land hungry peasant, Socialism's greatest supporter." He argued that

any land reform policy must have the concrete backing of a definite class. To push a land reform program without a political class base is to initiate a vague land reform process which will have no backing should vested class interests resist that program. . . . The vacillating nature of the middle peasants needs to be exploited to enlist it on the side of a radical land reform policy. The middle peasant hates the rural bourgeoisie and the kulak farmer. But he does so in order to be bourgeois himself. Thus he should be mobilized with the poor peasant and rural proletariat for land reform. . . . He must also be won over for socialism in the countryside. . . . The landless poor, unemployed peasant, and the rural proletariat will be the most consistent supporter of socialism in the countryside. All land reforms will be supported by him.[44]

But the land reform policies actually now adopted by the Zimbabwean government certainly do not seek to vest themselves in the class backing of the landless poor. They are much likelier, indeed, greatly to increase their number, by allocating land rights only to "permanent" full-time farmers. The impulse behind land reform in the communal areas is a technocratic one, warmly supported by spokesmen for Zimbabwean commercial agriculture and for Western aid and fueled by all the old fallacies about communal tenure. It is worthwhile to trace briefly how this has come about, before examining the elements in the present policy of land reform.

In retrospect, a crucial role was played by the Commission of Inquiry into the Agricultural Industry, set up in March 1981. The importance of this commission for the communal areas was for a long time obscured, first by the fact that its terms of reference made no reference to them, and second by the fact that although the commission reported in June 1982, its findings were not made public until the end of 1984. The African membership of the commission was significant. Its chairman, Professor Gordon Chavunduka, was the son of Solomon Chavunduka, a pioneer farmer in the native purchase areas (land set aside for African individual tenure by the Land Apportionment Act of 1930), and brother to Dexter Chavunduka, who had long worked in the agricultural extension services. One member was Robinson Gapare, leader of the NFA, launched in 1980 with a membership of six hundred Master Farmer clubs. Gapare claimed that the NFA allowed "communal farmers to speak with one voice," but he made an implicit distinction between "farmers," progressives committed to modernizing change, and "peasants" devoted to traditionalism.[45] Another member was Dr. L. T. Chitsike, a senior civil servant who was to mastermind the reform plan for the communal areas in 1985. Together with the white members of the commission, these men turned the inquiry into a eulogy for commercial farming and a critique of communal tenure.

The attitude of the commissioners was given an early expression in the report when they declared on page 3, that "the use of the term 'commercial farmer' has been avoided since the Commission believes that a prime objective of agricultural policy must be to encourage all farmers to become commercial farmers. The assumption that the communal farms will remain at subsistence production levels is not appropriate." On this basis, the commission redefined the problem that had been put to it. The problem was not the inequity of landholding between black and white. Nor was it the wasteful use of land by commercial farmers. Instead, "at the heart of the problem lies the issue of improving small holder production, particularly in the communal lands." Finding that the commercial sector was extremely efficient, the commission directed most of its criticism and recommendations toward the communal areas, urging that there was little point in redistributing land to communal peasants until means had been found to increase their productivity.[46]

The commission believed that the communal areas were handicapped not only by a legacy of colonial neglect and discrimination but also by the continuance of "traditional" attitudes. "In many communal areas farming systems remain limited to practices evolved under traditional shifting cultivation." It found "disturbing long-term trends" in the decrease in the productivity of communal land and labor and in the fall through the 1970s in the proportion of grain marketed by peasants.[47]

The commission disliked the circulatory migrant labor system and the "fact that access to land in the communal areas is regarded as a 'right' to all males." It described peasant land hunger in the following terms:

The main demand for land arises from people with few economic resources who often fail to follow good farming practices. To give these people more land without taking into account the need for major agricultural change will fail to have any long term effect on rural poverty. . . . Because it is inevitable that relatively high population pressures will continue in many communal lands into the forseeable future, it is vital that farming in these areas be returned to a sustainable basis. It will be necessary both to identify those individuals and groups who have the will and ability to farm, and to create the circumstances which will enable them to farm successfully within the communal areas.[48]

The report was rapidly becoming a master farmers' charter. Nor did the commission duck the question of communal tenure:

In order to provide communal farmers with both the status and the means to acquire a personal responsibility for the land in their care, it will be essential for farmers individually or as groups to become identified with their land and live-stock. In regard to land, means must be found of ensuring security of tenure, so that there is a clear link between an area of land and an individual or a group, which will be recognizable in practice and in law.[49]

The commission found that this was demanded "by almost everyone," including the National Farmers Association. It therefore recommended "that the Government initiate, as a matter of urgency, a study to identify existing land tenure systems in the communal lands with the object of defining the future pattern of land tenure in those areas."[50] It gave a broad hint of its own conclusions in deploring the movement of men from the rural areas to the towns and back again, suggesting that what was needed instead were permanent rural and urban populations.

The Chavunduka commission could be—and later on was—criticized for repeating most of the fallacies about communal tenure and for ignoring the evidence of the sharp rise in the proportion of agricultural commodities marketed by peasants after 1980. After its submission in June 1982, the report vanished from sight for over two years while its recommendations were debated. But the commission's recommendation on tenure had immediate effect. In the second half of 1982, Robert Mugabe directed the Ministry of Lands, Resettlement and Rural Development "to prepare a planning document on the restructuring and development of the communal lands." The permanent secretary to the ministry was the same Dr. Chitsike who had been a member of the commission and a signatory of its report. On October 29, 1982, Chitsike issued a circular on the procedures to be followed in preparing the Communal Lands Development Plan.

Chitsike emphasized that "an overall aspect which will have to be investigated in depth, will be the land tenure problems for both the resettlement and communal areas." The coordination of the Communal Lands Development Plan would be the responsibility of the ministry's

Central Planning Unit, "albeit still in the stage of being established."[51] The exercise was to be completed in twelve months.

In fact, nothing more was to be heard about the plan for some two and a half years. Meanwhile, however, other agencies hurried to support the thrust of the Chavunduka report. Thus, USAID representative Roy Stacey later commented,

When I first came to Zimbabwe I was led to believe that the communal lands were infertile and that the primary objective of the government would have to be centered around resettlement. But now I don't think it is really necessary to settle these people and I think that the communal lands under individual tenure can be much more productive.[52]

A central purpose of American aid, therefore, was to ensure the reintroduction into the communal areas of the technocrats whose task it would be to modernize them. As a USAID summary stated,

The major gain for the bureaucrats was that it re-established them in the rural areas from which the war had driven them out. The aid gave them the means to induce acceptance in these areas while their alignment with the party (ZANU/ PF) gave them legitimacy.[53]

World Bank studies took the same line. A World Bank Land Subsector report in 1985 asserted that land redistribution and resettlement was irrelevant to the key question of land management. Even if the government's target of 162,000 families could be resettled, "it would not in all likelihood have had much impact on land use conditions in the communal areas." The report warned against further reduction of the land held by commercial farmers and stressed the need for "reform" of land use in the communal areas.[54]

Meanwhile, while Chitsike's technocrats proceeded in their slow manner toward a plan and while Western agencies sought behind the scenes to change the meaning of "land reform" from the redistribution of land to changes in its use, a public debate over the communal areas and over peasant farming methods continued. Three positions were argued. One was the technocratic position itself, which laid stress on "traditional" obstacles to modernizing change. Another was a populist position that argued that the ever-increasing marketed output from the communal areas proved that all that was needed was to give support to the dynamism of the communal tenure system. A third was a socialist position that stressed state farms and producer cooperatives. But these socialist ambitions were often stated in a way that allowed all too much scope for the technocratic ambition. Thus the Marxist-Leninist ZANU/PF Congress of August 1984 passed the following resolutions on "Agriculture and Land Reform":

The Congress, recognizing the importance of agriculture as the backbone of the economy . . . and conscious of the fact that increasing population pressure is likely to tax the communal areas more than is the case now; resolves as follows:

That Government takes land reform as the key element of its strategy and overhaul the land tenure system with a view to ensuring equity in land holdings as well as maximum productivity.

That Government intensifies its program of large-scale farming as one arm of socialist agriculture, where the means of production are directly owned by the state. That co-operative farming be promoted as the second arm of socialist agriculture.[55]

For Chitsike and the technocrats, the crucial thing about these resolutions was that they gave the seal of party approval to a redefinition of land reform, away from resettlement to tenurial change. The time had now come, it was thought, to release the Chavunduka report as a preliminary to the presentation of Chitsike's own draft Communal Lands Development Plan. The Chavunduka report was published in December 1984. It ran into a withering hail of fire in the press. On January 18, the *Herald* carried a long attack by Malachia Madimutsa. In his view, the report "reflects a deep-seated prejudice of detached critics of rural folk." Madimutsa thought it absurd to blame low productivity on the faults of the communal system rather than on the poor soils of the communal areas. He pointed out that even despite these poor soils, peasant farmers were now marketing more than half of Zimbabwe's maize:

Capable farmers from the communal lands . . . can put under-utilized land in the commercial sector to better use and revolutionize agricultural output in this country. There is widespread but nevertheless wrong belief that communal farmers are incompetent and are the main culprits in the wasting away of the natural resources in the countryside.[56]

Madimutsa, in short, was seeking to keep the focus of land reform on resettlement and redistribution rather than on tenurial and other changes in the communal areas themselves.

At the time, he seemed to have won the public argument. The assumptions of the Chavunduka commission seemed outdated. Even the *Financial Gazette,* sympathetic as it was to the commission's point of view, was forced to admit that

Zimbabwe's communal land farmers have become a major force in the nation's agricultural sector. Once regarded as subsistence farmers only, their contribution to output during the past season has surprised everyone, even the experts. . . . It is an illustration of how small units, worked mainly by family labor, often on small parcels of land which a commercial farmer could not afford to exploit, can in total produce substantial volumes. It has also shown that the communal farmer, given proper incentives, can make a significant contribution.[57]

When even the spokesmen of commercial farming were making such concessions, it looked as though advocates of sweeping "reform" in the communal areas had been undercut.

Chitsike and his planners remained unperturbed. In March 1985, he presented his draft "Communal Lands Development Plan: A 15-Year Development Strategy" to an interministerial workshop. The draft showed a heavy reliance on the Chavunduka report, which it often cited. It drew on statistics for communal production for the period 1969 to 1979 and paid little attention to increases since 1980. It found that communal tenure, while positive in its effects on equality, had negative impacts on productitity and initiative.

It listed "poor land husbandry techniques" and "land tenure systems not suited for production intensification" among the crucial problems of the communal areas. It found that "circular migration in Southern Africa has resulted in villagers neither becoming progressive farmers, nor efficient employees." Hence, central among its recommendations was land tenure reform. While urging government to refrain fron entering into any ideologically and politically biased discussion, it recommended that

Government should be given the right and power to change the structure of land holdings to improve land productivity and to broaden the distribution of benefits from land. Land should be allocated by the state and held . . . on a leasehold basis. . . . Land rights should be legally vested in the People of Zimbabwe. . . . The land tenure system should place control over the agricultural land in the hands of those who actively farm and manage the land and who get an income from it. It should encourage productive land use. It should impose stringent conditions of land occupation . . . and prohibit absenteeism. It should allow for the consolidation of fragmented holdings, for the introduction of land management schemes and conservation measures.[58]

Land tenure should also enable the farm holder to give security for loans.

In practical terms, these principles would mean a survey of communal areas, after which the state would allocate sufficiently large areas of land to provide a decent income, subject to proper land use planning. Leaseholders would not be able to subdivide the land or to sell it. Common areas, forests, and so on, would be managed under an overall plan to be laid down and supervised by government officials. According to Chitsike, these recommendations would maintain the best features of communal tenure—establishing family farms of roughly equal size and a collective responsibility for common land—while eliminating its constraints on productivity and improvement. These reforms, however, would have to take place in the context of broader development priorities, the most important of which was "consolidated village development." These consolidated villages would meet "the need to restructure and reorganize the existing dispersed and isolated peasant settlements, to make cost-effective provision of social and physical infrastructure and services, and to release additional land for agricultural development." Village consolidation implied "resource use consolidation" and constituted "an agrarian reform strategy." Chitsike recommended that "with the consolidated village model . . . only those people who actively earn their living from farming [would] be given arable land use rights."[59]

There was plenty of emphasis in the draft plan on local participation in implementing these recommendations. Chitsike's assumption was that since they were manifestly in the interest of communal cultivators, they would be warmly endorsed. But this was an assumption held in the past by colonial advocates first of centralization and then of land husbandry, schemes that in fact met fierce peasant opposition but elements of which feature prominently in Chitsike's fifteen-year plan. At any rate, Chitsike had learned something from hostile press response to the Chavunduka report. He did not intend to leave the press free to report selectively on his plan. Instead, and unprecedentedly, he took out an advertisement in the *Sunday Mail* of June 30, 1985, so that he could summarize the results of the March workshop. Land reform and village and land consolidation were the crucial issues. "The land tenure system, therefore, needs to be revised [and] land tenure reform must be supplemented by a land use program based on proper land use planning, land consolidation, efficient land management, soil conservation, and use of scientific methods of farming."[60]

Chitsike's program was clear enough. But there was still some official hesitation. Chitsike's advertisement, after all, had been issued in the midst of an election campaign in which ZANU/PF was anxious to reassure the peasantry and even the chiefs. It was decided to launch yet another review of "all existing data, information, studies and research on land tenure and agrarian questions in Zimbabwe." The FAO was asked to provide a consultant to prepare a "Policy Options Paper for Agrarian Reform in Zimbabwe." The FAO selected Lionel Cliffe to carry out the consultancy; his discussions began in August 1985, and his report on policy options was submitted in February 1986. Cliffe's report made some effective critical points on Chitsike's assumptions. On villagization, Cliffe remarked that "whatever benefit in social infrastructure provision, its contribution to *agrarian* transformation is not obvious; it may obscure the issue of *production,* which ought to be first priority, and may in fact disrupt production." The idea of establishing individual titles in the communal areas based on a survey would involve "a costly and time-consuming operation" and not be "readily acceptable" to the people. It would not necessarily "guarantee security nor access to credit" and would lead to "loss of land of poorer households." As for the idea of attaching conditions to leases, such conditions would have to be policed, "and they could lead to nepotism . . . and could undermine households' security." Cliffe's preference was for "communal control of land allocation and land use," an extension of the inherited system "which would democratize the allocation of land rights" and entrust it to village committees. These committees would decide *who* should be given rights, and in Cliffe's view, it would be unjustifiable for them to exclude the dependents of urban migrants.[61]

As will have become clear from the introduction to this chapter, I believe Cliffe's recommendation to be *historically* as well as democratically grounded. I have argued that the classic period for the operation of "communal tenure" was one in which precisely this sort of local, village-level control over land was exercised. Cliffe's recommendations also seem to fit—at any rate, better than other proposals—with the realities on the ground of Murasi village as described by Pankhurst. His report is free of the routine fallacies about communal tenure, and it is acutely conscious of cautionary lessons from "land reform" elsewhere in Africa. Cliffe's recommendations have not been adopted as government policy, but they seem to have renewed debate.

Since 1986, there has been no legislation relating to communal tenure, nor has there been any coherent statement of the government's land reform program for the communal areas. The Five-Year National Development Plan for the period 1986 to 1990 speaks of "the reorganization of settlement patterns in the Communal Areas" and of "the replanning of land-use patterns," but it says nothing in detail about how this is to be done.[62] Robert Mugabe's New Year message on January 1, 1986, did little to clarify the matter.

In the peasant sector, the Government will, in the context of the new five-year national development plan due to begin in operating soon, try to accelerate the resettlement program and revolutionize peasant agriculture and the peasant style of life in many ways that will become clearer and clearer as the plan unfolds.[63]

Like most others, I have been reduced to watching the plan unfold in press reports so as to seek to guess *how* government intends to revolutionize peasant society. It has become clear that government backs the technocratic solutions of villagization and consolidation, with the necessary reallocation of land that these entail. In July 1987, for instance, Goodson Sithole, ZANU/Sithole member for Chipinge, asked in parliament whether "home owners displaced through villagization in the communal lands would be compensated." Mugabe replied that the present situation was "chaotic," with people building homes and plowing lands haphazardly. "The villagization program is meant to bring benefit to our people by bringing about a clear demarcation between arable and grazing areas and areas where business and growth points can be put."[64] In the same month, the *Herald* threw a rare light on the villagization process in one area—Gandanzara in Makoni District. According to a letter from a Gandanzara resident, people disliked the idea. It meant "uprooting a family which had been settled for, say, 30 years"; moreover, the ten hectares that fortunate residents in the new consolidation were to be given were "too large for a peasant considering the inputs (financial and labor) required for its maximum utilization."[65] The *Sunday Mail* of September 13, 1987, referred to "educational seminars to convince the villagers of Makoni District about the importance of consolidated gardens."[66]

Further signs of discontent appeared in *Parade* of August 1987. A correspondent from Binga complained,

Most people have been forced to leave their usual places to live in line resettlements along the main roads. . . . When we asked our local councillor and Vidcos, they simply told us it was the Government's policy. . . . We parents need ploughing and grazing land. So how come we were told to settle along the roads where conditions are unsuitable for ploughing and grazing? Can't the road follow the people, instead of people going to the road?[67]

He was given short shrift by the district administrator, who dismissed his complaints as "bogus and of first class rubbish." The writer should

get it clear that this administration is here to implement the policy of Government, there are no two ways about that, and get it clear also that when we talk about Government we talk about the people themselves.[68]

The district administrator objected to sorting out "developmental issues through the press," but nevertheless, occasional press reports continue to offer insights. Thus, the *Herald* of October 29, 1987, carried a long report entitled "Putting the Land Reform Program into Action." It is vivid enough to cite as a conclusion to this discussion.

The local district administrator alights from the Government truck and finds a crowd patiently waiting under a muhacha tree. They number more than a thousand, and more are still streaming to the venue. . . . Some sun-scorched figures scratch at their skins, having travelled many kilometers to come and verify this rumor about the Government wanting to take away their cattle, shorten their stands and their fields. One peasant stands up, accuses the Government of trying to bring back the "Smith days." . . . Another peasant asks what this whole idea of land reorganization is about. Cde Daniel Machakaire, a civil servant from the Government's Department of Physical Planning repeats what has been explained already. "We want to ensure that your homesteads are removed from grazing land, that your cattle graze where there is suitable land for grazing." . . . The meeting is soon over. There are mixed feelings about the land reform program. Some amid the crowd feel enlightened that they had in fact built their huts where cattle should be grazing. Others feel that they should stay where they are, since land reform means they must move their homesteads some hundreds of meters away.[69]

The *Herald* writes of how "the gospel of land reorganization is being taken to the various provinces."[70]

Conclusion

The present position of "land reform" in Zimbabwe is thus a confused one. There is plainly little "socialist" about it. Cooperatives are decreasingly spoken of. Equally plainly, what *is* being attempted is part of the technocratic program. What remains unclear is how much of that technocratic program government is committed to. Is village consolidation a first step, or does it in itself now constitute "the gospel" of land reform? Will the government go further and take the risk of tenurial legislation?

It seems clear that this still remains a matter for debate. In October 1987, for example, the National Symposium on Agrarian Reform in Zimbabwe was held in Nyanga under the joint sponsorship of the Department of Rural Development and the FAO. Delegates discussed Cliffe's report, and Cliffe himself was present. In December, a report on the discussions and recommendations was produced and circulated to all district administrators. The symposium committed itself to the following view:

There was need for a new deal over land within the Communal Areas through a modification of those rules, customs and procedures governing how people get access to land and who should get that access, the conditions under which they use it, and retain it. In line with the desire for land use rationalization, it was felt that means had to be found to allow and encourage users to make good use of land and improve it, but that "good land use" also meant in the interest of the community and future generations, not just of the individual, thus implying some "management" of land by the community.[71]

The symposium thus sought to replace "communal tenure" by "community control."

The report declared that some consensus had been achieved around "some general guidelines for a modified communal tenure system." It had been agreed that "individual freehold titles would not be appropriate as they would generate inequality, landlessness, indebtedness and ultimately . . . a lack of the very security that the system sought to create as peasants lose the land through mortgages. It was also felt that there should be some degree of community supervision of family (or group) arable land use." It was therefore agreed that a system of conditional permits to use land should be introduced. Such permits should be allocated—and withdrawn where necessary—at the village development committee level, "where there are direct users of land." VIDCOs should be reconstituted so as to represent "complete village head units" and "avoid fragmenting communities"; headmen should be members ex officio so as to avoid conflict. VIDCOs would give long-term leases on arable land and would themselves manage the grazing "commons." People who did not make use of their lease to cultivate would lose it, and the land would be reallocated to "more deserving members of the village." VIDCOs would have to take into account inequalities of income and cattle holding, giving more land to those without off-farm incomes, assisting female-headed households, protecting widows, and promoting village oxen teams.[72]

These recommendations plainly backed Cliffe's recommendations rather than Chitsike's. The problem is whether they can be made consistent with the other technocratic dimensions of "land reform," with contempt for peasant conservatism and ignorance such as comes out so clearly in the *Herald*'s report on the sun-scorched, scratching figures, groping with rumor and tradition. Can genuine control of land by VIDCOs be matched with implementation of the whole series of transformations from above to which the government appears committed?

In August 1988, there was a seminar on communal lands reorganization in Harare, at which F. T. Gonese, a leading rural development bureaucrat, presented a paper. Gonese emphasized strongly the role of central planning and concluded that planners could do the job of transforming the communal areas without needing to resort to tenurial reform, whether in the direction of individual titles or in the direction of community control. He wrote,

The question of entitlement to land is a burning issue. . . . A free-for-all situation has problems . . . while the resettlement model with "qualification criteria" does pose its own limitations, especially in a communal area situation where members may have enjoyed residence from time immemorial.[73]

"Traditional communal landholding" meant that no one had specific responsibility for grazing land; individual tenure posed enormous logistical difficulties; leases "too do not provide any solution." Gonese's own solution to this predicament was to bypass it. With proper planning, villagization, and so on, the question of tenure per se does fall off."[74]

In the light of the other contributions to this book, one must welcome any decision not to proceed with tenurial legislation. But I confess I am still alarmed at the terms of Gonese's dismissal of the necessity. It seems to me that the democratic community control proposed by Cliffe and endorsed by the Nyanga symposium must necessarily involve the capacity of the village development committees to *dissent* from proposals for "land reform" urged from above. Gonese's notion of bypassing tenure and achieving one's ends precisely through the implementation of "reform" seems to negate the very notion of local community control. Michael Drinkwater has recently criticized the land reform plans of Zimbabwe's agrarian bureaucrats as "flawed even in their own technical and economic terms"; as ignorant of society and culture; as careless of history; and hence as dangerously repetitive of the very colonial interventions that in the past aroused such strong peasant opposition.[75] Democratic community control could be a real option, based in a real, if relatively recent, tradition and drawing on the flexibilities of the system. It would be tragic if peasant resistance to statist imposition now takes the form of support for chiefs and the whole apparatus of bogus "traditionalism."

Notes

This paper was presented in the spring of 1988, and has not been revised since the original conference.
1 *Herald,* 15 January 1981.
2 Hans Holleman, *Chief, Council and Commissioner* (Assen, 1969): 62.
3 A. Mafeje, "South Africa: The Dynamics of a Beleaguered State," *African Journal of Political Economy* 1 (1986): 97.
4 M. Yudelman, *Africans on the Land* (Cambridge, Mass., 1964): 109.
5 Memorandum by L. J. de Bruijn, Acting Provincial Commissioner, Manicaland, "Weya Tribal Trust Land: Makoni District, 1971," file "Weya," District Commissioners Office, Rusape.
6 Holleman, *Chief.*
7 Communal Lands Development Plan: A 15-Year Development Strategy"

(Ministry of Lands, Resettlemnent and Rural Development, Harare, February 1985): 16–18.

8 A. K. H. Weinrich, *African Farmers in Rhodesia: Old and New Peasant Communities in Karangaland* (Oxford, 1975): 70.

9 Memorandum by W. G. Swanson, Assistant Native Commissioner, Wedza, to the Native Trade and Production Commission, 31 May 1944, file ZBJ 1/2/2, National Archives, Harare.

10 D. B. Scholz, "Report on the Conducted Tour of the Chiweshe T.T.L.," 10 September 1974, file "Catholic Commission of Justice and Peace," 7–8, Centre of Southern African Studies, York.

11 A. K. H. Weinrich, "Agricultural Reconstruction in Zimbabwe," ms., 1977.

12 *Herald,* 8 August 1984.

13 Holleman, *Chief.*

14 R. Mtetwa, "The Political and Economic History of the Duma People of South-Eastern Rhodesia" (Ph.D. dissertation, University of Rhodesia, 1976); D. B. Scholz, "Report on the Conducted Tour."

15 E. Chiviya, "Land Reform in Zimbabwe: Policy and Implementation" (Ph.D. dissertation, Indiana University, 1982): 245–246.

16 "Communal Lands Development Plan," 61–62.

17 T. Ranger, *Peasant Consciousness and Guerrilla War in Zimbabwe* (London, 1985); L. Besant, "Going into the Lines: Centralization and the Perception of Land Shortage in the Chiweshe Reserve, 1940–1944," University of Zimbabwe seminar paper, Pay 1985; W. Depke and B. Davis, "Survival and Accumulation in Gutu," University of Zimbabwe seminar paper, July 1985; W. Dopke, "State and Peasants in Mazoe District in the 1930s," University of Zimbabwe seminar paper, 1985.

18 *Report of the Commission of Inquiry into the Agricultural Industry,* June 1982, 29.

19 *Herald,* 12 June 1982; "Communal Lands Development Plan," 19–20.

20 Interview with Angela Cheater, 21 August 1987.

21 *Herald,* 28 July 1983.

22 D. Lan, *Guns and Rain* (London, 1985).

23 W. Beinart and C. Bundy, *Hidden Struggles in Rural South Africa: Politics and Popular Movements in the Transkei and Eastern Cape, 1890–1930* (Berkeley, 1986).

24 *Herald,* 8 August 1984.

25 *Herald,* 27 July 1982.

26 *Sunday Mail,* 17 March 1985.

27 *Herald,* 9 September.

28 *Herald,* 14 October 1987.

29 *Herald,* 19 November 1987.

30 *Herald,* 24 February 1988.

31 *Herald,* 17 February 1988.

32 D. N. Beach, "Re-reading Traditional Traditional History: The Mangwende Dynasty of Zimbabwe," ms., 1988, 10.

33 *Herald,* 13 January 1988.

34 *Herald,* 6 December 1985.

35 *Herald,* 16 October 1984.

36 D. Potts, "Recent Rural-Urban Migrants to Harare: The Maintenance of Rural Ties," Seminar paper, SOAS, 20 November 1987.

37 *Herald,* 7 March 1989.

38 *Herald,* 6 March 1989.

39 *Herald,* 13 March 1988.

40 *Herald,* 10 April 1989.

41 D. Pankhurst, "The Dynamics of the Social Relations of Production and Reproduction in Zimbabwe's Communal Areas" (Ph.D. dissertation, University of Liverpool, 1989): 230, 232, 238, 241–243.

42 Ibid.

43 Ibid.

44 "Land-Hungry Peasants, Socialism's Greatest Supporter," *Moto* 18 (November 1983): 7–10.

45 *Herald,* 4 January 1985.

46 *Report of the Commission of Inquiry into the Agricultural Industry* (Harare, 1982): 3,7.

47 Ibid., 29, 35.

48 Ibid., 62.

49 Ibid., 63.

50 Ibid., 63.

51 L. Chitsike, circular, 20 October 1982.

52 This citation is from Kathy Boraine, "The Path of No Return?" (Honors thesis, Economic History, Cape Town, 1983): 108.

53 Ibid., 109.

54 World Bank, "Zimbabwe Land Subsection Study," 1985, 37, as cited in Michael Drinkwater, "Technical Development and Peasant Impoverishment: Land Use Policy in Zimbabwe's Midlands Province," *Journal of Southern African Studies* 15, 2 (January 1989): 291.

55 Congress resolutions were reproduced in *Zimbabwe Pressespiegel,* 3 August 1984.

56 *Herald,* 18 January 1985.

57 *Financial Gazette,* 14 December 1984.

58 "Communal Lands Development Plan," 40, 47, 73, 75, 76.

59 Ibid., 79, 121–124.

60 "Government Prepares the Communal Lands Development Program," *Sunday Mail,* 30 June 1985.

61 L. Cliffe, "Policy Options," February 1986, xiv–xv.

62 *Republic of Zimbabwe: First Five-Year National Development Plan, 1986–1990,* Jarare, 1986, 28.

63 *Herald,* 1 January 1986.

64 *Herald,* 9 July 1987.

65 *Herald,* 1 July 1987.

66 *Sunday Mail,* 13 September 1987.
67 *Parade,* August 1987, 6.
68 Ibid.
69 *Herald,* 20 October 1987.
70 Ibid.
71 *Report on National Symposium on Agrarian Reform in Zimbabwe* (Harare, December 1987): 26–28.
72 Ibid.
73 F. T. Gonese, "A Framework for Communal Lands Reorganization," 4 August 1988.
74 Ibid.
75 M. Drinkwater, "Technical Development and Peasant Impoverishment: Land Use Policy in Zimbabwe's Midlands Province," *Journal of Southern African Studies* 15, 2 (1989): 287–305.

SELECTED BIBLIOGRAPHY
INDEX

Selected Bibliography

Adams, A. *Le long voyage des gens du fleuve*. Paris, 1977.

Adams, A. *La terre et les gens du fleuve*. Paris, 1985.

Adedeji, A., and T. Shaw, eds. *Economic Crisis in Africa*. Boulder, 1985.

Almagor, U. "Pastoral Identity and Reluctance to Change: The Mbanderu of Ngamiland," in R. Werbner, ed. *Land Reform in the Making*. London, 1982.

Anderson, D., and R. Grove, eds. *Conservation in Africa: People, Policies and Practice*. Cambridge, 1987.

Arrighi, G. "Labour Supplies in Historical Perspective: A Study of the Proletarianisation of the African Peasantry in Rhodesia." *Journal of Development Studies* VI, 3 (1970): 197–234.

Ashton, B., K. Hill, A. Piazza, and R. Zeitz. "Famine in China, 1958–61." *Population and Development Review* X, 4 (1984): 613–645.

Ault, D. E., and G. L. Rutman. "The Development of Individual Rights to Property in Tribal Africa." *Journal of Law and Economics* 22 (1979): 163–182.

Barett, H. *The Marketing of Foodstuffs in The Gambia 1400–1980*. Avebury, 1988.

Barrows, R. "African Land Reform Policies: The Case of Sierra Leone." *Land Economics* 50 (1974): 402–410.

Barry, M. "Les Peuls en Côte d'Ivoire." *Cahiers Ivoriens de la Recherche Economique et Sociale* (CIRES) 5 (1978): 75–81.

Bassett, T. "Fulani Herd Movements." *Geographical Review* 76, 3 (1986): 233–248.

Bassett, T. "The Development of Cotton in Northern Ivory Coast, 1910–1965." *Journal of African History* 29 (1988): 267–284.

Bassett, T. "The Political Ecology of Peasant-Herder Conflicts in the Northern Ivory Coast." *Annals of the Association of American Geographers* 78, 3 (1988): 453–472.

Bates, R. "The Agrarian Origins of Mau Mau." *Agricultural History* 61 (1987): 1–28.

Baulin, J. *La Politique Intérieure d'Houphouet-Boigny*. Paris, 1980.

Bedjaoui, M. *Towards a New International Economic Order*. Paris, 1979.

Beech, M. W. "Kikuyu System of Land Tenure." *Journal of the African Society* 17, 65 (1917): 46–59.

Beinart, W. "Soil Erosion, Conservationism and Ideas about Development: A Southern African Exploration, 1900–1960." *Journal of Southern African Studies* XI, 1 (1984): 52–83.

Beinart, W., and C. Bundy. *Hidden Struggles in Rural South Africa: Politics and Popular Movements in the Transkei and Eastern Cape, 1890–1930.* Berkeley, 1986.

Beneria, L., and M. Roldan. *The Crossroads of Class and Gender: Industrial Homework, Subcontracting, and Household Dynamics in Mexico City.* Chicago, 1987.

Benoit, M., *Le Chemin des Peul de Boobola.* Paris, 1977.

Berger, M., P. Belem, D. Dakou, and V. Hien. "La maintien de la fertilité des sols dans l'ouest du Burkina Faso et la nécessité de l'association agriculture-élevage." *Coton et Fibres Tropicales* 42, 3 (1987): 201–210.

Bernal, V., "Losing Ground—Women and Agriculture on Sudan's Irrigated Schemes: Lessons from a Blue Nile Village." In J. Davison, ed., *Agriculture, Women and Land: The African Experience.* Boulder, 1988. Pp. 131–156.

Bernardet, P. "Dix ans de développement de l'élevage en Côte d'Ivoire. Stratégie et organisation de l'encadrement: Réalisations et échecs." *Cahiers Ivoiriens de Recherche Economique et Sociale* 1 (1987): 41–56.

Bernardet, P. *Association Agriculture-Élevage en Afrique: Les Peuls semi-transhumants de Côte d'Ivoire.* Paris, 1984.

Bernstein, H., and B. Campbell, eds. *Contradictions of Accumulation in Africa.* Beverly Hills, 1985.

Berry, A. R., and W. F. Cline. *Agrarian Structure and Productivity in Developing Countries.* Baltimore, 1979.

Berry, S. *Cocoa, Custom, and Socio-Economic Change in Rural Western Nigeria.* Oxford, 1975.

Berry, S. "The Food Crisis and Agrarian Change in Africa." *African Studies Review* 27, 2 (1984): 59–112.

Berry, S. "Property Rights and Rural Resource Management: The Case of Tree Crops in West Africa." *Cahiers d'ORSTOM Sciences Humains* 24, 1 (1988): 3–16.

Berry, S. "Concentration Without Privatization? Some Consequences of Changing Patterns of Land Control in Africa." In S. P. Reyna and R. E. Downs, eds., *Land and Society in Contemporary Africa.* Hanover, 1988. Pp. 53–75.

Biebuyck, D., ed. *African Agrarian Systems.* Oxford, 1963.

Blaikie, P. *The Political Economy of Soil Erosion.* London, 1985.

Blaikie, P., and H. Brookfield, eds. *Land Degradation and Society.* London, 1987.

Bohannan, P. " 'Land,' 'tenure' and land-tenure." In D. Biebuyck, ed., *African Agrarian Systems.* Oxford, 1963. Pp. 101–115.

Boserup, E. *The Conditions of Agricultural Growth: The Economics of Agrarian Change under Population Pressure.* Chicago, 1965.

Bourdieu, P. "The Social Space and the Genesis of Groups." *Theory and Society* XIV, 6 (1985): 723–744.

Boutillier, J.-L. "Les structures agraires en Haute Volta." *Etudes Voltaïques, mémoires,* 5. Ouagadougou, 1964.

Boutrais, J. "L'expansion des éléveurs peul dan les savanes humides de Cameroun." In M. Adamu and A. H. M. Kirk-Greene, eds., *Pastoralists of the West African Savanna.* Manchester, 1986. Pp. 145–160.

Braun, J. von, and P. Webb. "The Impact of New Crop Technology on the Agricultural Divison of Labor in a West African Setting." *Economic Development and Cultural Change* 37, 3 (1989): 513–534.

Brenner, R. "Social Basis of Economic Development." In J. Roemer, ed., *Analytical Marxism.* Cambridge, 1985. Pp. 23–53.

Bruce, J. *Land Tenure Issues in Project Design and Strategies for Agricultural Development in Sub-Saharan Africa.* Land Tenure Center Paper 128. Madison, 1986.

Burawoy, M. *The Politics of Production.* London, 1985.

Burnham, P. "Changing Agricultural and Pastoral Ecologies in the West African Savanna Region." In D. Harris, ed., *Human Ecology in Savanna Environments.* New York, 1980. Pp. 147–170.

Campbell, D. "Land-Use Competition at the Margins of the Rangelands: An Issue in Development Strategies for Semi-Arid Areas." In G. Norcliffe and T. Pinfold, eds., *Planning African Development.* Boulder, 1981. Pp. 39–61.

Carney, J. "Struggles over Crop Rights and Labor with Contract Farming Households in a Gambian Irrigated Rice Project." *Journal of Peasant Studies* 15 (1988): 334–349.

Carney, J. "Struggles over Land and Crops in an Irrigated Rice Scheme: The Gambia." In J. Davidson, ed., *Agriculture, Women and Land: The African Experience.* Boulder, 1988. Pp. 59–78.

Carney, J., and M. Watts. "Manufacturing Dissent." *Africa* 60, 2 (1990): 207–241.

Carney, J., and M. Watts. "Disciplining Women?" *Signs* 16, 41 (1991): 651–681.

Chanock, M. *Law, Custom and Social Order: The Colonial Experience in Malawi and Zambia.* Cambridge, 1985.

Chanock, M. "A Peculiar Sharpness: An Essay on Property in the History of Customary Law in Colonial Africa." *Journal of African History* 32, 1 (1991): 65–88.

Chauveau, J.-P., J.-P. Dozon, E. Le Bris, E. Le Roy, G. Salem, and F. G. Snyder. "Rapport introductif au journés d'études." In E. Le Bris, E. Le Roy, and F. Leimforfer, eds., *Enjeux fonciers en Afrique noire.* Paris, 1983. Pp. 17–43.

Chazan, N., and T. Shaw, eds. *Coping with Africa's Food Crisis.* Boulder, 1988.

Cheung, N. S. S. "Private Property Rights and Sharecropping." *Journal of Political Economy* 76 (1968): 1107–1122.

Clark, T. J. *The Painting of Modern Life.* New York, 1984.

Clark, C. M. "Land and Food, Women and Power, in Nineteenth-Century Kikuyu." *Africa* 50, 4 (1980): 357–370.

Clayton, E. S. *Agrarian Development in Peasant Economies.* Oxford, 1964.

Cliffe, L. "The Conservation Issue in Zimbabwe." *Review of African Political Economy* 42 (1988): 48–58.

Cliffe, L. "Zimbabwe's Agricultural 'Success' and Food Security in Southern Africa." *Review of African Political Economy* 43 (1988): 4–25.

Cohen, J. "Land Tenure and Rural Development in Africa." In R. Bates and M. Lofchie, eds., *Agricultural Development in Africa*. New York, 1980. Pp. 349–389.

Cohen, J. M., and N.-I. Isakson. "Smallholder vs. Agricultural Collectivization: Agricultural Debates in Ethiopia since the Revolution; Paper for the Conference on Problems of the Horn of Africa." *World Development* XVI, 3 (1988): 323–348.

Colburn, F. *Post-Revolutionary Nicaragua: State, Class and the Dilemmas of Agrarian Policy*. Berkeley, 1986.

Colclough, C., and S. McCarthy. *The Political Economy of Botswana*. Oxford, 1980.

Coldham, S. F. R. "The Effect of Registration of Title upon Customary Land Rights in Kenya." *Journal of African Law* 22 (1978): 91–111.

Colson, E. "The Impact of the Colonial Period on the Definition of Land Rights." In V. Turner, ed., *Colonialism in Africa 1870–1960*, vol. 3, *Profiles of Change: African Society and Colonial Rule*. Cambridge, 1971. Pp. 193–215.

Comaroff, J. *The Structure of Agricultural Transformation in Barolong: Towards an Integrated Development Plan*. Good Hope, 1977.

Comaroff, J. "Class and Culture in a Peasant Economy: The Transformation of Land Tenure in Barolong." In R. Werbner, ed., *Land Reform in the Making*. London, 1982.

Conze, P., and T. Labahn, eds. *Somalia: Agriculture in the Winds of Change*. Saarbrucken-Schafbrucke, W. Germany, 1986.

Cooper, F. "From Free Labor to Family Allowances." *American Ethnologist* 16, 4 (1989): 745–765.

Cotran, E. "The Development and Reform of the Law in Kenya." *Journal of African Law* 27, 1 (1983): 42–61.

Coulibaly, S. *Le Paysan Sénufo*. Abidjan, 1978.

Coulson, A. "Agricultural Policies in Mainland Tanzania." *Review of African Political Economy* 10 (1977): 74–100.

Cowen, M. "The Early Years of the Colonial Development Corporation." *African Affairs* 83, 330 (1984): 63–75.

Croll, E. *The Family Rice Bowl: Food and the Domestic Economy in China*. Geneva, 1982.

Cummins, S. K., M. Lofchie, and R. Payne. *African Agrarian Crisis: The Roots of Famine*. Boulder, 1986.

Davies, R. W. *The Socialist Offensive: The Collectivisation of Soviet Agriculture 1929–1930*. London, 1980.

Davis, J. "Capitalist Agricultural Development and Exploitation of the Propertied Laborer." In F. Buttel and H. Newby, eds., *The Rural Sociology of Advanced Societies: Critical Perspectives*. London, 1980.

Davison, J. " 'Without Land We Are Nothing': The Effect of Land Tenure Policies and Practices upon Rural Women in Kenya." *Rural Africana* 27 (1987): 19–33.

Davison, J., ed. *Agriculture, Women and Land: The African Experience.* Boulder, 1988.

Dejene, A. *Peasants, Agrarian Socialism and Rural Development in Ethiopia.* Boulder, 1987.

Denman, D. R., and S. Prodano. *Land Use—An Introduction to Proprietary Land Use Analysis.* London, 1972.

Dessalegn, R. *Agrarian Reform in Ethiopia.* Uppsala, 1984.

Dessalegn, R. "The Political Economy of Development in Ethiopia." In E. Keller and D. Rothchild, eds., *Afro-Marxist Regimes: Ideology and Public Policy.* Boulder, 1987.

Dey, J. *Gambian Women and Rice in The Gambia.* Unpublished Ph.D. dissertation, Reading University (1980).

Dey, J. "Development Planning in the Gambia: The Gap Between Planners' and Farmers' Perceptions, Expectations and Objectives." *World Development* 10, 5 (1982): 377–396.

Dickenson, J. P., C. G. Clarke, W. T. S. Gould, R. M. Prothero, D. J. Siddle, C. I. Smith, E. M. Thomas-Hope, A. G. Hodgkiss, eds., *A Geography of the Third World.* New York, 1983.

Downs, R., and S. Reyna, eds. *Land and Society in Contemporary Africa.* Hanover, N.H., 1988.

Drinkwater, M. "Technical Development and Peasant Impoverishment: Land Use Policy in Zimbabwe's Midlands Province." *Journal of Southern African Studies* 15, 2 (1989): 287–305.

Dumont, R. *False Start in Africa.* London, 1966.

Duncan, P. *Sotho Laws and Customs.* Cape Town, 1960.

Ellman, M. "Did the Agricultural Surplus Provide the Resources for the Increase in Investment in the USSR during the First Five-Year Plan?" *Economic Journal* 85 (1975): 844–864.

Ellman, M. *Socialist Planning.* Cambridge, 1979.

Fagen, R. R., C. D. Deere, and J. K. Coraggio, eds. *Transition and Development: Problems of Third World Socialism.* New York, 1986.

Falloux, F. "Land Management, Titling and Tenancy." In T. Davis and I. Schirmer, eds. *Sustainability Issues in Agricultural Development.* Washington, D.C., 1987. Pp. 190–208.

Famoriyo, S. "Land Transactions and Agricultural Development in Nigeria." *East African Journal of Rural Development* 7 (1974).

Fauvet, P. "Roots of Counter-Revolution: The Mozambique National Resistance." *Review of African Political Economy* 41 (1984): 108–121.

Feldman, R. "Custom and Capitalism: Changes in the Basis of Land Tenure in Ismani, Tanzania." *Journal of Development Studies* 10, 3 & 4 (1974): 305–320.

First, R. *Black Gold.* Brighton, Sussex, 1983.

Fleuret, A. "Some Consequences of Tenure and Agrarian Reform in Taita,

Kenya." In R. Downs and S. Reyna, eds., *Land and Society in Contemporary Africa*. Hanover, N.H., 1988. Pp. 136–158.

Fortmann, L., and J. W. Bruce, eds. *Whose Trees? Proprietary Dimensions of Forestry*. Boulder, 1988.

Francisco, R., B. Laird, and R. Laird, eds. *The Political Economy of Collectivized Agriculture*. New York, 1979.

Frantz, C. "Contraction and Expansion in Nigerian Bovine Pastorialism." In T. Monod, ed., *Pastoralism in Tropical Africa*. London, 1975. Pp. 338–352.

Friedman, H. "Patriarchy and Property." *Sociologica Ruralis* 26, 2 (1986): 186–193.

Gallais, J. "Essai sur la situation actuelle des relations entre pasteurs et paysans dans le Sahel ouest-african." In *École Pratiques des Hautes Études, Études de géographie tropicale offerts à Pierre Gourou*. Paris, 1972. Pp. 301–313.

Gamble, D. *Contributions to a Socio-Economic Survey of The Gambia*. London, 1949.

Gamble, D. *Economic Conditions in Two Mandinka Villages*. London, 1955.

Gershenberg, I. "Land Tenure as a Constraint to Rural Development: A Re-Evaluation." *East African Journal of Rural Development* 4 (1971): 51–62.

Glazier, J. *Land and the Uses of Tradition among the Mbeere of Kenya*. Lanham, Md., 1985.

Goheen, M. "Land Accumulation and Local Control: The Manipulation of Symbols and Power in Nso, Cameroon." In R. Downs and S. Reyna, eds., *Land and Society in Contemporary Africa*. Hanover, N.H., 1988. Pp. 280–308.

Gondwe, Z. S. "Agricultural Policy in Tanzania at the Crossroads." *Land Use Policy* 3, 1 (1986): 31–36.

Gourou, P. *L'Afrique Tropicale: Nain or géant agricole?* Paris, 1991.

Grigg, D. *The World Food Problem: 1950–1980*. Oxford, 1985.

Gritzner, J. *The West African Sahel: Human Agency and Environmental Change*. Chicago, 1989.

Gubrium, J. "The Family as Project." *The Sociological Review* 36, 2 (1988): 273–296.

Gulbrandsen, Ø. *Privilege and Responsibility*. Bergen, 1987.

Gunn, S. "Land Reform in Somalia." In J. P. Powelson and R. Stack, eds., *The Peasant Betrayed*. Cambridge, 1986. Pp. 109–124.

Guyer, J., and P. Peters. "Introduction to Conceptualizing the Household: Issues of Theory and Policy in Africa." *Development and Change* 18, 3 (1987): 197–214.

Hailey, Lord. *An African Survey*. London, 1957.

Hanlon, J. *Mozambique*. London 1984.

Hannerz, U. *Exploring the City*. New York, 1980.

Hansen, A., and D. McMillan, eds. *Food in Sub-Saharan Africa*. Boulder, 1986.

Hardin, G. "The Tragedy of the Commons." *Science* 162 (1968): 1243–1248.

Harris, J., and M. P. Todaro. "Migration, Unemployment and Development: A Two-Sector Analysis." *American Economic Review* 60 (1970): 126–142.

Harrison, P. *The Greening of Africa: Breaking through in the Battle for Land and Food*. New York, 1987.

Hart, K. *The Political Economy of West African Agriculture.* Cambridge, 1982.

Haugerud, A. "Land Tenure and Agrarian Change in Kenya." *Africa* 59, 1 (1989): 62–90.

Haugerud, A. "The Consequences of Land Tenure Reform among Smallholders in the Kenya Highlands." *Rural Africana* 15/16 (1983): 25–53.

Hay, M. J. "Women as Owners, Occupants, and Managers of Property in Colonial Western Kenya." In M. J. Hay and M. Wright, eds., *African Women and the Law: Historical Perspectives.* Boston, 1982. Pp. 110–123.

Hayami, Y., and V. W. Ruttan. *Agricultural Development: An International Perspective.* Baltimore, 1985.

Hecht, R. "Immigration, Land Transfer and Tenure Change in Divo, Ivory Coast, 1940-1980." *Africa* 55, 3 (1985): 319–336.

Hermele, K. *Contemporary Land Struggles on the Limpopo.* Uppsala, 1986.

Hermele, K. *Land Struggles and Social Differentiation in Southern Mozambique: A Case Study of Chokwe, Limpopo, 1950–1987.* Uppsala, 1988.

Hesseling, G. *Le droit foncier au Sénégal: L'impact de la réforme foncière en Basse Casamance.* Leiden, 1982.

Heyer, J. "The Origins of Regional Inequalities in Small-holder Agriculture in Kenya, 1920–1973." *East African Journal of Rural Development* VIII, 1–2 (1975).

Heyer, J., J. K. Maitha, and W. M. Senga, eds. *Agriculture Development in Kenya: An Economic Assessment.* Nairobi, 1976.

Hill, P. "Three Types of Ghanian Cocoa Farmer." In D. Biebuyck, ed., *African Agrarian Systems.* Oxford, 1963. Pp. 203–223.

Hitchcock, R. "Tradition, Social Justice and Land Reform." In R. Werbner, ed., *Land Reform in the Making.* London, 1982. Pp. 1–34.

Hoben, A. "Social Anthropology and Development Planning—A Case Study in Ethiopian Land Reform Policy." *Journal of Modern African Studies* 10 (1972): 561–583.

Hoben, A. "The Political Economy of Land Tenure in Somalia." In R. Downs and S. Reyna, eds., *Land and Society in Contemporary Africa.* Hanover, N.H., 1988. Pp. 192–220.

Hobswan, E., and T. Ranger, eds. *The Invention of Tradition.* Cambridge, 1983.

Holm, J. "Botswana: A Paternalistic Democracy." In L. Diamond, J. Linz, and S. Lipset, eds., *Democracy in Developing Countries,* II, *Africa.* Boulder, 1988. Pp. 179–216.

Homan, F. D. "Consolidation, Enclosure and Registration of Title in Kenya." *Journal of Local Administration Overseas* 1 (1962): 4–14.

Horowitz, M., and P. Little. "African Pastoralism and Poverty: Some Implications for Drought and Famine." In M. Glantz, ed., *Drought and Hunger in Africa: Denying Famine a Future.* Cambridge, 1987. Pp. 59–82.

Hunt, D. *The Impending Crisis in Kenya: The Case for Land Reform.* Aldershot, 1984.

Hunter, J., and G. K. Ntiri. "Speculations on the Future of Shifting Agriculture in Africa." *Journal of Developing Areas* 12 (1978): 183–208.

Hussain, A., and K. Tribe. *Marxism and the Agrarian Question.* London, 1983.

Hyden, G. *Beyond Ujamaa in Tanzania: Underdevelopment and the Uncaptured Peasantry.* Berkeley, 1980.

Hynes, W. G. *The Economics of Empire: Britain, Africa and the New Imperialism 1870–95.* London, 1979.

Igbozurike, M. U. "Fragmentation in Tropical Agriculture: An Overrated Phenomenon." *Professional Geographer* 22 (1970): 321–325.

Jacoby, E. *Man and Land: The Fundamental Issue in Development.* London, 1971.

Jacoby, E. H., and C. F. Jacoby. *The Essential Revolution: Man and Land.* New York, 1971.

Jean, S. *Les jachères en Afrique tropicale: Interprétation technique et foncière.* Paris, 1975.

Johnston, B. F., and P. Kilby. *Agriculture and Structural Transformation: Economic Strategies in Late-Developing Countries.* New York, 1975.

Johnson, O. E. G. "Economic Analysis, the Legal Framework and Land Tenure Systems." *Journal of Law and Economics* 15 (1972): 259–276.

Jones, C. "Intra-Household Bargaining in Response to the Introduction of New Crops: A Case Study from North Cameroon." In J. L. Moock, ed., *Understanding Africa's Rural Households and Farming System.* Boulder, 1986. Pp. 105–123.

Kanogo, T. *Squatters and the Roots of Mau Mau 1905–1963.* London, 1987.

Kautsky, K. *La question agraire.* Paris, 1906.

Kershaw, G. "The Changing Role of Men and Women in the Kikuyu Family by Socioeconomic Strata." *Rural Africana* 19 (1974–75): 173–194.

Killick, A. *Readings in the Political Economy of Kenya.* Nairobi, 1981.

King, R., and S. Burton. "Land Fragmentation: Notes on a Fundamental Rural Spatial Problem." *Progress in Human Geography* 6 (1982): 475–495.

Kitching, G. *Class and Economic Change in Kenya: The Making of an African Petite Bourgeoisie.* New Haven, 1980.

Knowles, J., and K. Cloud. "Where Can We Go From Here? Recommendations for Action." In J. Davison, ed., *Agriculture, Women, and Land: The African Experience.* Boulder, 1988. Pp. 250–264.

Köbben, A. "Land as an Object of Gain in a Non-Literate Society: Land-Tenure among the Bété and Dida (Ivory Coast, West Africa)." In D. Biebuyck, ed., *African Agrarian Systems.* Oxford, 1963. Pp. 245–264.

Kuper, A. *Kalahari Village Politics.* Cambridge, 1970.

Laitin, D. "The Political Economy of Military Rule in Somalia." *Journal of Modern African Studies* 14, 3 (1976): 449–468.

Lamb, G. *Peasant Politics.* Lewes, 1974.

Lambert, H. E., and W. Harris. *The Kikuyu Lands.* Nairobi, 1945.

Lan, D. *Guns and Rain.* London, 1985.

Lawrence, P., ed. *World Recession and the Food Crisis in Africa.* London, 1986.

Leakey, L. S. B. *The Southern Kikuyu before 1903.* 3 vols. London, 1977.

Le Bris, E., E. Le Roy, and F. Leimforfer, eds. *Enjeux fonciers en Afrique noire.* Paris, 1983.

Lehmann, D. "Sharecropping and Capitalist Transition in Agriculture." *Journal of Development Economics* 23 (1986): 333–354.

Le Moal, G. *Les Bobo: Nature et fonction des masques.* Paris, 1980.

Lennihan, L. "Rights in Men and Rights in Land." *Slavery and Abolition* 3 (1982): 111–139.

Leo, C. *Land and Class in Kenya.* Toronto, 1984.

Levi, J., and M. Havinden. *Economics of African Agriculture.* Harlow, 1982.

Ley, A. "L'expérience Ivoirienne." In E. Le Bris, et al., eds., *Enjeux fonciers en Afrique noire.* Paris, 1983. Pp. 135–141.

Linares, O. "Cash Crops and Gender Constructs: The Jola of Senegal." *Ethnology* XXIV, 2 (1985): 83–94.

Little, P. "Absentee Herdowners and Part-Time Pastoralists: The Political Economy of Resource Use in Northern Kenya." *Human Ecology* 13, 2 (1985): 131–151.

Mackenzie, F. "Local Organization: Confronting Contradiction in a Smallholdings District of Kenya." *Cahiers de Géographie du Québec* 31, 83 (1987): 273–286.

McDowell, C. M. "The Breakdown of Traditional Land Tenure in Northern Nigeria." In D. Biebuyck, ed., *African Agrarian Systems* London, 1963. Pp. 266–278.

McNamara, R. *One Hundred Countries, Two Billion People.* London, 1973.

Mafeje, A. "South Africa: The Dynamics of a Beleaguered State." *African Journal of Political Economy* 1 (1986).

Manghezi, A. "Ku Thekela: Estratégia de Sobrevivência contra a Fome no Sul de Moçambique." *Estudos Moçambicanos* 4 (1983).

Manners, R. A., ed. *Process and Pattern in Culture.* Chicago, 1974.

Medick, H., and D. Sabean. Introduction. In H. Medick and D. Sabean, eds., *Interest and Emotion.* Cambridge, 1984.

Medick, H. "Missionaries in a Row Boat? Ethnological Ways of Knowing as a Challenge to History." *Comparative Studies in Society and History* XXIX, 1 (1987): 76–98.

Meillassoux, C. Introduction. In *The Development of Indigenous Trade and Markets in West Africa.* Oxford, 1971.

Merry, S. E. "The Articulation of Legal Spheres." In M. J. Hay and M. Wright, ed., *African Women and the Law: Historical Perspectives.* Boston, 1982. Pp. 68–89.

Michael, H. W. "Zemacha: An Attempt at Rural Transformation in Ethiopia." In H. W. O. Okoth-Ogendo, ed., *Approaches to Rural Transformation in Eastern Africa.* Nairobi, 1981. Pp. 77–105.

Migot-Adholla, S., P. Hazzell, B. Blarel, and F. Place. "Indigenous Land Rights Systems in Sub-Saharan Africa: A Constraint on Productivity?" *The World Bank Economic Review* 5, 1 (1991): 155–175.

Millar, J. R. "Soviet Rapid Development and the Agricultural Surplus Hypothesis." *Soviet Studies* XXII, 1 (1970): 77–93.

Molutsi, P. "The State, Environment and Peasant Consciousness in Botswana." *Review of African Political Economy* 42 (1988): 40–47.

Moore, F. *Travels in the Inland Parts of Africa*. London, 1738.

Moore, H. *Space, Text and Gender: An Anthropological Study on the Marakwet of Kenya*. Cambridge, 1986.

Moore, S. F. "Explaining the Present: Theoretical Dilemmas in Processual Ethnography." *American Ethnologist* XIV (1987): 727–736.

Moore, S. F. *Social Facts and Fabrications: "Customary" Law on Kilimanjaro, 1880-1980*. Cambridge, 1988.

Muriuki, G. *A History of the Kikuyu 1500–1900*. Nairobi, 1974.

Murray, C. "Land, Power and Class in the Thaba Nchu District, Orange Free State 1884 to 1983." *Review of African Political Economy* 29 (1984): 30–48.

Mwaniki, N. "Against Many Odds: The Dilemma of Women's Self-Help Groups in Mbiri, Kenya." *Africa* 56, 2 (1986): 210–227.

Nolan, P., and G. White. "Socialist Development and Rural Inequality: The Chinese Countryside in the 1970s." *Journal of Peasant Studies* VII, 1 (1979): 3–48.

Noronha, R. *A Review of the Literature on Land Tenure Systems in Sub-Saharan Africa*. World Bank, Research Unit, Agricultural Development Department. Washington, D.C., 1985.

Nothale, D. W. "Land Tenure Systems and Agricultural Production in Malawi." In J. W., Arntzen, et al., eds., *Land Policy and Agriculture in Eastern and Southern Africa*. New York, 1986. Pp. 127–132.

Nyerere, J. K. "Africa and the Debt Crisis." *African Affairs* 84, 337 (1985). Pp. 489–98.

Nyerere, J. K. *Freedom and Unity*. Dar-es-Salaam, 1986.

Obbo, C. "Dominant Male Ideology and Female Options: Three East African Case Studies." *Africa* 46 (1976): 371–389.

Obol-Ocholla, J. ed. *Land Law Reform in East Africa*. Kampala, 1986.

O'Brien, D. "Female Husbands in Southern Bantu Societies." In A. Schlegel, ed., *Sexual Stratification: A Cross-Cultural View*. New York, 1977. Pp. 109–126.

Okali, C. *Cocoa and Kinship in Ghana*. London, 1983.

Okeya Pala, A. "The Joluo Equation: Land Reform = Lower Status for Women." *Ceres* (May–June 1980): 37–42.

Okeyo, A. P. "Daughters of the Lakes and Rivers: Colonization and the Land Rights of Two Women." In M. Etienne and E. Leacock, eds., *Women and Colonization and Colonization: Anthropological Perspectives*. New York, 1980. Pp. 186–213.

Okoth-Ogendo, H. W. O. "African Land Tenure Reform." In J. Hayer, J. K. Maitha, and W. M. Senga, eds., *Agricultural Development in Kenya: An Economic Assessment*. Oxford, 1976. Pp. 152–186.

Okoth-Ogendo, H. W. O. "Property Theory and Land Use Analysis: An Essay in the Political Economy of Ideas." *Journal of Eastern African Research and Development* V, 1 (1976): 37–53.

Okoth-Ogendo, H. W. O. "The Perils of Land Tenure Reform: The Case of Kenya." In J. Arntzen, L. Ngcongco, and S. Turner, eds., *Land Policy and Agriculture in Eastern and Southern Africa*. Tokyo, 1986. Pp. 79–92.

Okoth-Ogendo, H. W. O. "Some Issues of Theory in the Study of Tenure Relations in African Agriculture." *Africa* 59, 1 (1989): 6–17.

O'Fahey, R. *Land in Dar Fur: Charters and Reliable Documents from the Dar Fur Sultanate.* Cambridge, 1983.

O'Laughlin, B. "A Questão Agrária em Moçambique." *Estudos Moçambicanos* 3 (1981): 9–32.

Palmer, R., and N. Parsons, eds. *The Roots of Rural Poverty in Central and Southern Africa.* London, 1977.

Parkin, D. J. *Palms, Wine and Witnesses: Public Spirit and Private Gain in an African Farming Community.* San Francisco, 1972.

Parson, J. "Cattle, Class and the State in Rural Botswana." *Journal of Southern African Studies* VII (1981).

Parsons, N. "Settlement in East-Central Botswana, c. 1800–1920." In R. R. Hitchcock and M. Smith, eds., *Settlement in Botswana.* Gaborone, 1982.

Pearsc, A. *Seeds of Plenty, Seeds of Want: Social and Economic Implications of the Green Revolution.* Geneva, 1980.

Peters, P. "Struggles over Water, Struggles over Meaning: Cattle, Water and the State in Botswana. *Africa* 54 (1987): 24–59.

Peters, P. "Embedded Systems and Rooted Models." In B. McKay and J. Acheson, eds., *The Question of the Commons: The Culture and Ecology of Communal Resources.* Tucson, 1987. Pp. 171–194.

Phillips, A. *The Enigma of Colonialism: British Policy in West Africa.* London, 1989.

Picard, L. "Bureaucrats, Cattle and Public Policy. " *Comparative Political Studies* 13 (1980): 313–356.

Platon, P. "The OMVS program." *Marchés Tropicaux et Méditéranéens*, special issue. Paris. 1981.

Pollet, E., and G. Winter. *La société Soninké (Dyahunu, Mali).* Bruxelles, 1971.

Quéant, T , and C. de Rouville. *Agriculteurs et éleveurs de la région du Gondo-Sourou.* Ouagadougou, 1969.

Radwan, S. *Agrarian Reform and Rural Poverty: Egypt 1951–1975.* Geneva, 1977.

Raikes, P. "Food Policy and Production in Mozambique Since Independence." *Review of African Political Economy* 29 (1984): 95–107.

Ranger, T. *Peasant Consciousness and Guerrilla War in Zimbabwe.* London, 1985.

Rattray, R. S. *Ashanti Law and Constitution.* London, 1920.

Raup, P. M. "The Contribution of Land Reforms to Agricultural Development: An Analytical Framework." *Economic Development and Cultural Change* 12 (1963): 1-21.

Raynaut, C. "Aspects of the Problem of Land Concentration in Niger." In R. Downs and S. Reyna, eds., *Land and Society in Contemporary Africa.* Hanover, 1988. Pp. 221–242.

Redfield, R., and M. Singer. "The Cultural Role of Cities." *Economic Development and Cultural Change* 3 (1954): 53–73.

Richards, A. "Some Effects of the Introduction of Individual Freehold into

Buganda." In D. Biebuyck, ed., *African Agrarian Systems*. Oxford, 1963. Pp. 267–280.

Robertson, C., and I. Berger. "Introduction: Analyzing Class and Gender-Africa Perspectives." In C. Robertson and I. Berger, eds., *Women and Class in Africa*. New York, 1986. Pp. 3–24.

Robertson, A. F. *The Dynamics of Productive Relationships: African Share Contracts in Comparative Perspective*. Cambridge, 1987.

Roesch, O. "Peasants and Collective Agriculture in Mozambique." In J. Barker, ed., *The Politics of Agriculture in Tropical Africa*. Beverley Hills, 1985. Pp. 291–316.

Roesch, O. "Economic Reform in Mozambique: Notes on Stabilization, War and Class Formation." *Taamuli* 1 (forthcoming).

Saith, A., ed. *The Agrarian Question in Socialist Transition*. London, 1985.

Sanderson, S. *The Transformation of Mexican Agriculture: International Structure and the Politics of Rural Change*. Princeton, 1986.

Şaul, M. "Money and Land Tenure as Factors in Farm Size Differentiation." In S. P. Reyna and R. E. Downs, eds., *Land and Society in Contemporary Africa*. Hanover, 1988. Pp. 243–279.

Şaul, M. "Corporate Authority, Exchange, and Personal Opposition in Bobo Marriages." *American Ethnologist* XVI (1989): 57–74.

Şaul, M. "Farm production in Bare, Burkina Faso: The Technical and Cultural Framework of Diversity." In G. Dupré, ed., *Savoirs Paysans et Développement*. Paris, 1990. Pp. 301–329.

Şaul, M. "The Bobo 'House' and the Uses of Categories of Descent." *Africa* 61 (1991): 71–97.

Sawyer, G. F. A. "Discriminatory Restrictions on Private Dispositions of Land in Tanganyika: A Second Look." *Journal of African Law* 13, 1–2 (1969): 2–27.

Schapera, I. *Native Land Tenure in the Bechuanaland Protectorate*. Alice, 1943.

Schapera, I. "The System of Land Tenure on the Barolong Farms (Bechuanaland Protectorate)." *Botswana Notes and Records* 15 (1983): 15–37.

Scott, J. "Resistance Without Protest and Without Organization." *Comparative Studies in Society and History* 29, 3 (1987): 417–452.

Sement, G. "Etude des effects secondaires de la fertilisation minérale sur le sol dans des systèmes culturaux à base de coton en Côte d'Ivoire: Première résultats en matière de correction." *Coton et Fibres Tropicales* 35, 2 (1980): 229–248.

Sement, G. "Le fertilité des systèmes culturaux à base de cotonnier en Côte d'Ivoire." Supplément à *Coton et Fibres Tropicales* (1983), Série *Documents, Etudes et Synthèses,* no. 4.

Shipton, P. "The Kenyan Land Tenure Reform: Misunderstandings in the Public Creation of Private Property." In R. Downs and S. Reyna, eds., *Land and Society in Contemporary Africa*. Hanover, 1988. Pp. 91–135.

Showers, K. "Soil Erosion in the Kingdom of Lesotho: Origins and Colonial Response, 1830–1950s." *Journal of Southern African Studies* 15, 2 (1989): 263–286.

Simmance, A. J. F. "Land Redemption among the Fort Hall Kikuyu." *Journal of African Law* 5, 2 (1961): 75–81.

Simpson, S. R. *Land Law and Registration*. Cambridge, 1976.

Sorrenson, M. P. K. *Land Reform in Kikuyu County: A Study in Government Policy*. London, 1967.

Synder, F. "Colonialism and Legal Form: The Creation of 'Customary Law' in Senegal." *Journal of Legal Pluralism* 19 (1981): 49–90.

Snyder, F. *Capitalism and Legal Change*. London, 1981.

Stamp, P. "Kikuyu Women's Self-Help Groups: Toward an Understanding of the Relation Between Sex-Gender System and Mode of Production in Africa." In I. Berger and C. Robertson, eds., *Women and Class in Africa*. London, 1986. Pp. 27–46.

Stamp, P. "Perceptions of Change and Economic Strategy among Kikuyu Women in Mitero, Kenya." *Rural Africana* 29 (1975–1976): 19–44.

Stenning, D. *Savannah Nomads*. London, 1959.

Stocking, M. "Soil Conservation Policy in Colonial Africa." *Agricultural History* 59, 2 (1985): 148–161.

Storper, M., and A. Scott, eds. *Production, Work and Territory*. London, 1986.

Sutherland, A. "Grass Roots Land Tenure Among Yeyi of North-Western Botswana." In R. Werbner, ed., *Land Reform in the Making*. London, 1982. Pp. 62–84.

Swedish International Development Agency, *Proposal for SIDA Support to Rural Development in Arssi and Bale 1986/87-1988/89*. Stockholm, 1985.

Swindell, K. "Searwoolies, Tillibunkas and Strange Farmers." *Journal of African History* 21, 1 (1980): 93–104.

Swindell, K. *The Strange Farmers of the Gambia*. Norwich, 1981.

Swindell, K., and A.B. Mamman. "Land Expropriation and Accumulation in the Sokoto Periphery, Northwest Nigeria, 1976–86." *Africa* 60, 2 (1990): 173–187.

Tambiah, S. *Culture, Thought and Social Action*. Cambridge, 1985.

Tardits, C. "Développement du Régime d' Appropriation Privée des Terres de la Palmeraie du Sud Dahomey." In D. Biebuyck, ed., *African Agrarian Systems*. London, 1963. Pp. 297–313.

Thomas, M. F., and G. W. Whittington. *Environment and Land Use in Africa*. London, 1969.

Thomas, B. P. *Politics, Participation and Poverty: Development Through Self-Help in Kenya*. Boulder, 1985.

Timberlake, L. *Africa in Crisis: The Causes, the Cures of Environmental Bankruptcy*. London, 1985.

Toulmin, C. "Herders and Farmers or Farmer-Herders and Herder-Farmers?" *Pastoral Network Paper* 15d (1983): 1–22.

Tuma, E. H. *Twenty-Six Centuries of Agrarian Reform, A Comparative Analysis*. Berkeley, 1965.

Uchendu, V. "The Impact of Changing Agricultural Technology on African Land Tenure." *Journal of Developing Areas* 4 (1970): 477–486.

United Nations Food and Agricultural Organization, *Apartheid, Poverty and Malnutrition*. Rome, 1982.

Vail, L., ed. *The Creation of Tribalism in Southern Africa*. London, 1989.

Verhelst, T. "Customary Land Tenure as a Constraint on Agricultural Development: A Re-Evaluation." *Cultures et Développement* 2 (1969-70): 627–656.

Vergopolous, K. "Capitalisme difformé." In S. Amin and K. Vergopolous, *La Question Paysanne et le Capitalisme*. Paris, 1974.

Vergopolous, K. "The End of Agribusiness or the Emergence of Biotechnology?" *Journal of International Social Science* 37 (1985): 89–400.

Wadekin, K. E. *Agrarian Policies in Communist Europe*. The Hague, 1982.

Wardman, A. "The Co-operative Movement in Chokwe, Mozambique." *Journal of Southern African Studies* 11, 2 (1985): 294–304.

Watts, M. *Silent Violence: Food, Famine, and Peasantry in Northern Nigeria*. Berkeley, 1983.

Watts, M. " 'Good try, Mr. Paul': Populism and the Politics of African Land Use." *African Studies Review* 26, 2 (1983): 73–83.

Watts, M. "Drought, Environment and Food Security: Some Reflections on Peasants, Pastoralists and Commoditization in Dryland W. Africa." In M. Glantz, ed., *Drought and Hunger in Africa: Denying Famine a Future*. Cambridge, 1987. Pp. 171–211.

Watts, M. "Peasants under Contract." In H. Bernstein and B. Crow, eds., *The Food Question: Profits versus People?* New York, 1990. Pp. 149–162.

Watts, M. *Manufacturing Dissent: Production Politics and Rice in The Gambia*. London, forthcoming.

Weigel, J.-Y. *Migration et production domestique des Soninké du Sénégal*. Travaux et Documents de l'ORSTOM, no. 116. Paris, 1982.

Weil, P. "Wet Rice, Women, and Adaptation in The Gambia." *Rural Africana* 19 (1973): 20–29.

Weinrich, A. K. H. *African Farmers in Rhodesia: Old and New Peasant Communities in Karangaland*. Oxford, 1975.

Werbner, R. "Local Adaptation and the Transformation of an Imperial Concession in North-Eastern Botswana." *Africa* 41: (1971): 32–41.

Werbner, R. "Land, Movement and Status among Kalanga of Botswana." In M. Fortes and S. Patterson, eds., *Essays in African Social Anthropology*. London, 1975. Pp. 95–120.

Werbner, R. "Small Man Politics and the Rule of Law: Center-Periphery Relations in East-Central Botswana." *Journal of African Law* XXI (1977): 24–39.

Werbner, R. Introduction. In R. Werbner, ed., *Land Reform in the Making*. London, 1982. Pp. i–xii.

Werbner, R. "The Quasi-Judicial and the Experience of the Absurd: Remaking Land Law in North-Eastern Botwsana." In R. Werbner, ed., *Land Reform in the Making*. London, 1982. Pp. 131–150.

Werbner, R. "Production and Reproduction: The Dynamics of Botswana's North-Eastern Micro-Regions." In R. R. Hitchcock and M. Smith, eds., *Settlement in Botswana*. Gaborone, 1982. Pp. 264–277.

Werbner, R. *Ritual Passage, Sacred Journey*. Washington, D.C., 1989.

Whitaker, J. S. *How Can Africa Survive?* New York, 1988.

White, C. "Factors Determining the Content of African Land Tenure Systems in Northern Rhodesia." In D. Biebuyck, ed., *African Agrarian Systems*. Oxford, 1962. Pp. 364–337.

White, G., and E. Croll, eds., *Agriculture in Socialist Development*. Oxford, 1985.

White, G., R. Murray, and C. White, eds. *Revolutionary Socialist Development in the Third World*. Sussex, 1983.

Willis, P. *Learning to Labor*. New York, 1981.

Wolff, R. D. *The Economics of Colonialism: Britain and Kenya 1870–1930*. New Haven, 1976.

Wood, A. P. "Spontaneous Agricultural Resettlement in Ethiopia, 1950–1974." In J. I. Clarke and L. A. Kosinski, eds., *Redistribution of Population in Africa*. London, 1982. Pp. 157–165.

Wood, A. P. "Population Redistribution and Agricultural Settlement Schemes in Ethiopia 1958–80." In J. I. Clarke, et al., eds., *Population and Development Projects in Africa*. Cambridge, 1985. Pp. 84–111.

Wood, E. M. "Capitalism and Human Emancipation." *New Left Review* 167 (1988): 1-21.

Wood, S. "The Deskilling Debate, New Technology and Work Organization." *Acta Sociologia* 30 (1987): 3–24.

World Bank. *Accelerated Development in Sub-Saharan Africa: An Agenda for Action*. Washington, D.C., 1981.

World Bank. *Financing Adjustment with Growth in Sub-Saharan Africa, 1986–90*. Washington, D.C., 1986.

World Bank. *Ethiopia*. Washington, D.C., 1987.

World Bank. *Sub-Saharan Africa: From Crisis to Sustainable Growth*. Washington, D.C., 1989.

Yudelman, M. *Africans on the Land*. Cambridge, 1964.

Zwanenberg, R. van. *Colonial Capitalism and Labour in Kenya*. Nairobi, 1974.

Index